Illustrated AutoCAD®

For All Versions Through Release 9

Dr. Tom W. Berghauser
and
Dr. Paul L. Schlieve

Dallas, Texas

Library of Congress Cataloging-in-Publication Data

Berghauser, Tom W.
Illustrated AutoCAD

Includes index.
1. AutoCAD (Computer program language). 2. Computer graphics. I. Schlieve, Paul L. II. Title.
T385.B465 1988 604.2'4'028553 87-31714
ISBN 1-55622-015-4

1506 Capital Ave.
Plano, Texas 75074

Printed in the United States of America

ISBN 1-55622-015-4

10 9 8 7 6 5 4 3 2 1

All inquiries for volume purchases of this book should be addressed to Wordware Publishing, Inc., at one of the above addresses. Telephone inquiries may be made by calling:

(214) 423-0090

Contents

Contents (Continued)

RECOMMENDED LEARNING SEQUENCE

Recommended Learning Sequence (Continued)

FOREWORD

As the designer of the organizational concept within the *Illustrated Series* from Wordware Publishing, I salute the authors of this book, Doctors Tom Berghauser and Paul Schlieve. I believe that every reader will agree *Illustrated AutoCAD* applies the essence of the illustrated concept to a premier computer-aided design tool — AutoCAD from Autodesk.

In addition to vouching for the book's organization, I also commend its readability, instructional value, and ease of reference. Using the manuscript, it took only a few short days to work through the recommended learning sequence.

I truly enjoyed the reading and learning process. Although this is a technical book, the experience was akin to reading a great novel. I could not put the book down. I found myself working into the early morning hours, looking forward to a new AutoCAD revelation on every page.

The reward of reading and performing the hands-on learning material was a working knowledge of AutoCAD. I now use it to create office layouts, design furniture, and prepare other types of artwork used in daily business operations.

The book lives on as a convenient quick reference tool. Each AutoCAD command and function is encapsulated in an alphabetized module that includes practical working examples.

As for AutoCAD the product, it is a testimony to the dedication and talent of the development and support team at Autodesk. In particular, I wish to extend my gratitude on behalf of the authors and myself to the people at Autodesk for their enthusiastic encouragement and support. Thanks, also, to Joseph Oakey for his help in reviewing this book.

Russell A. Stultz
President and Chief Executive Officer
Wordware Publishing, Inc.

Module 1

ABOUT THIS BOOK

INTRODUCTION

This book describes the AutoCAD computer aided drafting system. It covers AutoCAD versions through Release 9, which introduces an optional pull-down menu interface and network support. If you own Release 9, you may wish to review Appendix A for information about the Release 9 user interface and other features.

The AutoCAD software system, a product of Autodesk, Inc., represents the state of the art in computer-aided drafting. This book presents detailed information about AutoCAD, and each command and technique is illustrated with examples.

This book is designed for a broad range of users. It is designed for first-time users of CAD systems who need a sequential introduction to the system; for users who are familiar with AutoCAD, it serves as a reference manual with numerous examples to extract the full benefits of this complex software system.

A logical learning sequence is provided to guide you through the text. This sequence follows a computerized version of the paper-and-pencil procedures you would use to develop a drawing, from selection of the paper size, pencil hardness, and scale; to 3-dimensional rotation and production of finished drawings on paper.

Updated features introduced in AutoCAD versions 2.5, 2.6, and Release 9 have been clearly identified in the book. Therefore, if you are using version 2.18 or earlier, the book is designed to let you bypass the update information. If you are following the learning sequence and encounter version 2.5 or later command modules, simply move to the next module in the learning sequence.

ORGANIZATION

This book is not designed to be read in page-number order. If you are learning AutoCAD, follow the *Recommended Learning Sequence* printed in the front of the book.

After a brief introduction to AutoCAD in Modules 1 through 3, Modules 4 through 95 are arranged alphabetically by command group. The alphabetical sequence is provided so that, in addition to serving as a guide for learning AutoCAD, the book can continue serving you as a convenient command reference.

If you are like most computer users, you are probably in a hurry to see your software in action. Does this description fit you? If so, then Module 2 is for you. Module 2 provides a step-by-step sample session in which you use AutoCAD to draw the walls of an office and then draw and position the office furniture. This experience gives you insight into the power of AutoCAD, and lets you use many of its commands in a matter of minutes. It will also point out something else. You will quickly realize that AutoCAD is a complex tool—efficient use requires understanding. Every command used in the sample session is presented in this book to ensure that you have a working knowledge.

STYLE CONVENTIONS

Knowing a few practices followed in the book can make your understanding of its content clearer.

- Discussion of AutoCAD features, procedures, and applications is presented in paragraph form. Steps which you perform in the Typical Operations are numbered.
- Keys that are typed or pressed are indicated by bold type.
- Two-key combinations are indicated by a statement such as "Press **Ctrl-C** to cancel the operation." The word *press* is your clue that you must use a function key or key combination. The notation **Ctrl-C** means that you press and hold the key marked **Ctrl**, then press and release the key for typing the letter **c**, and finally release the **Ctrl** key.
- The notation <**CR**> stands for the "Carriage Return" key on your computer. The key cap notation used by computer manufacturers differ for this key. The key may be engraved with "Return" or "Enter." Some computers, such as the Texas Instruments Professional, have both a **Return** key and an **Enter** key. Both are identical for AutoCAD applications and are used interchangably. The IBM PC uses the symbol ↵ to designate the **Enter** or **Return** key and does not provide a printed legend.

BEFORE YOU BEGIN

AutoCAD supports a wide variety of computers, input devices, display screens, printers, and plotters. One of the fastest changing portions of the AutoCAD program is the portion to configure it for specific hardware. As a result, no attempt has been made to describe the procedures for configuring AutoCAD for specific pieces of hardware. The authors assume that you, or someone working with you, has configured AutoCAD for your particular computer configuration and that you can start at the AutoCAD Main Menu.

THE MAIN MENU

By typing **ACAD** and pressing **Return** you start the AutoCAD program. Once started, the AutoCAD Main Menu appears on the screen.

The Main Menu lists two groups of activities. The first group of five functions, numbered 0-4 (computer people like to start counting with 0 instead of 1), describe familiar drafting activities. The second group of options, numbered "5" through "8" provide the mechanism for taking care of computer related tasks. The Main Menu options in both groups are briefly described in the following list.

0. Exit AutoCAD—Provides an orderly way for you to end your work session and return to DOS.
1. Begin a NEW drawing—Displays the equivalent to a blank sheet of drawing paper.
2. Edit an EXISTING drawing—Allows you to make additions and changes to a drawing that was created in an earlier work session.
3. Plot a drawing—Options 3 and 4 are both used to produce paper output. Option 3 (Plot a drawing) is designed to produce output on a pen plotter.
4. Printer plot a drawing—Used to plot a drawing on a graphics-capable printer.
5. Configure AutoCAD—Allows you to setup the AutoCAD software to match changes in your computer configuration.
6. File Utilities—Provides access to a variety of file utilities that are commonly used for drawing file maintenance.
7. Compile shape/font description file—Lets you define alternate character sets and shapes to include in your drawings (in addition to a wide variety of character sets which are included when you purchase AutoCAD).
8. Convert old drawing file—Provides a mechanism to automatically convert drawings which were produced with an earlier version of AutoCAD to the internal format used by the current version of the software.

```
                    A U T O C A D
          Copyright (C) 1982,83,84,85,86,87 Autodesk, Inc.
          Release X.XXz (MM/DD/YY) IBM PC
          Advanced Drafting Extensions 3
          Serial Number: 99-999999


          Main Menu

            0.  Exit AutoCAD
            1.  Begin a NEW drawing
            2.  Edit an EXISTING drawing
            3.  Plot a drawing
            4.  Printer Plot a drawing

            5.  Configure AutoCAD
            6.  File Utilities
            7.  Compile shape/font description file
            8.  Convert old drawing file

          Enter selection:
```

Module 2

SAMPLE SESSION

DESCRIPTION

This sample session guides you through the steps required to produce an AutoCAD drawing. This session introduces you to many of the most popular AutoCAD commands. The following commands are used to produce a typical office floor plan:

- LIMITS
- SNAP
- GRID
- ZOOM
- LINE
- COPY
- FILLET
- BREAK
- REDRAW
- PAN
- ARC
- BLOCK
- INSERT
- TEXT

Carefully follow each numbered step to produce the finished office layout. Although you shouldn't have any problems following the steps, if you get lost, just move on to another module in the learning sequence. Later, after gaining confidence in your ability to use the power of AutoCAD, return to this sample session and complete all the steps.

TYPICAL OPERATION

Use AutoCAD to design the interior layout of an office.

1. Type **ACAD** from the DOS prompt and press **Return** to display AutoCAD's Main Menu.
2. Type **1** and press **Return** to begin a new drawing.

NOTE

If you plan to save your drawing on another disk drive, preface your drawing name with the drive designator. For example, if you want to save your drawing on drive B, type **B:SAMPLE**.

3. Type **SAMPLE** and press **Return** to name the new drawing SAMPLE.DWG.

After AutoCAD loads the Drawing Editor, the Command prompt is displayed at the bottom of your graphics screen. Always look for the Command prompt at the bottom of the screen before entering a new command.

Before beginning the first numbered step on the office drawing, you must determine the size of your drawing sheet. One of the major differences between AutoCAD and manual drafting is that you always work with full scale in AutoCAD. In the case of our office layout, the sheet of paper must be large enough for a drawing of 120 X 144 inches plus some border area. At the Command prompt, type the bold letters shown in the following line.

NOTE

<CR> means to press **Return** (or *Carriage Return*).

Take a look at the office illustration. Each operation is numbered to correspond to a step in the session.

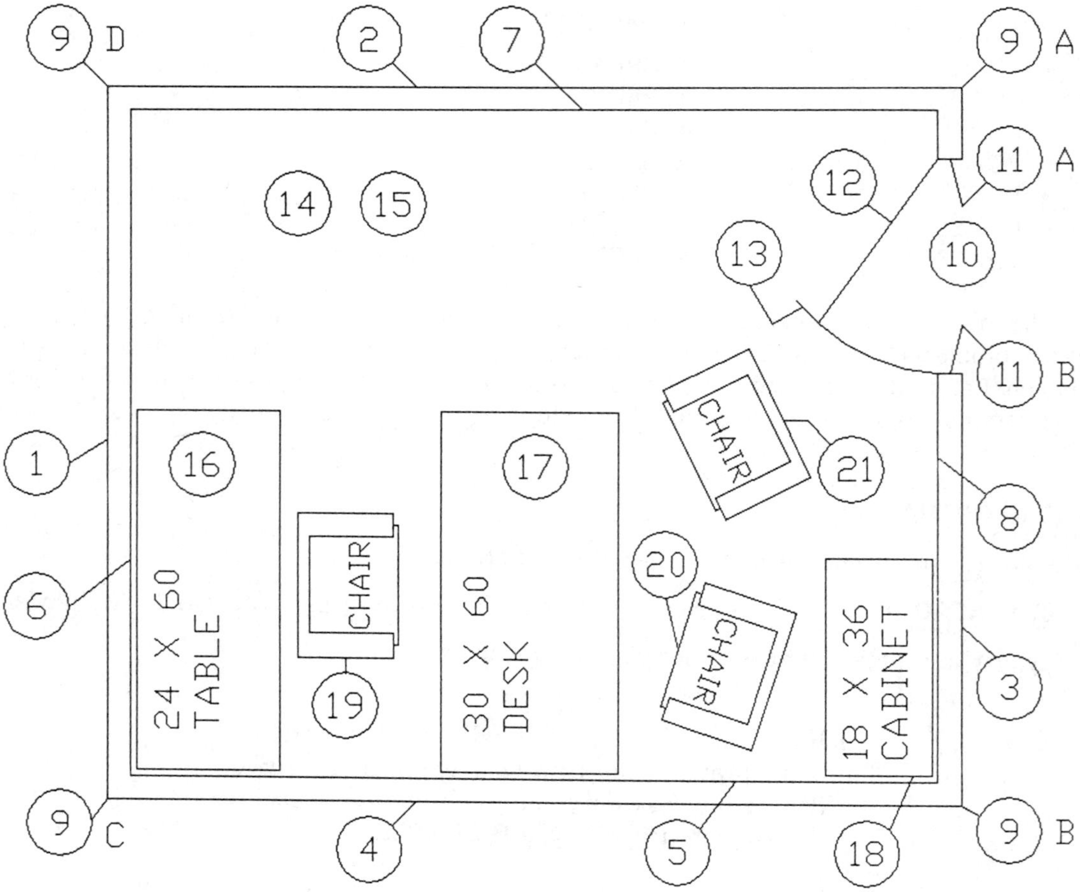

Perform the following setup procedure.

1. Set the drawing dimension.

```
Command: LIMITS <CR>
ON/OFF/Lower left corner <0.0000,0.0000>: <CR>
Upper right corner <12.0000,9.0000>: 192,168 <CR>
```

2. Designate the SNAP value for the drawing screen. A SNAP value of 4 inches is designated with the following entry.

```
Command: SNAP <CR>
Snap spacing or ON/OFF/Aspect/Rotate/Style <1.0000>: 4 <CR>
```

3. Turn the GRID on.

```
Command: GRID <CR>
Grid spacing(X) or ON/OFF/Snap/Aspect <0.0000>: ON <CR>
```

4. Before beginning the actual drawing activity shown on the sample graphics screen, zoom the screen to show the drawing at its maximum view.

```
Command: ZOOM <CR>
All/Center/Dynamic/Extents/Left/Previous/Window/<Scale(X)>: A <CR>
```

Start the drawing by performing the following steps.

1. Draw the first line of the outer wall.

```
Command: LINE <CR>
From point: 24,28 <CR>
To point: @112<90 <CR>  (This notation means 112 units at a 90-
                          degree angle.)
To point: <CR>
```

NOTE

If you make a mistake, you can erase the last line or object with EDIT Erase Last.

2. Draw a line.

```
Command: LINE <CR>
From point: 28,144 <CR>
To point: @136<0 <CR>
To point: <CR>
```

3. Draw a line.

```
Command: LINE <CR>
From point: 168,140 <CR>
To point: @112<270 <CR>
To point: <CR>
```

4. Draw a line to finish the outer wall.

```
Command: LINE <CR>
From point: 164,24 <CR>
To point: @136<180 <CR>
To point: <CR>
```

NOTE

The gaps in the corners are only temporary. These disappear as you continue your work.

5. The inner walls are drawn by copying the outer walls in the following four steps.

```
Command: COPY <CR>
Select objects: L <CR>
1 found.
Select objects: <CR>
Base point or displacement: 28,24 <CR>
Second point of displacement: @4<90 <CR>
```

6. Copy a second line.

```
Command: COPY <CR>
Select objects: 24,44 <CR>
1 selected, 1 found.
Select objects: <CR>
Base point or displacement: 24,44 <CR>
Second point of displacement: @4<0 <CR>
```

7. Copy a third line.

```
Command: COPY <CR>
Select objects: 100,144 <CR>
1 selected, 1 found.
Select objects: <CR>
Base point or displacement: 100,144 <CR>
Second point of displacement:  100,140 <CR>
```

8. Copy the last line.

```
Command: COPY <CR>
Select objects: 168,100 <CR>
1 selected, 1 found.
Select objects: <CR>
Base point or displacement: 168,100 <CR>
Second point of displacement: 164,100 <CR>
```

9. Use the FILLET command to close the outer wall lines as instructed in the next four steps (labeled 9a through 9d in the example).

```
a.  Command: FILLET <CR>
    Polyline/Radius/<Select two objects>: 168,128 <CR>
    152,144 <CR>

b.  Command: <CR>
    FILLET Polyline/Radius/<Select two objects>: 168,36 <CR>
    152,24 <CR>

c.  Command: <CR>
    FILLET Polyline/Radius/<Select two objects>: 40,24 <CR>
    24,36 <CR>

d.  Command: <CR>
    FILLET Polyline/Radius/<Select two objects>: 24,128 <CR>
    40,144 <CR>
```

10. Remove a section of two lines to form a door opening by using the BREAK command. Then redraw the screen.

```
Command: BREAK <CR>
Select object: 168,132 <CR>
Enter second point or F: 168,96 <CR>
```

```
Command: <CR>
BREAK Select object: 164,96 <CR>
Enter second point or F: 164,132 <CR>

Command: REDRAW <CR>
```

11. Use the ZOOM and PAN commands to improve your view of the drawing. This lets you see the work area. Then add two lines to close and complete the outer wall.

```
Command: ZOOM <CR>
All/Center/Dynamic/Extents/Left/Previous/Window/<Scale(X)>: W <CR>
First point: 124,76 <CR>
Second point: 172,148 <CR>

Command: PAN <CR>
Displacement: 128,116 <CR>
Second point: 156,116 <CR>

Command: LINE <CR>
From point: 164,132 <CR>
To point: 168,132 <CR>
To point: <CR>

Command: <CR>
LINE From point: 168,96 <CR>
To point: 164,96 <CR>
To point: <CR>
```

12. Add the door.

```
Command: LINE <CR>
From point: 164,132 <CR>
To point:  @34.4093<234 <CR>
To point: <CR>
```

13. Complete the schematic door symbol with the ARC command.

```
Command: ARC <CR> Center/<Start point>:  164,96 <CR>
Center/End/<Second point>: end <CR>
of 144,104 <CR>
End point: DRAG 140,108 <CR>
Command: ZOOM <CR>
All/Center/Dynamic/Extents/Left/Previous/Window/<Scale(X)>: A <CR>
```

14. Draw a 1-inch square box.

NOTE

The box is used to produce the table, desk, and cabinet. It is saved as a block and does not appear again on the drawing in its original size. It is inserted with different X and Y scale factors in later steps to obtain the necessary dimensions.

```
Command: LINE <CR>
From point: 32,132 <CR>
To point: @1<0 <CR>
To point:   @1<90 <CR>
To point: @1<180 <CR>
To point: @1<270 <CR>
To point: <CR>
```

15. Now save the 1-inch square box as a block.

NOTE

This operation causes the box to disappear from the screen. The box is saved on your disk.

```
Command: BLOCK <CR>
Block name (or ?): BOX <CR>
Insertion base point: 32,132 <CR>
Select objects: W <CR>
First point: 32,132 <CR>
Second point: 36,136 <CR>
4 found.
Select objects or Window or Last: <CR>
```

16. Insert the block as a table.

```
Command: INSERT <CR>
Block name (or ?): BOX <CR>
 Insertion point: 29,29 <CR>
 X scale factor <1> / Corner / XYZ: 24 <CR>
 Y scale factor (default=X): 60 <CR>
 Rotation angle <0>: <CR>
```

17. Insert the block as a desk.

```
Command: INSERT <CR>
Block name (or ?) <BOX>: <CR>
 Insertion point: 80,29 <CR>
 X scale factor <1> / Corner / XYZ: 30 <CR>
 Y scale factor (default=X): 60 <CR>
 Rotation angle <0>: <CR>
```

18. Insert the block as a cabinet.

```
Command: INSERT <CR>
Block name (or ?) <BOX>: <CR>
 Insertion point: 163,29 <CR>
 X scale factor <1> / Corner / XYZ: -18 <CR>
 Y scale factor (default=X): 36 <CR>
 Rotation angle <0>: <CR>
```

19. Zoom to a specific area. Draw a chair and save it as a block named CHAIR.

```
Command: ZOOM <CR>
All/Center/Dynamic/Extents/Left/Previous/Window/<Scale(X)>: W <CR>
First point: 48,20 <CR>
Second point: 88,96 <CR>

Command: LINE <CR>
From point: 72,48  <CR>
To point: 56,48 <CR>
To point: 56,72 <CR>
To point: 72,72 <CR>
To point: 72,68 <CR>
To point: 58,68 <CR>
To point: 58,52 <CR>
To point: 72,52 <CR>
To point: 72,52 <CR>
To point: 72,48 <CR>
To point: <CR>

Command: LINE <CR>
From point: 72,50 <CR>
To point: 73,50 <CR>
To point: 73,70 <CR>
To point: 72,70 <CR>
To point: <CR>

Command: TEXT <CR>
Start point or Align/Center/Fit/Middle/Right/Style: A <CR>
First text line point: 68,53 <CR>
Second text line point: 68,67 <CR>
Text: CHAIR <CR>

Command: REDRAW <CR>

Command: BLOCK <CR>
Block name (or ?): CHAIR <CR>
Insertion base point: 56,48 <CR>
Select objects: W <CR>
First point: 56,48 <CR>
Second point: 76,76 <CR>
13 found.
Select objects: <CR>
Command: OOPS <CR>
```

20. Zoom back out to view the entire drawing. Insert the block named CHAIR and rotate it to a suitable angle.

```
Command: ZOOM <CR>
All/Center/Dynamic/Extents/Left/Previous/Window/<Scale(X)>: A <CR>

Command: INSERT <CR>
Block name (or ?) <BOX>: CHAIR <CR>
 Insertion point: 140,56 <CR>
 X scale factor <1> / Corner / XYZ: <CR>
 Y scale factor (default=X): <CR>
 Rotation angle <0>: 162 <CR>
```

21. Insert the block named chair again.

```
Command: INSERT <CR>
Block name (or ?) <CHAIR>: <CR>
 Insertion point: 132,100 <CR>
 X scale factor <1> / Corner / XYZ: <CR>
 Y scale factor (default=X): <CR>
 Rotation angle <0>: 206 <CR>
```

22. Add text to complete the drawing.

```
Command: TEXT <CR>
Start point or Align/Center/Fit/Middle/Right/Style: 36,36 <CR>
Height <XXXXXX>: 4 <CR>
Rotation angle <0>: 90 <CR>
Text: 24 X 60 <CR>
Command: <CR>
TEXT
Text: TABLE <CR>

Command: TEXT <CR>
Start point or Align/Center/Fit/Middle/Right/Style: 88,36 <CR>
Height <XXXXXX>: 4 <CR>
Rotation angle <90>: <CR>
Text: 30 X 60 <CR>
Command: <CR>
```

```
TEXT
Text: DESK <CR>

Command: TEXT <CR>
Start point or Align/Center/Fit/Middle/Right/Style: 152,32 <CR>
Height <4.0000>: 4 <CR>
Rotation angle <90>: <CR>
Text: 18 X 36 <CR>
Command: <CR>
TEXT
Text: CABINET <CR>
```

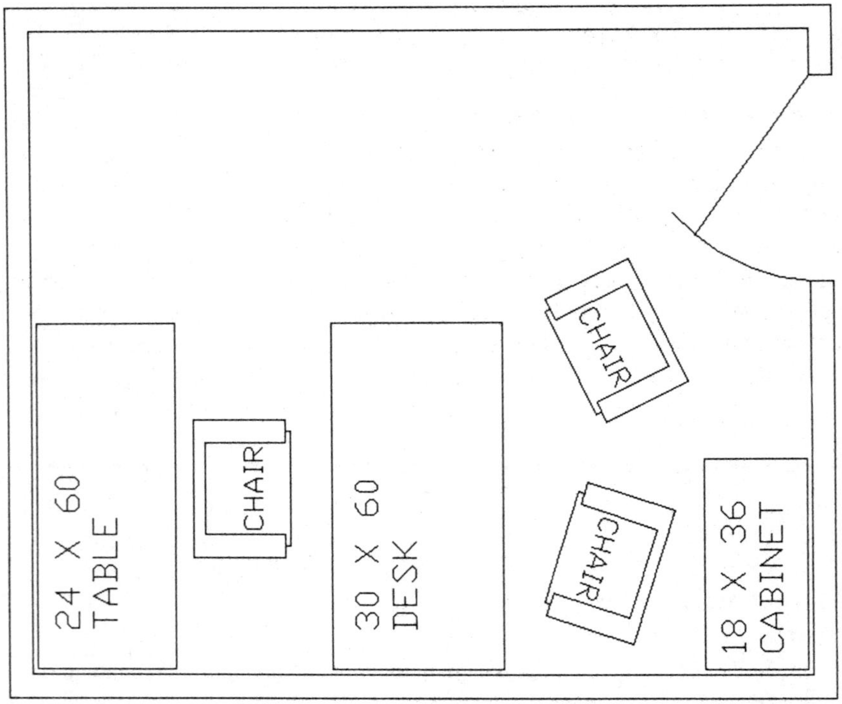

23. If you want to save the drawing, type **END**; otherwise type **QUIT** and press **Return**. Then type **Y** and press **Return** to redisplay the Main Menu.

Module 3

HARDWARE AND SOFTWARE

AutoCAD would be a far simpler program to learn if Autodesk, the company responsible for the program, would limit your choices to only a few computers, displays, digitizers, and hard-copy output devices. The advantages, however, far outweigh some minor inconveniences in learning the commands. AutoCAD is used with many different computers, displays, digitizers, and output devices. Through the installation procedure, you can modify AutoCAD to respond to the hardware configuration you choose as most suitable for your particular application.

MONITORS AutoCAD is designed to operate with two screens—a text screen and a graphics screen. You are not obligated, however, to have two physical monitors. If you prefer, you can purchase a computer system configured with two monitors. One monitor is used for text, and the other for drawings. Using AutoCAD with a single monitor is perfectly acceptable, however, and is typical of the majority of AutoCAD installations. With a single monitor system, you reserve the bottom several lines of the display for a command area. When you need to see the entire screen of text, either enter the TEXTSCREEN command, or press the Flip-Screen function key. The function (toggle) keys, including the Flip-Screen key differ from computer to computer. Following is a list of keys used with different computers.

Computer	*FLIP SCREEN*	*COORDS*	*GRID*	*ORTHO*	*SNAP*
Apricot	F1	^D	^G	^O	^B
Data General	F1	F6 or ^G	F7 or ^G	F8 or ^O	F9 or ^B
DEC Rainbow	PF1	F6 or ^D	F7 or ^G	F8 or ^O	F9 or ^B
Fujitsu Micro 16	CLS	^D	^G	^O	^B
Hewlett Packard	F1	F2	F3	F4	F5
IBM	F1	F6 or ^D	F7 or ^G	F8 or ^O	F9 or ^B
NCR & DEC Mate V	F1	F11	F9 or ^G	F8 or ^O	F7 or ^B
NEC APC III	PF1	PF6 or ^D	PF2 or ^G	PF3 or ^O	PF4 or ^B
Tandy 2000	F1	F1	^D	^O	^B
Texas Instruments	F1	F2 or ^D	F3 or ^G	F4 or ^B	F5 or ^B
Wang P.C.	PF7	PF6 or ^D	PF3 or ^G	PF2 or ^O	PF3 or ^B
Zenith Z-100	F10	F5 or ^D	F6 or ^G	F7 or ^O	F8 or ^B

A typical single screen AutoCAD configuration follows.

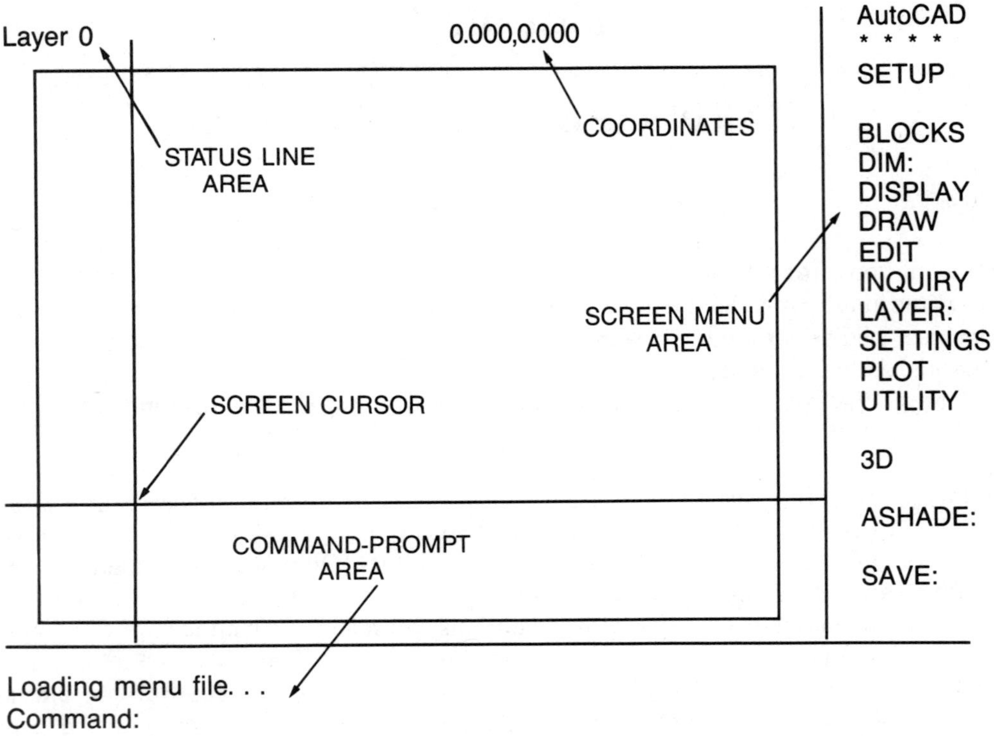

Depending upon your hardware choice and personal preferences, your screen setup may vary. The AutoCAD Main Menu Configuration option lets you make a number of choices about how your screen looks. If you are using a printed menu overlay with a digitizing tablet as an input device, the screen menu may be redundant. If you are performing all AutoCAD input from the keyboard, the screen menu is inconvenient. AutoCAD allows you to turn the screen menu off, providing additional space for drawing.

If you choose a two-monitor hardware system, one monitor is used for text and the other for graphics. In this case, the Command Area at the bottom of the screen is not needed. You may eliminate these lines from the bottom of your screen when you configure or reconfigure AutoCAD. Removing the text at the bottom of the screen provides additional area to view your drawing.

As you progress through this book, realize that there may be some minor variations between the sample screens in the book and what appears on your drawing screen. In general, the screen illustrations show only the graphics portion of the Drawing Editor, and the text screens display the text as it appears on a separate monitor, or as it scrolls by on the bottom lines of a single monitor system.

AutoCAD Release 9 adds additional features to the user interface including a menu bar, drop-down menus, icon menus, and dialogue boxes. Not all graphics adapters and displays that support AutoCAD benefit from these features. To take advantage of these features you must have one of the following display devices: IBM Enhanced Graphics Adapter (EGA), IBM Video Graphics Array (VGA), IBM Color Graphics Adapter (CGA) operating in monochrome mode, a Hercules Graphics Card, or a graphics adapter with a display driver for the Autodesk Device Interface (ADI™).

INPUT DEVICES It is possible to perform all AutoCAD input operations from the keyboard. The cursor control keys on your keyboard control the screen cursor. Pressing **Ctrl-Up Arrow** causes the screen cursor to move more rapidly. Pressing **Ctrl-Down Arrow** causes the screen cursor to move more slowly. There are several speed levels available. The cursor control keys can be used in addition to a mouse or digitizer.

If you attach a mouse to your computer system, you can control the screen cursor with both the mouse and the keyboard. In addition, you can use the mouse to select AutoCAD commands and options from the screen menu. With Release 9, you can also select commands and options from the drop-down menus and dialogue boxes. Use the method, or combination of methods, that is best for your hardware, software, and personal style.

If you add a digitizing tablet to your system, you can select points on the screen with the tablet's stylus, and select options from the screen menu. You can also develop printed overlays for your tablet for use with customized tablet menus. Printed overlays and preprogrammed menus are available for specialized AutoCAD applications both from Autodesk and other vendors.

All typical operations in this book can be performed with a single monitor system using only the keyboard as an input device. However, if your system has advanced input devices, such as a mouse or a digitizer, you may use them in performing the exercises.

Turn to Module 38 to continue the learning sequence.

Module 4

3DFACE

```
Command: 3DFACE
First point:
Second point:
Third point:
Fourth point:
```

NOTE

If you are following the recommended learning sequence through the book, Module 38 follows Module 3 in learning sequence order. 3DFACE is an advanced 3-dimensional command that is near the end of the learning sequence.

DESCRIPTION

The 3DFACE command and entity, introduced in AutoCAD 2.6, is a three-dimensional parallel to the two-dimensional SOLID command and entity. The prompts are the same, but 3DFACE accepts X, Y, and Z-coordinates for each point. A major difference in the construction of a 3DFACE is that, unlike the SOLID construction, the points for a 3DFACE are entered in a natural clockwise or counterclockwise order.

In the construction of three-dimensional objects, the midpoint, endpoint, and intersection OSNAP modes are available for determining locations on the edges of a 3DFACE.

3DFACES are displayed as wire frames; they are not filled. However, when VPOINT is used to rotate a construction for three-dimensional visualization, the HIDE command treats a 3DFACE as an opaque entity and removes lines passing behind the 3DFACE.

APPLICATIONS

The 3DFACE is essential for constructing diagonal planes for three-dimensional visualization. Consider the external view of a typical house with a pitched roof. You can use the 3DFACE command to depict the sloped roof. A 3DFACE command is ideal for depicting constructions like geodesic domes or the facets on gemstones. While SOLID is appropriate for three-dimensional objects with vertical lines in the Z-dimension, the 3DFACE is most appropriate for diagonals in the Z-dimension. There is no requirement that the vertices of a 3DFACE be co-planar, although practical applications of nonplanar surfaces are elusive.

TYPICAL OPERATION

In this session you draw a pyramid in three dimensions. The object constructed is similar to the pyramid constructed in the 3DLINE module. However, when rotated for three-dimensional visualization, the HIDE command recognizes the faces as opaque and performs hidden line removal. Begin a new drawing named 3DFACE.

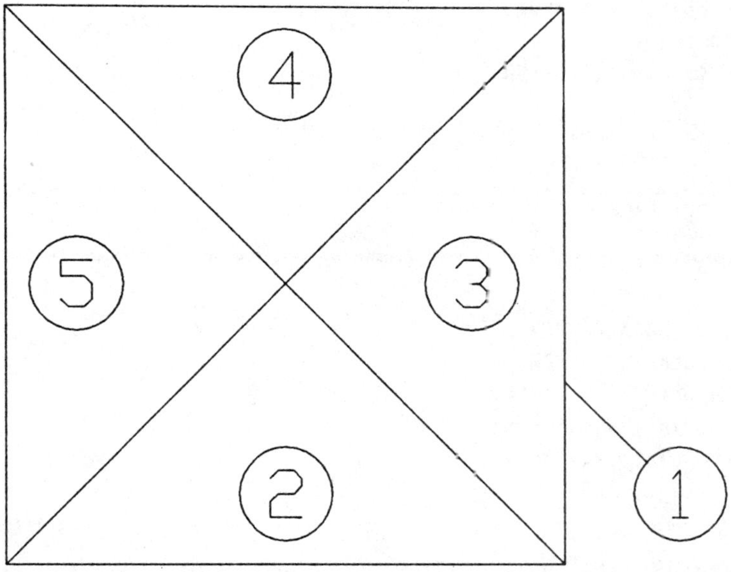

1. Draw the rectangular base of the pyramid as a 3DFACE. With the elevation at its default value of 0, you do not need to enter the Z-dimension.

```
Command: 3DFACE <CR>
First point: 1,1 <CR>
Second point: 7,1 <CR>
Third point: 7,7 <CR>
Fourth point: 1,7 <CR>
Third point: <CR>
```

2. Draw the front face of the pyramid. Only the vertex point requires the entry of the Z-axis point.

```
Command: 3DFACE
First point: 1,1 <CR>
Second point: 7,1 <CR>
Third point: 4,4,5 <CR>
Fourth point: 1,1 <CR>
Third point: <CR>
```

3. Draw the right face of the pyramid.

```
Command: 3DFACE <CR>
First point: 7,1 <CR>
Second point: 7,7 <CR>
Third point: 4,4,5 <CR>
Fourth point: 7,1 <CR>
Third point: <CR>
```

4. Draw the back face of the pyramid.

```
Command: 3DFACE <CR>
First point: 7,7 <CR>
Second point:  1,7 <CR>
Third point: 4,4,5 <CR>
Fourth point: 7,7 <CR>
Third point: <CR>
```

5. Draw the left face of the pyramid.

```
Command: 3DFACE <CR>
First point: 1,7 <CR>
Second point: 1,1 <CR>
Third point: 4,4,5 <CR>
Fourth point: 1,7 <CR>
Third point: <CR>
```

6. Rotate the pyramid and remove the hidden lines for a 3-dimensional visualization.

```
Command: VPOINT <CR>
Enter view point <0.0000,0.0000,1.0000>: 1,-1.5,1 <CR>
Regenerating drawing.
Command: HIDE <CR>
Regenerating drawing.
```

Your three-dimensional visualization looks similar to the following illustration.

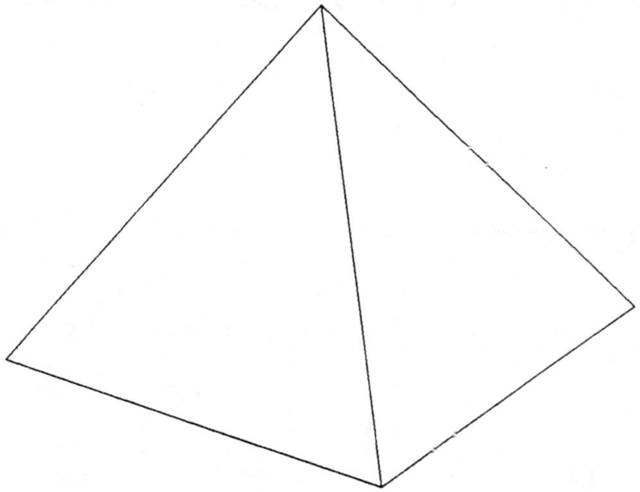

Compare this visualization with the visualization produced in the 3DLINE module. Notice that the fundamental difference is that the 3DLINE drawing is a hollow construction formed of lines, while the 3DFACE drawing recognizes the surfaces of the object and treats them as opaque faces, removing hidden lines.

7. Type **QUIT** and press **Return**; then type **Y** and press **Return** to display the Main Menu.
8. This is the last module of the learning sequence.

Module 5

3DLINE

```
Command: 3DLINE
From Point:
To Point:
```

DESCRIPTION

The 3DLINE command, introduced in AutoCAD 2.6, allows the construction of lines in three-dimensional space. Using the plan view, which is the default view, the third (or Z) dimension extends away from you, toward the rear of your display screen. A 3DLINE is an extension of a standard LINE entity with the addition of the third dimension.

You respond to the LINE prompt with an X, Y, and Z value. You can specify points using relative coordinates in the form @1,2,3. Specifying only an X and Y coordinate for a 3DLINE constructs a line using your X and Y coordinates and the Z coordinate from the current elevation (set with the ELEV command).

Polar coordinates are meaningful in only two dimensions. Specifying a point using polar coordinates (e.g., @56 < 90) supplies the X and Y coordinates, but assumes the Z-coordinate from the current elevation.

The points of a 3DLINE are manipulated in all three dimensions with the COPY, MOVE, and STRETCH commands. You can manipulate the X and Y dimensions of a 3DLINE with the ARRAY, MIRROR, and ROTATE commands. When you SCALE a 3DLINE, the scale factor is applied to the X, Y, and Z-axes.

The CHANGE command is used to modify 3DLINES. You must, however, explicitly enter the Z coordinate if you want to CHANGE the Z dimension of a 3DLINE. Otherwise, only the X and Y values are changed.

APPLICATIONS

The 3DLINE command brings to AutoCAD the ability to construct a diagonal line in the Z dimension. It is ideal for angular construction, such as buildings and cabinets, and enhances visualization when the VPOINT command is used. When drawing in three dimensions with only elevation and thickness specifications, all lines in the Z axis are constructed perpendicular to both X and Y axes. The 3DLINE allows the construction of lines that have any desired orientation in three-dimensional space; they are not limited to constructions perpendicular to the X and Y axes. When constructing drawings with 3DLINE, object snap is available to identify endpoints and midpoints in three dimensions. Modifying your point of view with the VPOINT command makes it easier to pick points on the screen when drawing in three dimensions.

TYPICAL OPERATION

In this session you construct a wire frame pyramid in three dimensions. Begin a new drawing named 3DLINE.

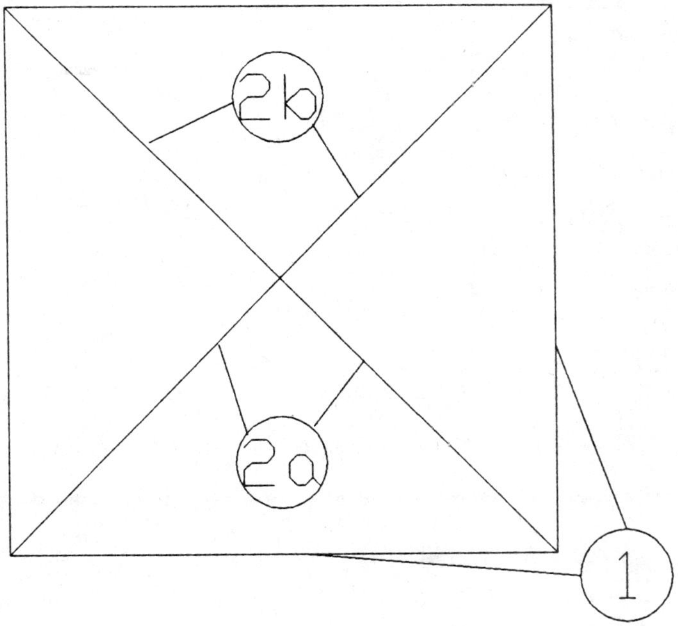

1. Start by drawing the square base of the pyramid in the X and Y axes. You could use 3DLINES for this construction, but standard lines are just as good and require fewer coordinates for entry.

```
Command: LINE <CR>
From point: 1,1 <CR>
To point: 7,1 <CR>
To point: 7,8 <CR>
To point: 1,8 <CR>
To point: C <CR>
Command:
```

2. Construct the edges of the pyramid going into three-dimensional space. Construct the vertex of the pyramid at 4,4,5.

```
Command: 3DLINE <CR>
From point: 1,1,0 <CR>
To point: 4,4,5 <CR>
To point: 7,1,0 <CR>
To point:  <CR>
Command:  <CR>
3DLINE
From point: 7,8,0 <CR>
To point: 4,4,5 <CR>
To point: 1,8,0 <CR>
To point:  <CR>
Command:
```

3. Use VPOINT to change your point of view for a better three-dimensional visualization.

```
Command: VPOINT <CR>
Enter view point <0.0000,0.0000,1.0000>: 1,-1.5,1 <CR>
Regenerating drawing.
Command:
```

Your completed drawing should look like the following one. As you look at the drawing, remember that you are looking at lines in space. There are no defined solids or faces in the construction. As a result, you can see right through the construction.

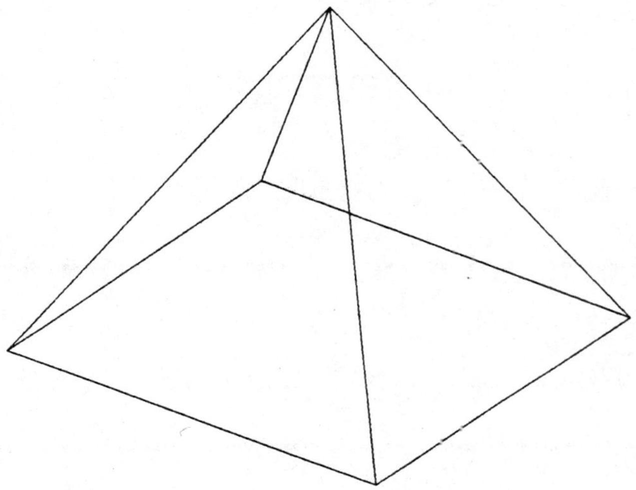

If you have difficulty visualizing the three-dimensional construction, use the VPOINT command to change your point of view to gain additional views.

4. Type **QUIT** and press **Return**; then type **Y** and press **Return** to display the AutoCAD Main Menu.
5. Turn to Module 4 to continue the learning sequence.

Module 6

APERTURE

```
Command: APERTURE
Object snap target height (1-50 pixels) <10>: 50
```

DESCRIPTION

The OSNAP command uses a special set of cross hairs with an aperture to pick drawing entities. The APERTURE command controls the size of the target cross hairs for object snap purposes.

APPLICATIONS

The size of the OSNAP target is expressed in pixels. Therefore, the physical size of the aperture depends directly upon the resolution of the display screen. The ideal target size is a function of hardware resolution, drawing complexity, and personal style. Selecting a target size that is too small requires additional effort in identifying points in the drawing with OSNAP. Selecting a target size that is too large may make it impossible to isolate a single drawing entity within a complex drawing. Experiment with various sizes of targets to determine the best size (or sizes) for your needs.

TYPICAL OPERATION

In this session you change the size of the OSNAP target with the APERTURE command. From the AutoCAD Main Menu, begin a new drawing named APERTURE and start the Drawing Editor.

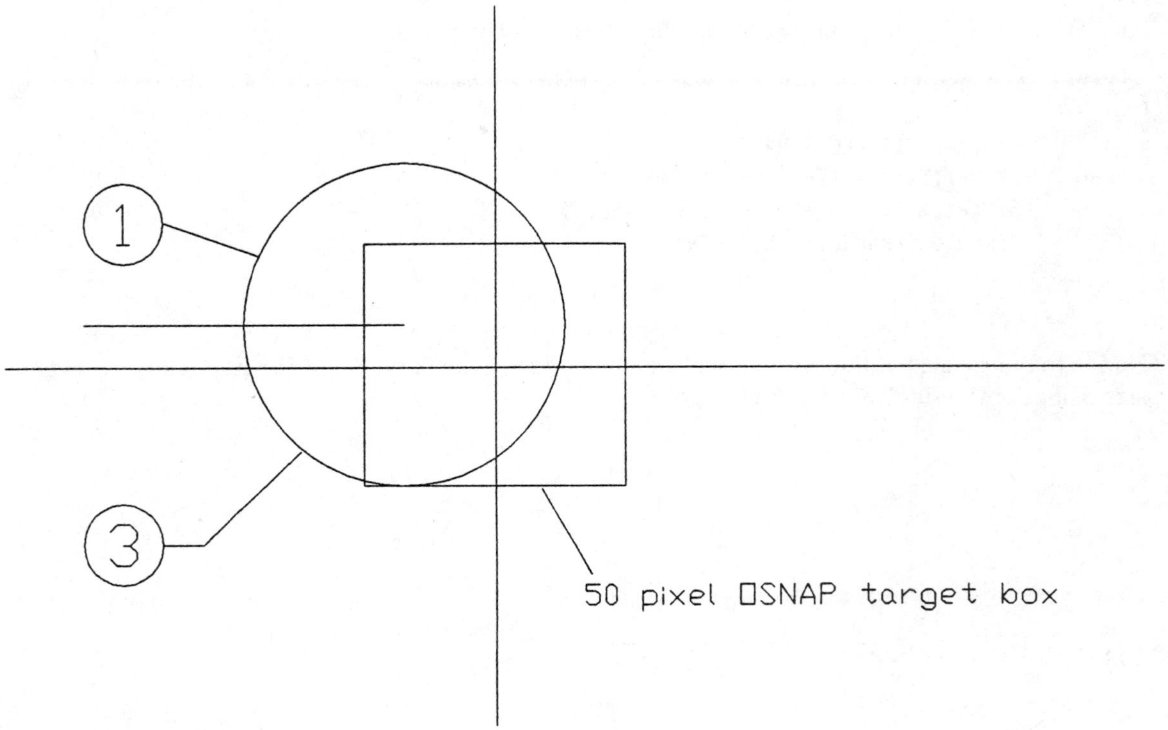

1. Draw a line.

```
Command: LINE <CR>
From point: 1,5 <CR>
To point: 5,5 <CR>
To point: <CR>
Command:
```

2. Use the APERTURE command to construct an OSNAP target as large as possible.

```
Command: APERTURE <CR>
Object snap target height (1-50 pixels) <10>: 50 <CR>
```

3. Draw a circle with the center at the endpoint of the line.

```
Command: CIRCLE <CR>
3P/2P/TTR/<Center point>: END <CR>
of (Pick the right end of the line.)
Diameter/<Radius>: 5,7 <CR>
```

Notice the large size of the target aperture as you select the endpoint of the line. The new target size remains in effect until you change it.

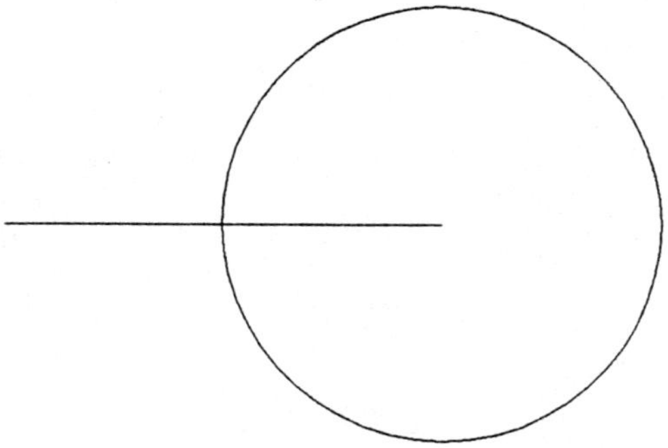

4. Type **QUIT** and press **Return**; then type **Y** and press **Return** to display the AutoCAD Main Menu.
5. Turn to Module 21 to continue the learning sequence.

Module 7

ARC

```
Command: ARC
Center/<Start point>:
```

DESCRIPTION

The ARC command is used for drawing incomplete circles.

Pick — Pick a point on the screen with the screen cursor or type its coordinates at the keyboard to specify the starting point for the arc.

Center — Specify the center of the circle containing the arc.

There are six option letters associated with the ARC command:

- A - included angle
- C - center
- D - starting direction
- E - end point
- L - length of chord
- R - radius

Prompts are provided at each step of arc construction to indicate what options are available. The AutoCAD ADE-2 software allows you to type "DRAG" when the last parameter prompt appears on the screen and then dynamically locate the last coordinate.

APPLICATIONS

Use the ARC command any time you need to draw a portion of a circle. It is quicker and easier to draw an arc than to draw a circle and break it.

There are eight ways of drawing arcs in AutoCAD. The eight ARC construction methods are:

1.	three points on arc	(3-point:)
2.	start point, center, end point	(S,C,E:)
3.	start point, center, included angle	(S,C,A:)
4.	start point, center, length of chord	(S,C,L:)
5.	start point, end point, radius	(S,E,R:)
6.	start point, end point, included angle	(S,E,A:)
7.	start point, end point, starting direction	(S,E,D:)
8.	continuation of previous line or arc	(Contin:)

The "three points on arc" method is the default for drawing arcs. The term "center" in methods 2, 3, and 4 refers to the center of the circle including the arc. Think of the center of the arc as the point where the steel point of the manual compass pierces the paper when drawing arcs and circles without the aid of a CAD system.

TYPICAL OPERATION

This session lets you use each of the arc construction methods. The numbered steps correspond to the arcs shown in the following drawing.

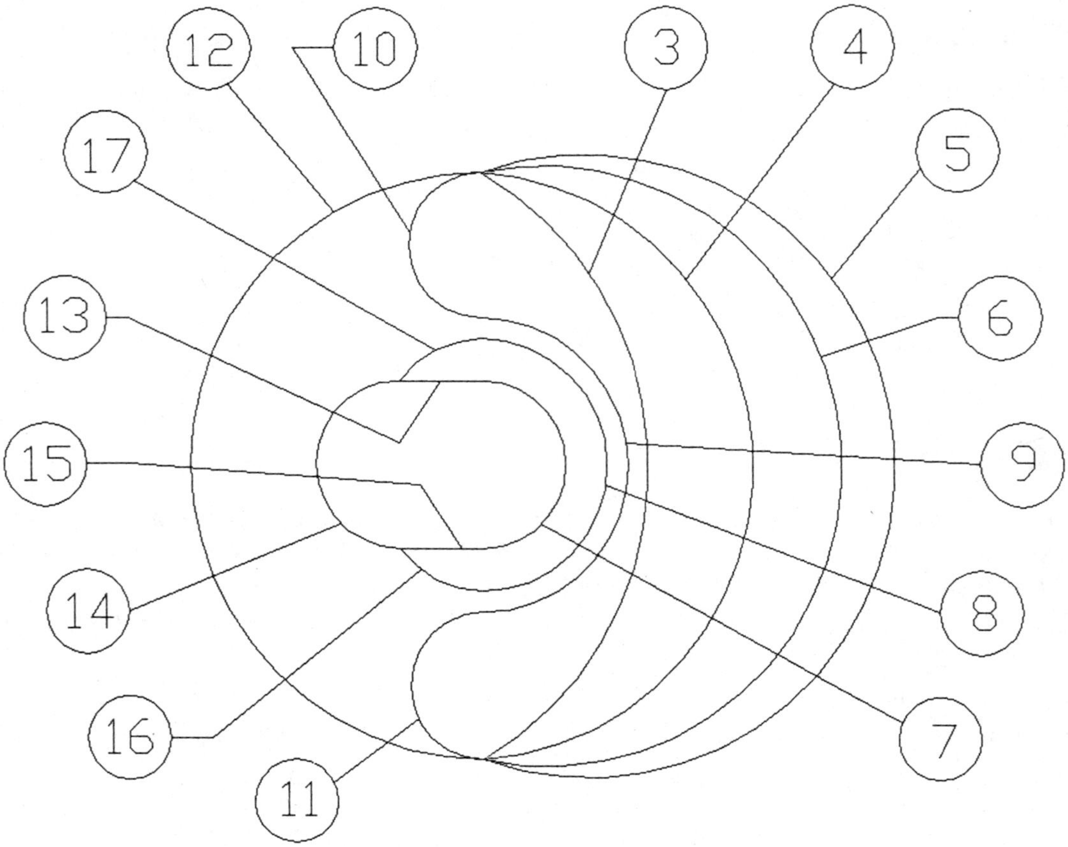

1. Starting at the Main Menu, begin a drawing named ARC. Set the SNAP and turn the GRID on:

```
Command: SNAP <CR>
Snap spacing or ON/OFF/Aspect/Rotate/Style <1.0000>: .25 <CR>

Command: GRID <CR>
Grid spacing(X) or ON/OFF/Snap/Aspect <0.0000>: on <CR>
```

2. Press **INS** and select DRAW from the AutoCAD Root Menu using the cursor keys or a mouse. From the DRAW submenu, pick ARC.
3. Select the 3-point ARC.

```
Command: ARC Center/<Start point>: 6.0,1.0 <CR>
Center/End/<Second point>: 8.0,4.5 <CR>
End point: DRAG 6.0,8.0 <CR>
```

4. Pick the ARC menu selection labeled as S,C,E.

```
Command: ARC Center/<Start point>: 6,1 <CR>
Center/End/<Second point>: C Center: 6.75,4.5 <CR>
Angle/Length of chord/<End point>: DRAG  6,8 <CR>
```

5. Pick the ARC menu selection labeled as S,C,A.

```
Command: ARC Center/<Start point>: 6,1 <CR>
Center/End/<Second point>: C Center: 7.25,4.5 <CR>
Angle/Length of chord/<End point>: <CR>
A Included angle: DRAG  219 <CR>
```

6. Pick the ARC menu selection labeled as S,C,L.

```
Command: ARC Center/<Start point>: 6,1 <CR>
Center/End/<Second point>: C Center: 5.75,4.5 <CR>
Angle/Length of chord/<End point>: <CR>
L Length of chord: DRAG @7.0<90 <CR>
```

7. Pick the ARC menu selection labeled as S,E,A.

```
Command: ARC Center/<Start point>: 6,3.5 <CR>
Center/End/<Second point>: E End point: 6,5.5 <CR>
Angle/Direction/Radius/<Center point>: <CR>
A Included Angle: 180 <CR>
```

8. Pick the ARC menu selection labeled as S,E,R.

```
Command: ARC Center/<Start point>: 6,3 <CR>
Center/End/<Second point>: E End point: 6,6 <CR>
Angle/Direction/Radius/<Center point>: <CR>
R Radius: 1.5 <CR>
```

9. Pick the ARC menu selection labeled as S,E,D.

```
Command: ARC Center/<Start point>: 6,2.75 <CR>
Center/End/<Second point>: E End point: 6,6.25 <CR>
Angle/Direction/Radius/<Center point>: <CR>
D Direction from start point: DRAG 0 <CR>
```

10. Pick the ARC menu selection labeled as C,S,E.

```
Command: ARC Center/<Start point>: C Center: 6.0,7.125 <CR>
Start point: 6,8 <CR>
Angle/Length of chord/<End point>: <CR>
DRAG   6,6.25 <CR>
```

11. Pick the ARC menu selection labeled as C,S,A.

```
Command: ARC Center/<Start point>: C Center: 6,1.875 <CR>
Start point: 6,2.75 <CR>
Angle/Length of chord/<End point>: <CR>
A Included angle: DRAG 180 <CR>
```

12. Pick the ARC menu selection labeled as C,S,L.

```
Command: ARC Center/<Start point>: C Center: 6,4.5 <CR>
Start point: 6,8 <CR>
Angle/Length of chord/<End point>: <CR>
L Length of chord: DRAG 6,1 <CR>
```

13. Draw a line.

```
Command: LINE <CR>
From point: 6,5.5 <CR>
To point: 5,5.5 <CR>
To point: <CR>
```

14. Pick the ARC menu selection labeled as Contin.

```
Command: ARC Center/<Start point>: <CR>
End point: DRAG   @2<270 <CR>
```

15. Draw a line.

```
Command: LINE <CR>
From point: 6,3.5 <CR>
To point: 5,3.5 <CR>
To point: <CR>
```

16. Pick the ARC menu selection labeled as S,E,D.

```
Command: ARC Center/<Start point>: 6,3 <CR>
Center/End/<Second point>: E End point: 5,3.5 <CR>
Angle/Direction/Radius/<Center point>: <CR>
D Direction from start point: DRAG 180 <CR>
```

17. Pick the ARC menu selection labeled as S,E,D.

```
Command: ARC Center/<Start point>: 6,6 <CR>
Center/End/<Second point>: E End point: 5,5.5 <CR>
Angle/Direction/Radius/<Center point>:<CR>
D Direction from start point: DRAG 180 <CR>
```

After completing all of the steps, your graphics screen should resemble the following drawing.

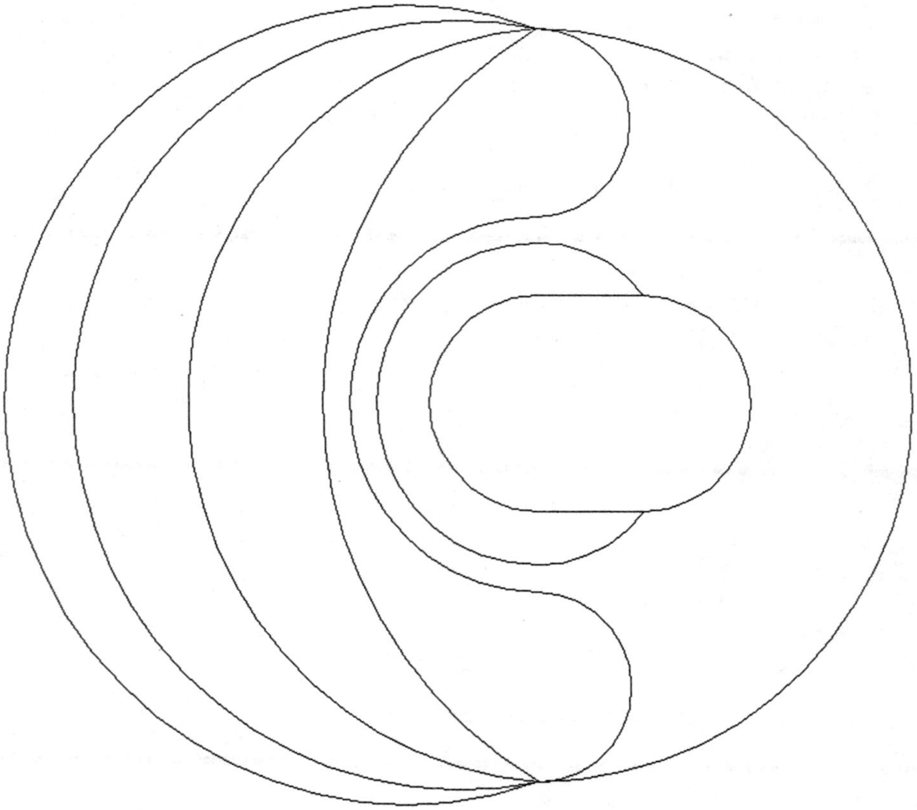

18. Type **QUIT** and press **Return**; then type **Y** and press **Return** to redisplay the Main Menu.
19. Turn to Module 10 to continue the learning sequence.

Module 8

AREA

```
Command: AREA
```

DESCRIPTION

The AREA command computes the area of an enclosed figure. With all versions of AutoCAD (2.18 +) you can describe a region by showing AutoCAD the area by picking the points on the screen or typing the points from the keyboard that define the area. Once the points are identified, AutoCAD computes the area.

Enhancements added with AutoCAD version 2.5 include the ability to pick a closed polyline or circle as an entity, as well as to add and subtract areas in the calculation of the area of complex regions. The area of all regions is expressed using the current drawing units.

APPLICATIONS

The AREA command is useful for computing the square footage in buildings. If you first determine the gross square footage of a house, you can use the AREA Subtract option to subtract the area of the garage. This process lets you determine the number of square feet of air-conditioned space, for instance. When parts are cut or machined from material of uniform thickness, the AREA command provides an easy way to determine the weight of the finished product. (Multiply the area by the weight per square unit.)

TYPICAL OPERATION

In this session you compute the area of several regions using a several variations of the AREA command. Begin a new drawing named AREA.

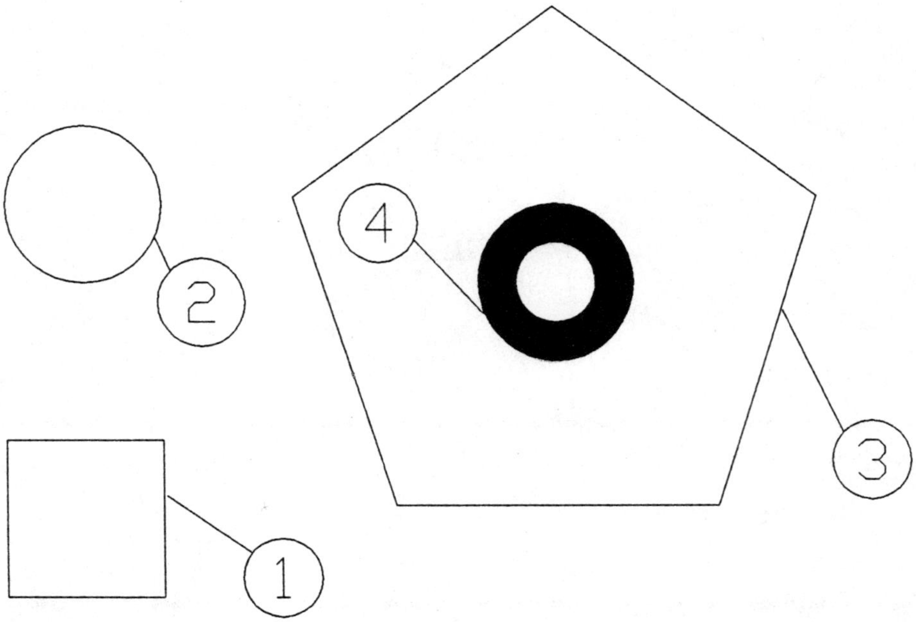

1. Draw a small box.

```
Command: LINE <CR>
From point: 1,1 <CR>
To point: 1,3 <CR>
To point: 3,3 <CR>
To point: 3,1 <CR>
To point: C <CR>
```

NOTE

If you are using a version of AutoCAD earlier than 2.5, skip to step 5.

2. Draw a circle.

```
Command: CIRCLE <CR>
3P/2P/TTR/<Center point>: 2,6 <CR>
Diameter/<Radius>: 1 <CR>
```

3. Draw a pentagon using the POLYGON command. A polygon is constructed as a polyline, therefore, the AREA command identifies it as a closed figure.

```
Command: POLYGON <CR>
Number of sides: 5 <CR>
Edge/<Center of polygon>: 8,5 <CR>
Inscribed in circle/Circumscribed about circle (I/C): I <CR>
Radius of circle:  3.5 <CR>
```

4. Draw a donut inside the pentagon. A donut is constructed of polyline segments, therefore, AutoCAD identifies it as a closed figure.

```
Command: DONUT <CR>
Inside diameter <0.5000>: 1 <CR>
Outside diameter <1.0000>: 2 <CR>
Center of doughnut: 8,5 <CR>
Center of doughnut: <CR>
Command:
```

5. Compute the area of the square.

```
Command: AREA <CR>
<First point>/Entity/Add/Subtract: 1,1 <CR>
Next point: 1,3 <CR>
Next point: 3,3 <CR>
Next point: 3,1 <CR>
Next point: 3,1 <CR>  (Version 2.5+ does not require this point)
Next point: <CR>
Area = 4.0000, Perimeter = 8.0000
```

NOTE

If you are using a version of AutoCAD prior to 2.5, skip to step 8.

6. Compute the area of the circle.

```
Command: AREA <CR>
<First point>/Entity/Add/Subtract: E <CR>
Select circle or polyline: (Pick the circle.) <CR>
Area = 3.1416, Circumference = 6.2832
```

7. Compute the area of the pentagon minus the area of the donut.

```
Command: AREA <CR>
<First point>/Entity/Add/Subtract: A <CR>
<First point>/Entity/Subtract: E <CR>
(ADD mode) Select circle or polyline: (Pick the pentagon.) <CR>
Area = 29.1261, Perimeter = 20.5725
Total area = 29.1261
(ADD mode) Select circle or polyline: <CR>
<First point>/Entity/Subtract: S <CR>
<First point>/Entity/Add: E <CR>
(SUBTRACT mode) Select circle or polyline: (Pick the donut.) <CR>
Area = 1.7671, Perimeter = 4.7124
Total area = 27.3590
(SUBTRACT mode) Select circle or polyline: <CR>
<First point>/Entity/Add: <CR>
Command:
```

Carefully examine the value derived for the area of the donut. AutoCAD figures the area based on the center of the polyline. This centerline has a diameter of 1.5 (radius of .75). The total area of 27.3590 is the area of the pentagon (29.1261) minus the area of the donut (1.7671). Remember that the area of all regions bounded by polylines is computed from the centerline of the polyline.

8. Type **QUIT** and press **Return**; then type **Y** and press **Return** to display the AutoCAD Main Menu.
9. Turn to Module 40 to continue the learning sequence.

Module 9

ARRAY

```
Command: ARRAY
Select objects:
Rectangular or Polar array (R/P):
```

DESCRIPTION

The ARRAY command is used to reproduce an object or group of objects in a rectangular or circular pattern. The command minimizes the effort required. After an array is produced, the resulting elements within the array may be manipulated independently. When using a rectangular array, AutoCAD prompts you for the number of rows and columns.

Rows are always horizontal and columns are always vertical. To help you remember the difference between a column and a row, think about the columns of a building to remember that columns are vertical. The default number of rows and columns is always 1. If you enter a row and column value of 1, the ARRAY command is meaningless to AutoCAD. You may enter either a row quantity of 1 or a column quantity of 1, but not both in the same ARRAY operation. Any time you enter values that produce extreme quantities in your array, AutoCAD displays the following prompt.

```
This command repeats the selected items nnn times.

    Do you really want to do this?
```

If you answer with Y, the array process continues.

RECTANGULAR ARRAY If the arrangement of drawing elements is to be arranged in vertical columns and horizontal rows, a rectangular array is required. There are two basic ways to indicate the distance between rows and columns. First, the values are entered by typing them individually from the keyboard. Second, they are specified by picking the opposite corners of a rectangle. The rectangle is similar to a window used in the ERASE or ZOOM commands.

POLAR ARRAY If the desired array is Polar and you reply to the ARRAY prompt with **P**, (**C** for circular in versions prior to 2.5), the following prompt is displayed.

```
Center point of array:
```

Either pick the center point with the screen cursor or type an absolute location from the keyboard. For circular arrays, the next prompt is:

```
Angle between items (+=CCW, -=CW):
```

A positive number produces a counterclockwise array. A negative number produces clockwise array. The angle is always greater than zero and less than 360 degrees.

The next prompt for a circular array is:

```
Number of items or -(degrees to fill):
```

The Polar array, introduced in AutoCAD version 2.5 has three potential parameters for specifying the construction of the array after you select the objects forming the array. These parameters are:

- Number of items
- Angle to fill
- Angle between items

You must specify two of the three parameters when responding to the ARRAY screen dialog. If you specify the number of items and the angle to fill, AutoCAD omits the prompt for the angle between items. If you provide a null response (press **Return**) for either the number of items or the angle to fill, AutoCAD prompts for the angle between items.

When AutoCAD constructs a Polar/circular array, a reference point for each entity or block is required.

Point	=	insertion point
Circle, Arc	=	center point
Block, Shape	=	insertion base point
Text	=	starting point
Line, Trace	=	one end point

Since the array process is complex, it is sometimes necessary to place the desired objects within a BLOCK. This preserves their relationship to one another during production of the array.

The last prompt in the series for a circular array is:

```
Rotate objects as they are copied? <N>
```

If you choose the default (no), then the object retains its original angle when drawn. If you respond with Y (yes), the original object (or group of objects) is rotated by the same number of degrees as the objects within the array.

APPLICATIONS

In printed circuit board design, draw one solder pad and then use ARRAY to make a rectangular array of pads for mounting an integrated circuit or socket. In mechanical design, draw a single tooth of a gear and use ARRAY to replicate the single tooth around the center point of the gear. In landscape design, draw a single bush, then use a rectangular array to produce a row of plantings along a drive. In architectural design, draw one side of a geodesic dome, then use a circular array to complete the drawing of the periphery of the dome. When drawing a suspended ceiling, draw one panel and replicate it over the entire open space.

TYPICAL OPERATION

In this session you produce both rectangular and circular arrays. Your final drawing should look like the one shown. The numbered balloons correspond to the steps in the operation. Begin a new drawing named ARRAY.

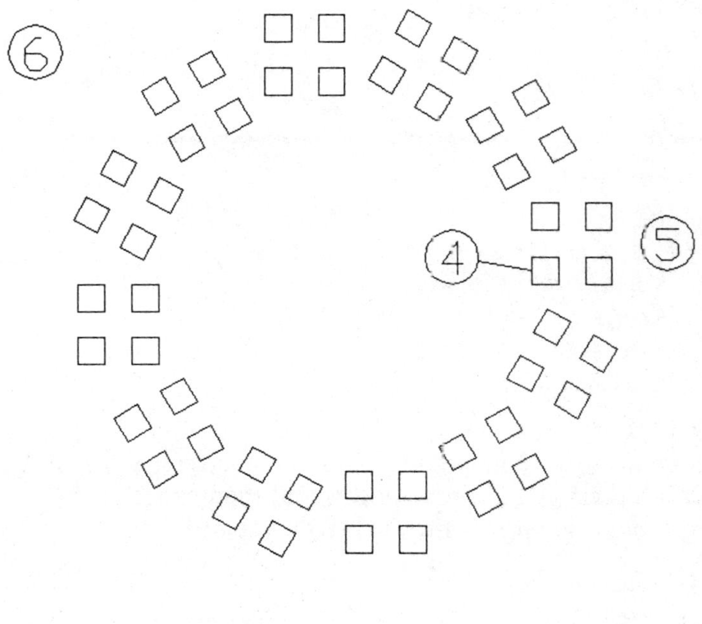

1. Set the SNAP to .25.

```
Command: SNAP <CR>
Snap spacing or ON/OFF/Aspect/Rotate/Style <1.0000>: .25 <CR>
```

2. Turn the GRID on.

```
Command: GRID <CR>
Grid spacing(X) or ON/OFF/Snap/Aspect <0.0000>: ON <CR>
```

3. ZOOM the screen with a Zoom window operation to magnify an area of the drawing before beginning the first part.

```
Command: ZOOM <CR>
All/Center/Dynamic/Extents/Left/Previous/Window/<Scale(X)>: W <CR>
First point: 7.75,3.75 <CR>
Second point: 10.0,5.75 <CR>
```

4. Draw a square box.

```
Command: LINE <CR>
From point: 8.5,4.25 <CR>
To point: 8.5,4.5 <CR>
To point: 8.75,4.5 <CR>
To point: 8.75,4.25 <CR>
To point: c <CR>
```

5. Now produce an array of four square boxes by choosing the ARRAY command. Place a window around the box you drew in step 4, and then choose a rectangular type array as shown. After producing the rectangular array, zoom the screen to its original view.

```
Command: ARRAY <CR>
Select objects: W <CR>
First point: (Pick a point below the lower-left corner of the block; do not
touch the block.)
Second point: (Pick a point above the upper-right corner of the block.)
4 found.
Select objects: <CR>
Rectangular or Polar array (R/P): R <CR>
Number of rows (---)  <1>: 2 <CR>
Number of columns (|||)  <1>: 2 <CR>
Unit cell or distance between rows: (Pick point at 8.5,4.25.)
Other corner: (Pick point at 9.0,4.75.)

Command: ZOOM <CR>
All/Center/Dynamic/Extents/Left/Previous/Window/<Scale(X)>: P <CR>
```

6. Now produce a circular array using the following entries.

```
Command: ARRAY <CR>
Select objects : W <CR>
First point: (Pick next pick window around the 4 blocks)
Second point:(Pick next pick window around the 4 blocks)
16 found.
```

You need to follow one of two different procedures to complete the Polar/circular array depending on your version of AutoCAD.

The dialog for performing this operation with the circular arrays of AutoCAD versions prior to 2.5 is shown in the following step.

```
Select objects: <CR>
Rectangular or circular array (R/C): C <CR>
Center point of array: {Pick center at 6.75,4.25}
Angle between items (+=CCW, -=CW): 30
Number of items or -(degrees to fill): 8 {or -360}
Rotate objects as they are copied? <N> Y <CR>
```

The dialog for performing this operation with the Polar arrays of AutoCAD versions 2.5 + is shown in the following step.

```
Rectangular or Polar array (R/P): P
Center point of array: 6.75,4.25
Number of items: <CR>
Angle to fill (+=ccw, -=cw) <360>: <CR>
Angle between items: 30 <CR>
Rotate objects as they are copied? <Y> <CR
```

Your drawing should look like the following one.

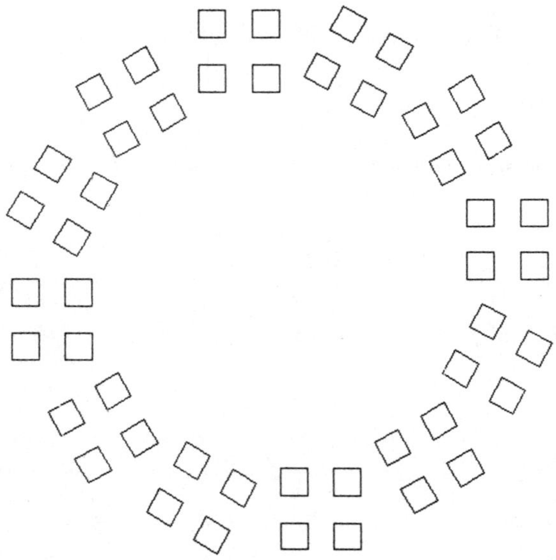

7. Use **QUIT** to redisplay the Main Menu.
8. Turn to Module 43 to continue the learning sequence.

Module 10

AXIS

```
Command: AXIS
Tick spacing(X) or ON/OFF/Snap/Aspect <0.0000>:
```

DESCRIPTION

The AXIS command places a ruler along the bottom and right sides of the drawing display. If the tick spacing exceeds the resolution of your screen, the ruler lines are turned off with the message:

```
Axis ticks too close to display.
Command:
```

This can happen when you specify numbers that are too small, or when zooming out to a larger display area. The Axis options are described in the following list.

On	Turns on the axis ruler line.
Off	Turns off the axis ruler line.
Tick spacing	Type a number to specify the spacing of the axis in terms of drawing units. The horizontal and vertical spacing is equal.
Tick spacing(X)	Type a number followed by X to specify the spacing of the axis in terms of a multiple of the SNAP resolution. 1X provides a tick spacing equal to the SNAP resolution. 10X provides a tick spacing equal to 10 times the SNAP resolution.
Aspect	Type "A" to specify different horizontal and vertical ruler tick spacing. (This option is not available when SNAP is isometric.)
Snap	(Version 2.5 +) Type **S** to specify that the axis should follow the snap resolution.

If you use the UNITS command to specify a feet and inches display (architectural), some of the tick marks are drawn double size to indicate whole feet or whole inches. Variable size tick marks are only used when the tick spacing corresponds to exact fractional inches or feet.

APPLICATIONS

If you like to use an architect's or engineer's scale, the AXIS command can be a valuable tool. The AXIS tick marks resemble the old, familiar scales found on every drafting board. Once you become comfortable with AutoCAD's X-Y coordinate system, you may find that you no longer depend on the AXIS scale. As you begin to think in terms of X-Y coordinates, you may wish to eliminate the use of the AXIS tick marks.

TYPICAL OPERATION

In this session you use the AXIS command. Begin a new drawing named AXIS.

1. Set the SNAP to .25.

```
Command:SNAP <CR>
Snap spacing or ON/OFF/Aspect/Rotate/Style <1.0000>: ON <CR>
Command:
```

2. Let the GRID follow the SNAP.

```
Command:GRID <CR>
Grid spacing(X) or ON/OFF/Snap/Aspect <0.0000>: 0 <CR>
Command:
```

3. Set the AXIS equal to the SNAP. Starting with version 2.5, you can also type S to set the AXIS equal to the SNAP.

```
Command:AXIS <CR>
Tick spacing(X) or ON/OFF/Snap/Aspect <0.0000>: 0 <CR>
Command:AXIS <CR>
Tick spacing(X) or ON/OFF/Snap/Aspect <0.0000>: ON <CR>
Command:
```

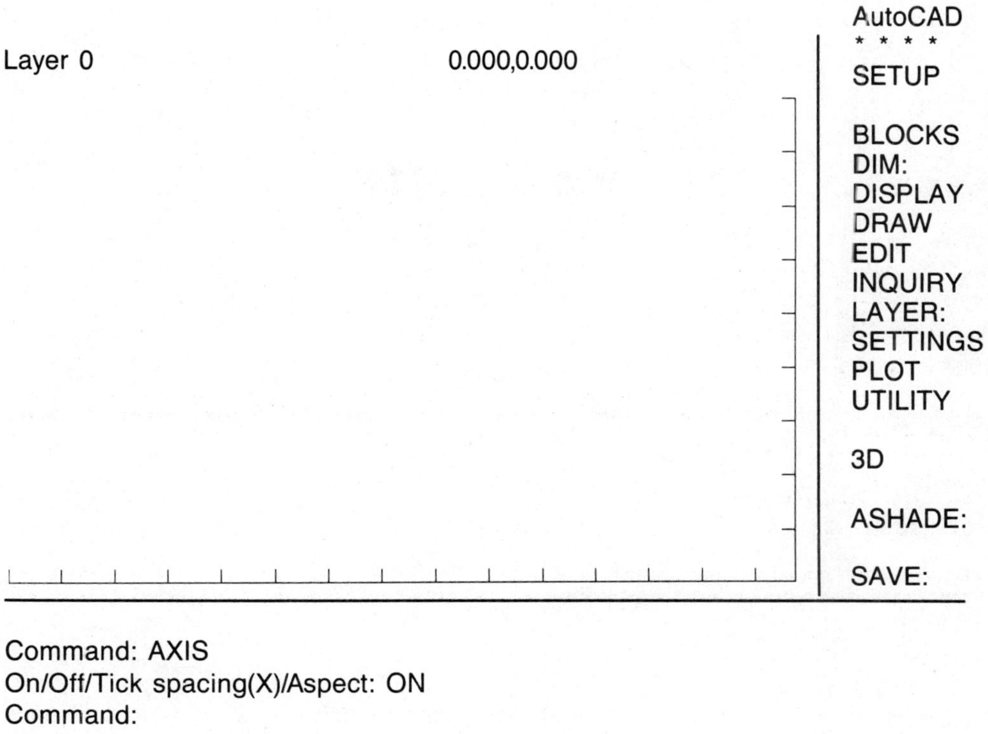

4. Type **QUIT** and press **Return**; then type **Y** and press **Return** to redisplay the Main Menu.
5. Turn to Module 29 to continue the learning sequence.

Module 11

BASE

```
Command: BASE
Base point <0.0000,0.0000,0.0000>:
```

DESCRIPTION

AutoCAD lets you insert one drawing into another even though the drawing to be inserted has not been designated as a block or a wblock. The major barrier to inserting a drawing that has not been saved as a wblock is that it does not have an insertion base point. You can remedy this by using the BASE command.

Therefore, if you plan to use a drawing as part of another drawing, you should designate a base point for insertion. If you do not specify a base point, AutoCAD assumes the 0,0 coordinate of the inserted drawing as the base point. Insertion of a drawing is similar to the insertion of a block or wblock.

Starting with AutoCAD version 2.6, the BASE command accepts 3-dimensional points including an X, Y, and Z-coordinate. For performing 2-dimensional work, you may safely ignore the 3-dimensional capability and allow the Z axis to default to 0, the X/Y plane.

APPLICATIONS

When producing a drawing, you can use the BASE command to assign a base point for future insertion. This point is usually the center of some meaningful entity (to aid in later rotation). You may wish to use the lower left-hand corner of the drawing. Consistent use of the lower left-hand corner helps you remember the location of the base point.

TYPICAL OPERATION

In this session you save the drawing of a face as a block. The insertion of the face is done with different X and Y scale factors and one different rotation angle.

The following drawing has numbered balloons that correspond to the following steps. Begin a new drawing named BASEAC.

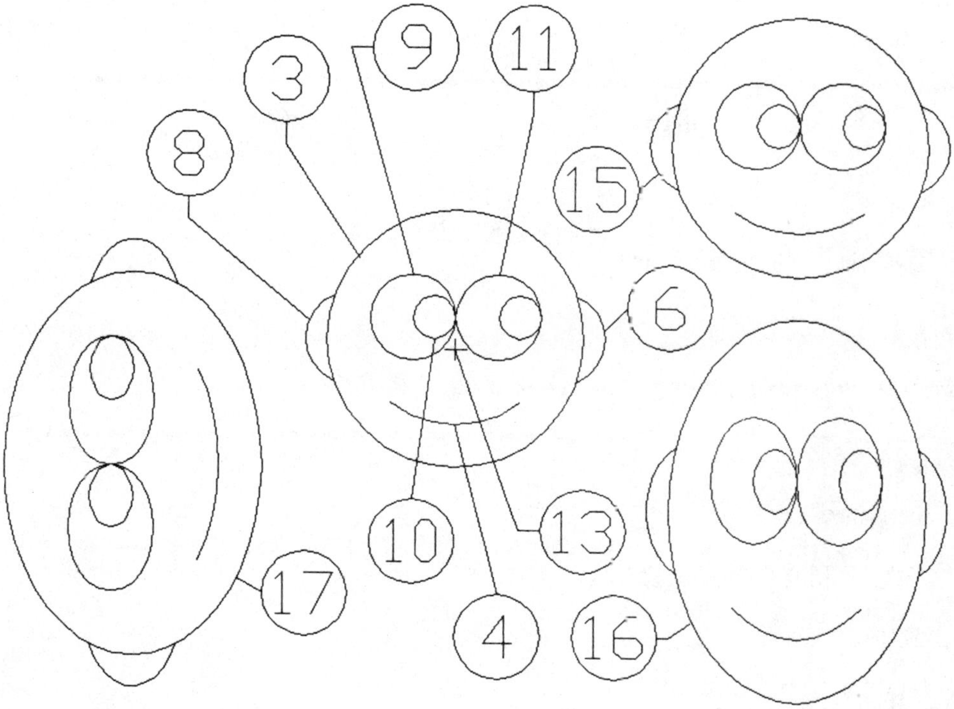

1. Set the SNAP distance.

Command: **SNAP <CR>**
Snap spacing or ON/OFF/Aspect/Rotate/Style <1.0000>: **.25 <CR>**

2. Turn the GRID on and ZOOM the screen.

Command: **GRID <CR>**
Grid spacing(X) or ON/OFF/Snap/Aspect <0.0000>: **ON <CR>**

Command: **ZOOM <CR>**
Magnification or type (ACELPW): **A <CR>**

3. Draw a circle.

Command: **CIRCLE <CR>**
3P/2P/<Center point>: **5.5,4.5 <CR>**
Diameter/<Radius>: **1.5 <CR>**

4. Draw an arc.

Command: **ARC <CR>**
Center/<Start point>: **4.75,3.75 <CR>**
Center/End/<Second point>: **5.5,3.5 <CR>**
End point: **6.25,3.75 <CR>**

5. ZOOM the screen to magnify the right side of the circle.

Command: **ZOOM <CR>**
All/Center/Dynamic/Extents/Left/Previous/Window/<Scale(X)>: **W <CR>**
First point: **6.5,3.75 <CR>**
Second point: **7.75,5.5 <CR>**

6. Draw an arc.

Command: **ARC <CR>**
Center/<Start point>: **NEA <CR>**
to {Pick close to coordinate 6.9150,4.0000}
Center/End/<Second point>: **7.25,4.5 <CR>**
End point: **NEA <CR>**
to {Pick close to coordinate 6.9134,5.0022}

7. ZOOM the screen back to the previous view.

Command: **ZOOM <CR>**
All/Center/Dynamic/Extents/Left/Previous/Window/<Scale(X)>: **P <CR>**

8. Mirror the last entity drawn (the arc).

```
Command: MIRROR <CR>
Select objects: L <CR>
1 found.
Select objects: <CR>
First point of mirror line: 5.5,6.25 <CR>
Second point: @3.75<270 <CR>
Delete old objects? <N> <CR>
```

9. Draw a circle.

```
Command: CIRCLE <CR>
3P/2P/<Center point>: 5.0,4.75 <CR>
Diameter/<Radius>: .5 <CR>
```

10. Draw a circle.

```
Command: CIRCLE <CR>
3P/2P/<Center point>: 5.25,4.75 <CR>
Diameter/<Radius>: .25 <CR>
```

11. Copy the two circles.

```
Command: COPY <CR>
Select objects: W <CR>
First point: 4.5,4.25 <CR>
Second point: 5.5,5.25 <CR>
2 found.
Select objects: <CR>
<Base point or displacement>/Multiple: 5.5,4.75 <CR>
Second point of displacement: @1.0<0 <CR>
```

12. Redraw the screen.

```
Command: REDRAW <CR>
```

13. Insert a base point into the drawing.

```
Command: BASE <CR>
Base point <0.0000,0.0000,0.0000>: 5.5,4.5 <CR>
```

14. Save the drawing as BASEAC.

```
Command: SAVE <CR>
File name <B:BASEAC>: <CR>
```

15. Insert the drawing.

```
Command: INSERT <CR>
Block name (or ?): BASEAC <CR>
 Insertion point: 9.5,6.75 <CR>
 X scale factor <1> / Corner / XYZ: <CR>
 Y scale factor (default=X): <CR>
 Rotation angle <0>: <CR>
```

16. Insert the drawing.

```
Command: INSERT <CR>
Block name (or ?) <BASEAC>: <CR>
 Insertion point: 9.5,2.5 <CR>
 X scale factor <1> / Corner / XYZ: <CR>
 Y scale factor (default=X): 1.5 <CR>
 Rotation angle <0>: <CR>
```

17. Insert the drawing.

```
Command: INSERT <CR>
Block name (or ?) <BASEAC>: <CR>
 Insertion point: 1.75,3.0 <CR>
 X scale factor <1> / Corner / XYZ: 1.5 <CR>
 Y scale factor (default=X): 1 <CR>
 Rotation angle <0>: 90 <CR>
```

Your drawing should look like the following one.

18. Use **QUIT** to redisplay the Main Menu.
19. Turn to Module 94 to continue the learning sequence.

Module 12

BLIPMODE

```
Command:BLIPMODE On/Off <current>:
```

DESCRIPTION

The BLIPMODE command lets you turn the screen blips (cross hairs) on and off. Review the effect of turning BLIPMODE on and off.

On — When you pick points on the screen, a small cross is placed on the screen to identify the point.

Off — When you pick points on the screen, nothing is drawn.

APPLICATIONS

The display of small markers on the screen tells you that AutoCAD has accepted your point. The markers are temporary. They do not become part of the drawing. They are erased automatically when a REDRAW, REGEN, ZOOM, or PAN command is issued. In most cases you want BLIPMODE on.

TYPICAL OPERATION

In this session two circles are drawn. One is drawn with BLIPMODE on and another with BLIPMODE off. Starting at the Main Menu, begin a new drawing named TEMP.

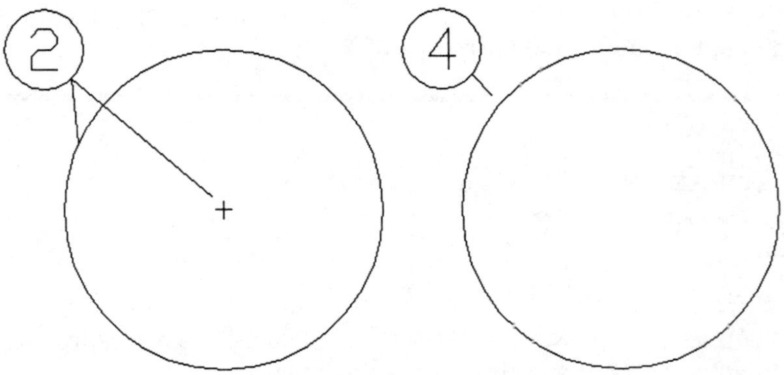

1. Type **BLIPMODE** and press **Return**. Then type **ON** and press **Return**.

```
Command:BLIPMODE <CR> On/Off <Off>: ON <CR>
Command:
```

2. Draw a circle. Specify the center point by picking it on the screen. A small mark appears, designating the center point. Enter a radius of 2.

```
Command:CIRCLE <CR> 3P/2P/<Center point>:
Diameter/<Radius>: 2 <CR>
Command:
```

3. Turn off BLIPMODE.

```
Command:BLIPMODE <CR>
On/Off <ON>:OFF <CR>
Command:
```

4. Draw a circle. Specify the center point by picking it on the screen. No mark appears to designate the center point. Enter a radius of 2.

```
Command:CIRCLE <CR> 3P/2P/<Center point>:
Diameter/<Radius>: 2 <CR>
Command:
```

5. Type **REDRAW** and press **Return**. Notice that the two circles are redrawn, but the marker showing the center point of the first circle disappears.

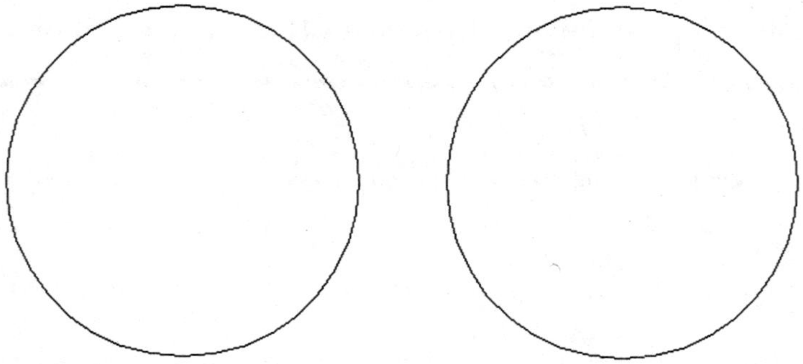

6. Type **QUIT** and press **Return**; then type **Y** and press **Return** to redisplay the Main Menu.
7. Turn to Module 63 to continue the learning sequence.

Module 13

BLOCK

```
Command: BLOCK
Block name (or ?):
```

DESCRIPTION

Typing ? produces a list of all blocks defined in the current drawing.

Each time you insert a block into your drawing, you may use a different scale factor and rotation.

Block is used to save one or more objects by naming it and then inserting it into the drawing. When inserted, you can give a block different X and Y scale and rotation values that differ from the original.

A block can contain entities from different layers on a drawing. When a block is inserted into your drawing, it is drawn on its original layer. There is one exception. If any of the entities within the block was originally on the 0 (zero) layer, then that entity is drawn on the active layer. The block is not generated if the insertion takes place upon a frozen layer.

APPLICATIONS

The BLOCK command is one of AutoCAD's most powerful commands. A block combines a group of entities to form a single object. AutoCAD considers a block as a primitive entity (like a line). These blocks can be gears, furniture, windows and doors, wheels, electrical and plumbing fixtures, etc. When you draw a subassembly that must be repeated several times in a drawing, the BLOCK command allows you to work with the entire subassembly as a single entity.

Blocks are used with the ERASE, LIST, or MOVE commands just as any other primitive entity. A block is defined from any set of objects on your drawing.

Use the BLOCK command to define a subassembly that is used only in the current drawing. Use the WBLOCK command to define a subassembly that must be used in several different drawings.

Once a block is defined, it is placed in a drawing with the INSERT command.

TYPICAL OPERATION

In this session you draw several objects and save them as a block called FRAMIS. The block is then inserted several times into the drawing. Begin a new drawing named BLOCK. When finished, your drawing should look like the following one; the numbered balloons correspond to the following steps.

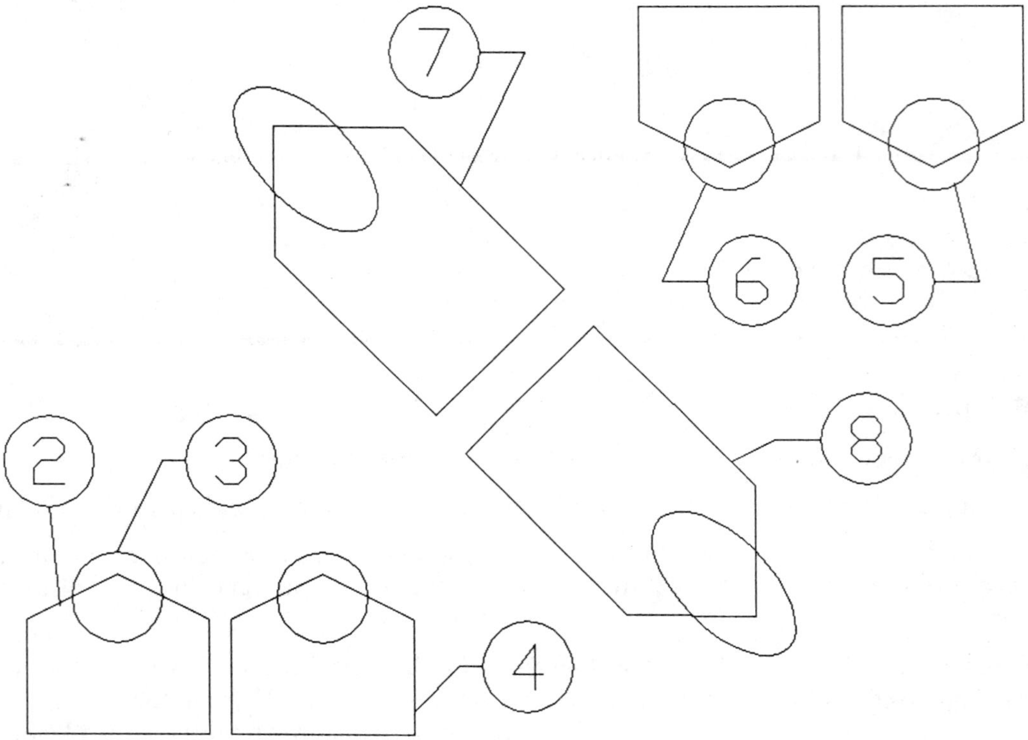

1. Set the SNAP distance, turn the GRID On, and ZOOM the display.

```
Command:  SNAP <CR>
Snap spacing or ON/OFF/Aspect/Rotate/Style <1.0000>: .25 <CR>
Command: GRID <CR>
Grid spacing(X) or ON/OFF/Snap/Aspect <0.0000>: ON <CR>
Command: ZOOM <CR>
All/Center/Dynamic/Extents/Left/Previous/Window/<Scale(X)>: A <CR>
```

2. Draw a 5-sided polygon.

```
Command: LINE <CR>
From point: .5,.5 <CR>
To point: @1.25<90 <CR>
To point: @1.1180<27 <CR>
To point: @1.1249<333 <CR>
To point: @1.2469<270 <CR>
To point: C <CR>
```

3. Draw a circle. Save the object as a block. Bring the object back to the screen with the OOPS command.

```
Command: CIRCLE <CR>
3P/2P/<Center point>: 2P <CR>
First point on diameter: MID <CR>
of 1,2 <CR>
Second point on diameter: MID <CR>
of 2,2 <CR>

Command: BLOCK <CR>
Block name (or ?): FRAMIS <CR>
Insertion base point: .5,.5 <CR>
Select objects or Window or Last: W <CR>
First point: .25,.25 <CR>
Second point: 2.75,2.75 <CR>
6 found.
Select objects: <CR>

Command: OOPS <CR>
```

4. Insert the block and redraw the screen.

```
Command: INSERT <CR>
Block name (or ?): FRAMIS <CR>
 Insertion point: 2.75,.5 <CR>
 X scale factor <1> / Corner / XYZ: <CR>
 Y scale factor (default=X): <CR>
 Rotation angle <0>: <CR>

 Command: REDRAW <CR>
```

5. Insert the block with a 180 degree rotation.

```
Command: INSERT <CR>
Block name (or ?) <FRAMIS>: <CR>
 Insertion point: 11.5,8.5 <CR>
 X scale factor <1> / Corner / XYZ: <CR>
 Y scale factor (default=X): <CR>
 Rotation angle <0>: 180 <CR>
```

6. Insert the block.

```
Command: INSERT <CR>
Block name (or ?) <FRAMIS>: <CR>
 Insertion point: 9.25,8.5 <CR>
 X scale factor <1> / Corner / XYZ: <CR>
 Y scale factor (default=X): <CR>
 Rotation angle <0>: 180 <CR>
```

7. Insert the block with a Y scale factor of 2 and a rotation angle of 45 degrees.

```
Command: INSERT <CR>
Block name (or ?) <FRAMIS>: <CR>
 Insertion point: 5.0,4.0 <CR>
 X scale factor <1> / Corner / XYZ: <CR>
 Y scale factor (default=X): 2 <CR>
 Rotation angle <0>: 45 <CR>
```

8. Insert the block one last time.

```
Command: INSERT <CR>
Block name (or ?) <FRAMIS>: <CR>
 Insertion point: 6.75,5.0 <CR>
 X scale factor <1> / Corner / XYZ: <CR>
 Y scale factor (default=X): 2 <CR>
 Rotation angle <0>: 225 <CR>
```

Your screen now looks like the following drawing.

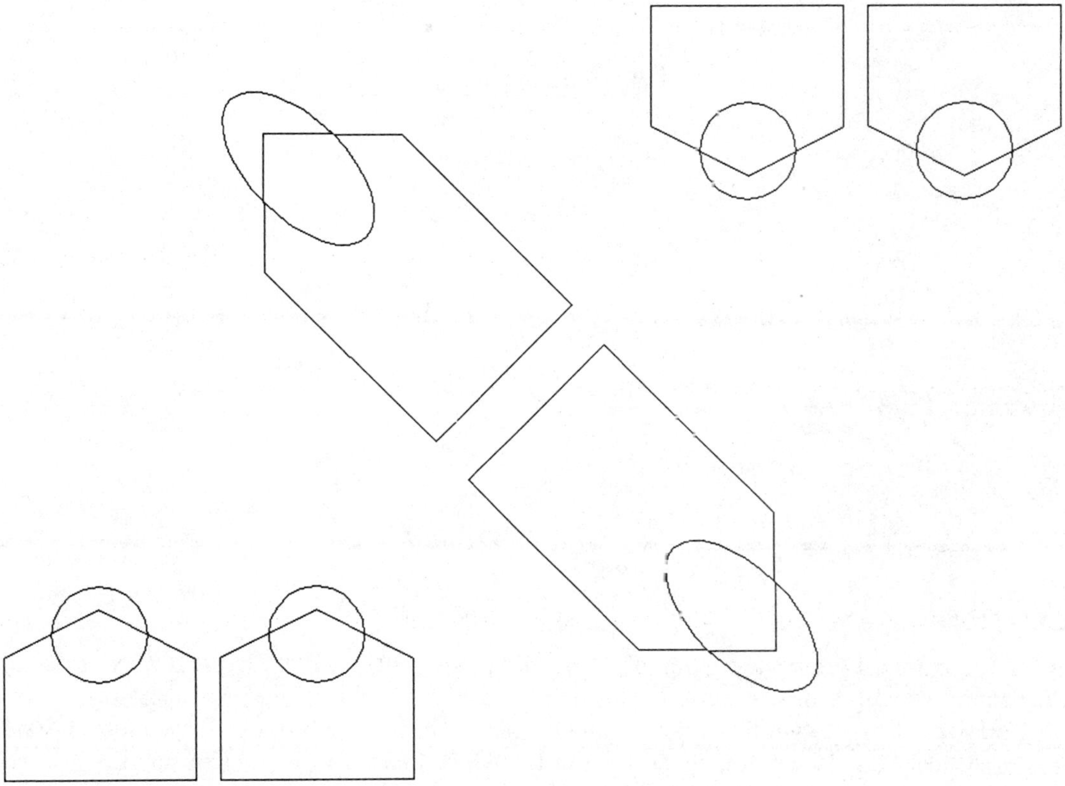

9. Use **QUIT** to redisplay the Main Menu.
10. Turn to Module 41 to continue the learning sequence.

Module 14

BREAK

```
Command: BREAK
Select object:
Enter second point or F:
```

DESCRIPTION

The BREAK command erases a portion of an existing entity, like a line. This is different from the ERASE command which erases an entire entity. The BREAK command works on lines, traces, circles, and arcs. Prior to version 2.5 of AutoCAD, BREAK did not work on polylines. In earlier editions of AutoCAD it is necessary to use the PEDIT command to BREAK a polyline. Starting with version 2.5, you can BREAK a polyline. The BREAK command can also split an object, such as a line or circle, into two parts without any erasure. When you use the BREAK command, ensure that you are at the command prompt. Then type **BREAK**, press **Return**, and check for the BREAK prompts.

To select the object to break, use the Point, Window, or Last options. When Point is used with the BREAK command, it works slightly different from other commands. The first point selected is assumed to be where you want the break to begin. If this is not your intention, you must type **F** and reselect the first point of the break. Then select the second point of the break. The second point of the break does not need to touch the object. For example, if you intend to cut off the end of a line, after you have pointed to the first point of the break, you may place the second point beyond the end of the line. AutoCAD understands that you want to eliminate all of the line beginning at the first selection point.

APPLICATIONS

The BREAK command is often used to place a gap in a drawn object or to erase a portion of an item. Sometimes the drawing activity requires that a line, circle, or arc be partially erased. Recall from the sample session in Module 2 how you used BREAK to make the door opening in a line.

TYPICAL OPERATION

In this session you draw several items and then break them. Additional items are inserted into the broken areas and combined to form a design. Starting at the Main Menu, begin a new drawing named BREAK.

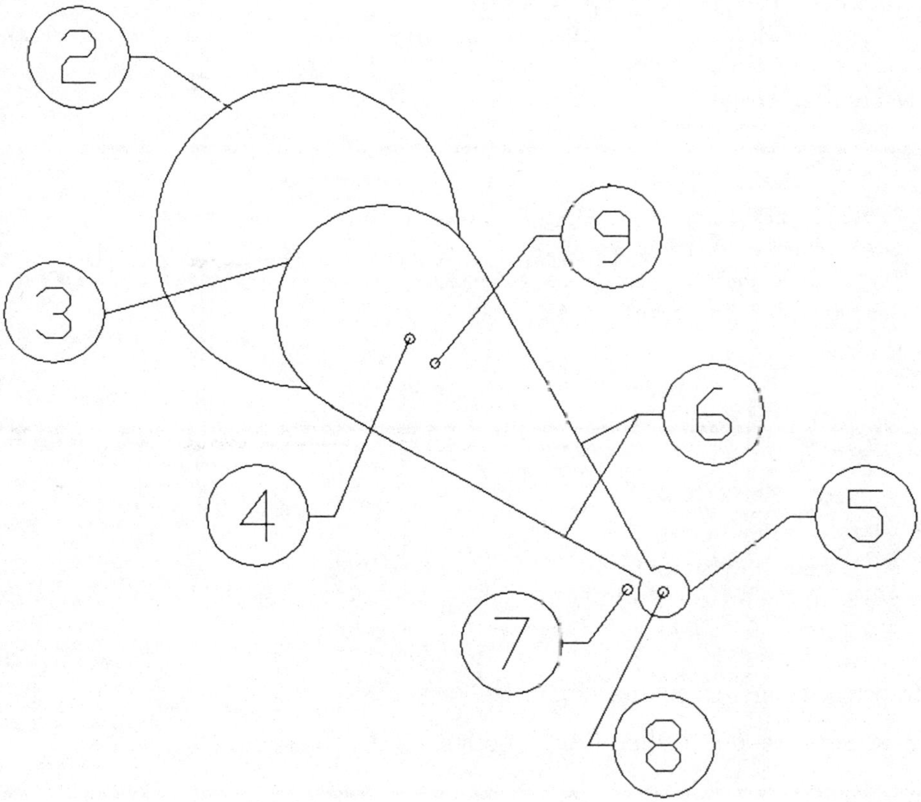

1. Set the SNAP value, turn the GRID on, and ZOOM the screen.

```
Command: SNAP <CR>
Snap spacing or ON/OFF/Aspect/Rotate/Style <1.0000>: .25 <CR>

Command: GRID <CR>
Grid spacing(X) or ON/OFF/Snap/Aspect <0.0000>: ON <CR>

Command: ZOOM <CR>
All/Center/Dynamic/Extents/Left/Previous/Window/<Scale(X)>: A <CR>
```

2. Draw a circle.

```
Command: CIRCLE <CR>
3P/2P/<Center point>: 6,4.5 <CR>
Diameter/<Radius>: 1.5 <CR>
```

3. Draw another circle.

```
Command: CIRCLE <CR>
3P/2P/<Center point>: 2p <CR>
First point on diameter: 7.5,4.5 <CR>
Second point on diameter: 6,3 <CR>
```

4. Break the circle labeled as No. 2.

```
Command: BREAK <CR>
Select object:  6,6 <CR>
Enter second point or F: f <CR>
Enter first point: 6,3 <CR>
Enter second point: 7.5,4.5 <CR>
```

Notice the break occurred counterclockwise.

5. Redraw the screen and then draw another circle.

```
Command: REDRAW <CR>

Command: CIRCLE <CR>
3P/2P/<Center point>: 9.5,1 <CR>
Diameter/<Radius>: .25 <CR>
```

6. Draw two lines from the center of the No. 5 circle tangent to the No. 3 circle.

```
Command: LINE <CR>
From point: 9.5,1 <CR>
To point: tan <CR>
```

```
to 7.75,4 <CR>
To point: <CR>

Command: LINE <CR>
From point: 9.5,1 <CR>
To point: tan <CR>
to 6.75,2.75 <CR>
To point: <CR>
```

7. ZOOM the screen to view the small circle and then break the circle No. 5.

```
Command: ZOOM <CR>
All/Center/Dynamic/Extents/Left/Previous/Window/<Scale(X)>: W <CR>
First point: 9,.5 <CR>
Second point: 10,1.5 <CR>

Command: BREAK <CR>
Select object: 9.75,1 <CR>
Enter second point or F: f <CR>
Enter first point: int <CR>
of 9.3795,1.2183 <CR>
Enter second point: int <CR>
of 9.2834,1.1232 <CR>
```

8. Break the lines from their intersection with circle No. 5 to the center of the same circle.

```
Command: BREAK <CR>
Select object: 9.3671,1.0739 <CR>
Enter second point or F: f <CR>
Enter first point: int <CR>
of 9.2883,1.1056 <CR>
Enter second point: 9.5,1 <CR>

Command: BREAK <CR>
Select object: 9.4189,1.1444 <CR>
Enter second point or F: f <CR>
Enter first point: int <CR>
of 9.3942,1.2077 <CR>
Enter second point: 9.5,1 <CR>
```

9. Zoom back out to view the entire drawing and then break the circle No. 3.

```
Command: ZOOM <CR>
All/Center/Dynamic/Extents/Left/Previous/Window/<Scale(X)>: A <CR>

Command: BREAK <CR>
Select object: 7.5,3 <CR>
Enter second point or F: F <CR>
Enter first point: nea <CR>
to  6.2430,2.8046 <CR>
Enter second point: NEA <CR>
to 7.7009,4.2402 <CR>
```

10. Redraw the screen.

```
Command: REDRAW <CR>
```

Your screen should resemble the following drawing.

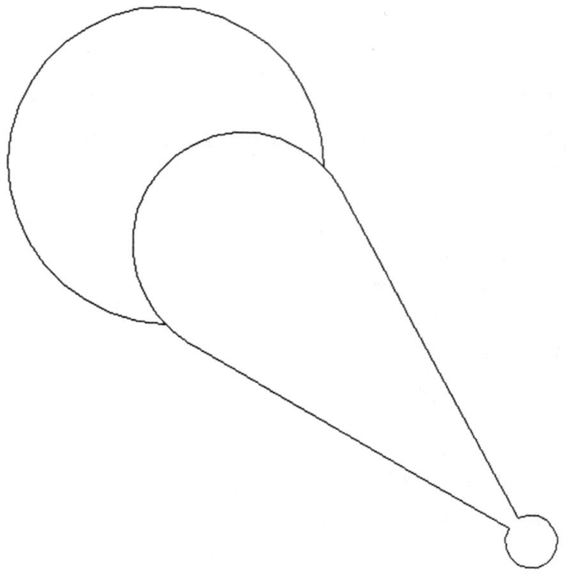

11. Type **QUIT** and press **Return**; then type **Y** and press **Return** to redisplay the Main Menu.
12. Turn to Module 26 to continue the learning sequence.

Module 15

CHAMFER

```
Command: CHAMFER
Polyline/Distances/<Select first line>:
```

DESCRIPTION

Pick — Select a line. You are then prompted to select a second line. The chamfer is created using the current value for *distance*.

Distances — You are prompted for the distance from the intersection to the bevel point for line 1 and line 2.

Polyline — Type **P** and press **Return**. You are prompted to select a Polyline. The CHAMFER operation progresses in a clockwise direction.

The CHAMFER command is used to bevel, or *chamfer*, sharp corners made of intersecting lines. CHAMFER is used on corners made from either lines or polylines.

APPLICATIONS

The obvious application of the CHAMFER command is to produce a bevel or sloping edge at the corner of an object. Specify the distance from the intersection for the bevel to begin for each line. When chamfering lines, the order in which you pick the lines determines which is "line 1" and "line 2" for application of different bevel distances to each line. When chamfering a polyline, the chamfer operation proceeds in a clockwise manner from the point you pick. Starting at the specified point, AutoCAD scans the polyline in a clockwise direction. When an intersection is encountered, the chamfer distance for line 1 is applied to the polyline segment between the start point and the intersection. The chamfer distance for line 2 is applied to the second polyline segment meeting at the intersection.

A less obvious application of the CHAMFER command is to extend two lines to their point of natural intersection. Specify a CHAMFER distance of 0, then chamfer the lines. Both lines are extended until they meet. This is an excellent technique to create clean intersections.

TYPICAL OPERATION

In this session you draw both lines and polylines and chamfer the corners. Begin a new drawing named CHAMFER.

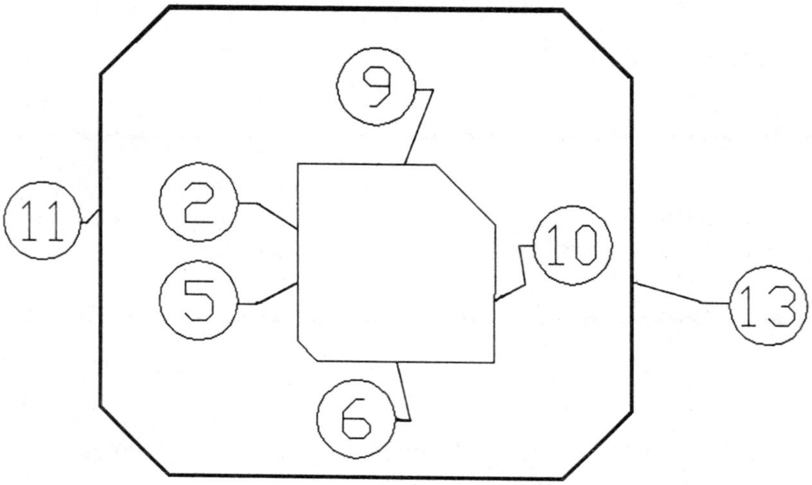

1. Turn on COORDS by pressing **F6**, set SNAP to .25, and turn GRID on.

```
Command:  <COORDS ON> SNAP <CR>
Snap spacing or ON/OFF/Aspect/Rotate/Style <1.0000>: .25 <CR>
Command: GRID <CR>
Grid spacing(X) or ON/OFF/Snap/Aspect <0.0000>: ON <CR>
```

2. Draw the inner rectangle.

```
Command: LINE <CR>
From point: 3.75,2.75 <CR>
To point: 3.75,5.25 <CR>
To point: 6.25,5.25 <CR>
To point: 6.25,2.75 <CR>
To point: C <CR>
```

3. Set the CHAMFER distances. For this example, chamfer each line the same amount.

```
Command: CHAMFER <CR>
Polyline/Distances/<Select first line>: D <CR>
Enter first chamfer distance <0.0000>: .25 <CR>
Enter second chamfer distance <0.2500>: <CR>
```

4. Chamfer the lower-left corner of the rectangle.

```
Command: CHAMFER <CR>
Polyline/Distances/<Select first line>:
```

5. Pick the line on the left side of the square.

```
Select second line:
```

6. Pick the line on the bottom of the square.
7. Set the distance for the next chamfer.

```
Command: CHAMFER <CR>
Polyline/Distances/<Select first line>: D <CR>
Enter first chamfer distance <0.2500>: .75 <CR>
Enter second chamfer distance <0.7500>: <CR>
```

8. Chamfer the upper-left corner of the cube.

```
Command: CHAMFER <CR>
Polyline/Distances/<Select first line>:
```

9. Pick the top line of the square.

```
Select second line:
```

10. Pick the line on the right side of the square.
11. Draw the outer square as a polyline.

```
Command: PLINE <CR>
From point: 1.25,1.25 <CR>
Arc/Close/Halfwidth/Length/Undo/Width/<Endpoint of line>: W <CR>
Starting width <0.0000>: .040 <CR>
Ending width <0.0400>: <CR>
Arc/Close/Halfwidth/Length/Undo/Width/<Endpoint of line>:
1.25,7.25 <CR>
Arc/Close/Halfwidth/Length/Undo/Width/<Endpoint of line>:
8.0,7.25 <CR>
Arc/Close/Halfwidth/Length/Undo/Width/<Endpoint of line>:
8.0,1.25 <CR>
Arc/Close/Halfwidth/Length/Undo/Width/<Endpoint of line>: C <CR>
```

12. Set the CHAMFER distance for chamfering the polyline.

```
Command: CHAMFER <CR>
Polyline/Distances/<Select first line>: D <CR>
Enter first chamfer distance <0.7500>: .875 <CR>
Enter second chamfer distance <0.8750>: <CR>
Command: CHAMFER <CR>
Polyline/Distances/<Select first line>: P <CR>
Select polyline:
```

13. Pick any line on the polyline rectangle.

```
4 lines were chamfered
```

The drawing is complete.

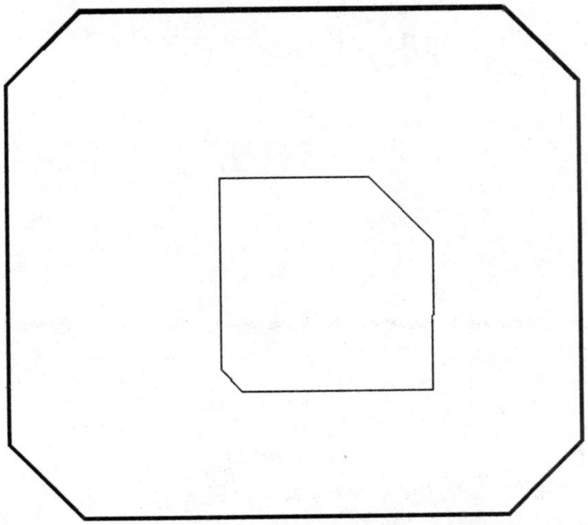

14. Type **QUIT** and press **Return**; then type **Y** and press **Return** to redisplay the Main Menu.
15. Turn to Module 88 to continue the learning sequence.

Module 16

CHANGE

```
Command: CHANGE
Select objects:
Change point (or Layer or Elevation):
Properties/<change point>:

Command: CHANGE
Select objects:
Properties/<change point>: P
Change what property (Color/Elev/Layer/LType/Thickness)?
```

DESCRIPTION

The CHANGE command alters the properties of the following entities:

line
circle
text
block

The CHANGE command also allows the alteration of attribute definitions. After creating an object in AutoCAD, you can change it with the CHANGE command. The five changes you can make to an object using this command are:

- thickness
- layer
- elevation
- color
- Ltype

CHANGING LAYERS To change a layer, respond to the "<Change point>:" prompt by typing **L** and pressing **Return**.

CHANGING ELEVATION To change an elevation, respond to the "<Change point>:" prompt by typing **E** and pressing **Return**.

CHANGING COLOR To change the color of an object, type **C** for color and press **Return**.

CHANGING LINES When using the CHANGE command to alter a line, the end point of the line closest to the change point is changed to that change point. If the Ortho mode is turned on, only orthogonal lines are drawn.

CHANGING LTYPE To change the LINETYPE of an object, type **LT** and press **Return**.

CHANGING CIRCLES When using the CHANGE command to alter a circle, a change point is picked. The change point becomes the new radius value of the circle as measured from the original center. The circumference of the circle passes through the change point.

CHANGING TEXT When Text is altered by the CHANGE command, the change point is picked and the text is moved to the new point. Pressing **Return** instead of picking a change point provides options for changing the text. You can change the text style, height, rotation angle, and the text string itself. To retain the current value for any attribute, press **Return**.

CHANGING BLOCKS When a block is altered by the CHANGE command, the change point is picked and the block is moved to the new point. If the **Return** key is pressed instead of picking a change point, options for changing the block are offered.

CHANGING THICKNESS To change the thickness of an object, type **T** at the properties prompt and press **Return**.

APPLICATIONS

If the world remained static, there would be little need for the CHANGE command. However, changes are inevitable in the design process. You could make changes by deleting the incorrect portion of the drawing and creating a new, correct version. It is easier to use the CHANGE command to modify the characteristics of the entity, retaining as much of the previous work as possible.

TYPICAL OPERATION

In this session you draw lines and circles and then use variations of the CHANGE command to modify them.

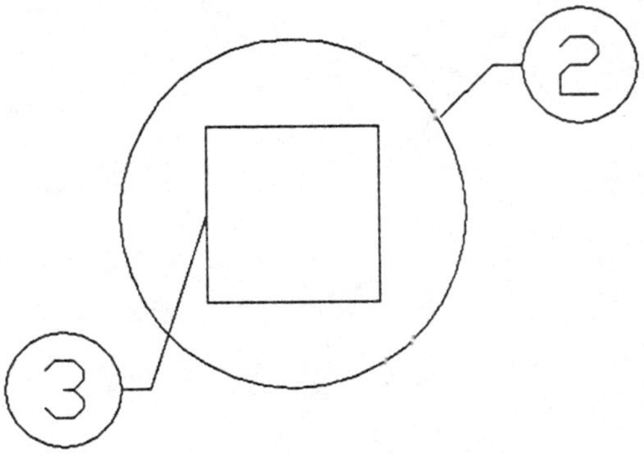

1. Begin a new drawing named CHANGE. Set the SNAP distance, turn the GRID on, and ZOOM the screen.

```
Command: SNAP <CR>
Snap spacing or ON/OFF/Aspect/Rotate/Style <1.0000>: .25 <CR>

Command: GRID <CR>
Grid spacing(X) or ON/OFF/Snap/Aspect <0.0000>: on <CR>

Command: ZOOM <CR>
All/Center/Dynamic/Extents/Left/Previous/Window/<Scale(X)>: A <CR>
```

2. Draw a circle.

```
Command: CIRCLE <CR>
3P/2P/<Center point>: 6,4.5 <CR>
Diameter/<Radius>: 1.5 <CR>
```

3. Draw four lines and redraw the screen.

```
Command: LINE <CR>
From point: 5.25,3.75 <CR>
To point: @1.5<90 <CR>
To point: @1.5<0 <CR>
To point: @1.5<270 <CR>
To point: C <CR>

Command: REDRAW <CR>
```

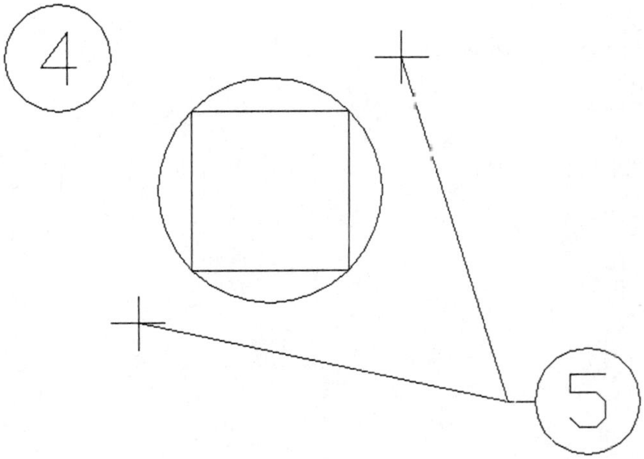

4. Change the radius of the circle.

```
Command: CHANGE <CR>
Select objects: (Pick on the circumferance of the circle.)
1 selected, 1 found.
Select objects: <CR>
Change point (or Layer or Elevation): (Pick on one of the corners
of the square.)
```

5. Save as a block.

```
Command: BLOCK <CR>
Block name (or ?): PEG <CR>
Insertion base point: 6,4.5 <CR>
Select objects: W <CR>
First point: 4.75,3.25 <CR>
Second point: 7.25,5.75 <CR>
5 found.
Select objects: <CR>
```

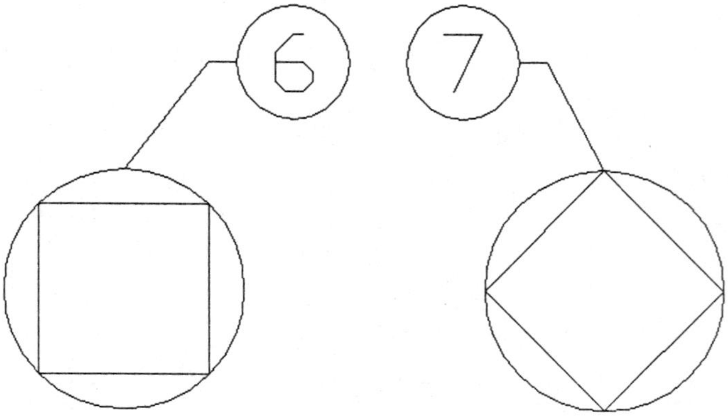

6. Insert a block.

```
Command: INSERT <CR>
Block name (or ?): PEG <CR>
 Insertion point: 2.5,4.25 <CR>
 X scale factor <1> / Corner / XYZ: <CR>
 Y scale factor (default=X): <CR>
 Rotation angle <0>: <CR>
```

7. Insert a block.

```
Command: INSERT <CR>
Block name (or ?) <PEG>: <CR>
 Insertion point: 6.75,4.25 <CR>
 X scale factor <1> / Corner / XYZ: <CR>
 Y scale factor (default=X): <CR>
 Rotation angle <0>: 45 <CR>
```

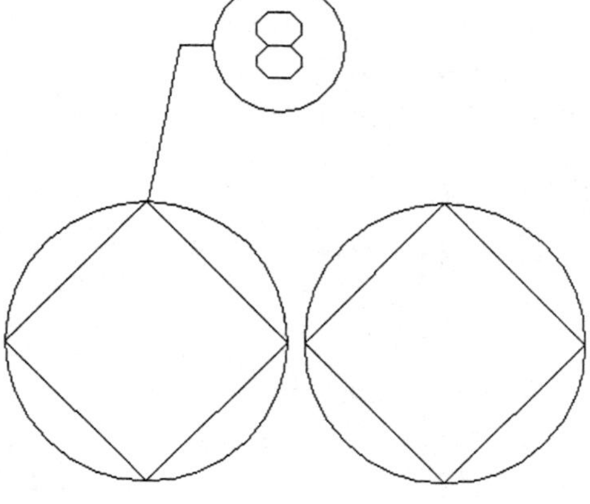

8. Change rotation angle of block and redraw the screen.

Command: **CHANGE <CR>**
Select objects: (Pick block at left.)
1 selected, 1 found.
Select objects: **<CR>**
Change point (or Layer or Elevation): **4.5,4.25 <CR>**
New rotation angle <0>: **45 <CR>**

Command: **REDRAW <CR>**

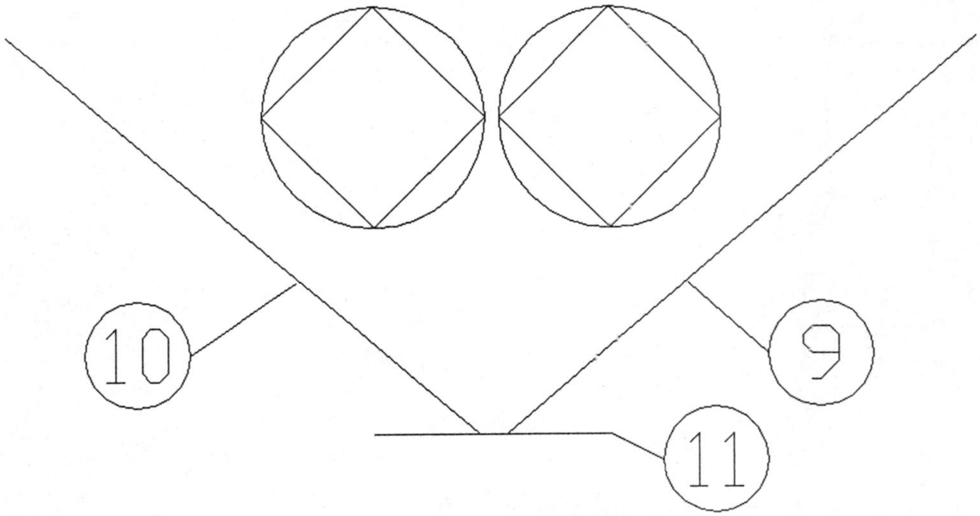

9. Draw a line.

Command: **LINE <CR>**
From point: **5.75,1.25 <CR>**
To point: **@5.8577<40 <CR>**
To point: **<CR>**

10. Draw a line.

Command: **LINE <CR>**
From point: **5.5,1.25 <CR>**
To point: **@5.8577<140 <CR>**
To point: **<CR>**

11. Draw a line.

```
Command: LINE <CR>
From point: 4.5,1.25 <CR>
To point: @2.25<0 <CR>
To point: <CR>
```

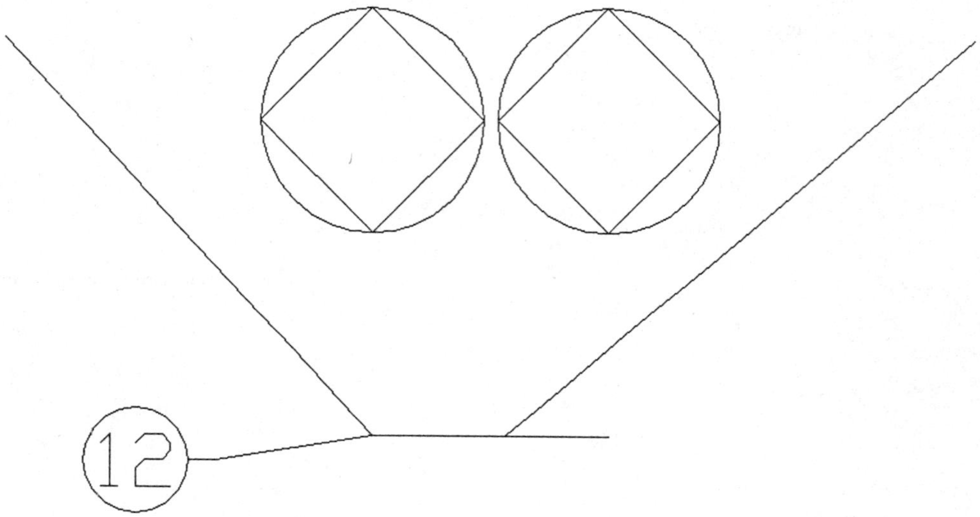

12. Change the end point of line drawn in step 10.

```
Command: CHANGE <CR>
Select objects: (Pick on line at left from step 10.)
1 selected, 1 found.
Select objects: <CR>
Properties/<Change point>:
(Pick on left end of horizontal line from step 11.)
```

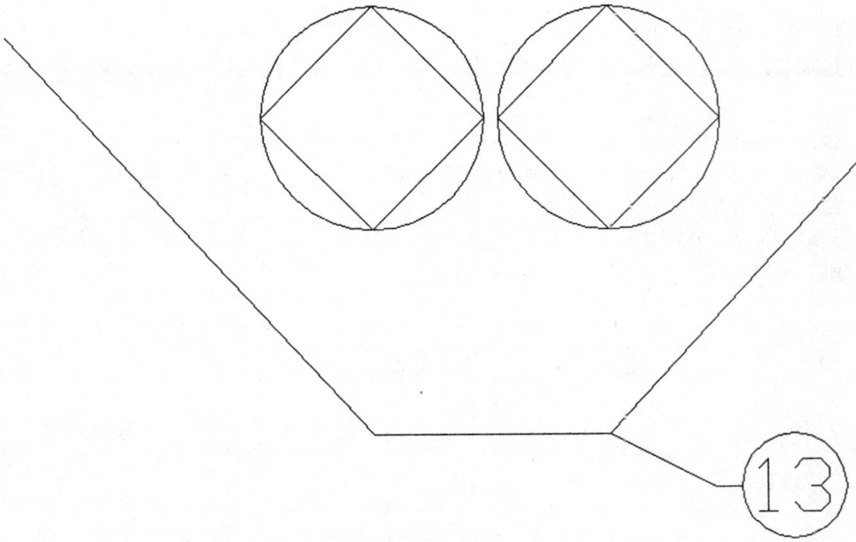

13. Change end of line drawn in step 9.

Command: **CHANGE <CR>**
Select objects: (Pick on line at right from step 9.)
1 selected, 1 found.
Select objects: **<CR>**
Properties/<Change point>: (Pick on right end of horizontal line
from step 11.)

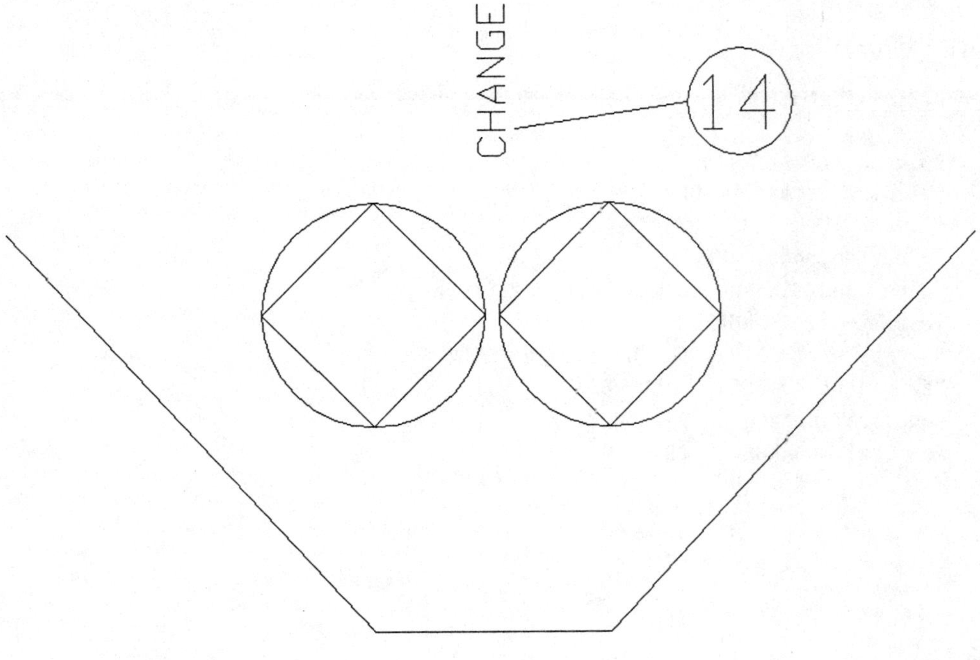

14. Add a line of text.

```
Command: TEXT <CR>
Start point or Align/Center/Fit/Middle/Right/Style: 5.75,5.75 <CR>
Height <0.200>: .25 <CR>
Rotation angle <0>: 90 <CR>
Text: CHANGE <CR>
```

15. Change the text.

```
Command: CHANGE <CR>
Select objects: L <CR>
1 found.
Select objects: <CR>
Properties/<Change point>: 4.5,2.25 <CR>
Text style: STANDARD
New style or RETURN for no change: <CR>
New height <0.2500>: .50 <CR>
New rotation angle <90>: 0 <CR>
New text <CHANGE>: <CR>
```

16. Move the text.

```
Command: MOVE <CR>
Select objects: L <CR>
1 found.
Select objects: <CR>
Base point or displacement: 4.5,2.25 <CR>
Second point of displacement:  @<25<180 <CR>
```

Your drawing now should resemble the one provided.

17. Use **QUIT** to redisplay the Main Menu.
18. Turn to Module 48 to continue the learning sequence.

Module 17

CIRCLE

```
Command: CIRCLE
3P/2P/TTR/<Center point>:
Diameter/<Radius>:
```

DESCRIPTION

A circle is a single drawing entity in the same way that a line is a single drawing entity. When the CIRCLE command is typed (or selected from the Screen Menu), there are three major methods of defining a circle.

- Press **Return** to specify the center point of the circle.
- Type **2P** to specify the endpoints of the diameter.
- Type **3P** to specify three points on the circumference.
- Type **TTR** to specify two tangents and the radius.

The location of points is either typed from the keyboard or picked from the screen using your cursor keys or a mouse.

If you specify the center of the circle, AutoCAD prompts you for the diameter or radius. If you type a number, the number is interpreted as the radius. If you want to specify the diameter, you must first type **D** and press **Return** (or pick Diameter from the submenu on the screen). You are then prompted for the diameter.

APPLICATIONS

CIRCLE is a frequently used command. It is used in the creation of mechanical, electrical, and architectural drawings. The ability to select diameter end points, the center point and a radius, or three points on the circumference provides a great deal of flexibility.

TYPICAL OPERATION

In this session you create a circle in each of three ways. Starting at AutoCAD's Main Menu, begin a new drawing named CIRCLE.

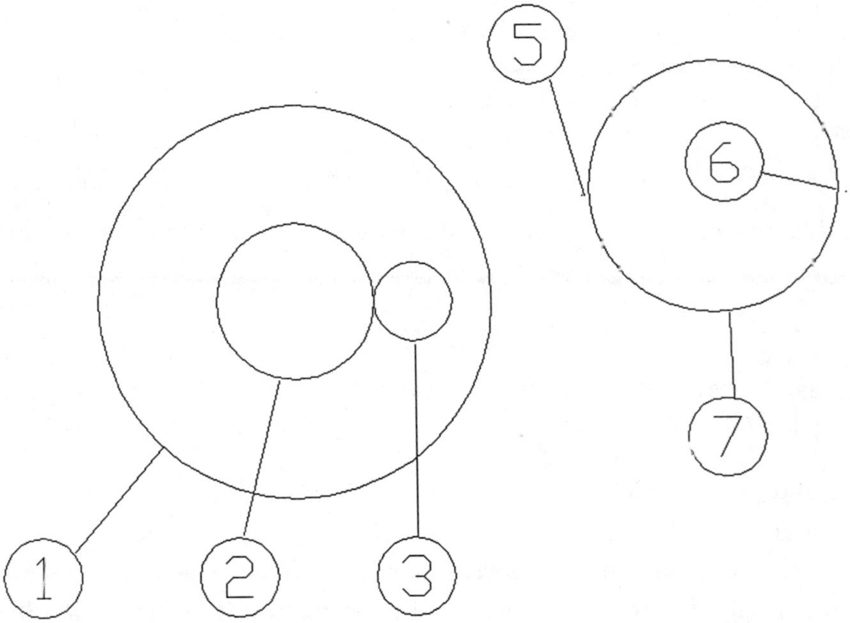

1. Create a circle by specifying the center and the radius.

```
Command: CIRCLE <CR>
3P/2P/TTR/<Center point>: 5,5 <CR>
Diameter/<Radius>: 2.5 <CR>
Command:
```

2. Create a circle by specifying the center and the diameter.

```
Command: <CR>
CIRCLE 3P/2P/TTR/<Center point>: 5,5 <CR>
Diameter/<Radius>: D <CR>
Diameter: 2 <CR>
Command:
```

3. Create a circle by specifying two points.

```
Command: <CR>
CIRCLE 3P/2P/TTR/<Center point>: 2P <CR>
First point on diameter: 6,5 <CR>
Second point on diameter: 7,5 <CR>
Command:
```

4. Create a circle by specifying three points, but use the screen cursor instead of the keyboard.

```
Command: <CR>
CIRCLE 3P/2P/TTR/<Center point>: 3P <CR>
```

5. Pick a point and press **Return**.
6. Pick a point and press **Return**.
7. Pick a point and press **Return**; notice that your circle is displayed on the screen.
8. Type **QUIT** and press **Return**; then type **Y** and press **Return** to redisplay the Main Menu.
9. Turn to Module 89 to continue the learning sequence.

Module 18

COLOR

```
Command: COLOR
New entity color <current>:
```

DESCRIPTION

Prior to AutoCAD version 2.5, the assignment of color to drawing entities was performed using the Color suboption of the LAYER command. You can still use this technique, and it is the method of choice for all but highly specialized applications.

There are three possible responses to the COLOR prompt "New entity color:." These are:

nnn	Type a number between 1 and 255 or a standard color name (RED, GREEN, BLUE, etc.) corresponding to the color you want to assign on a drawing entity basis. After using the COLOR command in this way, all future entities are drawn in the selected color, regardless of layer, until you use the COLOR command to change the color or color assignment method.
BYLAYER	This is the default method of assigning color to drawing entities. When you respond to the COLOR prompt with the word BYLAYER, all subsequent entities that you draw are assigned the color associated with their layer.
BYBLOCK	Entities are drawn in white until they are grouped as a block. Whenever the block is inserted, the objects inherit the color of the block insertion.

APPLICATIONS

CAUTION

The ability to assign color individually by entity is intended for highly specialized applications. This capability is an excellent case for the idea that the most powerful features of a program are also the most dangerous. Mixing color assignment by layer with color assignment by entity has the potential for creating total confusion, consternation, and frustration. For most applications, leave color assignment in its default setting of BYLAYER.

One interesting application of the COLOR command is in constructing an application that interfaces an AutoCAD drawing with remote temperature sensors. The application produces reports that display room temperatures within the building. It is useful to have all the text for the temperature report on the same layer. For clarity, rooms that are too cold are displayed in blue. Acceptable temperature readings are shown in green. Rooms that are too warm are shown in red. The ability to assign colors by entity is indispensable for this type of application.

TYPICAL OPERATION

In this session you create a series of entities in different colors on the same layer of a drawing using a technique that is not recommended for general applications. Begin a new drawing named COLOR.

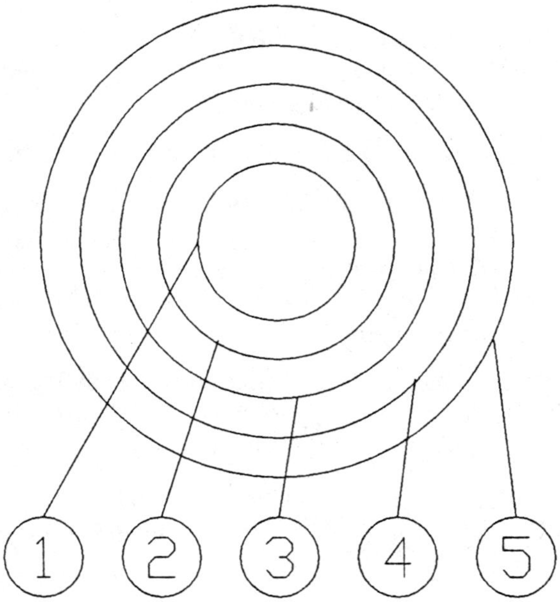

1. Draw a white (default color) circle on the 0 (default) layer.

```
Command: CIRCLE <CR>
3P/2P/TTR/<Center point>:  5,5 <CR>
Diameter/<Radius>: 1 <CR>
Command:
```

2. Change the drawing color to RED and draw another circle.

```
Command: COLOR <CR>
New entity color <BYLAYER>: RED <CR>
Command: CIRCLE <CR>
3P/2P/TTR/<Center point>: 5,5 <CR>
Diameter/<Radius>: 1.5 <CR>
```

3. Change the drawing color to GREEN and draw another circle.

```
Command: COLOR <CR>
New entity color <1 (red)>: GREEN <CR>
Command: CIRCLE <CR>
3P/2P/TTR/<Center point>: 5,5 <CR>
Diameter/<Radius>: 2 <CR>
```

4. Change the color to CYAN (color 4) and draw another circle.

```
Command: COLOR <CR>
New entity color <3 (green)>: 4 <CR>
Command: CIRCLE <CR>
3P/2P/TTR/<Center point>: 5,5 <CR>
Diameter/<Radius>: 2.5 <CR>
```

5. Change the color to BLUE (color 5) and draw another circle.

```
Command: COLOR <CR>
New entity color <4 (cyan)>: 5
Command: CIRCLE <CR>
3P/2P/TTR/<Center point>: 5,5 <CR>
Diameter/<Radius>: 3 <CR>
```

6. Type **QUIT** and press **Return**; then type **Y** and press **Return** to display the Main Menu.
7. Turn to Module 91 to continue the learning sequence.

Module 19

COPY

```
Command: COPY
Select objects:
<Base point or displacement>/Multiple:
```

DESCRIPTION

The COPY command has four options: Pick, Window, Last, and Multiple. These are described in the following list.

Pick	Select an object with the screen cursor.
Window	Type **W** and press **Return** (or pick "Window" on the screen menu) to specify copying all objects in a window. You are then prompted: First point: Second point: You may either type the coordinates on the keyboard, or pick them with the screen cursor.
Last	Selects the most recently used object for the copy operation.
Multiple	Creates a copy at each coordinate specified as a second point.

You use the COPY command to make an exact replica of an object. The original object remains undisturbed. To copy an item, verify that you are at the command prompt. Then type **COPY** and press **Return** or pick COPY from the EDIT submenu.

You may select more than one object in a single COPY operation. You may mix the Last, Pick, and Window options. To terminate the object selection process, press **Return**.

After selecting the object(s), AutoCAD confirms the selection with the message:

```
nn found.
Base point or displacement:
```

You must either select a reference point for your object, or specify a displacement in terms of a distance and an angle. You can either type the information on the keyboard, or you can pick a point on the screen.

If you choose to type the point, the following prompt appears:

```
Second point of displacement:
```

You may either type the position where the base point of the copy appears, or pick it on the screen.

APPLICATIONS

COPY is a convenient command for the reproduction of any entity or group of entities. The COPY and the MOVE commands are very similar. The major difference between the two commands is that the MOVE command moves one or more selected objects from one place to another, while the COPY command duplicates one or more selected objects.

TYPICAL OPERATION

This operation draws a picture of a "tank" and then generates a copy. Starting at the Main Menu, begin a new drawing named TEMP.

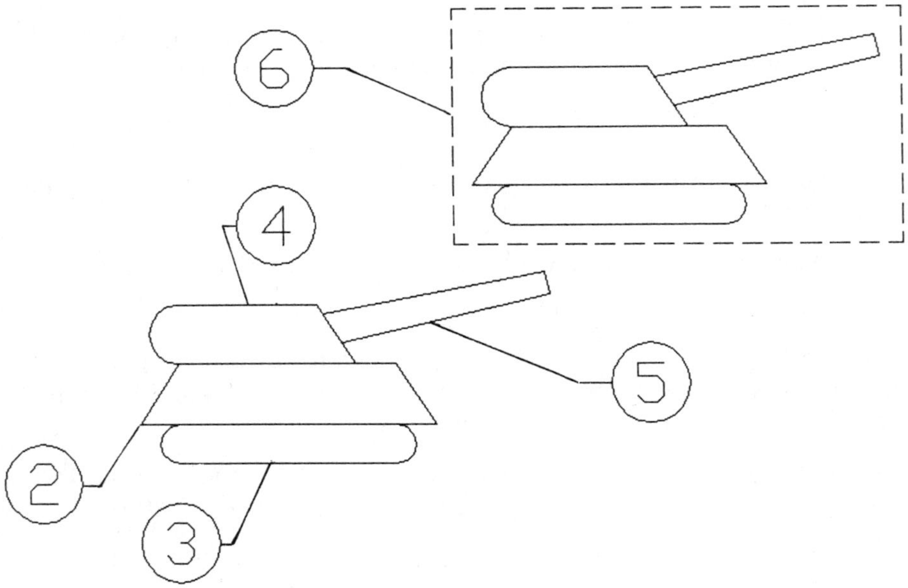

1. Set SNAP to .25 and turn GRID on.

Command: **SNAP <CR>**
Snap spacing or ON/OFF/Aspect/Rotate/Style <1.0000>: **.25 <CR>**
Command: **GRID <CR>**
Grid spacing(X) or ON/OFF/Snap/Aspect <0.0000>: **ON <CR>**

2. Draw the body of the tank.

Command: **LINE <CR>**
From point: **1.75,2.25 <CR>**
To point: **2.25,3 <CR>**
To point: **5,3 <CR>**
To point: **5.5,2.25 <CR>**
To point: **C <CR>**

3. Draw the track.

Command: **ARC <CR>**
Center/<Start point>: **C <CR>**
Center: **2.25,2 <CR>**
Start point: **2.25,2.25 <CR>**
Angle/Length of chord/<End point>: **@.25<270 <CR>**

Command: **ARC <CR>** Center/<Start point>: **C <CR>**
Center: **5,2 <CR>**
Start point: **5,1.75 <CR>**
Angle/Length of chord/<End point>: **@.25<90 <CR>**

Command: **LINE <CR>**
From point: **2.25,1.75 <CR>**
To point: **@2.75<0 <CR>**
To point: **<CR>**

Command: **REDRAW <CR>**

4. Draw the front and top of the turret.

```
Command: LINE <CR>
From point: 4.5,3 <CR>
To point: 4,3.75 <CR>
To point: 2.25,3.75 <CR>
To point: <CR>
```

5. Draw the rear of the turret.

```
Command: ARC <CR>
Center/<Start point>: 2.25,3.75 <CR>
Center/End/<Second point>: E <CR>
End point: 2.25,3 <CR>
Angle/Direction/Radius/<Center point>: A <CR>
Included Angle: 180 <CR>

Command: REDRAW <CR>
```

6. Draw the gun.

```
Command: LINE <CR>
From point: 4.3227,3.2629 <CR>
To point: @2.7088<13 <CR>
To point: @.2867<103 <CR>
To point: 4.0807,3.6217 <CR>
To point: <CR>

Command: REDRAW <CR>
```

7. Copy the tank.

```
Command: COPY <CR>
Select objects:W <CR>
First point: 1.5,1.25 <CR>
Second point: 7.5,4.75 <CR>
13 found.
Select objects: <CR>
Base point or displacement: 1.75,2.25 <CR>
Second point of displacement:  6,5.25 <CR>

Command: REDRAW <CR>
```

You now have two copies of the tank.

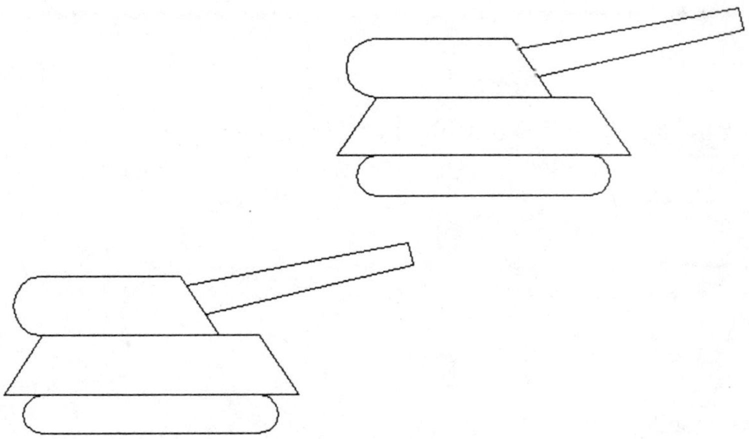

8. Type **SAVE** and press **Return**; then type **TANK** as the drawing name and press **Return** to redisplay the Main Menu. This drawing is used with the Typical Operation section of Module 53.

9. Turn to Module 53 to continue the learning sequence.

Module 20

DIM AND DIM1

```
Command: DIM
Dim:
```

DESCRIPTION

AutoCAD's ADE-1 package includes a semiautomatic dimensioning capability. This capability includes a number of dimensioning options. These are:

1. Linear
2. Angular
3. Diameter
4. Radius
5. Utility

Each option is described in the following list.

1. Linear suboptions:

HORIZONTAL	The linear dimension generated by this command has a horizontal dimension line.
VERTICAL	The linear dimension generated by this command has a vertical dimension line.
ALIGNED	The linear dimension generated by this command has a dimension line parallel to the points picked as the extension line origin points. This enables AutoCAD to align the dimension line with some part of the object being dimensioned.
ROTATED	The linear dimension generated by this command allows the dimension line to be rotated to a specified angle.

BASELINE	This command automatically stacks linear dimensions. It uses the first extension line as the baseline, and offsets each successive dimension line.
CONTINUE	This command chains linear dimensions. Each successive dimension uses the second extension line of the previous dimension. This method of dimensioning can cause tolerance build-up. In most instances, it should be avoided.
2. ANGULAR	This option draws an arc between two non-parallel lines to indicate the angle between them.
3. DIAMETER	This option is used to dimension a circle or an arc by indicating a diameter.
4. RADIUS	This option is used to dimension a circle or an arc by indicating a radius.
5. Utility suboptions:	
CENTER	This command draws center lines or marks the center of circles or arcs.
EXIT	This command works the same as **Ctrl-C** to return to the normal Drawing Editor mode.
LEADER	Draws leaders from simple to complex. Works like the LINE command. If the length of the first segment of a leader is longer than the length of two arrows, arrowheads are automatically added.
REDRAW	Same as the REDRAW command.
STATUS	Lists all current dimensioning variables.
UNDO	Erases the result of the most recent dimensioning activity.

Most AutoCAD commands are suppressed when using the DIM command. However, the mode toggle keys and the object snaps are still available.

Before dimensioning a drawing, you can adjust all of the dimensioning variables in AutoCAD. These variables are:

DIMSE1	Suppresses the first extension line when turned on. Default is equal to off.
DIMSE2	Suppresses the second extension line when turned on. Default is off.
DIMTIH	In linear dimensions, if the text is between the extension lines and DIMTIH is on, the text will be horizontal. If DIMTIH is off, the text is rotated to an angle equal to that of the dimension line. Default is on.
DIMTOH	This controls text located outside the extension lines in linear dimensions. The text is drawn horizontally if DIMTOH is turned on. Default is on.
DIMTAD	This variable places the text above the dimension line and does not break the dimension line. This is usually seen in architectural drawings. Default is off.
DIMTOL	If this variable is turned on, the tolerances specified by DIMTP and DIMTM are added to the dimensioning text. Default is off.

DIMLIM	If this variable is turned on, the dimension text is displayed as limit dimensions. Default is off.
DIMASZ	Specifies the length of an arrowhead. Default is .18 units.
DIMTSZ	If this variable is set to zero, arrowheads are drawn. If a unit value is provided, arrowheads are replaced by tick marks. Default is 0.
DIMTXT	This variable specifies the height of the dimension text unless the current text has a fixed height. Default is .18 units.
DIMCEN	Depending upon the value of the setting of this variable, it produces either center marks or center lines. The CENTER, DIAMETER, and RADIUS commands work with this variable. If the DIMCEN is set as zero, no center marks or lines are produced. If DIMCEN is given a positive value, then center marks of that length are drawn. If DIMCEN is given a negative value, then center lines are drawn with the center marks of the length set. Examples of this setting and their respective results are provided in the Typical Operation session. Default is .09 units.
DIMEXO	This variable determines the gap between the object line and the extension line. Default is .062 units.
DIMEXE	This variable determines how far extension lines extend beyond a dimension line. Default is .18 units.
DIMDLI	This variable controls the space between successive dimension lines. Default is .38 units.
DIMTP	This variable determines the plus tolerance that is added to dimensions when using the DIMTOL or DIMLIM variables. Default is 0 units.
DIMTM	This variable determines the minus tolerance that is added to dimensions when using the DIMTOL or DIMLIM variables. Default is 0 units.

The following dimensioning variables were introduced with AutoCAD versions 2.5 and 2.6.

DIMALT	Provides the simultaneous use of two different dimensioning systems. Both values are printed on each dimension location.
DIMSCALE	Controls the overall scale factor for specific dimensioning sizes.
DIMCEN	Controls the center mark size and style.
DIMTSZ	Controls the tick size.
DIMRND	Allows dimensions to be rounded off and does not effect angular dimensions.
DIMDLE	Controls the dimension line extension past the last extension line when using tick marks.
DIMZIN	Controls the inclusion zero inches/feet in dimensions.
DIMALTF	Produces an alternate unit scale factor to provide a value in an alternate system of measurement, such as mm.
DIMALTD	Controls the alternate unit decimal places.
DIMLFAC	Multiplied by all dimensions entered to provide a linear unit scale factor.

DIMBLK	Name of a block to replace all arrowheads.
DIMASO	Dimensions created with DIMASO turned On are associative in nature.
DIMSHO	When this variable is turned On, all associative dimensions are changed while dragging.
DIMPOST	Defines a character string to be added to a measurement.
DIMAPOST	Defines a character string to be added to an alternate measurement.

The following dimensioning subcommands became available with AutoCAD 2.6:

UPDATE	This command allows the updating of all existing dimensions to new DIMVAR settings.
HOMETEXT	Allows the repositioning of dimensioning text to its default position.
NEWTEXT	Provides for the redefinition of existing dimensioning text.

The following dimensioning layer command was introduced in AutoCAD 2.6

DEFPOINTS	A layer called DEFPOINTS is for storing all points drawn at locations used to create a dimension entity. These definitions points include: Angular, Diameter, Linear, and Radius.

You can review the dimensioning commands by typing **STATUS** and pressing **Return** from the DIM subsystem prompt. Several screens similar to the following version 2.6 screen, are displayed.

Before adjusting your dimensioning variables, you should use the STATUS command to display the following listing. It is obtained by typing **DIM** <**CR**>, **STATUS** <**CR**>.

```
DIMSCALE 1.0000      Overall scale factor
DIMASZ   0.1800      Arrow size
DIMCEN   0.0900      Center mark size
DIMEXO   0.0625      Extension line origin offset
DIMDLI   0.3800      Dimension line increment for
                     continuation
DIMEXE   0.1800      Extension above dimension line
DIMTP    0.0000      Plus tolerance
DIMTM    0.0000      Minus tolerance
DIMTXT   0.1800      Text height
DIMTSZ   0.0000      Tick size
DIMRND   0.0000      Rounding value
DIMDLE   0.0000      Dimension line extension
DIMTOL   Off         Generate dimension tolerances
DIMLIM   Off         Generate dimension limits
DIMTIH   On          Text inside extensions is horizontal
DIMTOH   On          Text outside extensions is horizontal
DIMSE1   Off         Suppress the first extension line
```

```
DIMSE2    Off          Suppress the second extension line
DIMTAD    Off          Place text above the dimension line
DIMZIN    0            Zero inches/feet control
DIMALT    Off          Alternate units selected
DIMALTF   25.4000      Alternate unit scale factor
DIMALTD   2            Alternate unit decimal places
DIMLFAC   1.0000       Linear unit scale factor
DIMBLK                 Arrow block name
DIMASO    On           Create associative dimensions
DIMSHO    Off          Update dimensions while dragging
DIMPOST                Default suffix for dimension text
DIMAPOST               Default suffix for alternate text
```

To return to the command prompt, type **Ctrl-C**.

When you are ready to dimension a drawing, make sure you are at the command prompt. Type **DIM** and press **Return**. The following prompt is displayed.

```
Command: DIM <CR>
Dim:
```

VERSIONS 2.5 and 2.6 AutoCAD versions later than 2.18 include the following features.

DIM1 The DIM1 command was introduced in AutoCAD 2.5. DIM1 lets you enter a single dimensioning command and then redisplays the Command line. In contrast, the DIM command displays an extensive dialogue, requiring you to type EXIT to redisplay the Command line.

Associative Dimensioning Another feature, called *Associative dimensionsing*, was introduced in AutoCAD 2.6. This feature automatically updates dimension lines and values when you change the size of an object on a drawing. Diminsioning changes as the size of the object is modified. Associative dimensioning is turned on unless you turn it off with the SETVAR command.

Consider the following example. A dimensioned line is lengthened using the STRETCH command. The dimension extension lines and dimension value are automatically updated to reflect the new line length.

APPLICATIONS

The DIM command is used to automatically add dimensions to a drawing. You can adjust the dimension presentation by using the DIM options and suboptions. Generally, you place dimensions in a layer by themselves. In this way, you can easily view the drawing either with or without dimensions by turning the dimension layer off and on. Freezing and thawing the dimension layer can speed drawing regeneration time when you must make modifications to your drawing. You can also take advantage of a separate dimension layer (or several dimension layers) to display or plot the dimensions in an alternate line type or color.

TYPICAL OPERATION

Several variations of the DIM command are illustrated in the following activities.

TYPICAL OPERATION 1 In this session you draw and dimension lines, arcs, and a circle. The following drawing shows the outcome of the session. Numbered balloons correspond to the operation steps.

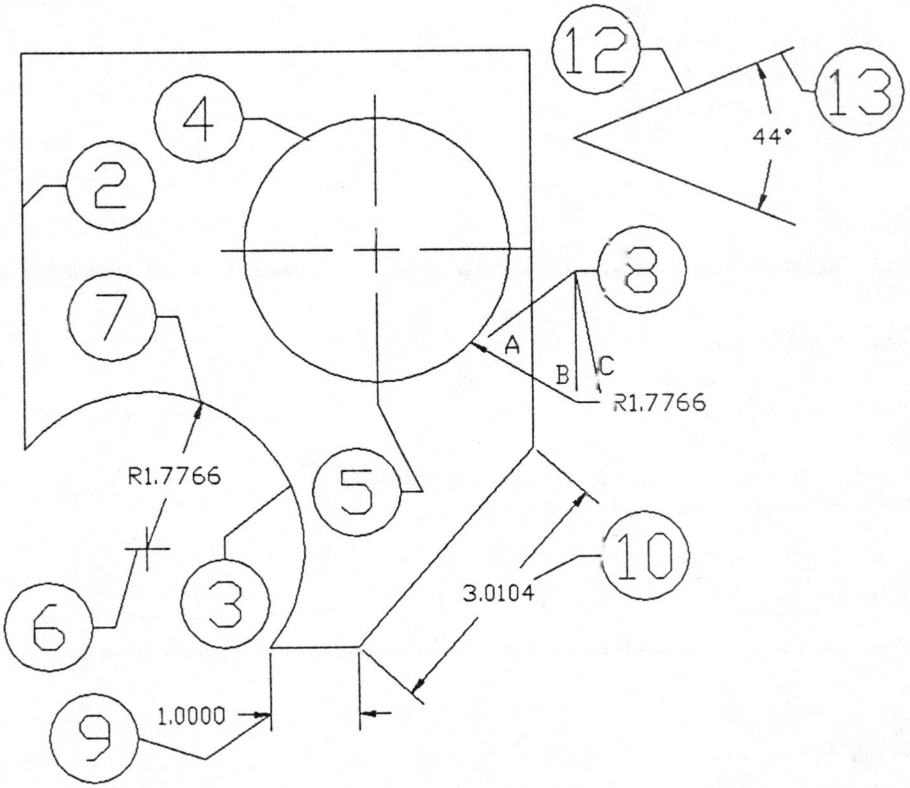

1. Begin a new drawing named DIMAC. Set the SNAP distance, turn the GRID on, and ZOOM the screen for maximum view.

```
Command: SNAP <CR>
Snap spacing or ON/OFF/Aspect/Rotate/Style <0.2500>: .25 <CR>

Command: GRID <CR>
Grid spacing(X) or ON/OFF/Snap/Aspect <0.0000>: ON <CR>

Command: ZOOM <CR>
All/Center/Dynamic/Extents/Left/Previous/Window/<Scale(X)>: A <CR>
Regenerating drawing.
```

2. Draw five lines.

```
Command: LINE <CR>
From point: .5,4 <CR>
To point:  .5,8.5 <CR>
To point: 6.25,8.5 <CR>
To point: 6.25,4 <CR>
To point: 4.25,1.75 <CR>
To point: 3.25,1.75 <CR>
To point: <CR>
```

3. Draw an arc.

```
Command: ARC <CR>
Center/<Start point>: 3.25,1.75 <CR>
Center/End/<Second point>: E <CR>
End point: .5,4 <CR>
Angle/Direction/Radius/<Center point>: A <CR>
Included Angle: 180 <CR>
```

4. Draw a circle with a 1.5-inch radius.

```
Command: CIRCLE <CR>
3P/2P/TTR/<Center point>: 4.5,6.25 <CR>
Diameter/<Radius>: 1.5 <CR>
```

5. Change the DIMCEN variable to -.25 and add center lines to the circle.

```
Command: DIM <CR>
Dim: DIMCEN <CR> Current value <0.0900> New value: -.25 <CR>
Dim: CENTER <CR> Select arc or circle:
(Pick on the circumference of the circle)
```

6. Change the DIMCEN variable to .25 and add center marks to the arc.

```
Dim: DIMCEN <CR>
Current value <-0.2500> New value: .25 <CR>
Dim: CENTER <CR>
Select arc or circle: (Pick on the arc)
```

7. Dimension the radius.

```
Dim: RAD <CR>
Select arc or circle: (Pick on the arc in the approximate location of the
arrowhead shown)
Dimension text <1.7766>: <CR>
```

8. Dimension the circle.

```
Dim: LEADER Leader start: NEA <CR>
to (Pick on circle at approximate location of arrowhead)
To point: (Pick at point approximately as shown)
To point: (Pick at point shown for end of LEADER)<CR>
Dimension text <1.7766>: <CR>
```

9. Dimension a short horizontal line.

NOTE

Since the dimension could not fit between the extension lines it is located closest to the second extension line location.

```
Dim: HOR <CR>
First extension line origin or RETURN to select: 4.25,1.75 <CR>
Second extension line origin: 3.25,1.75 <CR>
Dimension line location: 4,1 <CR>
Dimension text <1.0000>: <CR>
```

10. Dimension the angled line with an aligned dimension.

```
Dim: ALI <CR>
First extension line origin or RETURN to select: <CR>
Select line, arc, or circle: (Pick on the angled line)
Dimension line location: 5.75,2.25 <CR>
Dimension text <3.0104>: <CR>
```

11. Cancel dimensioning operations and get command prompt to return.

```
Dim: Ctrl-C *Cancel* (Pressing Ctrl-C exits DIM)
```

12. Draw two lines.

```
Command: LINE <CR>
From point: 9.25,8.5 <CR>
To point: 6.75,7.5 <CR>
To point: 9.25,6.5 <CR>
To point: <CR>
```

13. Dimension the two lines and cancel the dimensioning activity.

```
Command: DIM <CR>
Dim: ANGULAR <CR>
Select first line: (Pick at first line of two angled line)
Second line: (Pick at second of two angled line)
Enter dimension line arc location: 9,7.5 <CR>
Dimension text <44>: <CR>
Enter text location: <CR>

Dim: Ctrl-C *Cancel*
```

14. Save the drawing by typing **SAVE** <**CR**> and giving it a name such as **DIMAC**.

```
Command: SAVE <CR>
File name <DIMAC>: <CR>
```

If you have followed the numbered steps, your drawing looks like the following one.

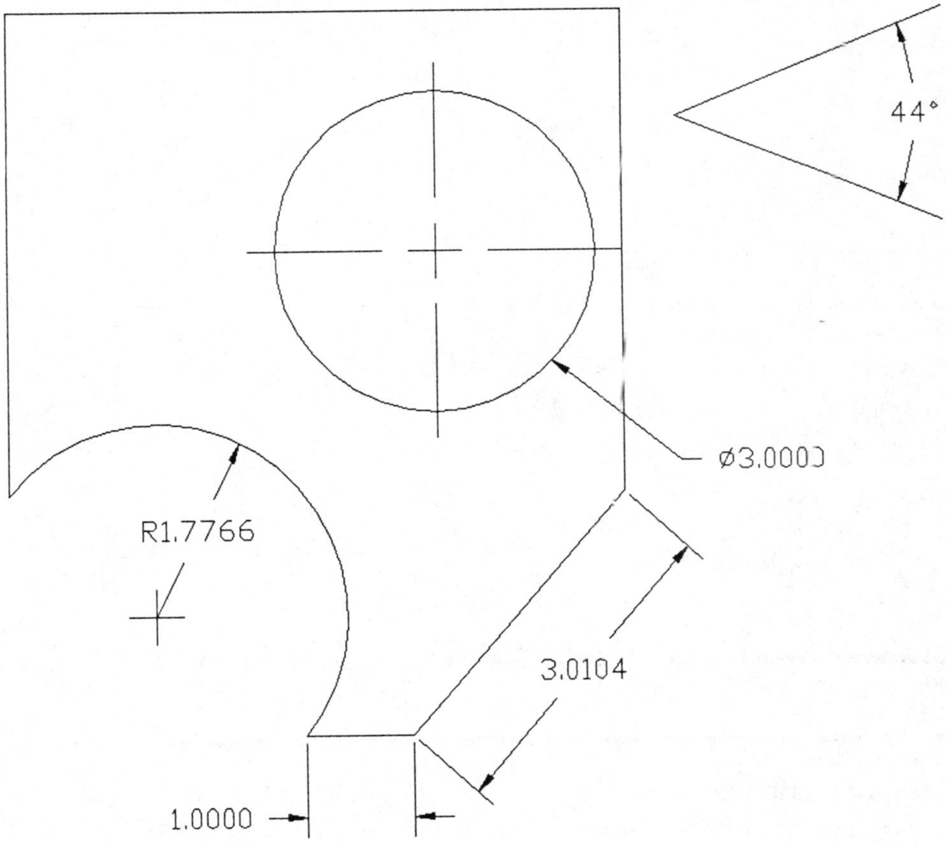

15. Type **QUIT** and press **Return**; then type **Y** and press **Return** to redisplay the Main Menu.

TYPICAL OPERATION 2 This session uses the dimensioning command to produce baseline dimensions, rotated dimensions, and other typical linear dimensioning. The following drawing includes numbered balloons that correspond to the numbered steps.

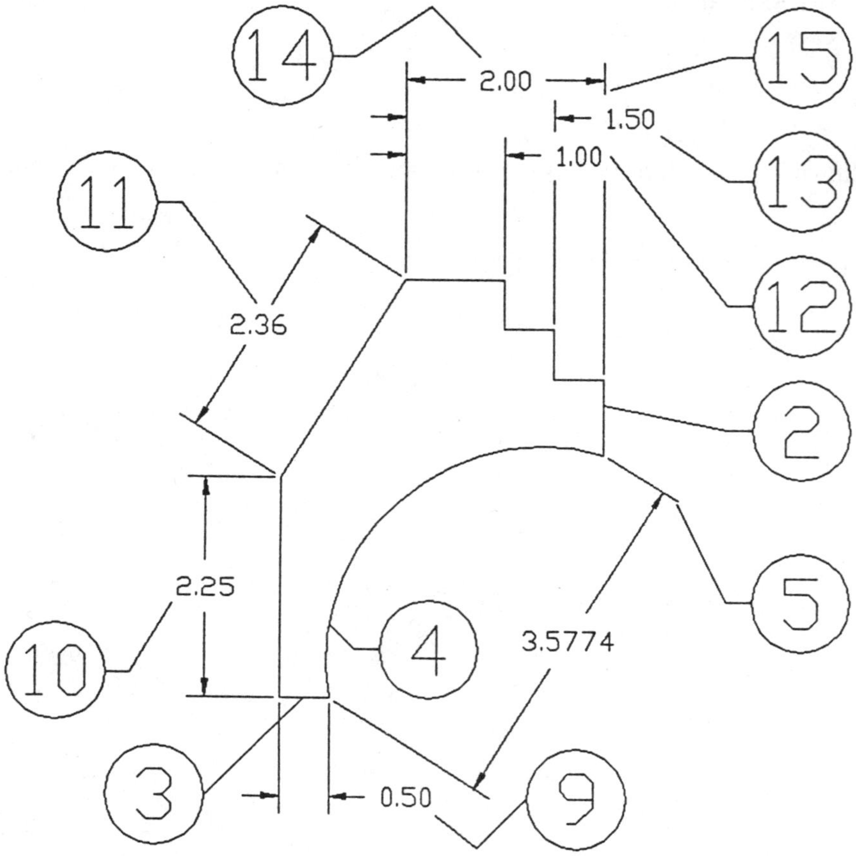

1. Begin a new drawing named DIMAC2. Set the SNAP distance, turn the GRID on, and ZOOM the screen.

```
Command: SNAP <CR>
Snap spacing or ON/OFF/Aspect/Rotate/Style <1.0000>: .25 <CR>

Command: GRID <CR>
Grid spacing(X) or ON/OFF/Snap/Aspect <0.0000>: ON <CR>

Command: ZOOM <CR>
All/Center/Dynamic/Extents/Left/Previous/Window/<Scale(X)>: A <CR>
```

2. Draw 8 lines.

```
Command:  LINE <CR>
From point: 1.25,1.5 <CR>
To point:  1.25,3.75 <CR>
To point: 2.5,5.75 <CR>
To point: 3.5,5.75 <CR>
To point: 3.5,5.25 <CR>
To point: 4,5.25 <CR>
To point: 4,4.75 <CR>
To point: 4.5,4.75 <CR>
To point: 4.5,4 <CR>
To point: <CR>
```

3. Draw one line.

```
Command: LINE <CR>
From point: 1.25,1.5 <CR>
To point: 1.75,1.5 <CR>
To point: <CR>
```

4. Draw an arc.

```
Command: ARC <CR>
Center/<Start point>: 4.5,4 <CR>
Center/End/<Second point>: 2.75,3.75 <CR>
End point: 1.75,1.5 <CR>
```

5. Draw a rotated dimension and then cancel dimensioning with **Ctrl-C**.

```
Command: DIM <CR>
Dim: ROT Dimension line angle <0>: 58 <CR>
First extension line origin or RETURN to select:
(Pick at one end of arc's intersection with a line)
Second extension line origin:
(Pick at other end of arc's intersection with a line)
Dimension line location:
(Pick at approximate location of dim line as shown on drawing)
Dimension text <3.5774>: <CR>

Dim: Ctrl-C *Cancel*
```

6. Save the drawing.

```
Command: SAVE <CR>
File name <B:DIMAC2>: (Give your DWG a name or press Return
to use the default name) <CR>
```

7. Use the UNITS command to change to two-place dimensions.

```
Command: UNITS <CR>

Systems of units:      (Examples)

    1.  Scientific      1.55E+01
    2.  Decimal         15.50
    3.  Engineering     1'-3.50"
    4.  Architectural   1'-3 1/2"
    5.  Fractional      15 1/2

Enter choice, 1 to 5 <2>: <CR>
Number of digits to right of decimal point (0 to 8) <4>: 2 <CR>
```

TIP: This is how you change the numerals past your decimal point.

```
Systems of angle measure:        (Examples)

    1.  Decimal degrees          45.0000
    2.  Degrees/minutes/seconds  45d0'0"
    3.  Grads                    50.0000g
    4.  Radians                  0.7854r
    5.  Surveyor's units         N 45d0'0" E

Enter choice, 1 to 5 <1>: <CR>
Number of fractional places for display of angles (0 to 8) <0>:
<CR>
```

With AutoCAD version 2.5 and later, you must respond to the following set of prompts.

```
Direction for angle 0:
   East    3 o'clock  =  0
   North  12 o'clock  =  90
   West    9 o'clock  =  180
   South   6 o'clock  =  270
Enter direction for angle 0 <0>: <CR> <CR>


Do you want angles measured clockwise? <N> <CR> <CR>
```

8. Press **F1** to return to the graphics screen.

```
Command: (Press display toggle switch to redisplay the drawing.
F1 on the IBM PC.)
```

9. Add a horizontal dimension.

```
Command: DIM <CR>
Dim: HOR <CR>
First extension line origin or RETURN to select: <CR>
Select line, arc, or circle: 1.5,1.5 <CR>
Dimension line location: 1.5,.5 <CR>
Dimension text <0.50>: <CR>
```

10. Add a vertical dimension.

```
Dim: VERT <CR>
First extension line origin or RETURN to select: 1.25,1.5 <CR>
Second extension line origin: 1.25,3.75 <CR>
Dimension line location: .5,2.5 <CR>
Dimension text <2.25>: <CR>
```

11. Add an aligned dimension.

```
Dim: ALI <CR>
First extension line origin or RETURN to select: <CR>
Select line, arc, or circle: 1.75,4.5 <CR>
Dimension line location: 1,5.25 <CR>
Dimension text <2.36>: <CR>
```

12. Add a horizontal dimension.

```
Dim: HOR <CR>
First extension line origin or RETURN to select: <CR>
Select line, arc, or circle: 2.75,5.75 <CR>
Dimension line location: 2.75,7 <CR>
Dimension text <1.00>: <CR>
```

13. Add a dimension using a baseline.

```
Dim: BASE <CR>
Second extension line origin: 4,5.25 <CR>
Dimension text <1.50>: <CR>
```

14. Add a dimension using a baseline and cancel dimensioning with **Ctrl-C**.

```
Dim: BASE <CR>
Second extension line origin: 4.5,4.75 <CR>
Dimension text <2.00>: <CR>

Dim: Ctrl-C *Cancel*
```

15. Zoom the screen, break two lines, and zoom back out to full screen view.

```
Command: ZOOM <CR>
All/Center/Dynamic/Extents/Left/Previous/Window/<Scale(X)>: W <CR>
First point: 3.75,6.50 <CR>
Second point: 5,8 <CR>
```

```
Command: BREAK <CR>
Select object: 4,6.75 <CR>
Enter second point or F: 4,7.25 <CR>

Command: BREAK <CR>
Select object: 4.5,6.75 <CR>
Enter second point or F: 4.5,7.625 <CR>

Command: ZOOM <CR>
All/Center/Dynamic/Extents/Left/Previous/Window/<Scale(X)>: A <CR>
```

Your drawing now looks like the following one.

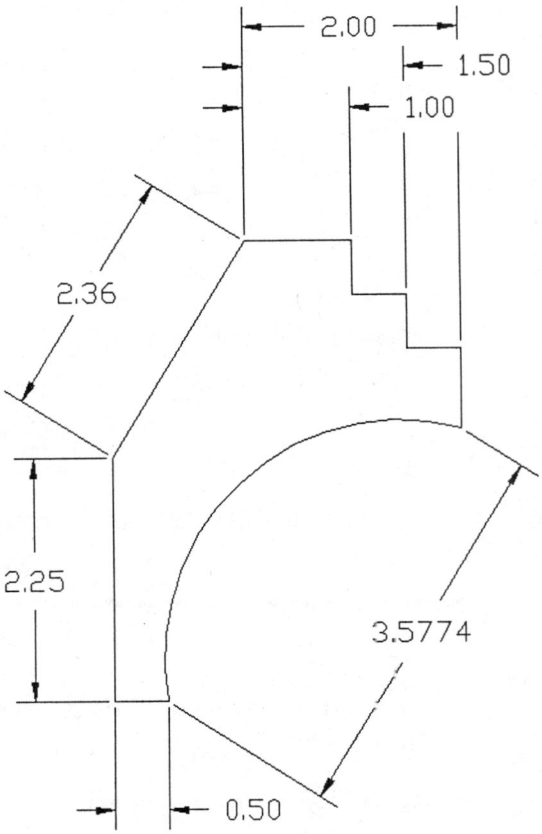

16. Type **SAVE** and press **Return** twice. Then **QUIT** to redisplay the Main Menu.

TYPICAL OPERATION 3 In this session you draw several figures and then dimension them with unidirectional and aligned text. The dimensions are placed within and above the dimension lines. You use two techniques for dimensioning angles. When complete, it should look like the following drawing.

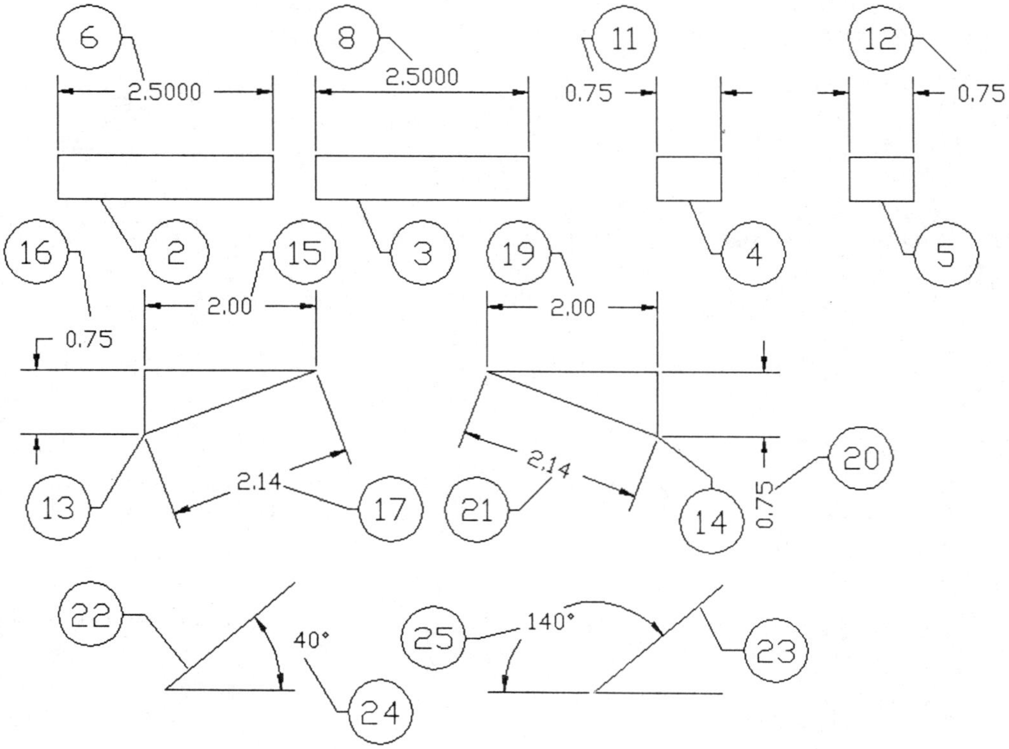

1. Begin a new drawing named DIMAC3. Set the SNAP distance, turn the GRID on, and ZOOM the screen.

```
Command: SNAP <CR>
Snap spacing or ON/OFF/Aspect/Rotate/Style <1.0000>: .25 <CR>

Command: GRID <CR>
Grid spacing(X) or ON/OFF/Snap/Aspect <0.0000>: ON <CR>

Command: ZOOM <CR>
All/Center/Dynamic/Extents/Left/Previous/Window/<Scale(X)>: A <CR>
```

2. Draw a rectangle.

```
Command: LINE <CR>
From point: .75,6.75 <CR>
To point: .75,7.25 <CR>
To point: 3.25,7.25 <CR>
To point: 3.25,6.75 <CR>
To point: C <CR>
```

3. Copy the rectangle.

```
Command: COPY <CR>
Select objects: W <CR>
First point: .5,6.5 <CR>
Second point: 3.5,7.5 <CR>
4 found.
Select objects: <CR>
Base point or displacement: .75,6.75 <CR>
Second point of displacement: 3.75,6.75 <CR>
```

4. Draw a small rectangle.

```
Command: LINE <CR>
From point: 7.75,6.75 <CR>
To point: 7.75,7.25 <CR>
To point: 8.5,7.25 <CR>
To point: 8.5,6.75 <CR>
To point: C <CR>
```

5. Copy the small rectangle.

```
Command: COPY <CR>
Select objects: W <CR>
First point: 7.5,6.5 <CR>
Second point: 8.75,7.5 <CR>
4 found.
Select objects: <CR>
Base point or displacement: 7.75,6.75 <CR>
Second point of displacement: 10,6.75 <CR>
```

6. Dimension the first rectangle with a broken dimension line.

```
Command: DIM <CR>
Dim: HOR <CR>
First extension line origin or RETURN to select: <CR>
Select line, arc, or circle: 1.25,7.25 <CR>
Dimension line location: 1.25,8 <CR>
Dimension text <2.5000>: <CR>
```

7. Turn on DIMTAD so that dimension text is placed above the dimension line.

```
Dim: DIMTAD Current value <Off> New value: On/Off: ON <CR>
```

8. Dimension the second rectangle and cancel dimensioning with **Ctrl-C**.

```
Dim: HOR <CR>
First extension line origin or RETURN to select: <CR>
Select line, arc, or circle: 5,7.25 <CR>
Dimension line location: 4.5,8 <CR>
Dimension text <2.5000>: <CR>

Dim: Ctrl-C *Cancel*
```

9. Type **UNITS** <**CR**>, **2**<**CR**>, <**CR**>, <**CR**>.

If you are using AutoCAD version 2.5 or later, press <**CR**>, <**CR**> to accept the defaults for the direction of angle 0 and to accept counterclockwise angle measure.

All users press **F1** to return to the graphics screen.

NOTE

The UNITS command is used to change the number of digits to right of decimal point from 4 to 2.

10. Turn off DIMTAD to break the dimension line for text.

```
Command: DIM <CR>
Dim: DIMTAD Current value <On> New value: On/Off: OFF <CR>
```

11. Dimension the third rectangle.

```
Dim: HOR <CR>
First extension line origin or RETURN to select: 8.5,7.25 <CR>
Second extension line origin: 7.75,7.25 <CR>
Dimension line location: 8,8 <CR>
Dimension text <0.75>: <CR>
(Text was located nearest the second extension line)
```

12. Dimension the fourth rectangle and redraw the screen.

```
Dim: HOR <CR>
First extension line origin or RETURN to select: <CR>
Select line, arc, or circle: 10.25,7.25 <CR>
```

TIP: The closest end of the line where you pick determines the location of the first extension line.

```
Dimension line location: 10.25,8 <CR>
Dimension text <0.75>: <CR>
```

NOTE

Text was located nearest the second extension line.

```
Dim: (Press REDRAW button on mouse or type Ctrl-C and type REDRAW
<CR>) *Cancel*
Command: REDRAW <CR>
```

13. Draw a triangle.

```
Command: LINE <CR>
From point: 1.75,4 <CR>
To point: 1.75,4.75 <CR>
To point: 3.75,4.75 <CR>
To point: C <CR>
```

14. Mirror the triangle.

```
Command: MIRROR <CR>
Select objects: W <CR>
First point: 1.5,3.75 <CR>
Second point: 4,5 <CR>
3 found.
Select objects: <CR>
First point of mirror line: 4.75,5 <CR>
Second point: 4.75,3.75 <CR>
Delete old objects? <N> <CR>
```

TIP: DIMTIH and DIMTOH are both turned on. This produces unidirectional type dimensioning.

15. Add a horizontal dimension.

```
Command: DIM <CR>
Dim: HOR <CR>
First extension line origin or RETURN to select: <CR>
Select line, arc, or circle: 3.25,4.75 <CR>
Dimension line location: 2.75,5.5 <CR>
Dimension text <2.00>: <CR>
```

16. Add a vertical, unidirectional dimension.

```
Dim: VERT <CR>
First extension line origin or RETURN to select: 1.75,4 <CR>
Second extension line origin: 1.75,4.75 <CR>
Dimension line location: .5,4.5 <CR>
Dimension text <0.75>: <CR>
```

17. Add an aligned, unidirectional dimension.

```
Dim: ALI <CR>
First extension line origin or RETURN to select: <CR>
Select line, arc, or circle: 2.5,4.25 <CR>
Dimension line location: 3.25,3.5 <CR>
Dimension text <2.14>: <CR>
```

TIP: To produce aligned type dimensioning (not unidirectional), DIMTIH and DIMTOH must be turned off.

18. Turn DIMTIH and DIMTOH off:

```
Dim: DIMTIH Current value <On> New value: On/Off: OFF
Dim: DIMTOH Current value <On> New value: On/Off: OFF
```

19. Add a horizontal dimension.

```
Dim: HOR <CR>
First extension line origin or RETURN to select: <CR>
Select line, arc, or circle: 7,4.75 <CR>
Dimension line location: 7,5.5 <CR>
Dimension text <2.00>: <CR>
```

20. Add a vertical dimension with aligned text.

```
Dim: VERT <CR>
First extension line origin or RETURN to select: 7.75,4.75 <CR>
Second extension line origin: 7.75,4 <CR>
Dimension line location: 9,4.25 <CR>
Dimension text <0.75>: <CR>
```

21. Add an aligned dimension with aligned (not horizontal) text. Redraw the screen.

```
Dim: ALI <CR>
First extension line origin or RETURN to select: <CR>
Select line, arc, or circle: 7,4.25 <CR>
Dimension line location: 6.25,3.75 <CR>
Dimension text <2.14>: <CR>

Dim: (Press REDRAW button on mouse or type Ctrl-C and type REDRAW)
<CR>) *Cancel*
Command: REDRAW
```

22. Draw two lines at an acute angle.

```
Command: LINE <CR>
From point: 3.5,2.25 <CR>
To point: 2,1 <CR>
To point: 3.5,1 <CR>
To point: <CR>
```

23. Copy the two lines.

```
Command: COPY <CR>
Select objects: W <CR>
First point: 1.75,.75 <CR>
Second point: 3.75,2.5 <CR>
2 found.
Select objects: <CR>
Base point or displacement: 2,1 <CR>
Second point of displacement: 7,1 <CR>
```

24. Add an angular dimension.

```
Command: DIM <CR>
Dim: ANGULAR <CR>
Select first line: 3.25,2 <CR>
Second line: 3.25,1 <CR>
Enter dimension line arc location: 3.25,1.5 <CR>
Dimension text <40>: <CR>
Enter text location: 3.5,1.5 <CR>
```

25. Add an angular dimension and cancel dimensioning.

```
Dim: ANGULAR <CR>
Select first line: 8.25,2 <CR>
Second line: 8.25,1 <CR>
Enter dimension line arc location: 6.25,1.75 <CR>
Dimension text <140>: <CR>
Enter text location: 6.25,1.75 <CR>

Dim: Ctrl-C *cancel*
```

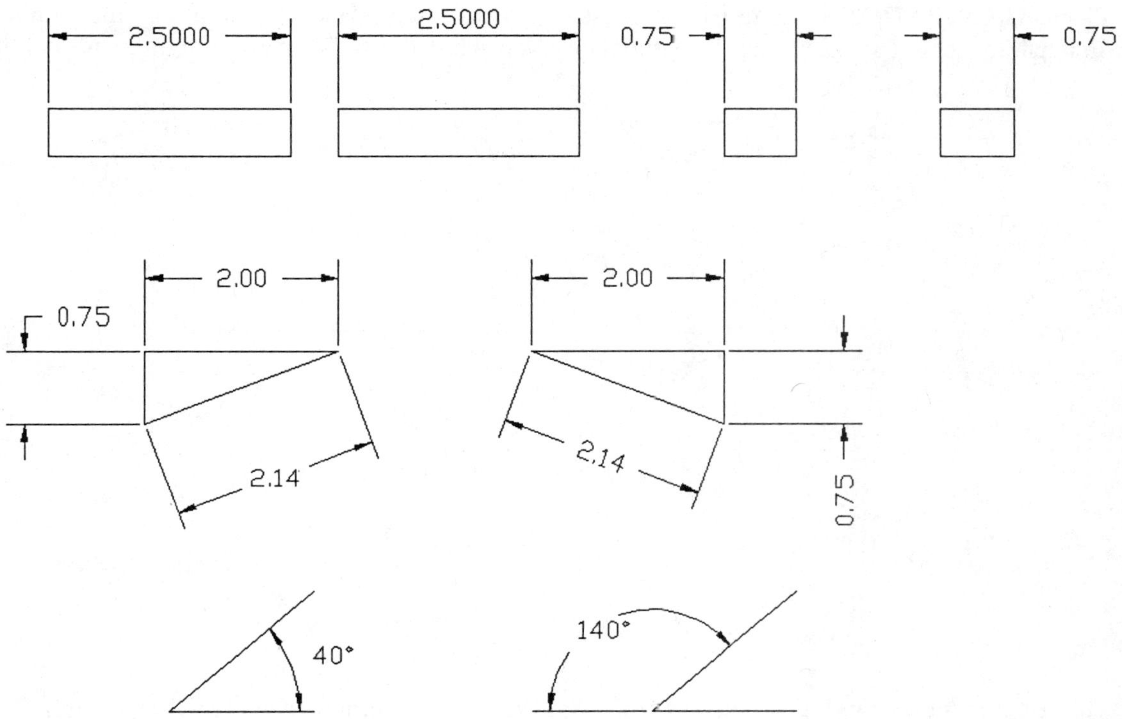

26. Save the drawing.

```
Command: SAVE <CR>
File name <B:DIMAC3>: (Give your DWG a name or press Return to
use the default name) <CR>
```

27. Use **QUIT** to redisplay the Main Menu.

TYPICAL OPERATION 4 In this fourth session, you draw three circles and a rectangle and then dimension them. The following drawing shows you what the finished drawing should look like.

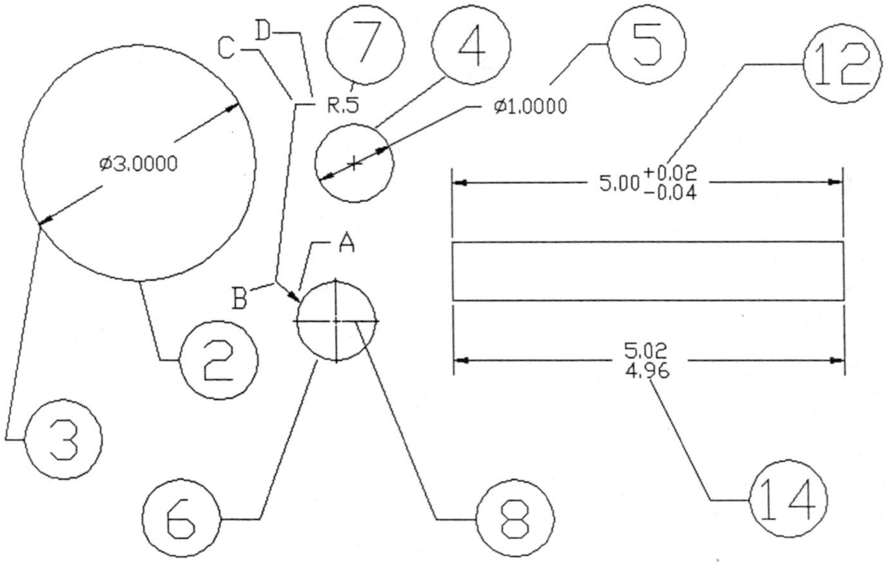

1. Begin a new drawing named DIMAC4. Set the SNAP distance, turn the GRID on, and ZOOM the screen.

```
Command: SNAP <CR>
Snap spacing or ON/OFF/Aspect/Rotate/Style <1.0000>: .25 <CR>

Command: GRID <CR>
Grid spacing(X) or ON/OFF/Snap/Aspect <0.0000>: ON <CR>

Command: ZOOM <CR>
All/Center/Dynamic/Extents/Left/Previous/Window/<Scale(X)>: A <CR>
Regenerating drawing.
```

2. Draw a circle.

```
Command: CIRCLE 3P/2P/<Center point>: 1.75,7 <CR>
Diameter/<Radius>: DRAG  <CR>
3.25,7 <CR>
```

3. Dimension the circle and redraw the screen.

```
Command: DIM <CR>
Dim: DIAM Select arc or circle: (Pick on circumference)
Dimension text <3.0000>: <CR>

Dim: (Press REDRAW button on mouse or type Ctrl-C and type REDRAW
<CR>) *Cancel*
Command: REDRAW
```

4. Draw a one-inch diameter circle.

```
Command:  CIRCLE <CR>
3P/2P/TTR/<Center point>: 4.5,7 <CR>
Diameter/<Radius>: 5,7 <CR>
```

5. Dimension the circle and redraw the screen.

```
Command: DIM <CR>
Dim: DIAM Select arc or circle: 5,7.25 <CR>
Dimension text <1.0000>: <CR>
Text does not fit.
Enter leader length for text: 5.75,8 <CR>

Dim: (Press REDRAW button on mouse or type Ctrl-C and type REDRAW
<CR>) *Cancel*
Command: REDRAW
```

6. Draw a circle with a .5-inch radius.

```
Command: CIRCLE <CR>
3P/2P/TTR/<Center point>: 4.25,5 <CR>
Diameter/<Radius>: .5 <CR>
```

7. Dimension the circle with a leader and redraw the screen.

```
Command: DIM <CR>
Dim: LEADER <CR>
Leader start: NEA <CR>
to (Pick on circumference of circle approx at point A)
To point: (Pick in location approx at point B)
To point: (Pick in location approx at point C)
To point: (Pick in location approx at point D)
To point: <CR>
Dimension text <>: R.5 <CR>

Dim: (Press REDRAW button on mouse or type Ctrl-C and type REDRAW
<CR> *Cancel*
Command: REDRAW
```

8. Add center lines to a circle and cancel dimensioning.

```
Command: DIM <CR>
Dim: DIMCEN Current value <0.0900> New value: -.040 <CR>
Dim: CENTER Select arc or circle: 4.75,5 <CR>

Dim: (Press REDRAW button on mouse or type Ctrl-C and type REDRAW
<CR> *Cancel*
```

9. Draw a rectangle.

```
Command: LINE <CR>
From point: 5.75,5.25 <CR>
To point: 5.75,6 <CR>
To point: 10.75,6 <CR>
To point: 10.75,5.25 <CR>
To point: C <CR>
```

10. Type **UNITS** <**CR**>, **2**<**CR**>, <**CR**>, <**CR**>.

If you are using AutoCAD version 2.5 or later, press <**CR**>, <**CR**> to accept the defaults for the direction of angle 0 and to accept counterclockwise angle measure.

All users press **F1** to return to the graphics screen.

11. Set dimensioning tolerances: DIMTP (plus tolerance) = .02 ; DIMTM (minus tolerance) = .04. Turn on dimensioning tolerance.

```
Command: DIM <CR>
Dim: DIMTP Current value <0.00> New value: .02 <CR>
Dim: DIMTM Current value <0.00> New value: .04 <CR>
Dim: DIMTOL Current value <Off> New value: On/Off: ON <CR>
```

12. Add horizontal dimension with a plus/minus tolerance.

```
Dim: HOR <CR>
First extension line origin or RETURN to select: <CR>
Select line, arc, or circle: 8,6 <CR>
Dimension line location: 8,6.75 <CR>
Dimension text <5.00>: <CR>
```

13. Turn DIMLIM on to produce limit dimensioning.

```
Dim: DIMLIM Current value <Off> New value: On/Off: ON <CR>
```

14. Add a horizontal dimension with limit dimensions and redraw the screen.

```
Dim: HOR <CR>
First extension line origin or RETURN to select: <CR>
Select line, arc, or circle: 8,5.25 <CR>
Dimension line location: 8,4.5 <CR>
Dimension text <5.00>: <CR>

Dim: (Press REDRAW button on mouse or type Ctrl-C and type REDRAW
<CR>)*Cancel*
Command: REDRAW
```

Your drawing now looks like the following one.

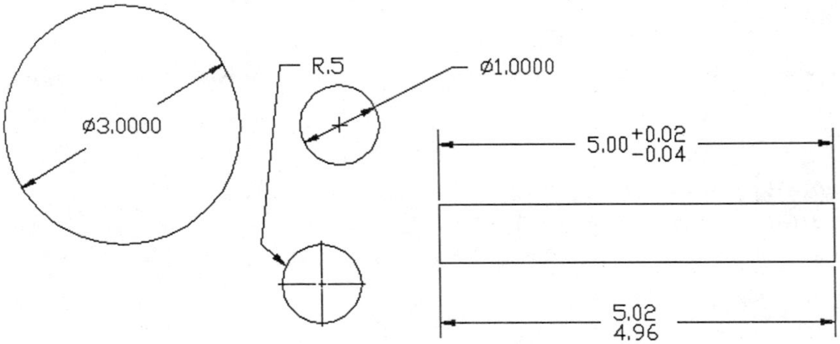

15. Use the SAVE command to save the drawing. Then **QUIT** to redisplay the Main Menu.
16. If you have AutoCAD 2.18 or earlier, turn to Module 13 to continue the learning sequence. Otherwise, perform the next activity.

TYPICAL OPERATION 5 This activity demonstrates the associative dimensioning feature introduced in AutoCAD version 2.6. The command name, DIMASO, is normally On unless you turn it Off, or change the parameters of your prototype drawing (ACAD.DWG). DIMASO is turned On or Off using the SETVAR command and then specifying DIMASO. If DIMASO has a value of 1, it is On; if the value is 0, it is Off. Begin a new drawing named DIMAC5.

1. Set the SNAP distance, turn on the GRID and ZOOM the screen.

```
Command: SNAP <CR>
Snap spacing or ON/OFF/Aspect/Rotate/Style <0.2500>: .25 <CR>

Command: GRID <CR>
Grid spacing(X) or ON/OFF/Snap/Aspect <0.0000>: ON <CR>

Command: ZOOM <CR>
All/Center/Dynamic/Extents/Left/Previous/Window/<Scale(X)>: A <CR>
Regenerating drawing.
```

2. Draw a polygon with the LINE command.

```
Command: LINE <CR>
From point: 2,2 <CR>
To point: @3<90 <CR>
To point: @3<0 <CR>
To point: @1<270 <CR>
To point: @1<0 <CR>
To point: 7,2 <CR>
To point: C <CR>
```

3. Dimension the polygon and redraw the screen.

```
Command: DIM <CR>
Dim: HOR <CR>
First extension line origin or RETURN to select: 2,2 <CR>
Second extension line origin: 7,2 <CR>
Dimension line location: 4,1 <CR>
Dimension text <5.0000>: <CR>
Dim: (type Ctrl-C)  *Cancel*
Command: REDRAW <CR>
```

4. Use the STRETCH command to see how the DIMASO feature automatically alters dimensions.

```
Command: STRETCH <CR>
Select objects to stretch by window...
Select objects: W <CR>
First corner: 3,0 <CR>
Other corner: 8,6 <CR>
3 found.
Select objects: 3,1 <CR>
1 selected, 1 found.
Select objects: 3,2 <CR>
1 selected, 1 found.
Select objects: 3,5 <CR>
1 selected, 1 found.
Select objects:
Base point: 7,2 <CR>
New point: 9,2 <CR>
```

5. Use the END command to save the drawing. Then QUIT to redisplay the Main Menu.
6. Turn to Module 13 to continue the learning sequence.

Module 21

DIST

```
Command: DIST
First point: (point)
Second point: (point)
Distance = <calculated distance> Angle = <angle>
Delta X = <change in X> Delta Y = <change in Y> Delta Z =
   <change in Z>
```

DESCRIPTION

The DIST command allows you to calculate the distance and angle between any two points on a drawing. The points may be specified by typing the coordinates from the keyboard, or picking them with the screen cursor. When picking points with the screen cursor, OSNAP is useful to ensure the accuracy of the referenced point, whether it is an endpoint, intersection, or a centerpoint.

Starting with version 2.6, the DIST command accepts 3-dimensional points.

APPLICATIONS

When you use the DIST command, the distance information is similar to the information provided by the dimensioning (DIM) commands, except that the DIST command does not change the drawing in any way.

TYPICAL OPERATION

In this session you calculate the distance between the points 1,1 and 2,2. Begin a new drawing named DIST.

1. Enter the two points and verify the distance between them.

```
Command: DIST <CR>
First point: 0,0,0 <CR>
Second point: 1,3,5 <CR>

Distance = 5.92   Angle = 72
Delta X = 1.00   Delta Y = 3.00,   Delta Z = 5.00

Command:
```

2. If you have AutoCAD 2.6 or later, compute the distance between the origin and the point 1,3,5.

```
Delta X = 1.0000   Delta Y = 1.0000   Delta Z = 0.0000
```

Notice that the angle measure is computed in the X/Y plane. The Z-coordinate is ignored in the computation of the angle measure.

The results are displayed in the current drawing units as specified by the UNITs command.

3. Type **Quit** and press **Return**; then type **Y** and press **Return** to display the Main Menu.
4. Turn to Module 8 to continue the learning sequence.

Module 22

DIVIDE

```
Command: DIVIDE
Select object to divide:   (point)
<Number of segments>/Block:
```

DESCRIPTION

The DIVIDE command, introduced with AutoCAD 2.5, divides an entity into equal portions. AutoCAD can divide lines, polylines, circles, and arcs. You may divide an entity into as few as two or as many as 32,767 parts. AutoCAD either places a point (the default) at each division boundary or marks the location with a block that you specify.

After issuing the DIVIDE command, you specify the object either by picking it with the screen cursor or typing a pair of coordinates the object contains. It makes no difference where on the object you pick. The option "<Number of segments>/Block:" presents you with two options. Typing a number divides the object into that number of equal segments, placing points at the division locations. Selecting "Block" produces an additional set of prompts. The first prompt, "Block name to insert:," asks you to enter the name of a block to use as the division marker. The next prompt, "Align block with object? <Y>," asks you to specify whether you want the block rotated to match the orientation of the divided object. Finally, the prompt "Number of segments:" provides the opportunity to specify the number of equal segments to create from the selected object.

APPLICATIONS

The DIVIDE command automates the division of an object into a specified number of segments. Use DIVIDE when the number of segments is the most important consideration. Use the MEASURE command when you want to divide an object into segments of a specific length, without regard to the number of segments required. Because of the high level of internal accuracy in AutoCAD, using the DIVIDE command to divide an object into equal parts is probably more accurate than performing the division manually and then placing the points or blocks. The DIVIDE command is certainly faster.

TYPICAL OPERATION

In this session you divide both a circle and a line, using blocks as the division markers. The numbered balloons correspond to the steps in the operation. Begin a new drawing named DIVIDE.

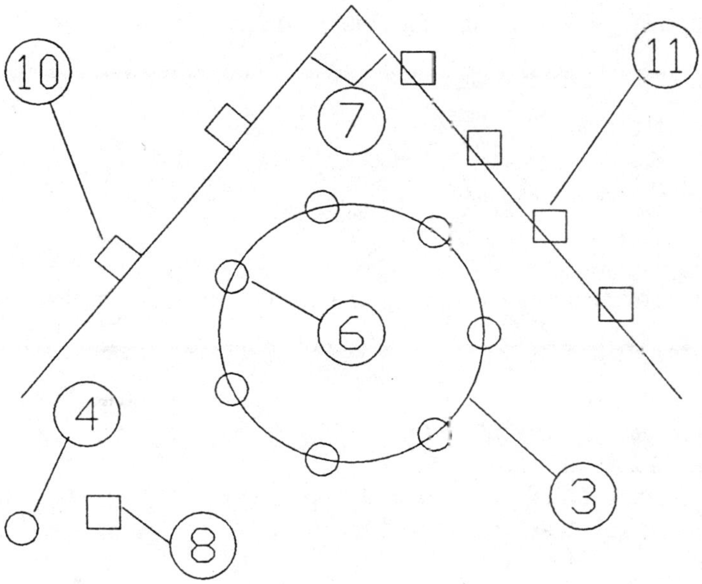

1. Turn on SNAP using the default setting of 1.00.

```
Command: SNAP <CR>
Snap spacing or ON/OFF/Aspect/Rotate/Style <1.0000>: ON <CR>
Command:
```

2. Turn the GRID on.

```
Command: GRID <CR>
Grid spacing(X) or ON/OFF/Snap/Aspect <0.0000>: ON <CR>
Command:
```

3. Draw a circle centered at 6,4 with a radius of 2.

```
Command: CIRCLE <CR>
3P/2P/TTR/<Center point>: 6,4 <CR>
Diameter/<Radius>: 2 <CR>
Command:
```

4. Create a small circle to use as the division marker.

```
Command: CIRCLE <CR>
3P/2P/TTR/<Center point>: 1,1 <CR>
Diameter/<Radius>: .25 <CR>
Command:
```

5. Make the circle a block named MARKER. Use the center of the circle as the insertion point.

```
Command: BLOCK <CR>
Block name (or ?): MARKER <CR>
Insertion base point: 1,1 <CR>
Select objects: (Turn off SNAP and pick the circle) 1 selected, 1 found.
Select objects: <CR>
Command:
```

The small circle disappears from the screen.

6. Divide the remaining circle into seven arcs. (The response to "Align block with object" makes no difference since rotating a circle has no effect on its appearance.)

```
Command: DIVIDE <CR>
Select object to divide: (Pick the circle.)
<Number of segments>/Block: B <CR>
Block name to insert: MARKER <CR>
Align block with object? <Y> <CR>
Number of segments: 7 <CR>
Command:
```

7. Draw two lines.

```
Command: LINE <CR>
From point: 1,3 <CR>
To point: 6,9 <CR>
To point: 11,3 <CR>
To point: <CR>
Command:
```

8. Draw a small box to use as a marker.

```
Command: LINE <CR>
From point: 2,1 <CR>
To point: 2,1.5 <CR>
To point: 2.5,1.5 <CR>
To point: 2.5,1 <CR>
To point: <CR>
Command:
```

9. Make the box a block named SQUARE. Make the midpoint of the bottom side be the insertion point.

```
Command: BLOCK <CR>
Block name (or ?): SQUARE <CR>
Insertion base point: 2.25,1 <CR>
Select objects: W <CR>
(Surround the square with a window)
First corner: (Pick a corner)
Other corner: (Pick a corner)
4 found.
Select objects: <CR>
Command:
```

The small box disappears from the screen.

10. Divide the left line into three parts. Rotate the block when it is inserted.

```
Command: DIVIDE <CR>
Select object to divide: (Pick the left line.)
<Number of segments>/Block: B <CR>
```

```
Block name to insert: SQUARE <CR>
Align block with object? <Y> <CR>
Number of segments: 3 <CR>
Command:
```

Notice that the blocks are drawn so the bottom of the blocks rests along the line.

11. Divide the right line into five parts. Do not rotate the block when it is inserted.

```
Command: DIVIDE <CR>
Select object to divide: (Pick the right line.)
<Number of segments>/Block: B <CR>
Block name to insert: SQUARE <CR>
Align block with object? <Y> N <CR>
Number of segments: 5 <CR>
Command:
```

Notice that when the blocks are not aligned, they are drawn in the same orientation as they were created. Your completed drawing should resemble the following illustration.

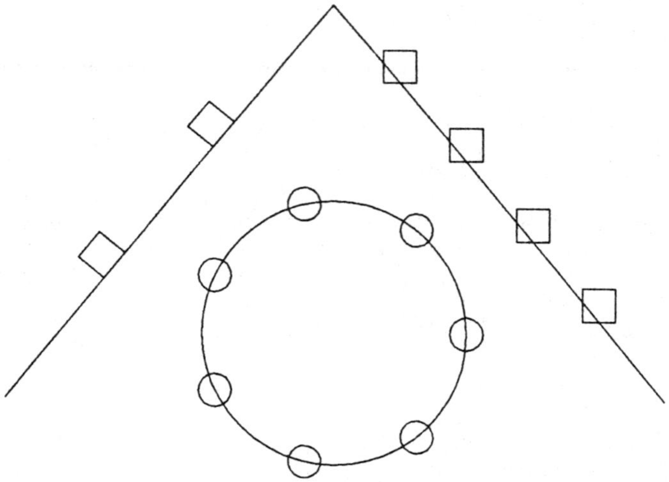

12. Type **QUIT** and press **Return**; then type **Y** and press **Return** to display the Main Menu.
13. Turn to Module 9 to continue the learning sequence.

Module 23

DONUT (or DOUGHNUT)

```
Command: DOUGHNUT
Inside diameter <last>: (value or two points)
Outside diameter <last>: (value or two points)
Center of doughnut: (two points)
```

DESCRIPTION

DONUT and DOUGHNUT, introduced with AutoCAD 2.5, are alternate spellings of the same command. This command produces a closed circular polyline, or doughnut-shaped, object. Because it is a polyline, PEDIT and other polyline editing commands are used to edit the resulting doughnut. The state of FILLMODE determines whether the doughnut appears filled. You have great flexibility in constructing the doughnut. To specify the inner and outer diameters you may either type values, or you can pick two points on the screen representing the value. You then specify the outer diameter either by typing the value or picking two points on the screen representing the value. AutoCAD then displays the resulting doughnut and allows you to dynamically locate the center point or type the coordinates from the keyboard. Once you use the DONUT command, AutoCAD remembers the values of the inner and outer radii and supplies them as the default values the next time you use the DONUT command.

APPLICATIONS

The DONUT command provides greater speed and flexibility in constructing doughnut-shaped entities than is possible through the use of more primitive drawing commands. For example, in the PLINE module you constructed a circuit board solder pad as a PLINE arc. While this construction is workable, it has some limitations. The position of a solder pad on a circuit board is most likely defined in terms of the center of the pad. To construct this pad as a PLINE arc, it is first necessary to compute a point offset from the center that describes the starting point of the polyline. The sequence of commands necessary to construct the doughnut as a PLINE arc is not easily remembered. In contrast, when constructing with the DONUT command, you start by specifying the inner and outer diameters of the circle and then specifying one or more locations in which to place the figure. If there are only a few locations, or the locations are not regularly placed, responding to the repeating "Center of doughnut" prompt may be quicker and easier than constructing an array.

TYPICAL OPERATION

In this section you use the DONUT command in constructing the following drawing of a truck. Starting at the Main Menu, begin a new drawing named DONUT.

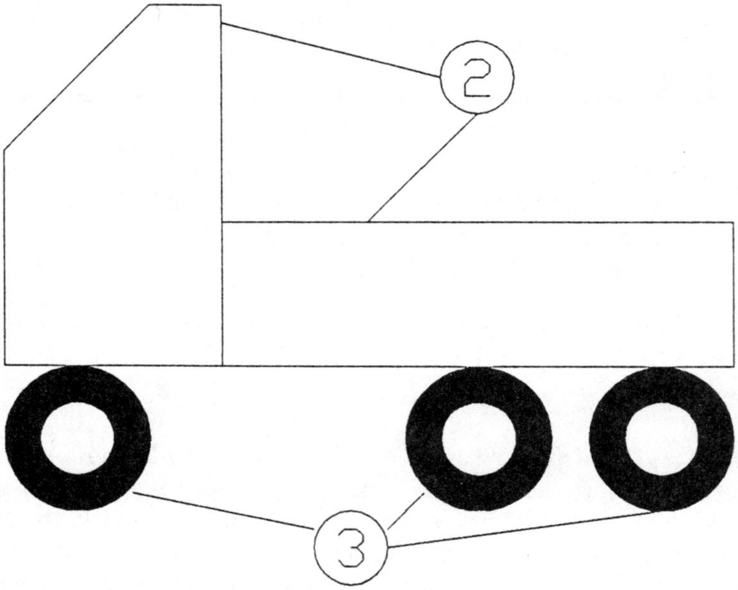

1. Set the SNAP to 1 and turn GRID on.

```
Command: SNAP <CR>
Snap spacing or ON/OFF/Aspect/Rotate/Style <1.0000>: ON <CR>
Command: GRID <CR>
Grid spacing(X) or ON/OFF/Snap/Aspect <0.0000>: ON <CR>
Command:
```

2. Draw the body of the truck. Either type the coordinates from the keyboard or pick them on the screen.

```
Command: LINE <CR>
From point: 4,3 <CR>
To point: 11,3 <CR>
```

```
To point: 11,5 <CR>
To point: 4,5 <CR>
To point: 4,8 <CR>
To point: 3,8 <CR>
To point: 1,6 <CR>
To point: 1,3 <CR>
To point: 4,3 <CR>
To point: 4,5 <CR>
To point:  <CR>
Command:
```

3. Use the DONUT command to construct and place the tires.

```
Command: DONUT <CR>
Inside diameter <0.5000>: 1 <CR>
Outside diameter<1.0000>: 1 <CR>
Center of doughnut: 2,2 <CR>
Center of doughnut: 7,2 <CR>
Center of doughnut: 10,2 <CR>
Center of doughnut: <CR>
Command:
```

Your completed drawing should resemble the following illustration.

4. Type **QUIT** and press **Return**; then type **Y** and press **Return** to display the Main Menu.
5. Turn to Module 64 to continue the learning sequence.

Module 24

DRAGMODE

```
Command: DRAGMODE
ON/OFF/Auto <Auto>:
```

DESCRIPTION

AutoCAD lets you drag many entities from one point to another. It also lets you expand and contract the size of entities during construction, such as circles and arcs. This provides excellent visualization and gives you the opportunity to complete construction when an entity is the proper size or in the desired location. However, when manipulating complex entities on slower hardware, the time required to display the drag display on the screen is annoying to some. Therefore, AutoCAD provides a system variable, DRAGMODE, to control dragging. You can modify this variable with either the DRAGMODE command or the SETVAR command from the AutoCAD drawing editor. DRAGMODE has three possible values:

ON	You may type **DRAG** in response to an AutoCAD prompt to allow you to drag your construction on the screen.
Auto	Dragging is enabled at every opportunity. You do not need to type **DRAG** to initiate dragging in response to an AutoCAD prompt.
OFF	Dragging is not allowed, not even if you type **DRAG** in response to a system prompt.

APPLICATIONS

On the slowest computer hardware, especially computer systems not equipped with a numeric co-processor, it is often easiest to work with DRAGMODE set to Off.

If you plan to drag objects infrequently, set DRAGMODE to On. This lets you activate the DRAGMODE feature when it is needed by typing DRAG and pressing Return in response to the appropriate drawing editor prompt.

If you wish to use drag most of the time, set DRAGMODE to Auto. When the manipulation of complex blocks or groups of entities makes dragging cumbersome, set DRAGMODE to Off until you resume work on simpler constructions.

TYPICAL OPERATION

In this session you draw a series of circles to explore the effect of different DRAGMODE settings on your editing display. From the AutoCAD Main Menu, select the new drawing DRAGMODE and start the Drawing Editor.

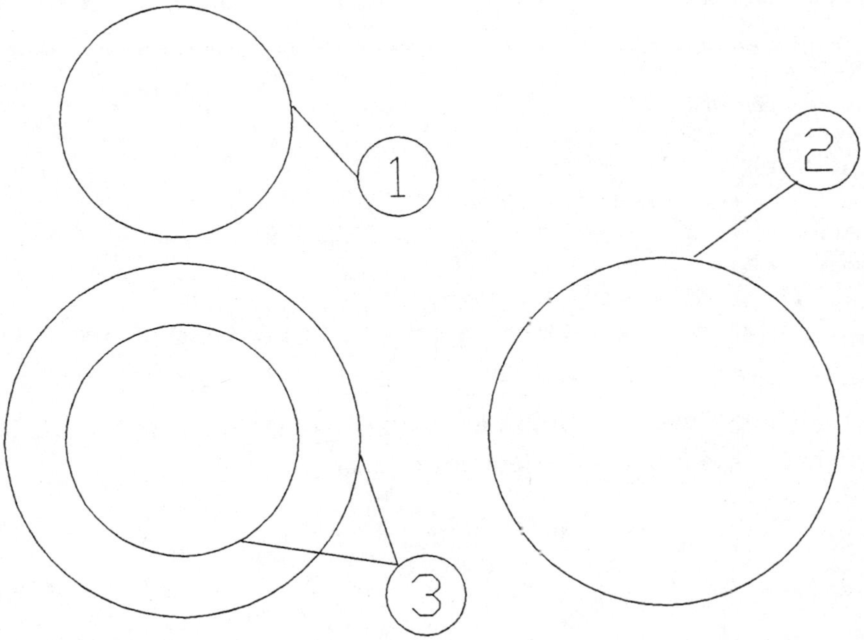

1. Draw a circle using the default DRAGMODE setting, Auto. Notice how the circle is displayed as you drag the radius with the screen cursor.

```
Command: CIRCLE <CR>
3P/2P/TTR/<Center point>: 3,7 <CR>
Diameter/<Radius>:  (Drag the radius with the screen cursor.) <CR>
```

2. Set DRAGMODE Off and construct a circle. Notice that although the radius displays on the screen, the circle is not displayed until you pick the second point.

```
Command: DRAGMODE <CR>
OFF/ON/Auto <Auto>: OFF <CR>
Command: CIRCLE <CR>
3P/2P/TTR/<Center point>: 9,3 <CR>
Diameter/<Radius>:  (Drag the radius with the screen cursor.)
```

3. Turn DRAGMODE On and draw two circles. Enable DRAG during the formation of the second circle. Notice that the outline of the circle changes as you move the screen cursor.

```
Command: DRAGMODE <CR>
OFF/ON/Auto <OFF>: ON <CR>
Command: CIRCLE <CR>
3P/2P/TTR/<Center point>: 3,3 <CR>
Diameter/<Radius>:  (Drag the radius with the screen cursor.) <CR>
Command: <CR>
3P/2P/TTR/<Center point>: 3,3 <CR>
Diameter/<Radius>:  DRAG (Drag the radius with the screen cursor.) <CR>
```

4. Type **QUIT** and press **Return**; then type **Y** and press **Return** to display the AutoCAD Main Menu.
5. Turn to Module 14 to continue the learning sequence.

Module 25

DTEXT

```
Command: DTEXT
Start point or Align/Center/Fit/Middle/Right/Style:
```

DESCRIPTION

The DTEXT command, introduced in AutoCAD 2.5, displays text on the screen as it is typed. In contrast, the TEXT command does not display the text on the graphic screen until you complete typing and press **Return**.

When you use DTEXT, the text is entered from the keyboard and menu picks are ignored. To terminate text entry using DTEXT, press **Return** at the "Text:" prompt. If the **Ctrl-C** key is pressed to terminate the DTEXT command, the text entered on the screen disappears.

You can move the screen cursor while DTEXT entry is in progress. If you move the cursor and pick a new position, text entry continues at the newly picked point.

DTEXT works best with left-justified text. You are encouraged to explore other types of justification before leaving this module. While you are experimenting with the DTEXT command, try the Backspace key to see its effect. The same "%%" control codes used in TEXT are used with DTEXT and produce the same results.

APPLICATIONS

The DTEXT command is useful for placing text in a drawing or illustration that requires text at some rotation angle other than zero. Before the availability of DTEXT, this process almost always required using the MOVE command or a combination of the BLOCK and INSERT commands to get the text moved and rotated into the desired position.

TYPICAL OPERATION

This activity introduces you to the benefits of the DTEXT command. You use the DTEXT command in two different ways. Begin a new drawing named DTEXT.

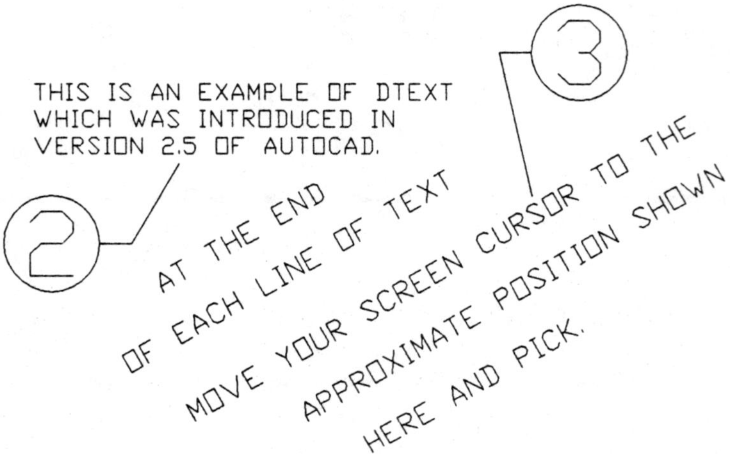

1. Set SNAP to .25, turn on the GRID, and ZOOM the screen.

```
Command: SNAP <CR>
Snap spacing or ON/OFF/Aspect/Rotate/Style <1.0000>: .25 <CR>

Command: GRID <CR>
Grid spacing(X) or ON/OFF/Snap/Aspect <0.0000>: ON <CR>

Command: ZOOM <CR>
All/Center/Dynamic/Extents/Left/Previous/Window/<Scale(X)>: A <CR>
Regenerating drawing.
```

2. Enter three lines of text using the DTEXT command.

```
Command: DTEXT <CR>
Start point or Align/Center/Fit/Middle/Right/Style: 1,6 <CR>
Height <0.2000>: .25 <CR>
Rotation angle <0>: <CR>
Text: THIS IS AN EXAMPLE OF DTEXT <CR>
Text: WHICH WAS INTRODUCED IN <CR>
Text: VERSION 2.5 OF AUTOCAD. <CR>
Text: <CR>
```

3. Enter text using the DTEXT command. Move the screen cursor to a different position after each line of text. Try to pick the same positions shown in the sample drawing.

```
Command: DTEXT <CR>
Start point or Align/Center/Fit/Middle/Right/Style: 3,3 <CR>
Height <0.2500>: .3 <CR>
Rotation angle <0>: 30 <CR>
Text: AT THE END (Pick a point.)
Text: OF EACH LINE OF TEXT (Pick a point.)
Text: MOVE YOUR SCREEN CURSOR TO THE (Pick a point.)
Text: APPROXIMATE POSITION SHOWN (Pick a point.)
Text: HERE AND PICK. <CR>
Text: <CR>
```

Your drawing should resemble the one shown at the beginning of this activity.

4. Type **Quit** and press **Return**; then type **Y** and press **Return** to display the Main Menu.
5. Turn to Module 61 to continue the learning sequence.

Module 26

ELEV

```
Command: ELEV
New current elevation <0.0000>:
New current thickness <0.0000>:
```

DESCRIPTION

The ELEV command provides for a Z dimension (or axis) in drawn objects. First you should set a value for the current elevation and extrusion thickness. The elevation is the original reference position. The thickness is the distance above or below the elevation. This gives the object height.If the thickness is input as a positive number, it is drawn above the elevation. If entered as a negative number, it is drawn below the elevation. You can also enter elevations as positive or negative numbers to achieve the same results.

The ELEV command is entered on the command prompt line by typing **ELEV** and pressing **Return**. The following prompts are displayed.

```
Command: ELEV <CR>
New current elevation <0.0000>:
New current thickness <0.0000>:
```

APPLICATIONS

The ELEV command is used for defining the third dimension in a drawing. AutoCAD does not have full three-dimension capabilities, but simulates the third dimension by assigning a fixed thickness to different drawing entities. In other words, a circle becomes a cylinder when a third dimension is added. The effect is like a geographic contour map. AutoCAD allows only vertical lines in the Z dimension. Through the use of many drawing layers which are sufficiently thin, excellent three-dimensional visualization can be realized, even for complex objects.

TYPICAL OPERATION

In this session you use the ELEV command in conjunction with a new drawing named ELEV.

1. Set the SNAP value to .25 and turn GRID on.

```
Command: SNAP <CR>
Snap spacing or ON/OFF/Aspect/Rotate/Style <1.0000>: .25 <CR>

Command: GRID <CR>
Grid spacing(X) or ON/OFF/Snap/Aspect <0.0000>: ON <CR>
```

2. Draw a rectangle.

```
Command: LINE <CR>
From point: .5,1.5 <CR>
To point: .5,6.5 <CR>
To point: 2,6.5 <CR>
To point: 2,1.5 <CR>
To point: C <CR>
```

3. Enter a line of text.

```
Command: TEXT <CR>
Start point or Align/Center/Fit/Middle/Right/Style: 1,2.5 <CR>
Height <0.1750>: .25 <CR>
Rotation angle <0>: 90 <CR>
Text: "BASE" Z PLANE <CR>
```

4. Set the elevation.

```
Command: ELEV <CR>
New current elevation <0.0000>: <CR>
New current thickness <0.0000>: -2.0 <CR>
```

5. Draw a rectangle.

```
Command: LINE <CR>
From point: 2.25,1.5 <CR>
To point: 2.25,6.5 <CR>
To point: 3.75,6.5 <CR>
To point: 3.75,1.5 <CR>
To point: C <CR>
```

6. Set the elevation and draw a third rectangle.

```
Command: ELEV <CR>
New current elevation <0.0000>: <CR>
New current thickness <-2.0000>: 2.0 <CR>
Command: LINE <CR>
From point: 4,1.5 <CR>
To point: 4,6.5 <CR>
To point: 5.5,6.5 <CR>
To point: 5.5,1.5 <CR>
To point: C <CR>
```

7. Set the elevation and draw a fourth rectangle.

```
Command: ELEV <CR>
New current elevation <0.0000>: 2 <CR>
New current thickness <2.0000>: 0 <CR>
Command: LINE <CR>
From point: 5.75,1.5 <CR>
To point: 5.75,6.5 <CR>
To point: 7.25,6.5 <CR>
To point: 7.25,1.5 <CR>
To point: C <CR>
```

8. Set the elevation and draw a fifth rectangle.

```
Command: ELEV <CR>
New current elevation <2.0000>: <CR>
New current thickness <0.0000>: 2 <CR>

Command: LINE <CR>
From point: 7.5,1.5 <CR>
To point: 7.5,6.5 <CR>
To point: 9,6.5 <CR>
To point: 9,1.5 <CR>
To point: C <CR>
```

9. Adjust the view point to see the thicknesses from an elevation.

```
Command: VPOINT <CR>
Enter view point <0.0000,0.0000,1.0000>: 1.5,-4.5,1.2566 <CR>
```

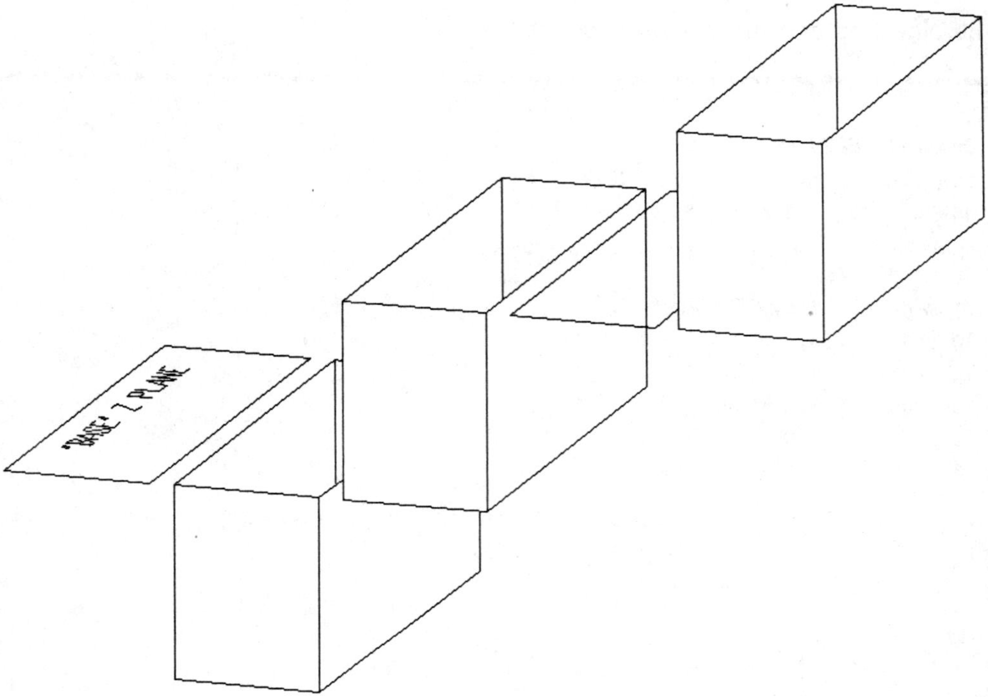

10. Use **QUIT** to redisplay the Main Menu.
11. Turn to Module 93 to continue the learning sequence.

Module 27

ELLIPSE

```
Command: ELLIPSE
<Axis endpoint 1>/Center: (point)
Axis endpoint 2: (point)
<Other axis distance>/Rotation:

Command: ELLIPSE
<Axis endpoint 1>/Center/Isocircle: I
Center of circle: (point)
<Circle radius>/Diameter: (radius distance or "D")
```

DESCRIPTION

The ELLIPSE command, introduced in AutoCAD 2.5, draws ellipses to meet a variety of drawing situations. You may specify the endpoints of the major axis of the ellipse, or you may specify the center point of the ellipse. Instead of specifying a second axis you can specify a rotation angle. When you specify a rotation angle, which must be between 0 and 89.4 degrees, the major axis of the ellipse is interpreted as the diameter line of a circle, and the ellipse produced is a representation of the circle rotated into the third dimension. When isometric snap is enabled, you can draw a circle in the selected isometric plane.

APPLICATIONS

Ellipses are often used to show a circle rotated into a third dimension. To accomplish this type of rotation, specify the diameter of the circle as the major axis. Then type **R** and specify a rotation angle.

One of the major uses of ellipses is the representation of circles in an isometric projection. When drawing an isometric circle, the circle is constructed in the active isometric plane. First use ISOPLANE to select the correct drawing plane; then use ELLIPSE to construct the isometric circle.

TYPICAL OPERATION

In this session you construct an isometric representation of a square block containing a circular hole in the right face as shown. Begin a new drawing named BOX.

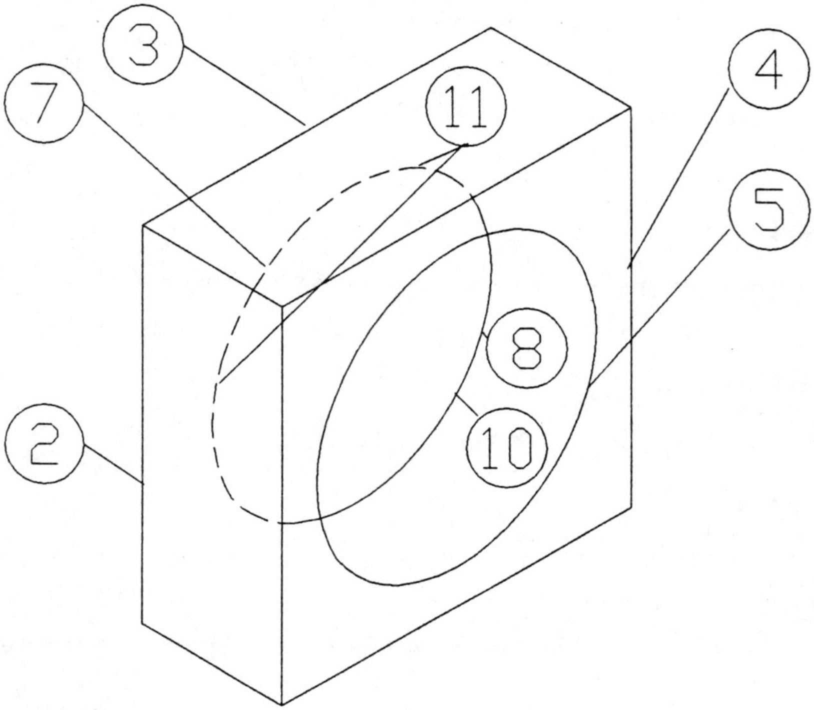

1. Set the SNAP for Isometric with a spacing of 0.5.

```
Command: SNAP <CR>
Snap spacing or ON/OFF/Rotate/Style <0.5000>: S <CR>
Standard/Isometric <I>: I <CR>
Vertical spacing <0.5000>: .5 <CR>
Command:
```

2. Draw the left face.

```
Command: ISOPLANE <CR>
Left/Top/Right/<Toggle>: L <CR>
Current Isometric plane is: Left
Command: LINE <CR>
From point: 3.4641,0 <CR>
```

```
To point: @5<90 <CR>
To point: @2<150 <CR>
To point: @5<270 <CR>
To point: c <CR>
Command:
```

3. Draw the top face.

```
Command: ISOPLANE <CR>
Left/Top/Right/<Toggle>: T <CR>
Current Isometric plane is: Top
Command: LINE <CR>
From point: 3.4641,5 <CR>
To point: @5<30 <CR>
To point: @2<150 <CR>
To point: @5<210 <CR>
To point: <CR>
Command:
```

4. Draw the right face.

```
Command: ISOPLANE <CR>
Left/Top/Right/<Toggle>: R <CR>
Current Isometric plane is: Right
Command: LINE <CR>
From point: 3.4641,0 <CR>
To point: @5<30 <CR>
To point: @5<90 <CR>
To point: <CR>
Command:
```

5. Draw the circle on the right face.

```
Command: ELLIPSE <CR>
<Axis endpoint 1>/Center/Isocircle: I <CR>
Center of circle: 5.6292,3.75 <CR>
<Circle radius>/Diameter: 2 <CR>
Command:
```

6. Create a layer for hidden lines. Name the layer HIDDEN and assign it the linetype HIDDEN.

```
Command: LAYER <CR>
?/Make/Set/New/ON/OFF/Color/Ltype/Freeze/Thaw: M <CR>
New current layer <0>: HIDDEN <CR>
?/Make/Set/New/ON/OFF/Color/Ltype/Freeze/Thaw: L <CR>
Linetype (or ?) <CONTINUOUS>: HIDDEN <CR>
Layer name(s) for linetype HIDDEN <HIDDEN>: <CR>
?/Make/Set/New/ON/OFF/Color/Ltype/Freeze/Thaw: <CR>
Command:
```

7. Draw the ellipse on the hidden face. (Note that you are still in the RIGHT Isoplane.)

```
Command: ELLIPSE <CR>
<Axis endpoint 1>/Center/Isocircle: I <CR>
Center of circle: 4.3301,4.5 <CR>
<Circle radius>/Diameter: 2 <CR>
Command:
```

8. Trim the hidden line ellipse to eliminate the hidden lines from the visible portion.

```
Command: TRIM <CR>
Select cutting edge(s)...  (Pick the continuous ellipse on the right face.)
Select objects: 1 selected, 1 found.
Select objects: <CR>
Select object to trim: (Pick the hidden ellipse inside the continuous ellipse.)
Select object to trim: <CR>
Command:
```

9. Freeze the hidden line layer.

```
Command: LAYER <CR>
?/Make/Set/New/ON/OFF/Color/Ltype/Freeze/Thaw: S <CR>
New current layer <HIDDEN>: 0 <CR>
?/Make/Set/New/ON/OFF/Color/Ltype/Freeze/Thaw: F <CR>
Layer name(s) to Freeze: HIDDEN <CR>
?/Make/Set/New/ON/OFF/Color/Ltype/Freeze/Thaw: <CR>
Command:
```

10. Draw a continuous ellipse on the hidden face.

```
Command: ELLIPSE <CR>
<Axis endpoint 1>/Center/Isocircle: I <CR>
Center of circle: 4.3301,4.5 <CR>
<Circle radius>/Diameter: 2 <CR>
Command:
```

11. Trim the part of the hidden face that is actually hidden.

```
Command: TRIM <CR>
Select cutting edge(s)... (Pick the ellipse on the right face.)
Select objects: 1 selected, 1 found.
Select objects: <CR>
Select object to trim: (Pick the top of the left most ellipse.)
Select object to trim: (Pick the left most ellipse.)
Select object to trim: <CR>
Command:
```

12. Thaw the hidden line layer.

```
Command: LAYER
?/Make/Set/New/ON/OFF/Color/Ltype/Freeze/Thaw: T
Layer name(s) to Thaw: HIDDEN
?/Make/Set/New/ON/OFF/Color/Ltype/Freeze/Thaw: <CR>
Regenerating drawing.
Command:
```

Your drawing should resemble the following illustration.

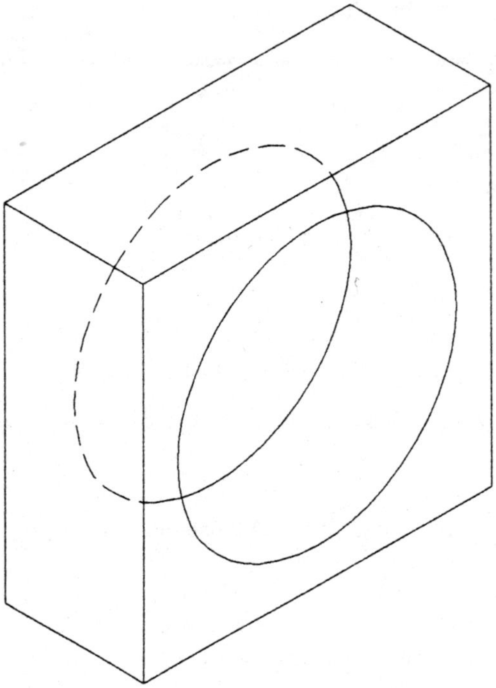

13. Type **QUIT** and press **Return**; then type **Y** and press **Return** to display the Main Menu.
14. Turn to Module 33 to continue the learning sequence.

Module 28

END AND ENDSV

```
Command: END
Command: ENDSV
```

DESCRIPTION

The END command exits the Drawing Editor and redisplays the Main Menu. The drawing is saved with the extension ".DWG". (The prior version of the drawing is renamed with the extension ".BAK".)

The ENDSV command performs all the functions of the END command. If you have not changed or deleted your drawing during the current editing session, it saves a vector file. The vector file lets AutoCAD reproduce the last view of the drawing rapidly when you re-enter the Drawing Editor. Vector files are saved with the extension ".$RF".

Support for the ENDSV command was dropped in AutoCAD version 2.5. In version 2.5 and later, the vector command is never saved, and ENDSV performs exactly the same function as END.

APPLICATIONS

If the drawing speed of the initial view of the drawing is important, use the ENDSV command to exit the Drawing Editor. If disk space is at a premium, use the END command, as vector files are often large. If you use the ENDSV command and later want to delete the vector file, you can use AutoCAD's file commands or the DOS ERASE command from the DOS prompt.

TYPICAL OPERATION

This operation uses the ENDSV command to create a vector file. Starting at AutoCAD's Main Menu, begin a new drawing named TEMP.

1. Type **ENDSV** and press **Return**.

```
Command:ENDSV
```

2. Type **0** to exit to DOS.
3. Type **DIR *.$RF** and notice that the file TEMP.$RF is displayed.
4. Turn to Module 45 to continue the learning sequence.

Module 29

ERASE

```
Command:ERASE
Select objects:
```

DESCRIPTION

The ERASE command is used to remove unwanted portions of a drawing. The ERASE command removes complete drawing entities. You can erase a line, but you cannot erase part of a line. To erase part of a line, use the BREAK command instead.

If you have defined a block, remember that a block is a single entity. If you pick a block, the entire block is erased, not just the line you picked.

Erase options are described in the following list.

Pick	You may pick the object on the screen.
W (Window)	You are prompted to supply a lower-left and an upper-right corner for a window. All objects in the window are erased.
L (Last)	The last object drawn is erased.

AutoCAD version 2.6 introduced the SELECT command for identifying a selection set. You may use SELECT to identify the selection set for erasure, or you may use any of the object selection techniques more fully described in the SELECT module.

APPLICATIONS

The Window option is used to remove several drawing elements that are close to each other.

The Last option erases the last object drawn. Repeated use of the ERASE Last command can erase an entire drawing, one element at a time. Each element is erased in the reverse order of its entry.

You can also use ERASE with the screen cursor. After typing **ERASE**, select an object with the screen cursor and press **Return**. The object is displayed in dashed lines. Pressing **Return** again finishes the ERASE operation.

TYPICAL OPERATION

In this session you erase two lines and a circle using each of the ERASE command options. Starting at the Main Menu, begin a new drawing named TEMP.

1. Type **LINE** and press **Return**. Enter the following points.

```
Command: LINE <CR>
From point: 5,5 <CR>
To point: 6,6 <CR>
To point: 5,7 <CR>
To point:<CR>
```

2. Type **CIRCLE** and press **Return**. Position the circle at 3,3 with a radius of 1.

```
Command: CIRCLE <CR>
3P/2P/<Center point>: 3,3 <CR>
Diameter/<Radius>: 1 <CR>
```

3. Type **ERASE** and press **Return**. Type **L** and press **Return** twice to erase the last item drawn. The circle is erased.

```
Command: ERASE <CR>
Select objects: L <CR>
1 found.
Select objects: <CR>
```

4. Press **Return** and select ERASE again. Then pick a point on the first line drawn and press **Return** to erase it.

```
Command: <CR>
ERASE
Select objects: (Pick the line)
1 selected, 1 found.
Select objects: <CR>
```

5. Press **Return**, type **W** and press **Return** again to choose the Window option.

```
Command:<CR>
ERASE
Select objects: W <CR>
```

6. Draw a window around the remaining line using your cursor keys or mouse to pick the lower left- and upper right-hand corners of the window.

```
First point: (Pick the corner)
Second point: (Pick the corner)
1 found.
Select objects: <CR>
```

7. Notice that pressing **Return** shows that the line is selected. Press **Return** again to erase it.
8. Type **QUIT** and press **Return**; then type **Y** and press **Return** to redisplay the Main Menu.
9. Turn to Module 56 to continue the learning sequence.

Module 30

EXPLODE

```
Command: EXPLODE
Select block reference, polyline, or dimension:
```

DESCRIPTION

The EXPLODE command was introduced in AutoCAD 2.5. This command changes a single entity block back into individual entities. After a block has been exploded, editing can be accomplished on individual parts. Occasionally it is necessary to use the EXPLODE command more than once, as it only removes one level of grouping at a time. EXPLODE does not work with blocks that have unequal X, Y, and Z scale factors, nor does it operate on blocks created with MINSERT. It is important for you to remember that attribute information associated with a block is lost when EXPLODE is used.

APPLICATIONS

The purpose of the EXPLODE command is to allow editing of blocks and polylines that could not previously be edited. In versions of AutoCAD prior to 2.5, the only way to edit a block was to use the INSERT command with an asterisk (*) prefixed to the block name. This inserted the block with all of its elements remaining as individual entities. If the asterisk was omitted before the block name, the block was inserted as one entire entity and could not be edited. If a block exists within a drawing that needs editing, the explode command is used first. After the use of the EXPLODE command, individual entities are easily edited.

TYPICAL OPERATION

In this exercise you construct a block from a polygon and circle. Next, you see how editing commands, such as BREAK, are used with EXPLODE to edit the block. Begin a new drawing named EXPLODE.

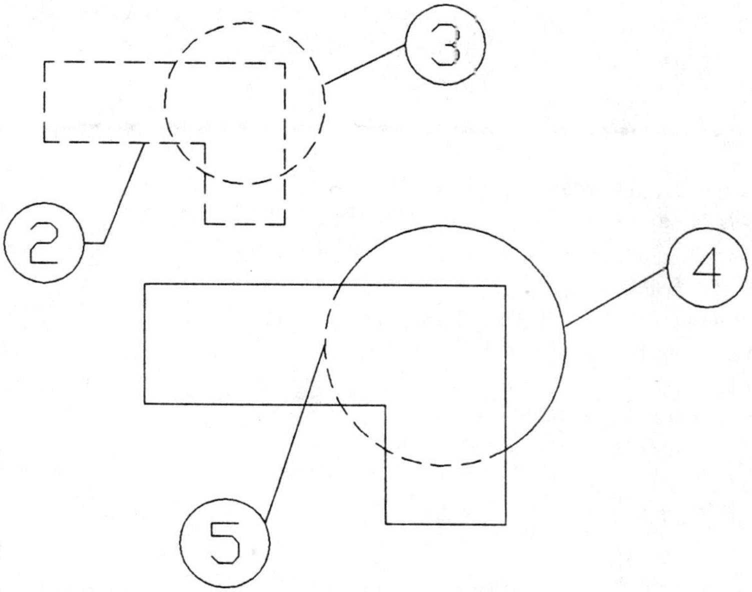

1. Set SNAP to .25 and turn on the GRID. ZOOM the screen to the drawing limits.

```
Command:  SNAP <CR>
Snap spacing or ON/OFF/Aspect/Rotate/Style <1.0000>: .25 <CR>
Command: GRID <CR>
Grid spacing(X) or ON/OFF/Snap/Aspect <0.0000>: ON <CR>
Command: ZOOM <CR>
All/Center/Dynamic/Extents/Left/Previous/Window/<Scale(X)>: A <CR>
Regenerating drawing.
```

2. Draw a polygon with the LINE command.

```
Command: LINE <CR>
From point: 1,8 <CR>
To point: 4,8 <CR>
To point: 4,6 <CR>
To point: 3,6 <CR>
To point: 3,7 <CR>
To point: 1,7 <CR>
To point: C <CR>
```

3. Draw a circle and save the object as a block named Gnarf. When the object disappears, this indicates it has been saved as a block and can be inserted into the drawing using the INSERT command.

```
Command: CIRCLE <CR>
3P/2P/TTR/<Center point>: 3.5,7.5 <CR>
Diameter/<Radius>:1 <CR>
Command: BLOCK <CR>
Block name (or ?): GNARF <CR>
Insertion base point: 3.5,7.5 <CR>
Select objects: W <CR>
First corner: 0,5 <CR>
Other corner: 5,9 <CR>
7 found.
Select objects: <CR>
```

4. Insert Gnarf using the INSERT command and then try to edit it using the BREAK command. Notice that the BREAK command will not work on a regular, single-entity block.

```
Command: INSERT <CR>
Block name (or ?): GNARF <CR>
 Insertion point: 6,4.5 <CR>
 X scale factor <1> / Corner / XYZ: 1.5 <CR>
 Y scale factor (default=X): <CR>
 Rotation angle <0>: <CR>

Command: BREAK <CR>
Select object: 7.5,4.5 <CR>
Can't break a block
*Invalid*
```

5. Use the EXPLODE command to break the block into its individual entities and then use the BREAK command to alter the object. Redraw the screen to clean up the stray blips.

```
Command: EXPLODE <CR>
Select block reference, polyline, or dimension: 7.5,4.5 <CR>
```

```
Command: BREAK <CR>
Select object: 6,6 <CR>
Enter second point (or F for first point): F <CR>
Enter first point: 4.75,5.25 <CR>
Enter second point: 6.75,3.25 <CR>
Command: REDRAW <CR>
```

6. Type **QUIT** and press **Return**; then type **Y** and press **Return** to display the Main Menu.

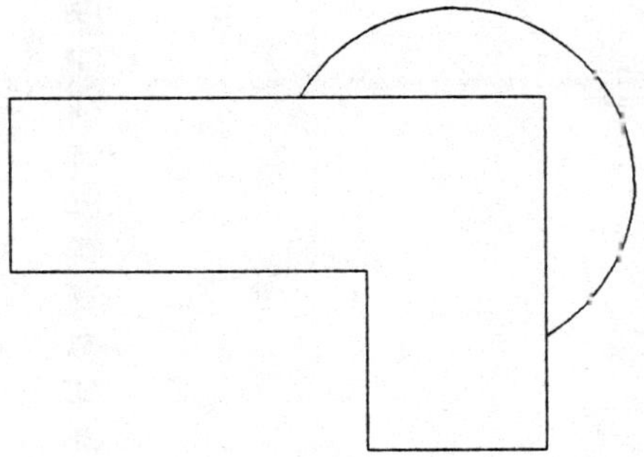

7. Turn to Module 11 to continue the learning sequence.

Module 31

EXTEND

```
Command: EXTEND
Select boundary edge(s)...
Select objects:
Select object to extend:
```

DESCRIPTION

The EXTEND command was introduced in AutoCAD 2.5. You can use the EXTEND command to extend a line, arc, or polyline until it meets another drawing entity to form a boundary. Lines, arcs, polylines, and circles serve as boundary edges. When a polyline is used as an edge, the boundary is defined as the centerline of the polyline. When you type EXTEND and press Return, the first prompt, "Select boundary edge(s). . . Select objects:" is displayed.

You may use any AutoCAD picking method to select one or more objects to serve as boundaries. When you complete selecting boundary objects, press Return. The second prompt, "Select object to extend:," lets you select the objects that should be extended to meet the boundaries. You may use any AutoCAD picking method to select objects for extension. When picking objects for extension, pick near an end that you want to extend. AutoCAD then extends the object until it meets the first object defined as a boundary. If the extended object does not meet a boundary, the drawing remains unchanged. When you have completed picking objects for extension, press Return to display the drawing editor command prompt.

APPLICATIONS

The EXTEND command is excellent for increasing the length of an existing line, arc, or polyline so that it meets another drawing entity in a precise manner.

When constructing a drawing, it is usually best to use OSNAP modes to ensure exact intersections. However, when making changes to existing drawings, EXTEND is invaluable in producing exact intersections.

Some users find it convenient to draw the entities short of an intersection point. They use the EXTEND command to "close the gap," thereby creating a precise intersection.

TYPICAL OPERATION

In this session you use EXTEND to ensure perfect intersections between lines, an arc, and a circle.

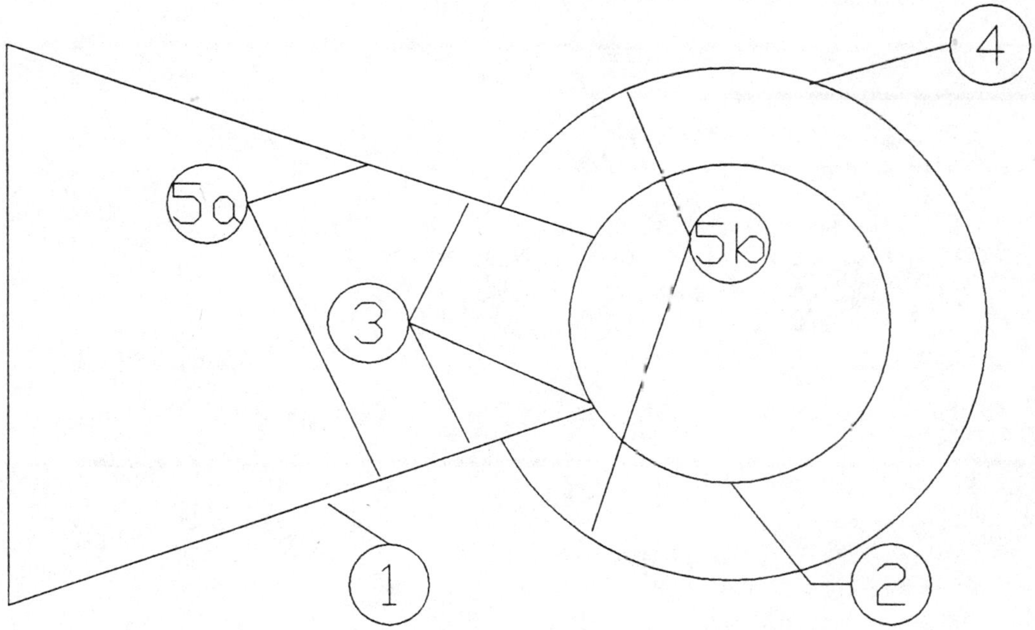

The same construction could be performed with OSNAP at the initial drawing phase, but the use of EXTEND in this activity simulates making modifications to an existing drawing. From the AutoCAD Main Menu select EXTEND as the current drawing and start the drawing editor.

1. Draw a series of three lines.

```
Command: LINE <CR>
From point: 7,3 <CR>
To point: 1,1 <CR>
To point: 1,8 <CR>
To point: 7,6 <CR>
To point: <CR>
Command:
```

2. Draw a circle. Note that the circle does not intersect the two lines as drawn.

```
Command: CIRCLE <CR>
3P/2P/TTR/<Center point>: 10,4.5 <CR>
Diameter/<Radius>:  2 <CR>
Command:
```

3. Extend the lines to intersect the circle.

```
Command: EXTEND <CR>
Select boundary edge(s) ...
Select objects: (Pick the circle)
1 selected, 1 found.
Select objects: <CR>
Select object to extend: (Pick a line)
Select object to extend: (Pick a line)
Select object to extend: <CR>
Command:
```

4. Construct the outer arc. Note that it does not meet the lines as constructed.

```
Command: ARC <CR>
Center/<Start point>: C <CR>
Center: 10,4.5 <CR>
Start point: 8,2 <CR>
Angle/Length of chord/<End point>:  8,8 <CR>
```

5. Extend the arc to meet the lines.

```
Command: EXTEND <CR>
Select boundary edge(s) ...
Select objects: (Pick one of the lines.)
1 selected, 1 found.
Select objects: (Pick one of the lines.)
1 selected, 1 found.
Select objects: <CR>
Select object to extend: (Pick the arc near one end.)
Select object to extend: (Pick the arc near the other end.)
Select object to extend: <CR>
```

Your completed drawing resembles the following illustration.

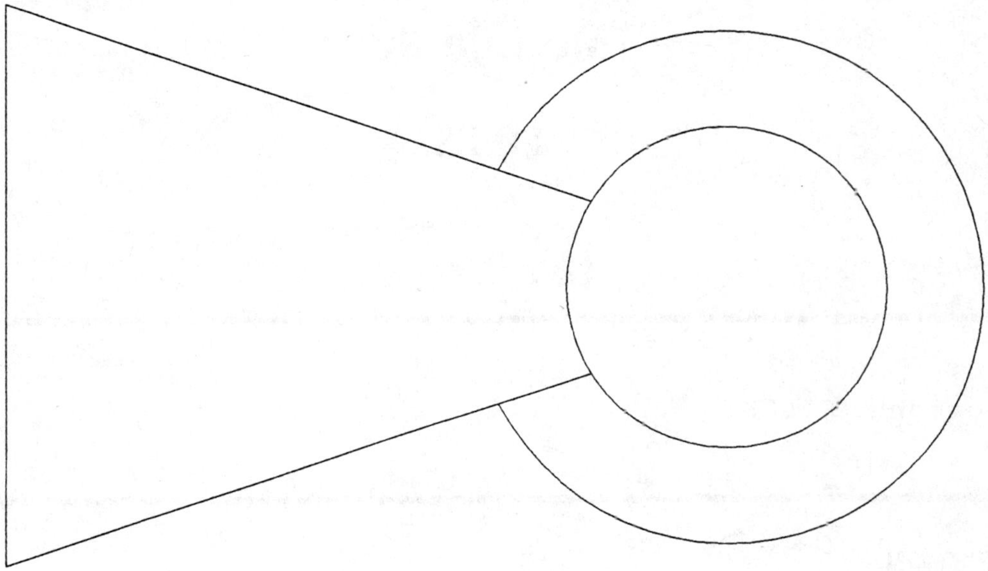

6. Type **QUIT** and press **Return**; then type **Y** and press **Return** to display the Main Menu.
7. Turn to Module 83 to continue the learning sequence.

Module 32

FILES

```
Command: FILES
```

DESCRIPTION

The FILES command displays the Files Utility Menu from the Drawing Editor, giving access to the AutoCAD file management features. Typing **FILES** and pressing **Return** presents the following choices.

```
              A U T O C A D
      Copyright (C) 1982,83,84,85,86,87 Autodesk, Inc.
      Release X.XXz (MM/DD/YY) IBM PC
      Advanced Drafting Extensions 3
      Serial Number: 99-999999

      File Utility Menu

        0.  Exit File Utility Menu
        1.  List Drawing files
        2.  List user specified files
        3.  Delete files
        4.  Rename files
        5.  Copy file

        Enter selection (0 to 5) <0>:
```

You can now type the number of your choice of activity and press **Return**.

APPLICATIONS

The AutoCAD FILES command lets you perform several file maintenance functions directly from the AutoCAD Drawing Editor. This eliminates the need to return to AutoCAD's Main Menu or to DOS (either by exiting AutoCAD, or through the SHELL command) to perform file maintenance.

TYPICAL OPERATION

In this session you display the drawing files on the current disk directory.

1. Begin a new drawing named TEMP.
2. Type **FILES** and press **Return**. Notice the following display.

```
          A U T O C A D
Copyright (C) 1982,83,84,85,86,87 Autodesk, Inc.
Release X.XXz (MM/DD/YY) IBM PC
Advanced Drafting Extensions 3
Serial Number: 99-999999


File Utility Menu

  0.  Exit File Utility Menu
  1.  List Drawing files
  2.  List user specified files
  3.  Delete files
  4.  Rename files
  5.  Copy file

  Enter selection (0 to 5) <0>:
```

3. Type **1** and press **Return** twice to display the drawing files on the current disk drive directory.

```
ELLIPSE.DWG    RECTANG.DWG    ACAD.DWG       CHROMA.DWG     COLORS.DWG
COLUMBIA.DWG   CONDO.DWG      COUNTER.DWG    CUBE.DWG       CURVES.DWG
FILE.DWG       GEO.DWG        HIGHWAY.DWG    ISOMECH.DWG    MPARTS.DWG
NOZZLE.DWG     OFFICE.DWG     PUMP.DWG       SOLAR.DWG      STAIR.DWG
SETUP-1.DWG    COPY.DWG       LAYERS.DWG     NEWHAT.DWG     HATCH.DWG
HIDE.DWG       HATTST.DWG     LINE.DWG       OOPS.DWG       GRID1.DWG
BLIPMODE.DWG   HIDE1.DWG      CHAMFER.DWG    MOVE.DWG       FILLET.DWG
TEXT.DWG       ZOOM.DWG       GRID25.DWG     CIRCLE.DWG     ZOOM1.DWG
40 files
Press RETURN to continue: <CR>
```

4. Press **Return**, type the number **0**, and press **Return** again to leave the file menu and return to the Drawing Editor.

```
            A U T O C A D
    Copyright (C) 1982,83,84,85,86,87 Autodesk, Inc.
    Release X.XXz (MM/DD/YY) IBM PC
    Advanced Drafting Extensions 3
    Serial Number: 99-999999


    File Utility Menu

      0.  Exit File Utility Menu
      1.  List Drawing files
      2.  List user specified files
      3.  Delete files
      4.  Rename files
      5.  Copy file

      Enter selection (0 to 5) <0>: 0 <CR>
```

The Drawing Editor is redisplayed.

5. Type **QUIT** and press **Return**; then type **Y** and press **Return** to redisplay the Main Menu.
6. Turn to Module 79 to continue the learning sequence.

Module 33

FILL

```
Command: FILL
ON/OFF <current>:

Remarks: Press Return to retain the current setting. Type
         ON or OFF and press Return to change the setting.
```

DESCRIPTION

Wide polylines, traces, and solids take a long time to fill on some displays and plotters. Turning FILL off allows you to speed display and plotting activities. The new FILL command setting does not take effect immediately. The new setting takes effect the next time you issue the REGEN command, or another command (such as ZOOM, PAN, or VIEW) that automatically performs a drawing regeneration. When the drawing is complete, set FILL on and perform a REGEN prior to plotting the final version of the drawing.

APPLICATIONS

The primary application of the FILL command is to increase the generation speed of the display and the plotting speed of the plotter. Typically, you draw a new portion of the drawing with FILL on for maximum visual feedback. Turning FILL off speeds redrawing operations when working on other elements in the drawing. FILL off also speeds the output of pen-type plotters, although it has little effect on printer plots.

TYPICAL OPERATION

In this session you draw the following figure using a wide polyline. Then compare the time it takes to refresh the screen with FILL on and FILL off. Begin a new drawing named FILL.

1. Draw the polyline as shown with a width of .75.

```
Command: PLINE <CR>
From point: 1,1 <CR>
Current line-width is 0.0000
Arc/Close/Halfwidth/Length/Undo/Width/<Endpoint of line>: W <CR>
Starting width <0.7500>: .75 <CR>
Ending width <0.7500>: <CR>
Arc/Close/Halfwidth/Length/Undo/Width/<Endpoint of line>: 1,8 <CR>
Arc/Close/Halfwidth/Length/Undo/Width/<Endpoint of line>: 4,8 <CR>
Arc/Close/Halfwidth/Length/Undo/Width/<Endpoint of line>: 4,3 <CR>
Arc/Close/Halfwidth/Length/Undo/Width/<Endpoint of line>: 8,3 <CR>
Arc/Close/Halfwidth/Length/Undo/Width/<Endpoint of line>: 8,8 <CR>
Arc/Close/Halfwidth/Length/Undo/Width/<Endpoint of line>: 11,8 <CR>
Arc/Close/Halfwidth/Length/Undo/Width/<Endpoint of line>: 11,1 <CR>
Arc/Close/Halfwidth/Length/Undo/Width/<Endpoint of line>: C <CR>
Command:
```

When you close, the polyline is redrawn on the screen.

2. Perform a REDRAW operation and observe the time required to display the drawing on the screen.

```
Command: REDRAW <CR>
Command:
```

3. Set FILL off.

```
Command: FILL <CR>
ON/OFF <On>: OFF <CR>
Command:
```

Notice that the drawing is unchanged on your screen. You must either explicitly perform a REGEN, or perform another command that in turn performs a REGEN for the change to appear in the drawing.

4. Issue a REGEN command, noticing the reduced time required to redraw the screen.

```
Command: REGEN <CR>
Command:
```

Notice that the polylines are represented by outlines.

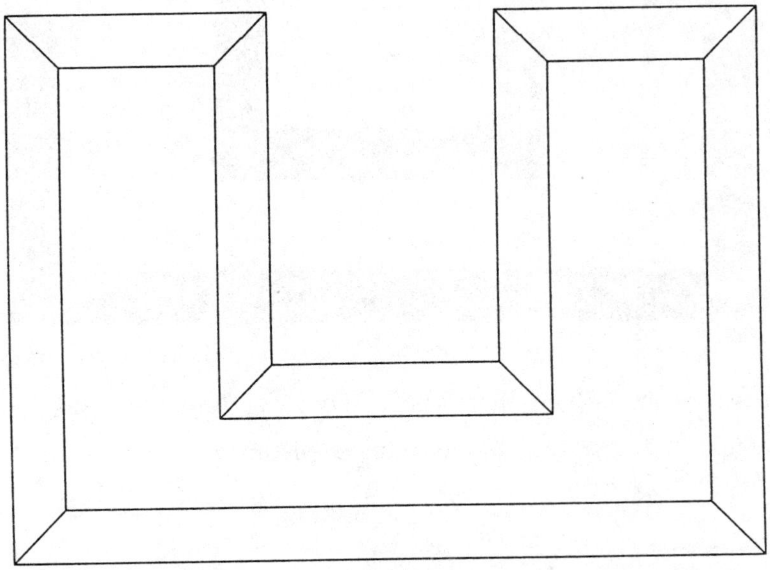

5. Set FILL on.

```
Command: FILL <CR>
ON/OFF <Off>: ON <CR>
Command:
```

Notice that there is no change in the screen.

6. Regenerate the drawing.

```
Command: REGEN <CR>
Command:
```

The drawing returns as before.

7. Type **QUIT** and press **Return**; then type **Y** and press **Return** to redisplay the Main Menu.
8. Turn to Module 81 to continue the learning sequence.

Module 34

FILLET

```
Command: FILLET
Polyline/Radius/<Select two objects>:
```

DESCRIPTION

Polyline — To perform a fillet of a polyline, type **P** and press **Return**. You are then prompted to select a polyline. All corners of the polyline are filleted in a single operation.

Radius — Type **R** and press **Return** to specify the radius for the fillet. Specify a radius of **0** if you want to extend two non-intersecting lines until they join.

Select two objects — Pick two lines, arcs, or circles with the creen cursor, or by typing the coordinates of a point on each line. (AutoCAD versions prior to version 2.5 can only FILLET lines.)

The FILLET command is used to round corners on a drawing. It is selected by typing **FILLET** and pressing **Return**.

APPLICATIONS

When you need to join two lines with a "fillet" or a "round", you should choose the FILLET command. Fillets are commonly used on mechanical and electrical drawings.

The FILLET command smoothly blends an arc between two lines, arcs, or circles. The lengths of the two objects are adjusted automatically according to the radius of the specified arc.

TYPICAL OPERATION

You can fillet lines, circles, arcs, and polylines. In this session you draw two lines and join them with a fillet. Then you place a fillet on a polyline. The complete drawing follows.

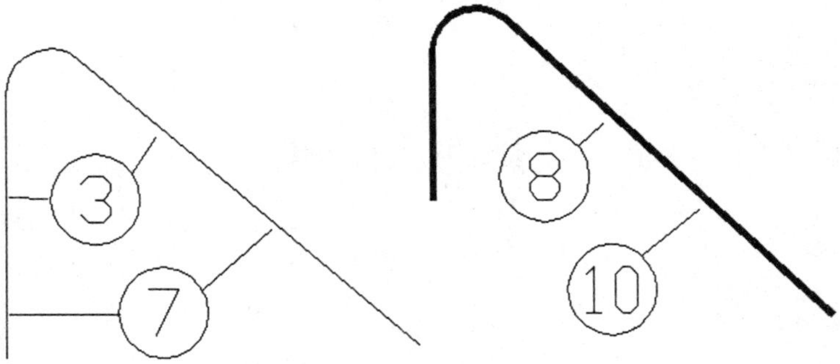

1. Begin a new drawing named FILLET. Turn SNAP on.

```
Command: SNAP <CR>
Snap spacing or ON/OFF/Aspect/Rotate/Style <1.0000>: .25 <CR>
```

2. Turn GRID on.

```
Command: GRID <CR>
Grid spacing(X) or ON/OFF/Snap/Aspect <0.0000>: ON <CR>
```

3. Draw two lines.

```
Command: LINE <CR>
From point: .5,.5 {PICK}
To point: @4<90 {PICK}
To point: @6<320 {PICK}
To point: <CR>
```

4. Specify the radius for FILLET.

```
Command: FILLET <CR>
Polyline/Radius/<Select two objects: R <CR>
Enter fillet radius <0.0 00>: .5 <CR>
```

5. Perform the FILLET.

```
Command: <CR>
FILLET Polyline/Radius/<Select two objects:
```

6. From the Root Menu, pick MODES, pick OSNAP, and pick Nearest. Press **Return**, type **FILLET**, and press **Return** again.
7. Pick one of the lines by placing the screen cross hairs on the line and pressing the pick button on the digitizer. Pick the other line in a similar manner. The arc is drawn automatically.
8. Draw the polyline.

NOTE

Use the Function key to turn COORDS on.

```
Command: PLINE <CR>
From point:  <Coords on> 5.75,2.75 <CR>
Current line-width is 0.0000
Arc/Close/Halfwidth/Length/Undo/Width/<Endpoint of line>: W <CR>
Starting width <0.0000>: .062 <CR>
Ending width <0.0620>: <CR>
Arc/Close/Halfwidth/Length/Undo/Width/<Endpoint of line>: @2.75<90
Arc/Close/Halfwidth/Length/Undo/Width/<Endpoint of line>: @6.0208<318
Arc/Close/Halfwidth/Length/Undo/Width/<Endpoint of line>: <CR>
```

9. Perform the FILLET.

```
Command: FILLET <CR>
Polyline/Radius/<Select two objects: P <CR>
Select polyline:
```

10. Pick the polyline.

```
1 line was filleted
```

After you pick the polyline the arc is drawn automatically.

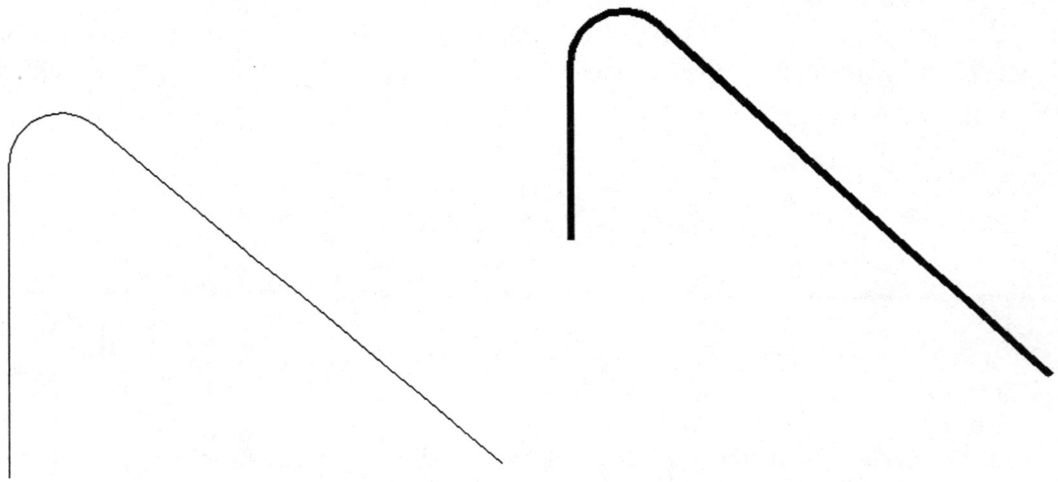

11. Type **QUIT** and press **Return**; then type **Y** and press **Return** to redisplay the Main Menu.
12. Turn to Module 38 to continue the learning sequence.

Module 35

GRAPHSCREEN

```
Command: GRAPHSCREEN
```

DESCRIPTION

The GRAPHSCREEN command shifts you between text screens and the Drawing Editor screen. Typically, you toggle between the text display and the graphics display by pressing a function key. A list of common microcomputers and the corresponding GRAPHSCREEN keys are contained in the following list.

Apricot	F1
Data General	F1
Dec Rainbow	PF1
Fujitsu Multi 16	CLS
Hewlett Packard	F1
IBM	F1
NCR	F1
DECMATE V	F1
NEC APC	FUNCTION 17
NEC APCIII	PF1
Tandy 2000	F1
Texas Instruments PC	F1
Wang PC	PF7
Zenith Z-100	F10

When writing menus, you are unable to use function key toggles. Therefore, the GRAPHSCREEN command switches you from the text screen to the graphics screen. Of course, the GRAPHSCREEN command can also be typed from AutoCAD's command line.

Starting with AutoCAD version 2.5, GRAPHSCREEN can be used during another command. At any text prompt, type **GRAPHSCREEN** and press **Return** to switch to the graphics screen.

APPLICATIONS

Occasionally, a command displays a list of text information. To redisplay the drawing, press the GRAPHSCREEN function key.

TYPICAL OPERATION

Because use of the GRAPHSCREEN command consists of a single keystroke, a practice session is not required.

Turn to Module 44 to continue the learning sequence.

Module 36

GRID

```
Command: GRID
Grid spacing(X) or ON/OFF/Snap/Aspect <0.0000>:
```

DESCRIPTION

The GRID command is most often used when you begin a new drawing. As implied by its name, it displays a coordinate system, or grid, to help you while producing a drawing. Grid options are described in the following list.

ON	Activates the grid.
OFF	Deactivates the grid.
Value(X)	Typing a value of 0 allows the grid spacing to automatically follow the SNAP spacing. The SNAP is a function of AutoCAD that is toggled on and off to allow the screen cursor to *snap* (or jump) to established grid coordinates. For example, a SNAP setting of .25 causes the screen cursor to jump by .25-inch increments. Typing a non-zero number specifies the coordinate spacing for the grid. It is possible, although not especially useful, to specify grid and snap coordinates which are completely unrelated using this method. A more common application is to specify the grid spacing as a multiple of the snap resolution. This is accomplished by typing a number followed by X.
Aspect	Aspect or A allows you to specify different horizontal and vertical spacings for the grid. The Aspect option is not available if the SNAP style has been set to isometric.
Snap	Typing **S** for Snap is the same as specifying a grid spacing of 0, it locks the grid to the snap resolution. In this way, changes to the SNAP specification are automatically reflected in the grid.

APPLICATIONS

The GRID command displays a visual grid, or matrix of dots, on the screen. It has no effect on the drawing and does not force alignment of any type. It is purely a visual reference. Usually, you want the visible grid to follow the snap resolution. However, if the snap resolution is small, it is often more useful to have the visible grid appear at some multiple of the snap resolution.

TYPICAL OPERATION

Typically, you draw with the GRID set to 0. This forces the displayed grid to follow whatever parameters you set for SNAP. Begin a new drawing named TEMP.

1. Set SNAP to .25.

```
Command: SNAP <CR>
Snap spacing or ON/OFF/Aspect/Rotate/Style <1.0000>:  .25 <CR>
```

2. Use the GRID command to let the grid follow the snap.

```
Command: GRID <CR>
Grid spacing(X) or ON/OFF/Snap/Aspect <0.0000>: 0 <CR>
Command:
```

The grid is now set to follow the specification for SNAP. Any changes in the SNAP specifications also change the grid.

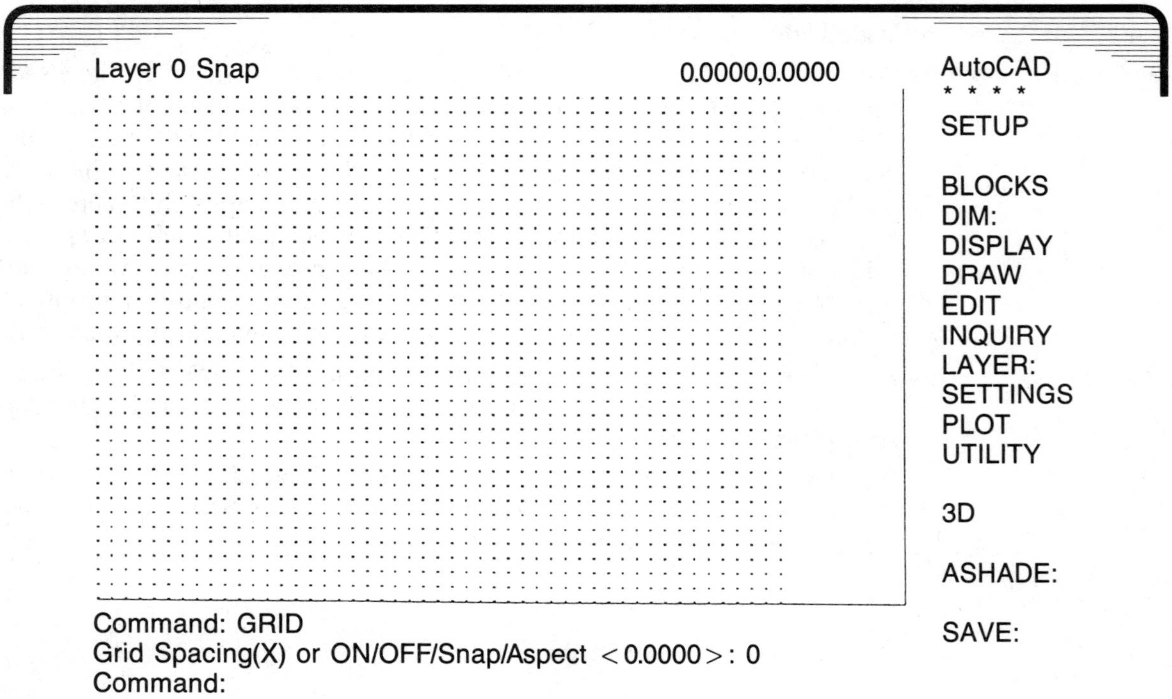

There are times when you do not want the GRID to follow the SNAP. In a drawing with the SNAP set to 0.25, the grid may be too dense. You may want to set the visible grid at 1, and then place points at each 0.25 increment visually. Here the SNAP feature is used to align the points correctly.

3. Set the grid to 1. Leave the snap at .25.

```
Command: GRID <CR>
Grid spacing(X) or ON/OFF/Snap/Aspect <0.0000>: 1 <CR>
Command:
```

The grid changes to a larger spacing. The snap remains unchanged.

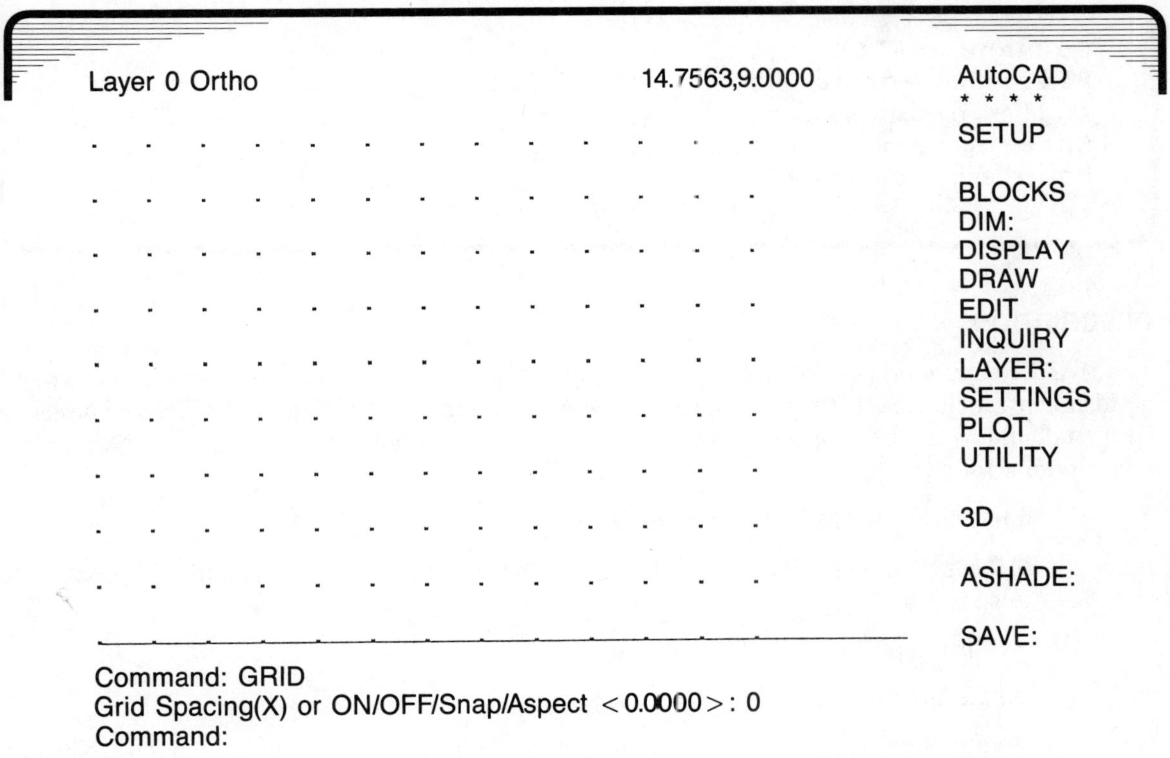

4. Type **QUIT** and press **Return**; then type **Y** and press **Return** to redisplay the Main Menu.
5. Turn to Module 80 to continue the learning sequence.

Module 37

HATCH

```
Command: HATCH
Pattern (? or name/U,style) <default>:
Angle for crosshatch lines <0>:
Spacing between lines <1.0000>:
Double hatch area? <N>
```

DESCRIPTION

The HATCH command is used to fill selected objects with patterns that represent some type of material, or that let you distinguish one object or section from another. Typing **HATCH** and pressing **Return** display a series of option prompts. A list of HATCH command options and corresponding descriptions follows.

? Lists the AutoCAD standard patterns.

name Allows you to specify a pre-defined pattern. You then have two additional prompts to respond to:

Scale for pattern <default>:

Angle for pattern <default>:

U Requires you to specify a simple line pattern in terms of angle of lines, spacing between lines, and whether or not to double hatch the area. You are prompted for:

Angle for crosshatch lines <default>:
Spacing between lines <default>:
Double hatch area? <default>

When you select the HATCH command from the drop-down menu (Release 9 and later) the available patterns are displayed on the screen. Pick the desired pattern with the screen cursor.

The style specification is one of three letters:

N Normal hatching. This is the default value.

O Outermost area. Fills only the outermost area.

I Ignore structure. Does not pay any attention to closed figures within the hatched area.

When sectional views of drawings are produced, the portions of the object which come in contact with the "cutting plane" are traditionally filled with "crosshatching." In AutoCAD, this is referred to as *hatching*. Hatching consists of parallel lines spaced at convenient intervals or of any number of special patterns of lines that represent some particular material.

When AutoCAD hatches an area, the involved lines or patterns are stored as a block. This block does not appear on the "INSERT ?" list as normal blocks do.

Consideration of the designation of layer properties for doing hatching should always include the use of *continuous* line type.

For hatching to honor boundaries properly, it is important to recognize that specific entities must exist. For example, separate entities such as lines, arcs, circles, traces, and polylines must be used for the correct boundaries to be recognized. Specific examples are included in the typical operation of this module to illustrate this point. Entities should have no overhanging portions and should intersect at their endpoints.

In the following examples, the three hatching styles are illustrated. These styles are called Normal, Outermost, and Ignore.

The Normal style begins hatching at the outermost boundary. Each time it encounters a new boundary, it toggles the hatching process off and on.

The Outermost style begins hatching at the outermost boundary and turns off the hatching process at the first internal boundary encountered.

The Ignore style simply hatches everything inside the first boundary.

If you want to edit individual hatch lines, you can suppress the inclusion of normal hatch lines into a block by typing an asterisk (*) before defining the hatching pattern. This is similar to the block insert operation.

APPLICATIONS

The HATCH command is often used in mechanical drawing to depict sectional views. When mechanical drawings are sectioned, the portion of the object sliced by the cutting plane is usually filled with crosshatching. The crosshatching also helps to differentiate one part from another in an assembly that has been sectioned. The HATCH command draws the crosshatching.

In architectural drawings, crosshatching is used to specify the type of material used by selecting the appropriate crosshatch pattern. This allows you to distinguish one section of material from another. The HATCH command lets you choose from a large number of stored hatching patterns. In addition, AutoCAD lets you design your own crosshatching patterns.

TYPICAL OPERATION

In this session you use a variety of hatching methods. Begin a new drawing named HATCH.

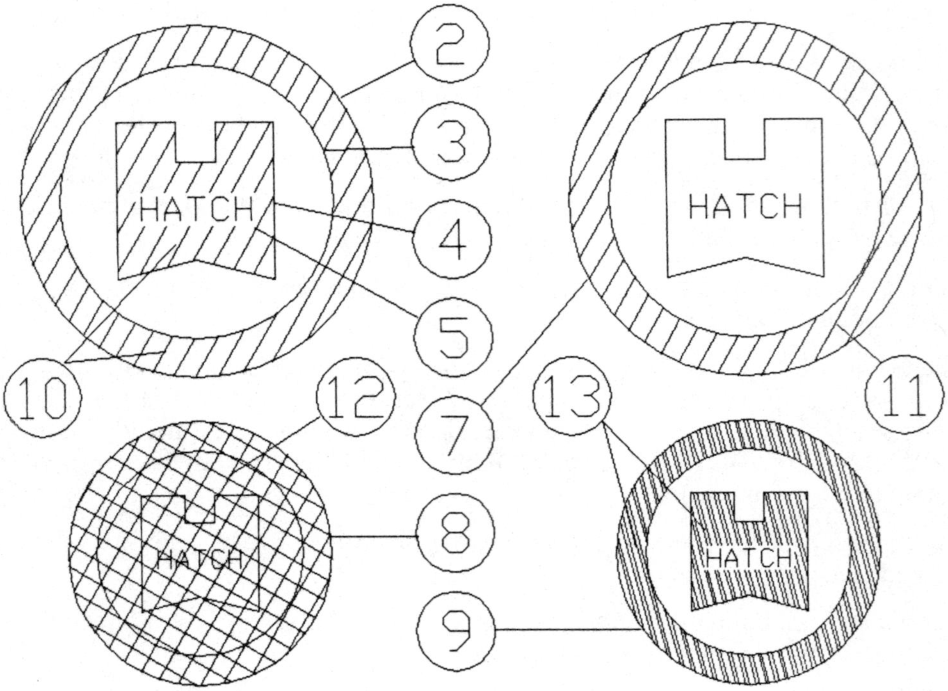

1. Set the SNAP to .25 and let the GRID follow the SNAP.

```
Command: SNAP <CR>
Snap spacing or ON/OFF/Aspect/Rotate/Style <1.0000>: .25 <CR>

Command: GRID <CR>
Grid spacing(X) or ON/OFF/Snap/Aspect <0.0000>: ON <CR>
```

2. Draw the outer circle of the figure.

```
Command: CIRCLE <CR>
3P/2P/<Center point>: 2.5,6.5 <CR>
Diameter/<Radius>: 2.25 <CR>
```

3. Draw the inner circle of the figure.

```
Command: CIRCLE <CR>
3P/2P/<Center point>: 2.5,6.5 <CR>
Diameter/<Radius>: 1.75 <CR>
```

4. Draw the closed figure in the center of the design.

```
Command: LINE <CR>
From point: 1.5,5.5 <CR>
To point: 1.5,7.5 <CR>
To point: 2.25,7.5 <CR>
To point: 2.25,7 <CR>
To point: 2.75,7 <CR>
To point: 2.75,7.5 <CR>
To point: 3.5,7.5 <CR>
To point: 3.5,5.5 <CR>
To point: 2.5,5.75 <CR>
To point: C <CR>
```

5. Center the word HATCH in the figure.

```
Command: TEXT <CR>
Start point or Align/Center/Fit/Middle/Right/Style: C <CR>
Center point: 2.5,6.25 <CR>
Height <0.200>: .3 <CR>
Rotation angle <0>: <CR>
Text: HATCH <CR>
```

6. Define the figure as a block.

```
Command: BLOCK <CR>
Block name (or ?): FIGURE <CR>
Insertion base point: 2.5,6.5 <CR>
Select objects: W <CR>
First point: 0,4 <CR>
Second point: 5,9 <CR>
12 found.
Select objects: <CR>
Command: OOPS <CR>
```

7. Insert the block in the upper-right corner of the screen.

```
Command: INSERT <CR>
Block name (or ?): FIGURE <CR>
 Insertion point: 9.5,6.5 <CR>
 X scale factor <1> / Corner / XYZ: <CR>
 Y scale factor (default= X): <CR>
 Rotation angle <0>: <CR>
```

8. Insert the block at 75% of size in the lower-left corner of the screen.

```
Command: INSERT <CR>
Block name (or ?) <FIGURE>: <CR>
 Insertion point: 2.5,2 <CR>
 X scale factor <1> / Corner / XYZ: .75 <CR>
 Y scale factor (default= X): .75 <CR>
 Rotation angle <0>: <CR>
```

9. Insert the block again in the lower-right corner of the screen.

```
Command: INSERT <CR>
Block name (or ?) <FIGURE>: <CR>
 Insertion point: 9.5,2 <CR>
 X scale factor <1> / Corner / XYZ: .75 <CR>
 Y scale factor (default= X): <CR>
 Rotation angle <0>: <CR>
```

10. Hatch the upper-left block with normal hatching. Use a user-specified pattern of lines .25 inches apart at a 60 degree angle.

```
Command: HATCH <CR>
Pattern (? or name/U,style): U <CR>
Angle for crosshatch lines <0>: 60 <CR>
Spacing between lines <1.0000>: .25 <CR>
Double hatch area? <N> <CR>
Select objects: W <CR>
First point: 0,4 <CR>
Second point: 5,9 <CR>
12 found.
Select objects: <CR>
```

11. Hatch the upper-right block with outermost-only hatching. Use the same pattern.

```
Command: HATCH <CR>
Pattern (? or name/U,style) <U>: U,O <CR>
Angle for crosshatch lines <60>: <CR>
Spacing between lines <0.2500>: <CR>
Double hatch area? <N> <CR>
Select objects: W <CR>
First point: 7,4 <CR>
Second point: 12,9 <CR>
1 found.
Select objects: <CR>
```

12. Hatch the lower-left block with double hatching. Furthermore, ignore the internal structure of the figure.

```
Command: HATCH <CR>
Pattern (? or name/U,style) <U,O>: U,I <CR>
Angle for crosshatch lines <60>: <CR>
Spacing between lines <0.2500>: <CR>
Double hatch area? <N> Y <CR>
Select objects: W <CR>
First point: 0,0 <CR>
Second point: 5,4 <CR>
1 found.
Select objects: <CR>
```

13. Hatch the lower-right block with STEEL hatching, one of AutoCAD's pre-defined hatch patterns.

```
Command: HATCH <CR>
Pattern (? or name/U,style) <U,0>: STEEL <CR>
Scale for pattern <1.0000>: <CR>
Angle for pattern <60>: <CR>
Select objects: W <CR>
First point: 7,0 <CR>
Second point: 12,4 <CR>
1 found.
Select objects: <CR>
```

Your drawing should look like the following one.

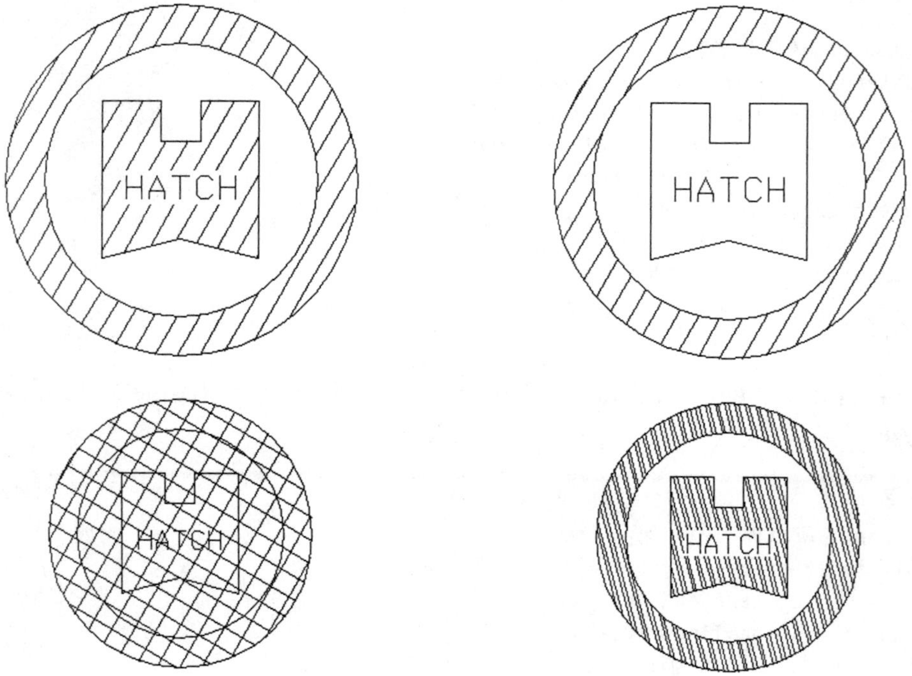

14. Use **QUIT** to redisplay the Main Menu.

Turn to Module 85 to continue the learning sequence.

The standard AutoCAD HATCH styles are as follows:

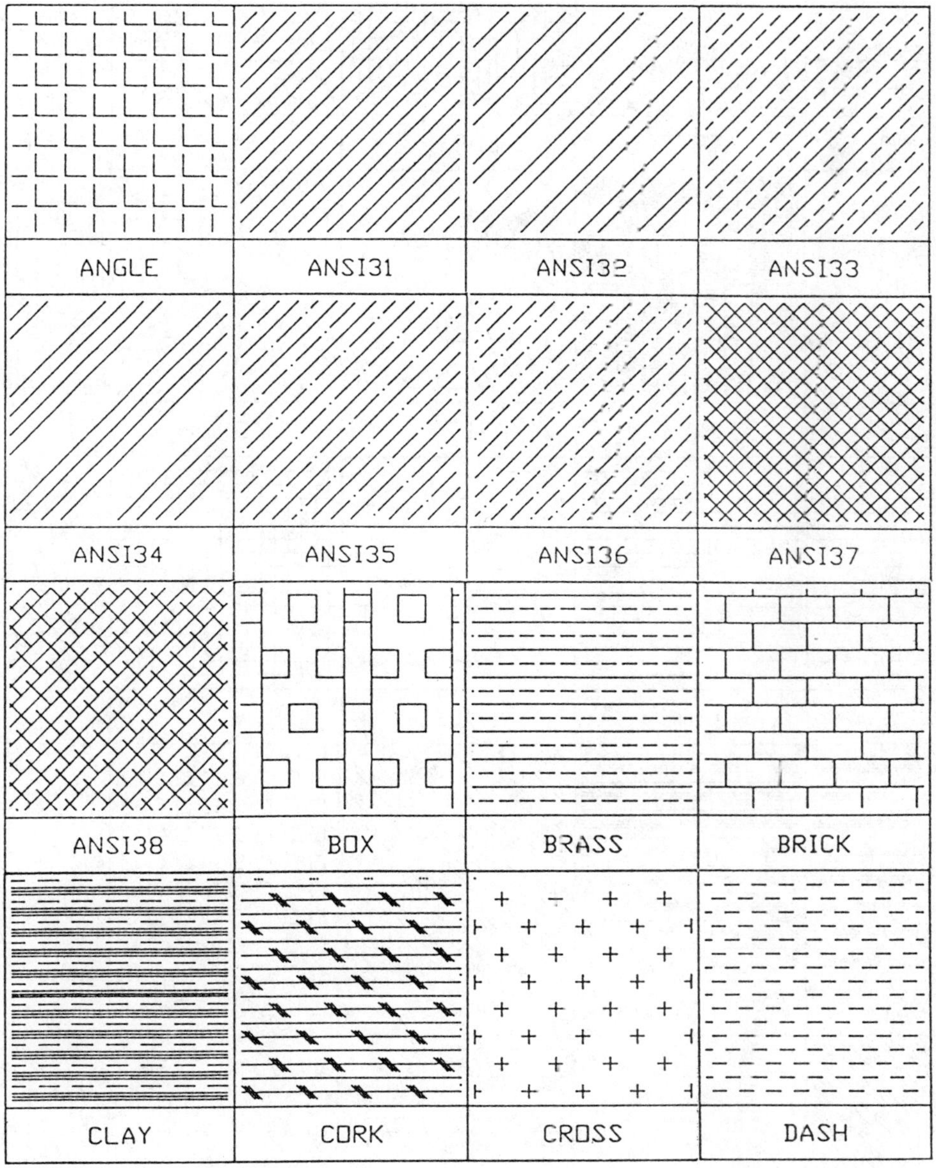

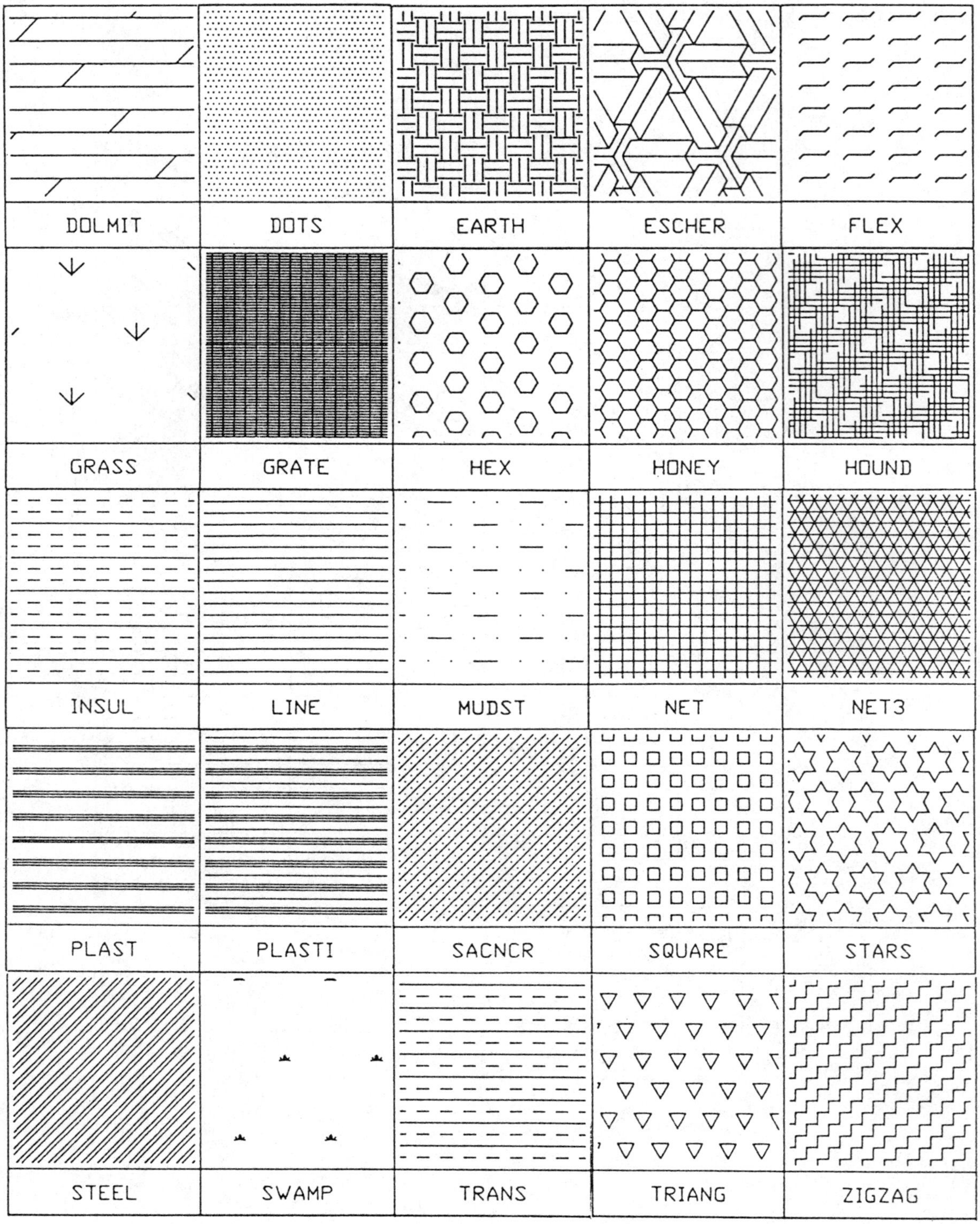
DOLMIT
DOTS
EARTH
ESCHER
FLEX
GRASS
GRATE
HEX
HONEY
HOUND
INSUL
LINE
MUDST
NET
NET3
PLAST
PLASTI
SACNCR
SQUARE
STARS
STEEL
SWAMP
TRANS
TRIANG
ZIGZAG

Module 38

HELP

```
Command: HELP (or ?)
Command name (RETURN for list):
```

DESCRIPTION

The HELP command displays on-screen help information. It is displayed by typing **HELP** or **?** and pressing **Return** from the command line. You can type **HELP** and press **Return** twice to list all AutoCad commands. You can type the name of any command and then press **Return** for information about a specific command. Press **Ctrl-C** to interrupt help at any point and return to your drawing by pressing the GRAPHSCREEN key. (See Module 35 for a list of GRAPHSCREEN keys.)

APPLICATIONS

Selecting **HELP** and pressing **RETURN** is an excellent way to refresh your memory if you simply forget the name of a command, or how to enter a point, distance, or angle specification.

TYPICAL OPERATION

In this operation AutoCAD's HELP information is displayed. Begin with the AutoCAD Main Menu displayed.

1. Type **1** and press **Return**; then type **TEMP** as the filename, and press **Return** again.
2. Type **HELP** and press **Return** twice.

```
Command List  (+n = ADE-n feature, ' = transparent command)

APERTURE +2  DELAY        FILLET +1    MENU         REDO          STRETCH +3
ARC          DIM/DIM1 +1  'GRAPHSCR    MINSERT      'REDRAW       STYLE
AREA         DIST         GRID         MIRROR +2    REGEN         TABLET
ARRAY        DIVIDE +3    HATCH +1     MOVE         REGENAUTO     TEXT
ATTDEF +2    DONUT +3     'HELP / '?   MSLIDE +2    RENAME        'TEXTSCR
ATTDISP +2   DOUGHNUT +3  HIDE +3      OFFSET +3    'RESUME       TIME
ATTEDIT +2   DRAGMODE +2  ID           OOPS         ROTATE +3     TRACE
ATTEXT +2    DTEXT +3     IGESIN +3    ORTHO        RSCRIPT       TRIM +3
AXIS +1      DXBIN +3     IGESOUT +3   OSNAP +2     SAVE          U
BASE         DXFIN        INSERT       'PAN         SCALE +3      UNDO
BLIPMODE     DXFOUT       ISOPLANE +2  PEDIT +3     SCRIPT        UNITS +1
BLOCK        ELEV +3      LAYER        PLINE +3     SELECT        'VIEW +2
BREAK +1     ELLIPSE +3   LIMITS       PLOT         'SETVAR       VIEWRES
CHAMFER +1   END          LINE         POINT        SHAPE         VPOINT +3
CHANGE       ERASE        LINETYPE     POLYGON +3   SHELL/SH +3   VSLIDE
CIRCLE       EXPLODE +3   LIST         PRPLOT       SKETCH +1     WBLOCK
COLOR        EXTEND +3    LOAD         PURGE        SNAP          'ZOOM
COPY         FILES        LTSCALE      QTEXT        SOLID         3DFACE
DBLIST       FILL         MEASURE +3   QUIT         STATUS        3DLINE

At the "Command:" prompt, you can enter RETURN to repeat the last command.

Press RETURN for further help.
```

3. Press **Return** to see the rest of the basic HELP screen.

```
You can enter points, or coordinates, in any of the following ways:

   Absolute:  x,y
   Relative:  @deltax,deltay
   Polar:     @dist<angle

For the commands that accept 3D points, you can include a Z coordinate
in the absolute and relative formats:

   Absolute:  x,y,z
   Relative:  @deltax,deltay,deltaz
```

```
If you omit the Z coordinate, the current elevation is used.

X/Y/Z filters can be used to compose a full point from the X, Y, and
Z components of intermediate points.  For instance, the filter ".X"
will instruct AutoCAD to use just the X coordinate of the following
point.  The Y (and possibly Z) values will then be requested.

See also:   Section 2.9 of the Reference Manual, and
            the version 2.6 supplement.

Press RETURN for further help.


Object selection:  ("Select objects:")

   (point)  =  One object
   M        =  Multiple objects
   L        =  Last object
   W        =  Objects within Window
   C        =  Objects within or Crossing window
   A        =  Add mode: add following objects
   R        =  Remove mode: remove following objects
   U        =  Undo/remove last

When you are satisfied with the selection-set as it stands, enter RETURN.


Command:
```

NOTE

To look at the HELP screen for a specific command, type **HELP**, press the **Spacebar**, then type the name of the command.

4. Type **?** and press the **Spacebar**.
5. Type **HELP** to see information on the use of the HELP command.

```
The  HELP  (or "?")  command displays help information.

Formats:    HELP (or ?)
            Command name (RETURN for list):
```

```
If you reply with a command name, information about that command is displayed.
Otherwise, the display consists of a list of valid commands, and a brief
reminder of the methods of point specification.

If the help information does not fit on one screen, AutoCAD will pause and
display:

            Press RETURN for further help.

To continue the help display, press RETURN.  If you want to cancel the help
display, enter CTRL-C.

Command:
```

HELP is available for all AutoCAD commands.

6. Press the GRAPHSCREEN key to redisplay the drawing screen.

NOTE

Leave the drawing screen displayed. Refer to Module 68, which describes the QUIT command.

7. Turn to Module 35 to continue the learning sequence.

Module 39

HIDE

```
Command: HIDE
```

DESCRIPTION

The HIDE command is used with the VPOINT command. When a three-dimensional view is produced with the VPOINT command, the drawing resembles a "wire frame," where all lines are shown. To eliminate the lines that would normally be invisible (or hidden), the HIDE command is used.

The HIDE command considers the following entities as solid objects:

circles

solids

traces

wide polylines

30 faces

A cylinder open at each end is drawn with two arcs. A closed cylinder is drawn with a circle.

APPLICATIONS

After a three-dimensional view is rotated into the desired position using the VPOINT command, the HIDE command is used to remove all hidden lines. Eliminating hidden lines lets you see what the object really looks like, without the confusion caused by extra lines.

TYPICAL OPERATION

In this session you draw a solid object. The VPOINT command is used to rotate it. Finally, HIDE is used to suppress the hidden lines. Begin a new drawing named HIDE.

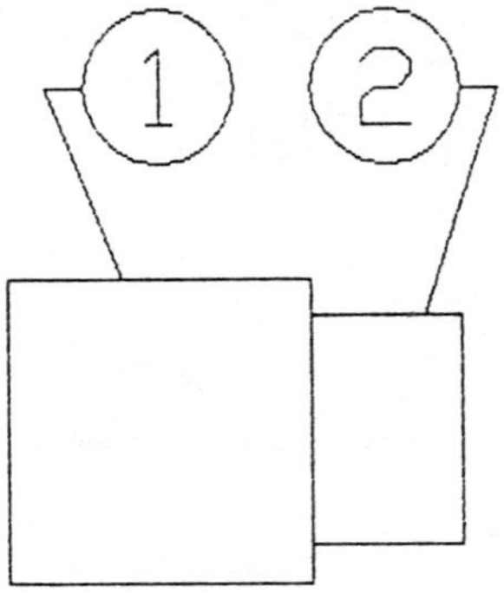

1. Draw the large solid.

```
Command: ELEV <CR>
New current elevation <0.0000>: <CR>
New current thickness <0.0000>: 4 <CR>
Command: SOLID <CR>
First point: 2,3 <CR>
Second point: 2,5 <CR>
Third point: 4,3 <CR>
Fourth point: 4,5 <CR>
Third point: <Ctrl-C> *Cancel*
```

2. Draw the smaller solid.

```
Command: ELEV <CR>
New current elevation <0.0000>: 1 <CR>
New current thickness <4.0000>: 2 <CR>
Command: SOLID <CR>
First point: 4,3.25 <CR>
Second point: 4,4.75 <CR>
Third point: 5,3.25 <CR>
Fourth point:5,4.75 <CR>
Third point: <Ctrl-C> *Cancel*
```

3. Rotate the drawing.

```
Command: VPOINT <CR>
Enter view point <0.0000,0.0000,1.0000>: 1,-1,1 <CR>
```

The view changes as shown:

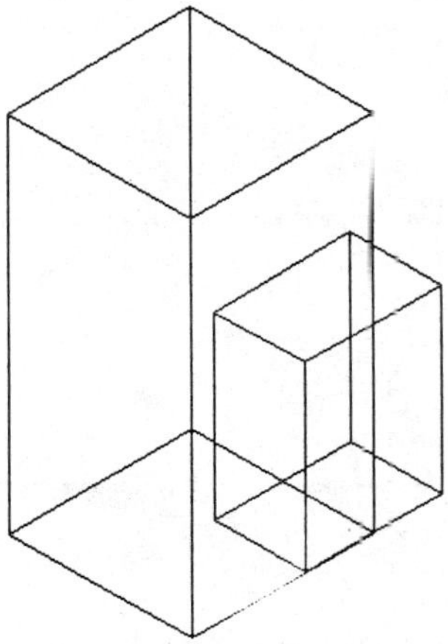

4. Remove the hidden lines.

```
Command: HIDE <CR>
```

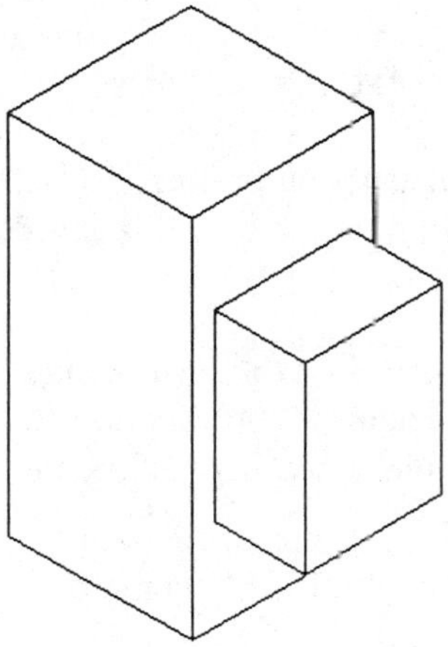

5. Use **QUIT** to redisplay the Main Menu.
6. Turn to Module 58 to continue the learning sequence.

Module 40

ID

```
Command: ID Point: (point to be displayed)
X = <X coordinate> Y = <Y coordinate> Z = <current elevation>
```

DESCRIPTION

The ID command gives you the location of a selected object or intersection within an AutoCAD drawing. There are two general ways to use the ID command. After typing **ID** and pressing **Return**, you can enter the X-Y coordinates of an object or intersection from the keyboard or pick it with a mouse or your cursor keys. The OSNAP options are available to make point selection easier. In particular, the NEA and INT options are quite helpful. In addition to these, you can use the MID, END, CEN, QUA, and NODE options. See Module 58 for a complete discription of each of these options. Because the NEA (near) option and INT (intersection) options are frequently used with ID, they are briefly described in the following two paragraphs.

NEA If you type **NEA** and press **Return**, you can pick a point close to the selected object, so that the target window (or aperature) surrounds the desired object. Pressing **Return** displays the exact location of the object for you.

INT If you want to determine the exact location of two intersecting lines, type **INT** and press **Return**. Then pick a point close to the desired intersection so that the target window surrounds the intersection. Pressing **Return** displays the coordinates of the intersection.

When a pick is made, AutoCAD displays a blip at the point (unless BLIPMODE is off). All blips are erased the next time the REDRAW or REGEN command is issued.

APPLICATIONS

Because the ID command shows you the precise coordinates of any selected object, it is a handy tool for finding dimensional reference points. For example, if you wish to know the exact location of an element within an architectural or geophysical drawing, ID is the command to use. Although you can see the X-Y position with the COORD function, you must use ID to determine the elevation (or Z coordinate) of an object. The NEA and INT options eliminate the need to enter or pick precise coordinates.

TYPICAL OPERATION

In this session you draw an elevated circle and then use the ID command to determine the coordinates of a point on the circumference. Begin a new drawing named ID.

1. Set the SNAP to .25 and turn the GRID on.

```
Command: SNAP <CR>
Snap spacing or ON/OFF/Aspect/Rotate/Style <1.0000>: .25 <CR>
Command: GRID <CR>
Grid spacing(X) or ON/OFF/Snap/Aspect <0.0000>: ON <CR>
```

2. Set the elevation at 1.5.

```
Command: ELEV <CR>
New current elevation <0.0000>: 1.5 <CR>
New current thickness <0.0000>: <CR>
```

3. Draw a circle located at 5,5 and having a radius of 1.25.

```
Command: CIRCLE <CR>
3P/2P/<Center point>: 5,5 <CR>
Diameter/<Radius>: 1.25 <CR>
```

4. Draw a line from 3,3 to 7,7.

```
Command: LINE <CR>
From point: 3,3 <CR>
To point: 7,7 <CR>
To point: <CR>
```

5. Determine the location of the intersection of the line and the lower left-hand side of the circumference.

```
Command: ID <CR>
Point: INT <CR>
to:     (Pick a point near the intersection of the line and
          circumference.)
Point:  X = 4.1161    Y = 4.1161    Z = 1.5000
```

6. Type **QUIT** and press **Return**; then type **Y** and press **Return** to display the Main Menu.
7. Turn to Module 37 to continue the learning sequence.

Module 41

INSERT

```
Command: INSERT
Block name (or ?):
```

DESCRIPTION

The INSERT command is used after a block or wblock has been defined. When you type **INSERT** at the command prompt, you must supply the block name in addition to several other items.

```
Insertion point:
X scale factor <1> / Corner / XYZ:
Y scale factor (default=X)
Rotation angle <0>:
```

Each INSERT command prompt is described in the following list.

Block name	The first prompt asks for the name of the block you wish to insert.
?	Displays a list of the available blocks.
Insertion point	The second prompt asks for the insertion point. You may pick the point or enter the coordinates from the keyboard. With version 2.6 and later, INSERT accepts 3-dimensional insertion points.
X scale factor	The default value is 1. If you press **Return**, the block is inserted using the original X value. If you provide a new X value, AutoCAD multiplies the X scale dimension of your block by the number. You may also use the screen cursor to simultaneously "show" AutoCAD both the X scale factor and the Y scale factor.

Y scale factor — The Y scale factor uses the same value entered for the X scale factor. Entering a Y scale factor value operates in the same way as the X scale factor. In summary, AutoCAD multiplies the X and Y values you enter times the original X and Y values of the block. When entering the X and Y scale factors, you can enter negative values to produce mirror images. The X and Y values may also be entered using the insertion point and another point as the corners of a box. To use this method, respond by typing **C** at the "X scale factor" prompt. Place the second point above and to the right of the insertion point unless you want to produce a mirror image of the block.

Rotation angle — The default rotation angle is zero. AutoCAD rotates the block by the number of degrees you enter. The rotation uses the insertion point as the center of rotation. If you repeat the whole insert process, some of the defaults are set to the last values used. This simplifies the insertion of identical blocks. You may also use the screen cursor to "show" AutoCAD the desired rotation.

If your block is simple, "Drag" is sometimes useful for the entry of the insertion point, the X scale factor, or the rotation angle. If Drag mode is turned on (or Auto in version 2.5 +), you can move the object and give it a scale or rotation value with your pointing device. If the block is complex, the Drag method is slow. When you insert a block, AutoCAD treats the block as an entity just as it treats a line as an entity. If you want to edit portions of a block after insertion, you should insert the block as a "*block." To do this, you respond to the block name prompt by preceding the block name with an asterisk. Only one scale factor is requested for a "*block" and it cannot be a negative value.

APPLICATIONS

The INSERT command is used to insert BLOCKS and WBLOCKS into AutoCAD drawings. This is an efficient way to repeat objects many times in a drawing. For example, you can draw the symbol of an electrical resistor and save it as a block. Then you can insert it as often as necessary on your electrical schematic diagram.

If you need to repeat a block several times in a rectangular or circular arrangement, use the ARRAY command instead of performing multiple insertions.

TYPICAL OPERATION

In this session you draw a circle and a square and identify each as a block. Each is inserted in various ways. The following drawing is the result of your work. Begin a new drawing named INSERT.

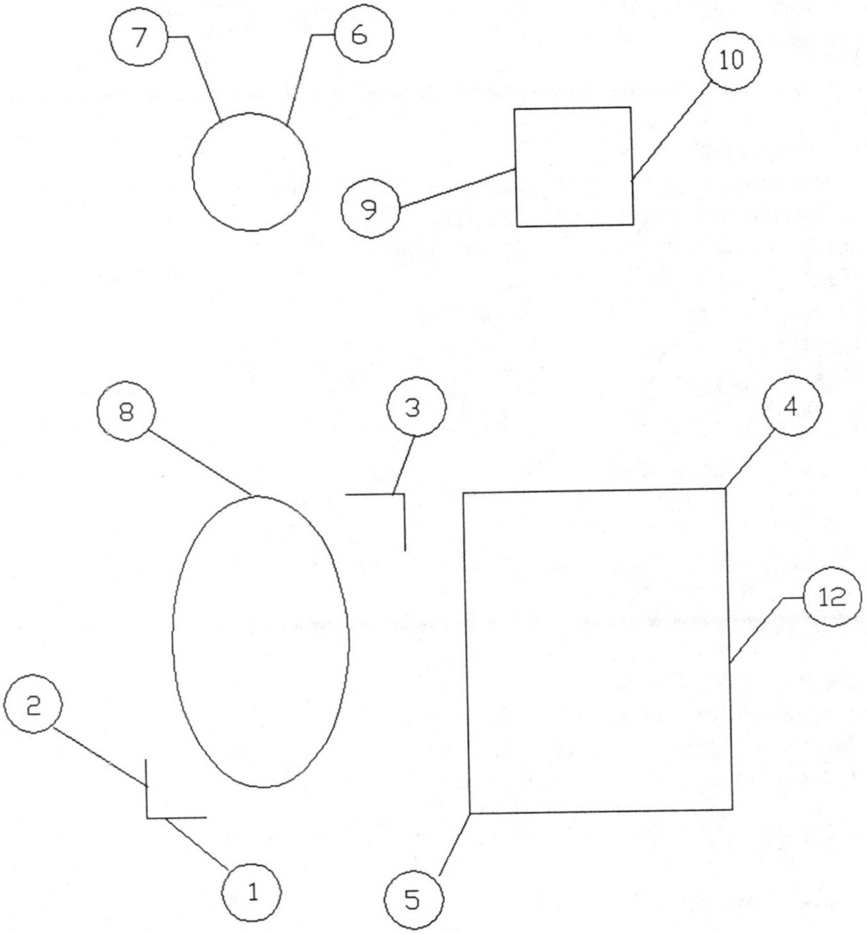

1. Draw lines and redraw the screen.

```
Command: LINE <CR>
From point: .25,.75 <CR>
To point: @.50<270 <CR>
To point: @.50<0 <CR>
To point: <CR>

Command: REDRAW <CR>
```

2. Make a block named CORNER and bring it back with the OOPS command and then redraw the screen.

```
Command: BLOCK <CR>
Block name (or ?): CORNER <CR>
Insertion base point: .25,.25 <CR>
Select objects: (Pick one of the lines)
1 selected, 1 found.
Select objects: (Pick the other line)
1 selected, 1 found.
Select objects: <CR>
Command: OOPS <CR>

Command: REDRAW <CR>
```

3. Insert the block and redraw the screen.

```
Command: INSERT <CR>
Block name (or ?): CORNER <CR>
 Insertion point: 2.5,3.0 <CR>
 X scale factor <1> / Corner / XYZ: -1 <CR>
 Y scale factor (default=X): -1 <CR>
 Rotation angle <0>: <CR>

Command: REDRAW <CR>
```

4. Insert the block.

```
Command: INSERT <CR>
Block name (or ?) <CORNER>: <CR>
 Insertion point: 5.25,3.0 <CR>
 X scale factor <1> / Corner / XYZ: -1 <CR>
 Y scale factor (default=X): <CR>
 Rotation angle <0>: <CR>
```

5. Insert the block and redraw the screen.

```
Command:  INSERT <CR>
Block name (or ?) <CORNER>: <CR>
 Insertion point: 3.0,.25 <CR>
 X scale factor <1> / Corner / XYZ: <CR>
 Y scale factor (default=X): <CR>
 Rotation angle <0>: <CR>

Command: REDRAW <CR>
```

6. Draw a circle.

```
Command: CIRCLE <CR>
3P/2P/TTR/<Center point>: 1.25,5.75 <CR>
Diameter/<Radius>: .5 <CR>
```

7. Save the circle as a block named ROUND. Bring it back to the screen with the OOPS command.

```
Command: BLOCK <CR>
Block name (or ?): ROUND <CR>
Insertion base point: 1.25,5.75 <CR>
Select objects: (Pick the circle)
1 selected, 1 found.
Select objects: <CR>

Command: OOPS <CR>
```

8. Insert the block named ROUND with an X scale factor of 1.5 and a Y scale factor of 2.5. Notice the resulting circle. The X value is 1.5 larger; the Y value is 2.5 larger.

```
Command: INSERT <CR>
Block name (or ?) <CORNER>: ROUND <CR>
 Insertion point: 1.25,1.75 <CR>
 X scale factor <1> / Corner / XYZ: 1.5 <CR>
 Y scale factor (default=X): 2.5 <CR>
 Rotation angle <0>: <CR>
```

9. Draw a 1-inch square box.

```
Command: LINE <CR>
From point: 3.5,5.25 <CR>
To point: @1<90 <CR>
To point: @1<0 <CR>
To point: @1<270 <CR>
To point: C <CR>
```

10. Make a block named SQUARE. Bring it back to the screen with the OOPS command.

```
Command: BLOCK <CR>
Block name (or ?): SQUARE <CR>
Insertion base point: 3.5,5.25 <CR>
Select objects: W <CR>
First point: 3.25,5 <CR>
Second point: 4.75,6.5 <CR>
4 found.
Select objects: <CR>

Command: OOPS <CR>
```

11. Insert the block again.

```
Command: INSERT <CR>
Block name (or ?) <ROUND>: SQUARE <CR>
 Insertion point: 3.0,.25 <CR>
 X scale factor <1> / Corner / XYZ: C <CR>
Other corner: 5.25,3 <CR>
 Rotation angle <0>: <CR>
```

Your final drawing should look like the following one.

The creation of a 1-inch square block is useful for knowing the exact scale factor to use. You may recall that the sample session in Module 2 used a 1 x 1 block to create rectangular furniture of varying dimensions.

12. Use **QUIT** to redisplay the Main Menu.
13. Turn to Module 51 to continue the learning sequence.

Module 42

ISOPLANE

```
Command: ISOPLANE
Left/Top/Right/(Toggle):
```

DESCRIPTION

To use the ISOPLANE command, you must first use the SNAP command. After typing **SNAP**, enter **S** for style, and **I** for isometric as shown.

```
Command: SNAP <CR>
Snap spacing or ON/OFF/Aspect/Rotate/Style <1.0000>: S <CR>
Standard/Isometric: I <CR>
Vertical spacing <1.0000>: .25 <CR>
```

After setting the isometric SNAP style, the ISOPLANE command is used to toggle the drawing axes to the proper rotation. When it becomes necessary to change the drawing axes, type **ISOPLANE**, and press **Return**. The following prompt is displayed.

```
Command: ISOPLANE <CR>
Left/Top/Right/(Toggle):
```

You can toggle the ISOPLANE axes without typing ISOPLANE. You press **Ctrl-E** to toggle the ISOPLANE axes. With Release 9 you can also toggle the ISOPLANE with the Drawing Aids option of the Mode drop-down menu.

APPLICATIONS

A multiview drawing makes it possible to accurately represent complex forms by showing a series of exterior views and sections. This representation has two limitations. First, creating the multiview drawing requires expertise in the principles of multiview projection; and second, reading the drawing requires both skill and imagination to properly visualize the design. The isometric drawing is a frequently used method to accurately represent a design in a way that is readily understood by people without technical training.

The classic isometric view of a cube reveals three faces. The three faces are the left side, right side, and top. The ISOPLANE command lets you choose one of the three faces on which to draw. The three faces are called planes. The face on the left side of the cube is the isometric plane produced by the 90-degree and the 150-degree axis pair. The face on the right side of the cube is the isometric plane produced by the 90-degree and the 30-degree axis pair. The face on the top is the isometric plane produced by the 30-degree and the 150-degree axis pair.

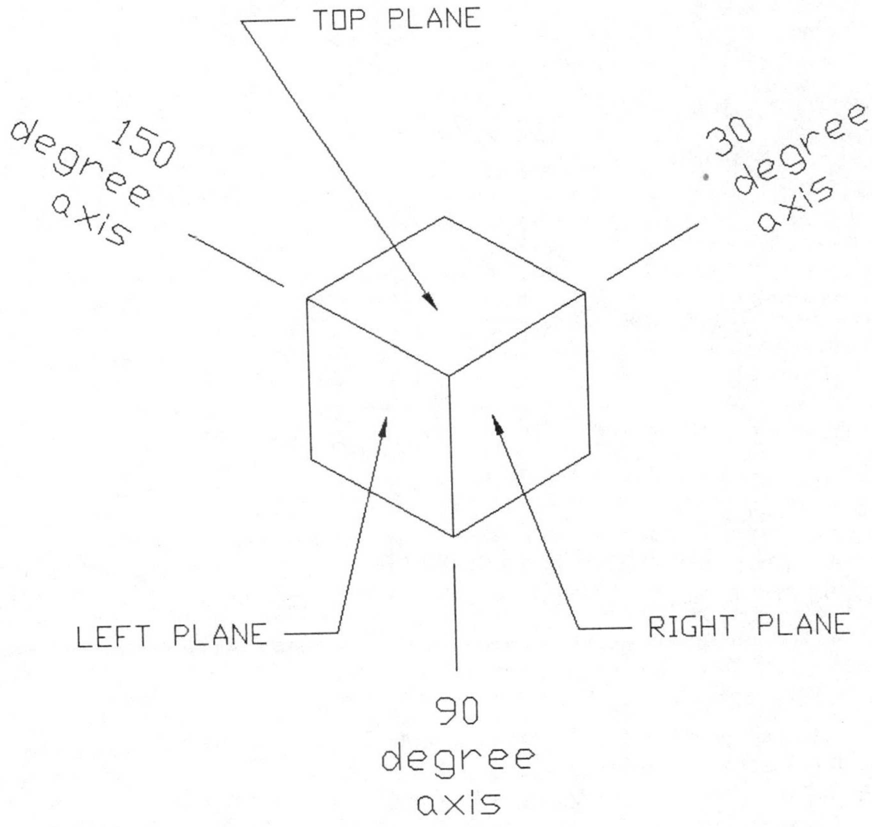

The ISOPLANE command is used to produce isometric drawings. Use ISOPLANE to switch from one set of isometric axes to another to draw on any of the three isometric planes.

TYPICAL OPERATION

In this session you toggle the isoplane three different ways. The session involves changing units to two decimal places and then drawing lines in each of the three planes. In the last portion of the session, you use the FILLET command in an isometric drawing, which should stimulate further experimentation.

The numbered balloons in the following drawing correspond to the steps in this session.

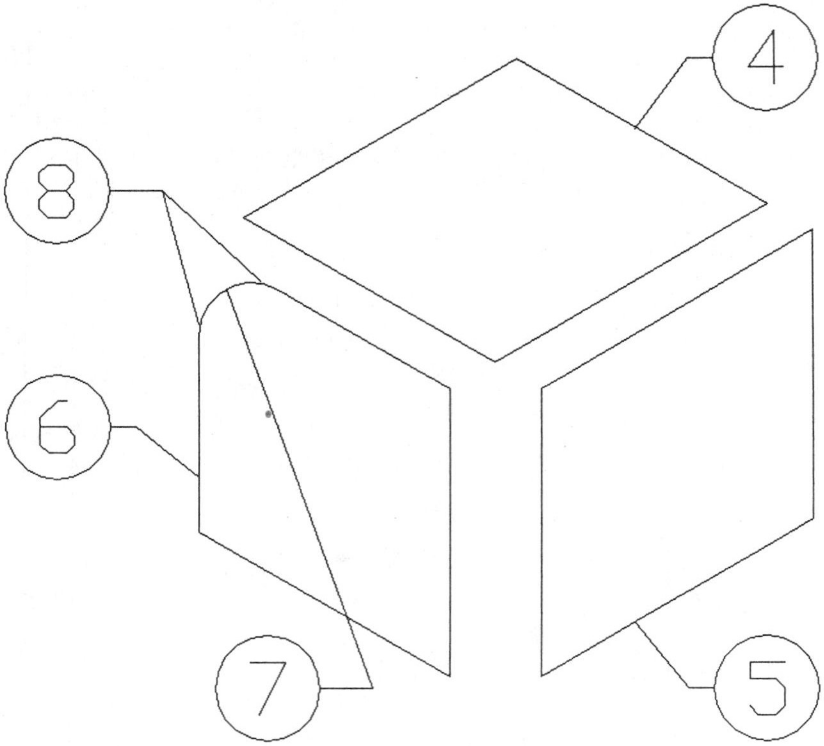

1. Begin a new drawing named ISOAC. Enter the **SNAP** command. (Pressing **Ctrl-E** three times rotates the following prompts: <Isoplane Left> <Isoplane Top> <Isoplane Right>)

```
Command: SNAP <CR>
Snap spacing or ON/OFF/Aspect/Rotate/Style <1.0000>: S <CR>
Standard/Isometric: I <CR>
Vertical spacing <1.0000>: .25 <CR>

Command: ISOPLANE <CR>
Left/Top/Right/(Toggle): L <CR>
Current Isometric plane is: Left
```

```
Command: <CR>
ISOPLANE Left/Top/Right/(Toggle): T <CR>
Current Isometric plane is: Top
Command: <CR>
ISOPLANE Left/Top/Right/(Toggle): R <CR>
Current Isometric plane is: Right
```

2. The ISOPLANE command is also toggled by pressing the **Return** key. Press **Return** to bring back the last command.

```
ISOPLANE Left/Top/Right/(Toggle): <CR>
Current Isometric plane is: Left
Command: <CR>
ISOPLANE Left/Top/Right/(Toggle): <CR>
Current Isometric plane is: Top
Command: <CR>
ISOPLANE Left/Top/Right/(Toggle): <CR>
Current Isometric plane is: Right
```

3. Change the number of decimal places.

```
Command: UNITS <CR>
Systems of units:       (Examples)

    1.   Scientific       1.55E+01
    2.   Decimal          15.50
    3.   Engineering      1'-3.50"
    4.   Architectural    1'-3 1/2"
    5.   Fractional       15 1/2

Enter choice, 1 to 5 <2>:
Number of digits to right of decimal point (0 to 8) <4>: 0 <CR>

Systems of angle measure:       (Examples)

    1.   Decimal degrees             45.0000
    2.   Degrees/minutes/seconds     45d0'0"
    3.   Grads                       50.0000g
    4.   Radians                     0.7854r
    5.   Surveyor's units            N 45d0'0" E
```

```
Enter choice, 1 to 5 <1>:
Number of fractional places for display of angles (0 to 8) <0>: <CR>


Direction for angle 0:
   East     3 o'clock  =  0
   North   12 o'clock  =  90
   West     9 o'clock  =  180
   South    6 o'clock  =  270
Enter direction for angle 0 <0>: <CR>

Do you want angles measured clockwise? <N> <CR>
```

4. Press **Ctrl-E** until <Isoplane Top> is displayed.

```
Command:  <Isoplane Top> LINE <CR>
From point: 3.03,5.75 <CR>
To point:   5.41,4.37 <CR>
To point: 8.01,5.87 <CR>
To point: 5.63,7.25 <CR>
To point: C <CR>
```

5. Press **Ctrl-E** until <Isoplane Right> is displayed.

```
Command:  <Isoplane Right> LINE <CR>
From point: 5.85,4.12 <CR>
To point: 8.44,5.62 <CR>
To point: 8.44,2.87 <CR>
To point: 5.85,1.37 <CR>
To point: C <CR>
```

6. Press **Ctrl-E** until <Isoplane Left> is displayed.

```
Command:  <Isoplane Left> LINE <CR>
From point: 4.98,4.12 <CR>
To point: 2.60,5.50 <CR>
To point: 2.60,2.75 <CR>
To point: 4.98,1.37 <CR>
To point: C <CR>
```

7. Use the FILLET command and adjust the fillet radius to ½ inch.

```
Command: FILLET <CR>
Polyline/Radius/<Select two objects>: R <CR>
Enter fillet radius <0.00>: .5 <CR>
```

8. Locate the cross hairs on one line in the left face and press **Return**. Repeat the process on a line that touches the previous line and press **Return** to complete the selection of two lines.

```
Command: <CR>
FILLET Polyline/Radius/<Select two objects>:
```

Compare your drawing to the following one.

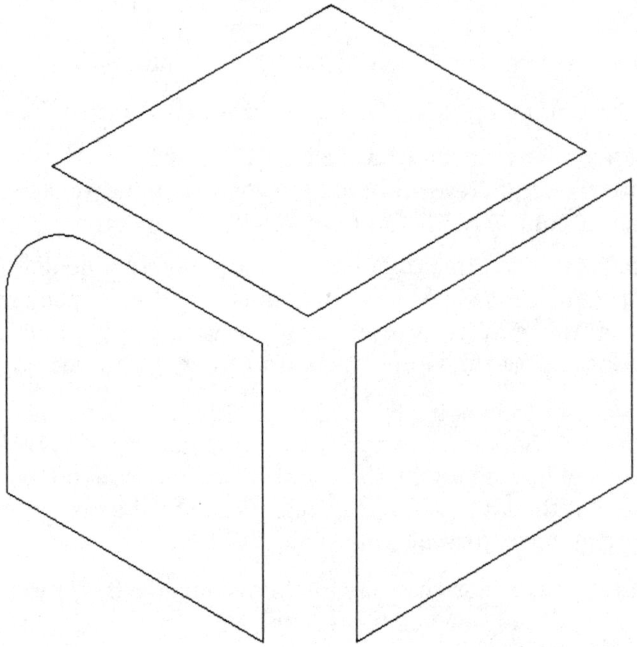

9. Use **QUIT** to redisplay the Main Menu.
10. Turn to Module 68 to continue the learning sequence.

Module 43

LAYER

```
Command: LAYER
?/Make/Set/New/ON/OFF/Color/Ltype/Freeze/Thaw: (select one)
```

DESCRIPTION

The LAYER command is used to draw objects having multiple planes.

The LAYER command has many options. These are described in the following list.

Make — Creates a new layer and assigns it as the current layer. It is, in effect, a combination of New and Set. The layer is initially set on, and drawing takes place in color 7 with the CONTINUOUS linetype.

? — Displays information about one or more layers. The list shows the layer name, color, and linetype. You are prompted for a layer name: Layer name(s) for listing <*>:. You may type either a layer name or an asterisk. The * acts as a "wildcard" and lists all layers and their characteristics.

Set — Allows you to specify the current layer. You may only draw on one layer at a time. The Set option is used to specify the active layer. The new current layer must exist (create it with the New option) and must not be frozen (see the Freeze option). If the layer is off (see the Off option), the Set option automatically turns the layer on before making it the current layer.

New — Creates one or more new layers. In response to the prompt: New layer name(s):, you can type either one layer name, or several names separated by a comma. The New option does not make the new layer the current layer—you must use the Set option to make it the current layer. All new layers are created with a continuous linetype in color 7 (white). If you want to change the linetype, use the Ltype option. If you want to change the color, use the Color option.

On/Off — Controls whether or not a particular layer is displayed. Turning a layer off helps to control the clutter on the screen. For example, you might turn off the mechanical layer of an architectural drawing while working on the plumbing layer. The On/Off option does not affect the computer time required to redraw a drawing. It only controls what is displayed. Compare the action with Freeze/Thaw.

Ltype — Changes the linetype used for specific layers of the drawing. In response to the prompt "Layer name(s) for linetype *xxx* <*current*>:", you can type either the name of a single layer, or several layer names separated by commas. You may use the wildcard characters ? (is matched by any single character) or * (is matched by any number of characters) when you specify any of the names in the list. (When using a linetype other than continuous for a layer, you must plot the layer using a continuous linetype. This is explained further in the PLOT module.)

Freeze/Thaw — The Freeze option causes AutoCAD to ignore one or more layers of your drawing. The frozen layers are not displayed, plotted, or regenerated when you ZOOM, PAN, VPOINT, or REGEN the drawing. As a result, the speed of these drawing operations is significantly increased. The Thaw option causes AutoCAD to resume processing of the specified layers. The difference between On/Off and Freeze/Thaw is that when a layer is off, calculations are performed on the entities in that layer when the drawing is redrawn. When the layer is frozen, no calculations are performed on the layer.

LAYER NAMES You refer to an AutoCAD layer by its name. AutoCAD does not limit the number of layers in a drawing. The layer name can include up to 31 characters. It may contain letters, digits, the dollar sign, hyphen, and underscore (no spaces are allowed). If you create a layer which you want to remove, use the PURGE command (see Module 49). The LAYER command creates and modifies layers, but cannot eliminate them.

LAYER COLORS AutoCAD references colors by numbers and defines the first seven color numbers as follows:

1	Red
2	Yellow
3	Green
4	Cyan
5	Blue
6	Magenta
7	White

If your graphics display is not capable of displaying these colors, AutoCAD makes substitutions. If you have a single-color monitor, all colors appear the same. The only guarantee is that any layer which is "On" is displayed on the monitor.

AutoCAD supports the numbers 1 to 255 as color numbers. The visual effect of colors 8 to 255 is entirely dependent on your particular hardware configuration.

The colors associated with a layer are used in two places. First, they are used for creating the visual display on your graphics monitor. Second, they are used for selecting the pen from a multi-pen plotter. The two functions are independent. It is not necessary to have a color monitor to produce color plots. You only need a plotter with multiple pens, or one that lets you change pen colors.

LINE TYPES The standard line types supplied with AutoCAD are stored on disk in the file ACAD.LIN. The line types you use are loaded into your drawing when you specify them as the line type for a layer. The standard supplied line types are as follows:

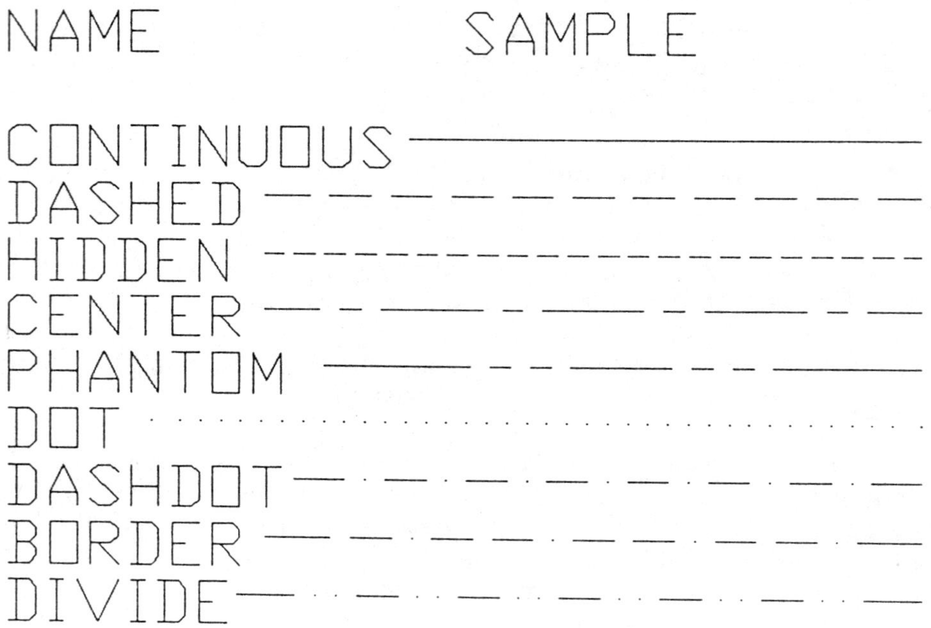

You use the LINETYPE command to create additional line types. You use the PURGE command to eliminate unused line types from your drawing file.

APPLICATIONS

The use of layers helps to organize your drawing by placing elements of the same type together. In a mechanical drawing, separate layers for the drawing sheet, the object, the dimensions, and the text can be used. For some applications, you might want separate layers for each of the three views of a three-view drawing. In an architectural drawing, the use of separate layers for the foundation, floor, walls, mechanical, electrical, plumbing, lighting, roof, interior design, and planting makes it straightforward to show only those elements of the drawing which pertain to a particular subcontractor:

TYPICAL OPERATION

The following operation includes making new layers of different colors and line types and using them to draw a stop sign and post. The steps that you follow to complete the operation are shown in the following graphics screen as numbered balloons.

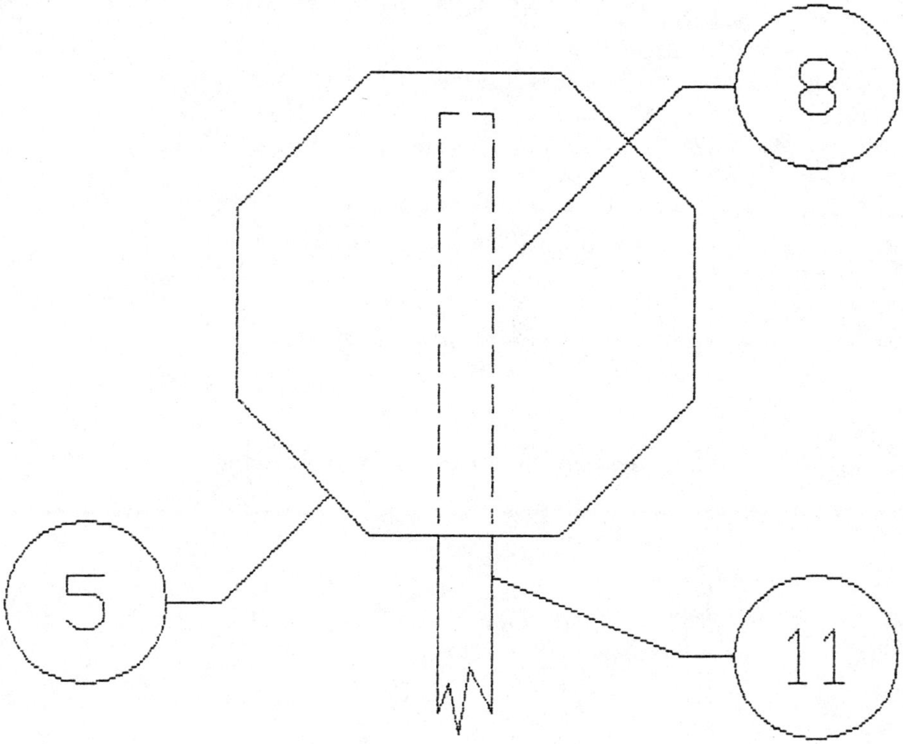

Begin a new drawing named LAYER.

1. Set SNAP to .25. Turn GRID on and ZOOM the screen to full view.

```
Command: SNAP <CR>
Snap spacing or ON/OFF/Aspect/Rotate/Style <1.0000>: .25 <CR>

Command: GRID <CR>
Grid spacing(X) or ON/OFF/Snap/Aspect <0.0000>: ON <CR>

Command: ZOOM  <CR>
All/Center/Dynamic/Extents/Left/Previous/Window/<Scale(X)>: A <CR>
```

2. Use the New option to create two new layers with different line types and colors.

```
Command: LAYER <CR>
?/Make/Set/New/ON/OFF/Color/Ltype/Freeze/Thaw: N <CR>
New layer name(s): SIGN <CR>
?/Make/Set/New/ON/OFF/Color/Ltype/Freeze/Thaw: N <CR>
New layer name(s): POST <CR>
?/Make/Set/New/ON/OFF/Color/Ltype/Freeze/Thaw: C <CR>
Color: RED <CR>
Layer name(s) for color 1 (red) <0>: SIGN <CR>
?/Make/Set/New/ON/OFF/Color/Ltype/Freeze/Thaw: C <CR>
Color: BLUE <CR>
Layer name(s) for color 5 (blue) <0>: POST <CR>
?/Make/Set/New/ON/OFF/Color/Ltype/Freeze/Thaw: <CR>
```

3. Ask AutoCAD to list the layers that now exist in your drawing.

```
Command: LAYER <CR>
?/Make/Set/New/ON/OFF/Color/Ltype/Freeze/Thaw: ? <CR>
Layer name(s) for listing <*>: * <CR>
```

After pressing **Return**, the following list appears on your text screen.

```
   Layer name        State     Color        Linetype
----------------- -------- ------------- ------------
0                 On        7 (white)    CONTINUOUS
SIGN              On        1 (red)      CONTINUOUS
POST              On        5 (blue)     CONTINUOUS

Current layer: 0

?/Make/Set/New/ON/OFF/Color/Ltype/Freeze/Thaw:
```

4. Set the layer named sign as the current layer and go back to the Graphics Editor by toggling the flip screen key (F1 on the IBM PC).

```
?/Make/Set/New/ON/OFF/Color/Ltype/Freeze/Thaw: S <CR>
New current layer <0>: SIGN <CR>
?/Make/Set/New/ON/OFF/Color/Ltype/Freeze/Thaw: <CR>
Command: (press Flip Screen Key)
```

5. Draw the outline of the stop sign.

The method you use depends on your version of AutoCAD. Select the correct procedure for your version of the software.

With versions prior to 2.5, use the CIRCLE, LINE, and ARRAY commands to perform the construction as shown in the following screen sequence.

```
Command: CIRCLE <CR>
3P/2P/<Center point>: 5.75,4.75 <CR>
Diameter/<Radius>: @2.1213<315 <CR>

Command: LINE <CR>
From point: 6.6287,2.6287 <CR>
To point: @1.7574<45 <CR>
To point: <CR>

Command: ARRAY <CR>
Select objects or Window or Last: L <CR>
1 found.
Select objects or Window or Last: <CR>
Rectangular or circular array (R/C): C <CR>
Center point of array: 5.75,4.75 <CR>
Angle between items (+=CCW, -=CW): 45 <CR>
Number of items or -(degrees to fill): 8 <CR>
Rotate objects as they are copied? <N> Y <CR>

Command: ERASE <CR>
Select objects or Window or Last: 7.75,4 <CR>
1 selected, 1 found.
Select objects or Window or Last: <CR>

Command: REDRAW <CR>
```

With version 2.5 + use the POLYGON command to draw the octagon at the required location, as shown in the following screen sequence.

```
Command: POLYGON <CR>
Number of sides: 8 <CR>
Edge/<Center of polygon>: 5.75,4.75 <CR>
Inscribed in circle/Circumscribed about circle (I/C): C <CR>
Radius of circle:  2 <CR>
```

7. Change the Ltype of the layer named POST to hidden and set the POST layer to the current layer.

```
Command: LAYER <CR>
?/Make/Set/New/ON/OFF/Color/Ltype/Freeze/Thaw: L <CR>
Linetype (or ?) <CONTINUOUS>: HIDDEN <CR>
Layer name(s) for linetype HIDDEN <SIGN>: POST <CR>
?/Make/Set/New/ON/OFF/Color/Ltype/Freeze/Thaw: S <CR>
New current layer <SIGN>: POST <CR>
?/Make/Set/New/ON/OFF/Color/Ltype/Freeze/Thaw:  <CR>
```

8. Draw the post hidden behind the sign by using the LINE command and then REDRAW the screen.

```
Command: LINE <CR>
From point: 5.5,2.75 <CR>
To point: 5.5,6.5 <CR>
To point: 6,6.5 <CR>
To point: 6,2.75 <CR>
To point: <CR>

Command: REDRAW <CR>
```

9. Refresh your memory of available layers by listing them again.

```
Command: LAYER <CR>
?/Make/Set/New/ON/OFF/Color/Ltype/Freeze/Thaw: ? <CR>
Layer name(s) for listing <*>: * <CR>
```

After pressing **Return** the following list appears on your text screen.

```
   Layer name       State        Color        Linetype
----------------- -------- ------------- ------------
0                 On        7 (white)    CONTINUOUS
SIGN              On        1 (red)      CONTINUOUS
POST              On        5 (blue)     HIDDEN

Current layer: POST

?/Make/Set/New/ON/OFF/Color/Ltype/Freeze/Thaw:
```

10. Set the layer named 0 (zero) as the current layer and go back to the Graphics Editor by toggling the flip screen key.

```
?/Make/Set/New/ON/OFF/Color/Ltype/Freeze/Thaw: S <CR>
New current layer <POST>: 0 <CR>
?/Make/Set/New/ON/OFF/Color/Ltype/Freeze/Thaw: <CR>
Command: (press Flip Screen key)
```

11. Draw the visible portion of the post with the LINE command and REDRAW the screen.

```
Command: LINE <CR>
From point: 5.5,2.6276 <CR>
To point: 5.5,1 <CR>
To point: 5.61,1.27 <CR>
To point: 5.7,.8 <CR>
To point: 5.8,1.4 <CR>
To point: 6,1 <CR>
To point: 6,2.6276 <CR>
To point: <CR>

Command: REDRAW <CR>
```

Your finished operation looks like the following:

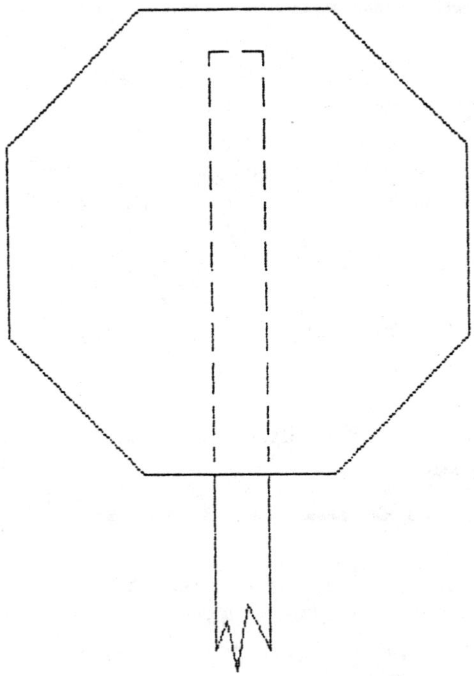

12. Type **QUIT** and press **Return**; then type **Y** and press **Return** to redisplay the Main Menu.
13. Turn to Module 46 to continue the learning sequence.

Module 44

LIMITS

```
Command: LIMITS
ON/OFF/<Lower left corner> <current value>:
```

DESCRIPTION

The LIMITS command is used to establish the size of your drawing. You may think of the LIMITS command as choosing the size of your drawing sheet in manual drafting. The drawing sheet in AutoCAD must be large enough to accommodate what you are drawing at full scale. The concept of always drawing in full scale is sometimes difficult for the AutoCAD novice. You can select one of the following options each time you issue the LIMITS command:

On — Turns on limit checking. If you attempt to specify a point outside the current limits, the point is rejected. You can, however, issue a command, such as CIRCLE, or a BLOCK command which starts within the limits and extends beyond the limits. Limits simply assists you in drawing "on the paper."

Off — Turns off limit checking. You may now draw anywhere. When you turn off limits, the old values of the limits are not forgotten, they are simply not enforced. Turning on limits at a later time restores the former values.

Lower left corner <*current value*>: — Allows you to specify a new set of drawing limits.

To reset the drawing limits you first specify the lower-left limit. If you want to accept the current value (shown in < >), press **Return**. If not, type two points separated by commas to specify the lower-left limit and press **Return**. The computer responds with "Upper right corner <*current value*>:." To accept the current value for the upper-right corner, press **Return**. Otherwise, enter values for the X and Y coordinates of the upper-right corner. All values are interpreted in terms of the current units.

APPLICATIONS

LIMITS is used to specify the size of your drawing using practical, every-day dimensions. You do not consider factors such as scale until you plot. You can reset drawing limits in the middle of your work if you find that your initial choices were inappropriate. When choosing LIMITS for your drawing, you must remember that in AutoCAD you are always drawing at full scale.

TYPICAL OPERATION

In this example begin a new drawing named TEMP. Then set the drawing limits for an A size drawing by performing the following steps.

1. Type **LIMITS** and press **Return**.

```
Command: LIMITS <CR>
ON/OFF/<Lower left corner> <curent value>:
```

2. Press **Return** to leave the lower-left corner at the <0,0> point.

```
Command: LIMITS <CR>
ON/OFF/<Lower left corner> <0.0000,0.0000>: <CR>
Upper right corner <12.0000,9.0000>:
```

3. Type **10.5,8** and press **Return**.

```
Command: LIMITS <CR>
ON/OFF/<Lower left corner> <0.0000,0.0000>: <0.0000,0.0000> <CR>
Upper right corner <12.0000,9.0000>: 10.5,8 <CR>
Command:
```

4. Press **Return** to redisplay the LIMITS command.

```
Command: <CR>
LIMITS
ON/OFF/<Lower left corner> <0.0000,0.0000>: <CR>
Upper right corner <10.50,8.00>: <CR>
Command: <CR>
LIMITS
ON/OFF/<Lower left corner> <0.0000,0.0000>:
Command:
```

5. Type **ON** and press **Return**.

Your limits are now set and active.

6. Type **QUIT** and press **Return**; then type **Y** and press **Return** to redisplay the Main Menu.
7. Turn to Module 90 to continue the learning sequence.

Module 45

LINE

```
Command: LINE From point:
To point:
To point: (Press Spacebar or Return to end the command.)
```

DESCRIPTION

The LINE command is used to draw a straight line. When drawing a line, you must designate its endpoints. There are several ways to designate a point.

- Drag the screen cursor to the desired position and pick the position from the screen.
- Type the X and Y coordinates of the point.
- Specify a distance and an angle from the last point.

APPLICATIONS

A line is one of the basic drawing elements. A line extends between two endpoints. AutoCAD treats a line as a single entity, not as a series of points.

TYPICAL OPERATION

In this example, a figure is drawn using a series of lines. Begin a new drawing named LINE.

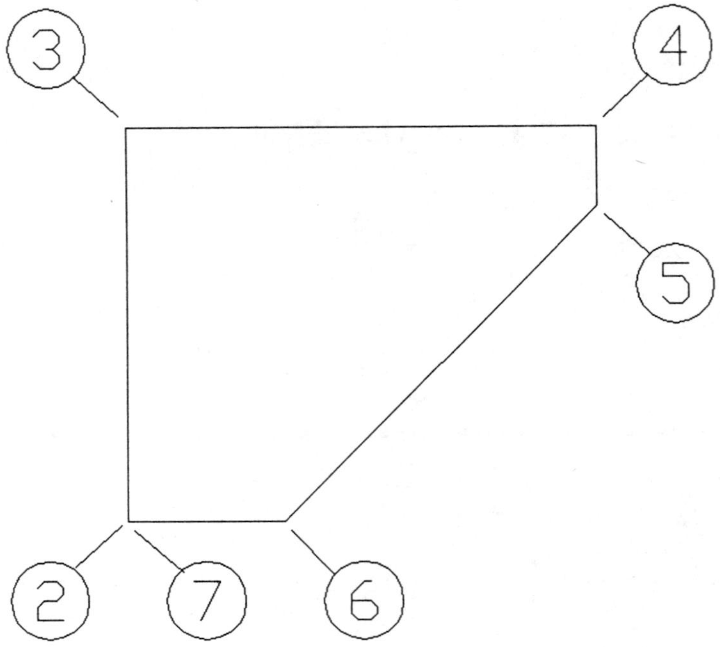

1. Set SNAP at 1 and let GRID follow the SNAP. Then type **LINE** at the command prompt and press **Return**.

```
Command: SNAP <CR>
Snap spacing or ON/OFF/Aspect/Rotate/Style <1.0000>: ON <CR>
Command: GRID <CR>
Grid spacing(X) or ON/OFF/Snap/Aspect <0.0000>: ON <CR>
Command: LINE <CR>
From point:
```

2. Type **1,1** and press **Return** to establish the lower-left corner of the figure.

```
Command: LINE <CR>
From point: 1,1 <CR>
To point:
```

AutoCAD assumes you want to continue drawing lines.

NOTE

If the screen cursor is moved to the desired location using the arrow keys on the keyboard, designate the point by pressing **Return**. If a mouse is used, the point is located by pressing the PICK button on the mouse.

3. Drag the screen cursor vertically five drawing units (to coordinates 1.0,6.0) and pick the point by pressing **Return**.

```
To point: (Pick 1,6)
```

4. Drag the screen cursor to the right six drawing units (to coordinates 7.0,6.0) and pick the point by pressing **Return**.

```
To point: (Pick 7,6)
```

5. Type @**1**<**270** and press **Return** to specify a line length of 1 and an angle of 270 degrees (which is straight down).

```
To point: @1<270
To point:
```

6. Select the next point by dragging the screen cursor (to coordinates 3.0,1.0) and pressing **Return**.

```
To point: (Pick 3,1)
```

7. Type **C** and press **Return** to close the figure. AutoCAD connects your current endpoint with the endpoint which started this LINE command.

```
To point: C <CR>
```

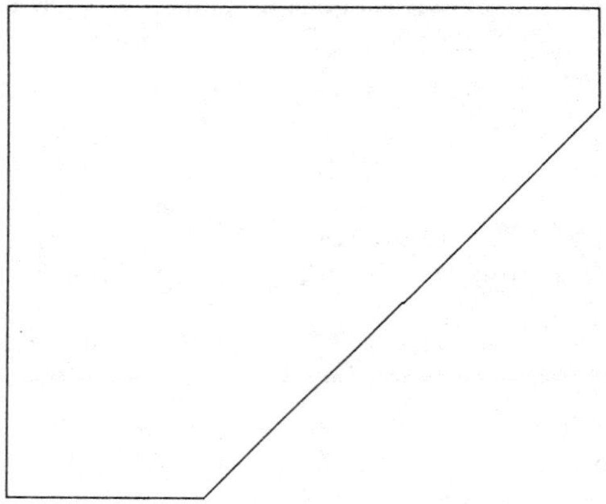

8. Type **QUIT** and press **Return**; then type **Y** and press **Return** to redisplay the Main Menu.
9. Turn to Module 87 to continue the learning sequence.

Module 46

LINETYPE

```
Command: LINETYPE
?/Load/Create: (select one)
```

DESCRIPTION

? Lists the line types loaded into the drawing.

Load Loads a line type into the drawing from a disk file.

Create Creates a new line type.

APPLICATIONS

USING PREDEFINED LINE TYPES Nine line types are provided with the AutoCAD software package. These line types are as follows:

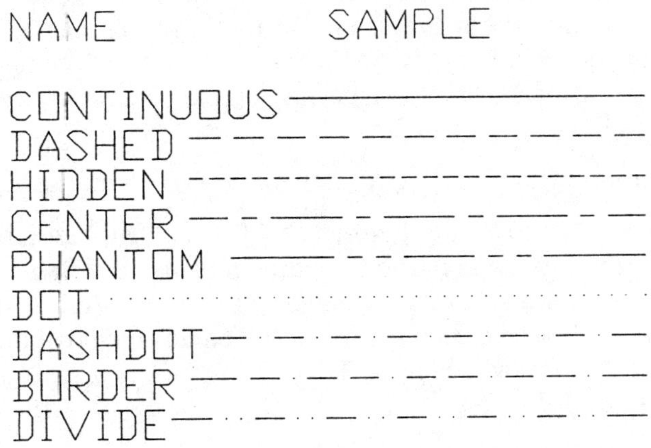

The LAYER command's LTYPE option automatically loads the desired line type from the above list. This group of line types is in a file named ACAD.LIN. If you only desire to use the line types supplied with AutoCAD, you may skip the remainder of this module. The LTYPE option in LAYER performs all the functions you require.

CREATING NEW LINE TYPES If you want to create additional line types, you must define them with the LINETYPE command.

The LINETYPE command is also capable of creating new line types. For most practical purposes, however, the LAYER command is all that is necessary to use different line types.

The LINETYPE command can be used to list existing line types, load existing line types from a disk file into the drawing, and create new line types. In normal operation, the LINETYPE command is seldom used. The LTYPE option of the LAYER command is used instead. The primary application of the LINETYPE command is the creation of new line type definitions.

The first step in the creation of a new line type is the specification of the line type name. Although it is possible to redefine one of the AutoCAD standard line types, this is inadvisable. A better strategy is the creation of a new line type with a new name.

The second step is to specify a disk file to save the line type definition. You have the option of adding the new line to an existing line type file, (including the file ACAD.LIN supplied with AutoCAD) or creating a new line type file.

NOTE

The line type files are stored on disk with the DOS file extension .LIN. However, when you specify the name of a line type file in AutoCAD, do not type the .LIN extension. Type only the file name, then press **Return.**

The third step in the process is creating the description of the line. The first entry on the line is the name assigned to the line type. This is the name you use when you load a line type with either the LINETYPE command or the LAYER command. The remainder of the line is the description that is placed on the screen when you list the available line types from within either LINETYPE or LAYER. This description may be up to 47 characters in length. Specifying a name is mandatory. Specifying a description is optional. If you choose not to specify a description, do not include the comma following the name.

The fourth step is the creation of descriptive text for the line type definition.

The fifth step is the creation of the actual pattern definition of the line type. There is no built-in relationship between the descriptive text and the pattern. You could, if confusion was your goal, create a pattern that had nothing to do with the descriptive text. AutoCAD would not generate any sort of error or warning. However, your system would be difficult to understand. The definition begins with the letter A, followed by a comma. This portion of the definition specifies alignment of the endpoints of the line of dashes.

The A and the comma are provided automatically by AutoCAD. Numeric values in the pattern definition specify the length of line segments in drawing units. The number 0 specifies a dot. Negative numbers mean to lift the pen before moving. Positive numbers mean to lower the pen onto the drawing surface before moving. Before using the newly defined line type, you must load it from the line type file into the drawing file. You can either use the LOAD option of the LINETYPE command, or the LTYPE option of the LAYER command to accomplish this task.

TYPICAL OPERATION

Create a new line type consisting of three dots, three dashes, and three dots. Call the new line type SOS.

1. Begin a drawing named LINETYPE.
2. Create a new line type named SOS in the file MYLINES.

```
Command: LINETYPE <CR>
?/Load/Create: C <CR>


Name of linetype to create: SOS <CR>

File for storage of linetype <ACAD>: MYLINES <CR>
Creating new file
Descriptive text: SOS,___ . . . ___ . . . <CR>
```

Even though the preceding text description of the line contains two complete sets of dots and dashes, the pattern need contain only one complete set of dots and dashes.

3. Enter the pattern definition for the SOS line type.

```
Enter pattern (on next line):
   A,0,-.1,0,-.1,0,-.1,.25,-.1,.25,-.1,.25,-.1 <CR>
New definition written to file.
?/Load/Create:
```

This definition specifies a pattern of three dots, designated by the number 0, and three dashes, designated by the number .25. Spacing between the dots and dashes is 0.1 drawing units.

4. Use the ? option to list the line types in MYLINES.

```
?/Load/Create: ? <CR>

File to list <MYLINES>: <CR>

Linetypes defined in file MYLINES.LIN:

      Name              Description
---------------- -------------------
SOS              SOS,_ _ _ . . . _ _ _ . . .

?/Load/Create:
```

5. Load the SOS line type into the drawing.

```
?/Load/Create: L <CR>

Name of linetype to load: SOS <CR>

File to search <MYLINES>: <CR>
Linetype SOS loaded.

?/Load/Create: <CR>

Command:
```

6. Use the LAYER command to specify the SOS line type for the layer 0 of the drawing.

```
Command: LAYER <CR>
?/Make/Set/New/ON/OFF/Color/Ltype/Freeze/Thaw: L <CR>

Linetype (or ?) <CONTINUOUS>: SOS <CR>

Layer name(s) for linetype SOS <0>: <CR>
?/Make/Set/New/ON/OFF/Color/Ltype/Freeze/Thaw: <CR>
Command:
```

7. Return to the graphics screen and draw a square in the new line type.

```
Command: LINE <CR>
From point: 1,1 <CR>
To point: 1,8 <CR>
To point: 10,8 <CR>
To point: 10,1 <CR>
To point: C <CR>
Command:
```

Your finished drawing displays the SOS line type.

8. **QUIT** the Drawing Editor and redisplay the Main Menu.
9. Turn to Module 16 to continue the learning sequence.

Module 47

LIST AND DBLIST

```
Command: LIST
Select objects or Window or Last:
```

DESCRIPTION

The LIST command allows you to view the exact AutoCAD description of one or more drawing entities. The DBLIST command lists the description of every element in the current drawing. The LIST command options are described in the following list.

Pick	Select an object with the screen cursor.
Window	Specify a window containing one or more objects. You can either type the coordinates of the upper-right and lower-left corners, or pick them on the screen with the screen cursor.
Last	Specifies the last-drawn object.

You are prompted repeatedly until you press **Return** for object selection.

Because DBLIST lists every entity in a drawing, no options are required.

APPLICATIONS

You can use LIST to check the dimensions and positions of objects on a drawing. You can also verify the accuracy of various parts. For a drawing of any size, the list of entities is lengthy. Selection of the LIST command is usually preferred for most applications, as it gives you more control relative to what you want to see.

With either command, you can use AutoCAD display controls to control the presentation of the information:

Ctrl-S Pauses the listing for your examination.

Ctrl-C Cancels the listing and returns to the Command prompt.

Ctrl-Q Toggles printer on and off to capture the listing on paper.

TYPICAL OPERATION

In this session you create an object from lines and arcs. You then examine a description of the entities in the drawing using the LIST command.

The following drawing contains numbered balloons that correspond to the steps in the session.

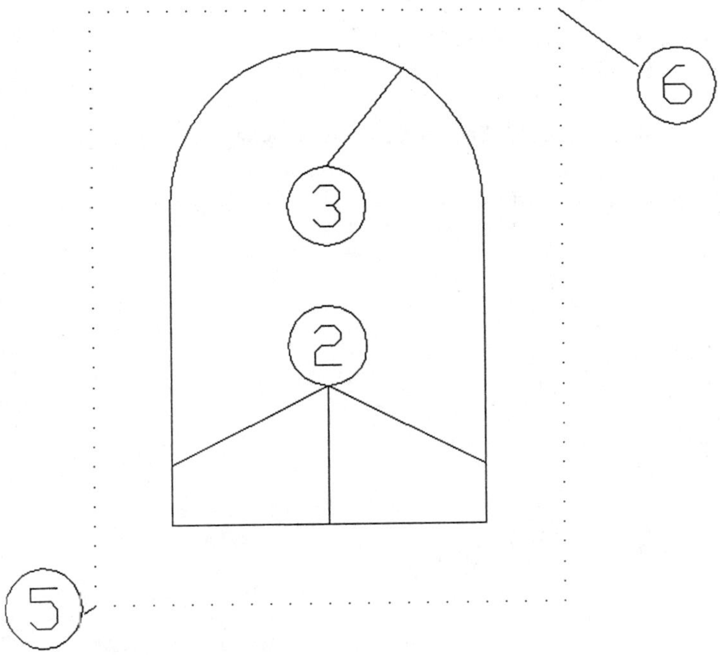

Begin a new drawing named LIST.

1. Set SNAP to .25, and turn GRID on.

```
Command: SNAP <CR>
Snap spacing or ON/OFF/Aspect/Rotate/Style <1.0000>: .25 <CR>

Command: GRID <CR>
Grid spacing(X) or ON/OFF/Snap/Aspect <0.0000>: ON <CR>
```

2. Draw the three lines.

```
Command: LINE <CR>
From point: 2,6 <CR>
To point: 2,2 <CR>
To point: 6,2 <CR>
To point: 6,6 <CR>
To point: <CR>
```

3. Draw the arc.

```
Command: ARC <CR>
Center/<Start point>: C <CR>
Center: 4,6 <CR>
Start point: 6,6 <CR>
Angle/Length of chord/<End point>: 2,6 <CR>
```

Your drawing should now resemble the following illustration.

4. Examine the description of the drawing entities.

```
Command: LIST <CR>

Select objects: W <CR>
```

5. Pick the lower-left corner of the window.

```
First point: .5,.5 <CR>
```

6. Pick the upper-right corner of the window; then press **Return** to display the list.

```
Second point: 7.5,8.75 <CR>
4 found.
Select objects: <CR>

                ARC         LAYER: 0
          center point, X=    4.0000   Y=    6.0000
          radius    2.0000
           start angle       0
             end angle     180

                LINE        LAYER: 0
            from point, X=    6.0000   Y=    2.0000
              to point, X=    6.0000   Y=    6.0000
                 Length  =    4.0000,  Angle =       90
                 Delta X =    0.0000,  Delta Y =     4.0000

                LINE        LAYER: 0
            from point, X=    2.0000   Y=    2.0000
              to point, X=    6.0000   Y=    2.0000
                 Length  =    4.0000,  Angle =        0
                 Delta X =    4.0000,  Delta Y =      0.0

                LINE        LAYER: 0
            from point, X=    2.0000   Y=    6.0000
              to point, X=    2.0000   Y=    2.0000
                 Length  =    4.0000,  Angle =      270
                 Delta X =    0.0000,  Delta Y =   -4.0000

Command:
```

You can examine the exact description of each drawing entity as defined by AutoCAD.

7. Use **QUIT** to redisplay the Main Menu.
8. Turn to Module 73 to continue the learning sequence.

Module 48

LTSCALE

```
Command: LTSCALE
New scale factor <default>:
```

DESCRIPTION

The LTSCALE command lets you adjust the scale of lines to fit the drawing size. The length of each line segment and open-space segment in the line type definition is increased or decreased proportionately. Dots in a line type definition have no width, and are plotted as the size of the pen installed in the plotter.

APPLICATIONS

When line types other than the *continuous* line type are used in a drawing, occasionally segments defining the line are too long or too short relative to the size of drawing being produced. Excessively long dashes in a line may give the impression of multiple lines, rather than a single, dashed line. Excessively short line segments in a line are sometimes indistinguishable from dots. Spacing between line segments are sometimes so small that the line looks continuous.

The LTSCALE command applies a scaling factor to all lines in a drawing. Its effect is not limited to only the current line type or the current layer, but affects all lines in all layers in the current drawing.

TYPICAL OPERATION

In this session you draw a 1-inch square box with a dashed line type. Then you use LTSCALE to improve the appearance of the dashed line. Begin a new drawing named LTSCALE.

1. Set the drawing limits to 1,1.5. Set SNAP to .1, turn GRID on, and ZOOM all.

```
Command: LIMITS <CR>
ON/OFF/<Lower left corner> <0.0000,0.0000>: <CR>
Upper right corner <12.0000,9.0000>: 1.5,1 <CR>
Command: SNAP <CR>
Snap spacing or ON/OFF/Aspect/Rotate/Style <1.0000>: .1 <CR>

Command: GRID <CR>
Grid spacing(X) or ON/OFF/Snap/Aspect <0.0000>: ON <CR>

Command: ZOOM <CR>
All/Center/Dynamic/Extents/Left/Previous/Window/<Scale(X)>: A <CR>
```

2. Set the current line type to DASHED.

```
Command: LAYER <CR>
?/Make/Set/New/ON/OFF/Color/Ltype/Freeze/Thaw: LTYPE <CR>
Linetype (or ?) <CONTINUOUS>: DASHED <CR>
Layer name(s) for linetype DASHED <0>: <CR>
?/Make/Set/New/ON/OFF/Color/Ltype/Freeze/Thaw: <CR>
```

3. Draw a square with 1-inch sides.

```
Command: LINE <CR>
From point: 0,0 <CR>
To point: 0,1 <CR>
To point: 1,1 <CR>
To point: 1,0 <CR>
To point: C <CR>
```

4. Use LTSCALE to modify the relative length of the dashes forming each line.

```
Command: LTSCALE <CR>
New scale factor <1.0000> .05 <CR>
```

Compare your drawing to the following illustration.

5. Type **QUIT** and press **Return**; then type **Y** and press **Return** to redisplay the Main Menu.
6. Turn to Module 78 to continue the learning sequence.

Module 49

MEASURE

```
Command: MEASURE
Select object to measure:
```

DESCRIPTION

The MEASURE command, introduced in AutoCAD 2.5, places markers along a line, arc, circle, or polyline at specific intervals. The markers may either be points, the default, or a block that you specify. To place blocks along a figure, first define the block and then use the MEASURE command to place them. The block must already be defined in the current drawing. Selection of the object to measure must be by "point" selection. You may type the coordinates of a point on the object, or you may pick the object with the screen cursor with or without OSNAP. You may *not* use other methods, such as a window, to pick objects for MEASURE.

APPLICATIONS

The MEASURE command is similar to the DIVIDE command. With MEASURE, you specify the length of each segment, and AutoCAD determines the number of segments to create. With DIVIDE, you specify the number of segments, and AutoCAD determines the length of each segment. MEASURE is useful any time a regularly spaced interval is needed. Using a block defined as the cross section of a stud, you can place studs on 16" centers in walls for framing. The perimeter of a piece of property can be measured with post-shaped blocks for speed in drawing a fence. Points, even when drawn in a contrasting color, tend to be invisible when shown on the screen. Modifying the variables PDMODE and PDSIZE with SETVAR allows you to see the position of points when using the MEASURE command.

TYPICAL OPERATION

In this session, you use the MEASURE command to construct an Archimedes spiral. A spiral is a curve that is generated by a point moving away from or toward a fixed point at a constant rate while the radius vector from the fixed point rotates at a constant rate. In spite of this esoteric definition, the spiral is a simple construction, useful in the design of many screws and drills. Begin a new drawing named MEASURE.

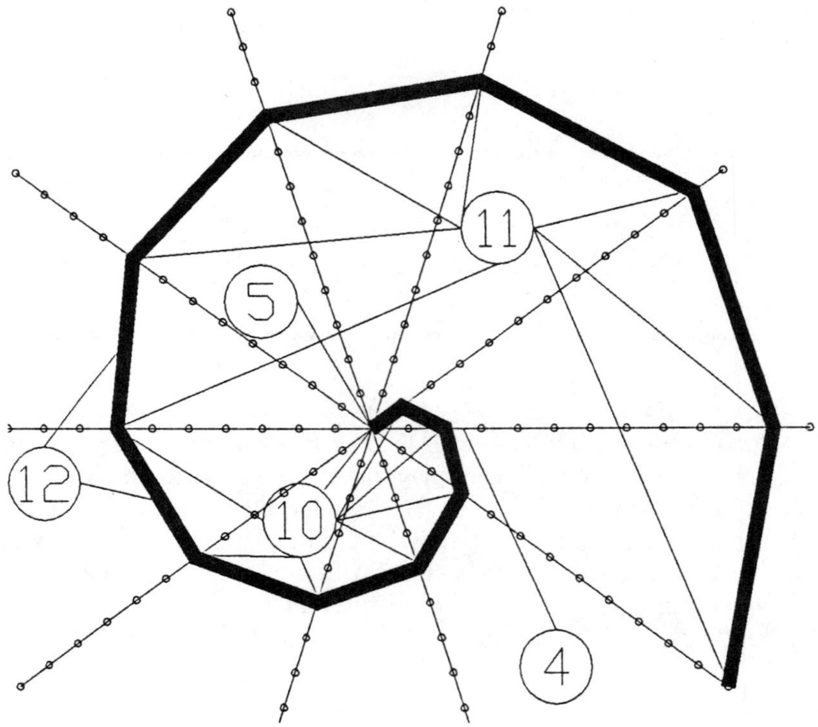

1. Set the SNAP to .25. Let the GRID follow the SNAP.

```
Command: SNAP <CR>
Snap spacing or ON/OFF/Aspect/Rotate/Style <1.0000>: .25 <CR>
Command: GRID <CR>
Grid spacing(X) or ON/OFF/Snap/Aspect <0.0000>: <CR>
Command:
```

2. Use SETVAR to change PDMODE and PDSIZE to make it possible to see the points on the screen.

```
Command: SETVAR <CR>
Variable name or ?: PDMODE <CR>
New value for PDMODE <0>: 32 <CR>
Command: SETVAR <CR>
Variable name or ?: PDSIZE <CR>
New value for PDSIZE <0.0000>: -2 <CR>
Command:
```

3. Create a CONSTRUCTION layer to contain the lines and points used in the construction of the spiral and set it as the current layer.

```
Command: LAYER <CR>
?/Make/Set/New/ON/OFF/Color/Ltype/Freeze/Thaw: N <CR>
New layer name(s): CONSTRUCTION <CR>
?/Make/Set/New/ON/OFF/Color/Ltype/Freeze/Thaw: S <CR>
New current layer <0>: CONSTRUCTION <CR>
?/Make/Set/New/ON/OFF/Color/Ltype/Freeze/Thaw: C <CR>
Color: RED <CR>
Layer name(s) for color 1 (red) <CONSTRUCTION>: <CR>
?/Make/Set/New/ON/OFF/Color/Ltype/Freeze/Thaw: <CR>
Command:
```

4. Draw a horizontal line.

```
Command: LINE <CR>
From point:  5,4 <CR>
To point:  11,4 <CR>
To point: <CR>
```

5. Use the MEASURE command to mark off .5 unit segments.

```
Command: MEASURE <CR>
Select object to measure: (Pick the left end of the line.)
&lt;Segment length&gt;/Block: 0.5 <CR>
```

6. Use the ARRAY command to create a polar array of the line and points.

```
Command: ARRAY <CR>
Select objects: W <CR>
First corner: 4,3 <CR>
Other corner: 12,5 <CR>
19 found.
Select objects: <CR>
Rectangular or Polar array (R/P): P <CR>
Center point of array: 5,4 <CR>
Number of items: 10 <CR>
Angle to fill (+=ccw, -=cw) <360>: <CR>
Rotate objects as they are copied? <Y> <CR>
```

7. Use the LAYER command to return to layer 0.

```
Command: LAYER <CR>
?/Make/Set/New/ON/OFF/Color/Ltype/Freeze/Thaw: S <CR>
New current layer <CONSTRUCTION>: 0 <CR>
?/Make/Set/New/ON/OFF/Color/Ltype/Freeze/Thaw: <CR>
Command:
```

8. Set the OSNAP mode to NODE to pick points.

```
Command: OSNAP <CR>
Object snap modes: INT,NOD <CR>
Command:
```

9. Zoom the center of the drawing.

```
Command: ZOOM <CR>
All/Center/Dynamic/Extents/Left/Previous/Window/<Scale(X)>: W <CR>
First corner: 1,1 <CR>
Other corner: 6.25,5 <CR>
Command:
```

10. Draw a polyline starting at the center and moving outward one point on each radial.

```
Command: PLINE <CR>
From point: (Pick the center of the radial lines.)
Current line-width is 0.0000
Arc/Close/Halfwidth/Length/Undo/Width/<Endpoint of line>: W <CR>
Starting width <0.2000>: 0.2 <CR>
Ending width <0.2000>: <CR>
Arc/Close/Halfwidth/Length/Undo/Width/<Endpoint of line>: (Pick)
Arc/Close/Halfwidth/Length/Undo/Width/<Endpoint of line>: (Pick)
Arc/Close/Halfwidth/Length/Undo/Width/<Endpoint of line>: (Pick)
Arc/Close/Halfwidth/Length/Undo/Width/<Endpoint of line>: (Pick)
Arc/Close/Halfwidth/Length/Undo/Width/<Endpoint of line>: (Pick)
Arc/Close/Halfwidth/Length/Undo/Width/<Endpoint of line>: (Pick)
Arc/Close/Halfwidth/Length/Undo/Width/<Endpoint of line>: (Pick)
Arc/Close/Halfwidth/Length/Undo/Width/<Endpoint of line>: <CR>
Command:
```

11. Zoom to the previous view; then continue picking until you run out of points.

```
Close/Join/Width/Edit vertex/Fit curve/Decurve/Undo/eXit <X>: F <CR>
Close/Join/Width/Edit vertex/Fit curve/Decurve/Undo/eXit <X>: X <CR>
```

12. Join the two polylines into one.

```
Command: LAYER <CR>
?/Make/Set/New/ON/OFF/Color/Ltype/Freeze/Thaw: F <CR>
Layer name(s) to Freeze: CONSTRUCTION <CR>
?/Make/Set/New/ON/OFF/Color/Ltype/Freeze/Thaw: <CR>
Command:
```

13. Smooth the segmented polyline into a curve.

```
Command: PLINE <CR>
From point: (Pick the endpoint of the first segment.)
Current line-width is 0.2000
Arc/Close/Halfwidth/Length/Undo/Width/<Endpoint of line>: (Pick)
```

```
Arc/Close/Halfwidth/Length/Undo/Width/<Endpoint of line>: (Pick)
Arc/Close/Halfwidth/Length/Undo/Width/<Endpoint of line>: (Pick)
Arc/Close/Halfwidth/Length/Undo/Width/<Endpoint of line>: (Pick)
Arc/Close/Halfwidth/Length/Undo/Width/<Endpoint of line>: (Pick)
Arc/Close/Halfwidth/Length/Undo/Width/<Endpoint of line>: (Pick)
Arc/Close/Halfwidth/Length/Undo/Width/<Endpoint of line>: <CR>
Command:
```

14. Freeze the construction layer.

```
Command: PEDIT <CR>
Select polyline: (Pick the polyline)
Close/Join/Width/Edit vertex/Fit curve/Decurve/Undo/eXit <X>: J <CR>
Select objects: (Pick the first segment) 1 selected, 1 found.
Select objects: (Pick the second segment) 1 selected, 1 found.
Select objects: <CR>
6 segments added to polyline
Close/Join/Width/Edit vertex/Fit curve/Decurve/Undo/eXit <X>:
```

Your drawing should resemble the following illustration.

15. Type **Q** and press **Return**; then type **Y** and press **Return** to return to the AutoCAD Main Menu.
16. Turn to Module 22 to continue the learning sequence.

Module 50

MENU

```
Command: MENU
File name:
```

DESCRIPTION

AutoCAD displays a series of standard drawing screen menus, which are normally adequate for most users. However, AutoCAD gives you the ability to modify the information within drawing screen menus. This module describes this process.

SPECIFYING A MENU FILE When AutoCAD begins a drawing, it looks for a file with the same name as the drawing, but with the extension .MNU. If no such file exists, it loads the supplied menu file ACAD.MNU.

When you type the name of an AutoCAD menu file, do not type the .MNU extension; use only the first portion of the file name. If you press **Return** in response to the "File name:" prompt, the menus are disabled.

The screen menu is normally displayed along the right edge of the Drawing Editor screen, the button menu corresponds to the buttons on a multi-button mouse, and the tablet menu corresponds to defined areas on an optional digitizing tablet. You may have a maximum of four rectangular areas defined as menu areas on your tablet.

CUSTOMIZING A MENU FILE An AutoCAD menu file is an ASCII text file containing text and special symbols. The menu file uses a number of special symbols to define certain menu items.

***	Used to start the name of a major section of a menu file.
**	Used to start the name of a subsection of a screen menu.
[ ]	The AutoCAD menu area provides for eight characters of menu display. Menu items cannot be more than 8 characters in length and are enclosed in square brackets.

$S = Causes AutoCAD to proceed to a new screen submenu. When used in the form $S = *XX*, it causes AutoCAD to proceed immediately to the submenu labeled ***XX*. When followed by spaces, ($S =   ), it causes AutoCAD to return to the previous menu. This technique is used to implement the LASTMENU feature of AutoCAD screen menus.

\ When used in conjunction with a screen menu, causes AutoCAD to pause to accept user input. When used in conjunction with the button menu, it causes AutoCAD to use the present location of the screen cursor as an input value.

; Equivalent to pressing **Return** on the keyboard.

+ The maximum length of lines in an AutoCAD menu line is 80 characters. If this is not sufficient to perform the operation, terminate the line with a plus sign, then continue on the next line.

^ When used in conjunction with another letter, the caret transmits control characters to AutoCAD. For example, character sequence ^C in an AutoCAD menu file performs the cancel function, identically to pressing **Ctrl-C** on the keyboard.

^C^C Automatic menu choice repetition, introduced in Release 9, is accomplished by beginning the menu item with the code sequence "^C^C," followed immediately (with no intervening space) by the command. For example, a menu entry for COPY could be implemented "[Copy   ]*^C^CCOPY Single Auto," specifying that the COPY command repeats indefinitely in single object automatic selection mode.

The original file ACAD.MNU is organized into three sections, ***BUTTONS, ***SCREEN, and ***TABLET1. The AutoCAD menu system can handle up to a maximum of seven menu sections. You can add sections labeled ***TABLET2 and ***TABLET3 if you want to provide more than one menu area on your digitizing tablet. You can add a section ***AUX1 to refer to an auxillary input device, such as a function key box, or a touch screen.

As a first step in creating or customizing an AutoCAD menu, print a copy of the file ACAD.MNU on your printer. This file is a standard ASCII text file, and can be printed from DOS by typing **TYPE ACAD.MNU > LPT1:** and pressing **Return**. The file is over 20 pages in length. It is far easier to start with a supplied file and perform modifications than to start from scratch. In addition to the file ACAD.MNU, AutoCAD provides menu files to accompany some of the sample drawings on the distribution diskettes. You can determine the names of other menu files by typing **DIR *.MNU** and pressing **Return** from the DOS prompt. Printing these additional files can provide other techniques for creating customized menus.

To create customized menus you need a word processor or text editor capable of editing ASCII text files.

CAUTION

Some word processors insert control characters in the text for use as formatting codes, or use nonstandard file formats. Check the documentation of your word processor to make certain it can read, modify, and write ASCII files.

Some word processors have options for working with ASCII files. For example, if you use the WordStar™ program, start the editing with the N command for "Open a non-document file."

If you have extremely limited resources, you can use the EDLIN program which is supplied as part of MS-DOS and PC-DOS to modify and create menu files.

Understanding the supplied menus provides the basis for making modifications and creating new menus. Using a word processor to inspect the file ACAD.MNU, you see the ***BUTTON section at the top of the file. Immediately following is the beginning of the text for the screen menu system.

```
***SCREEN
**S
[ R O O T]
[ M E N U]

[BLOCKS]$S=BL
[DIM:]$S=DIM ^CDIM
[DISPLAY]$S=DS
[DRAW]$S=DR
[EDIT]$S=ED
[HATCH:]^CHATCH $S=HATCH
[INQUIRY]$S=INQ
[LAYERS]$S=LY
[MODES]$S=MD
[PLOT]$S=PLOT
[UTILITY]$S=UT




**0
```

Notice the space between the line [UTILITY]$S = UT and the last line, **O. You can add additional items to the AutoCAD Root Menu in this space. Most of the commands on the Root Menu perform the single function of jumping to a submenu with the $S = code. Notice that both the [DIM] and [HATCH] entries also cancel the current operation with the ^ C function, and issue the DIM and HATCH commands respectively before branching to a submenu.

For example, follow through the sequence of events necessary to issue the OSNAP command with the Endpoint options. OSNAP is located on the MODES submenu. When you pick OSNAP from the screen menu, the code $S = MD causes AutoCAD to display the menu labeled **MD. Using a word processor to search through the menu file, you find the following.

```
**MD
[AXIS:]^CAXIS $S=AXIS
[BLIPS:]^CBLIPMODE $S=BLIPMODE
[COORDS:]^D
[DRAGMOD:]^CDRAGMODE $S=DRAGMODE
[ELEV:]^CELEV \\$S=
[GRID:]^CGRID $S=GRID
[ISOPLAN:]^CISOPLANE $S=ISOPLANE
[ORTHO:]^CORTHO $S=ORTHO
[OSNAP:]^COSNAP $S=OSNAP
[SNAP:]^CSNAP $S=SNAP
[TABLET:]^CTABLET $S=TABLET


[DISPLAY]$S=DS
[DRAW]$S=DR
[EDIT]$S=ED
[LAYERS]$S=LY

[LASTMENU]$S=
[ROOTMENU]$S=S
**AXIS 1
[AXIS:]^CAXIS
[on]ON $S=
```

Here, between **MD and **AXIS 1 you see the Mode submenu. Notice the empty space that is available in the menu area. You can add frequently used modes if you want in these locations. If you have no use for some options, like the table options, you can replace that line in the menu with spaces to enhance the readability of your customized AutoCAD menu. Placing the screen cursor on the OSNAP command activates the command string " ^ COSNAP $S = OSNAP." The ^ C cancels any operation in progress. The string "OSNAP " issues the OSNAP command. The characters $S = OSNAP cause AutoCAD to jump to the menu section labeled **OSNAP.

```
**OSNAP 1
[OSNAP:]^COSNAP
[center]CENTER\
[endpoint]ENDPOINT\
[insert]INSERT\
[intersec]INTERSEC\
[midpoint]MIDPOINT\
```

```
[nearest]NEAREST\
[node]NODE\
[perpend]PERPEND\
[quadrant]QUADRANT\
[tangent]TANGENT\

none

[,],\

[HELP:]^C? OSNAP
[CANCEL:]^C
**SNAP 1
[SNAP:]^CSNAP
[on]ON $S=
[off]OFF $S=
```

The heading of this submenu **OSNAP 1 illustrates an additional feature of the AutoCAD screen menu system. In this particular example, the 1, which is optional, specifies the beginning menu line for the new menu. The default is 1, so the 1 in this example simply confirms the default value. However, it is possible to use this technique to replace only a portion of a screen menu by using a number other than 1.

Picking [endpoint] on this menu sends the characters ENDPOINT to AutoCAD. The backslash allows additional input. The input can come either by typing it at the keyboard, or by picking another OSNAP option from this menu. If ENDPOINT is the only desired option, pressing Return on the keyboard terminates the command.

APPLICATIONS

Menus are provided to make the most commonly used AutoCAD functions readily accessible. The AutoCAD Menu capability lets you change or replace any portion of the screen, button, or tablet menu system.

If you decide to make your own AutoCAD menu, beware! Every line, space, and symbol in an AutoCAD menu is significant. The best way to proceed is to start with a copy of the supplied ACAD.MNU file. For your own protection, never modify the original file ACAD.MNU. Always make a copy of the file before attempting change.

TYPICAL OPERATION

NOTE

This Typical Operation requires that your machine be equipped with a multi-button mouse or digitizer. The second Typical Operation requires a digitizer, which can be any mouse or digitizer.

MODIFY THE BUTTON MENU Add a function to the AutoCAD button menu to draw a circle 0.1-inches in diameter at the current screen cursor location any time the second button is pressed.

The first step is to analyze the sequence of commands and prompts necessary to create the desired circle. It is easiest to start with the steps necessary to enter the command from the keyboard.

```
Command: CIRCLE <CR>
3P/2P/<Center point>: (Pick a point) Diameter/<Radius>: 1 <CR>
Command:
```

The steps are:

- Type **CIRCLE** and press **Return**.
- Pick a point.
- Type **1** and press **Return**.

The AutoCAD menu command to perform this sequence of operations is CIRCLE;\1;.

1. Use DOS or the AutoCAD file utilities to copy the file ACAD.MNU to MENU.MNU.
2. Use EDLIN or your personal word processor in non-document or ASCII file mode to edit the file MENU.MNU.
3. Replace the second line of the button menu with the statement **CIRCLE;\1;** as shown.

```
***BUTTONS
CIRCLE;\1;
^CREDRAW
^C
^B
^O
^G
^D
^E
^T
***SCREEN
**S
[ R O O T]
[ M E N U]

[BLOCKS]$S=BL
[DIM:]$S=DIM ^CDIM
[DISPLAY]$S=DS
[DRAW]$S=DR
[EDIT]$S=ED
[HATCH:]^CHATCH $S=HATCH
```

```
[INQUIRY]$S=INQ
[LAYERS]$S=LY
[MODES]$S=MD
```

4. Save the file and exit your text editor or word processor.
5. Start AutoCAD. Begin a new drawing named MENU.

NOTE

Because you created a menu file named MENU.MNU, AutoCAD loads your newly created menu instead of the default ACAD.MNU.

6. Move the screen cursor with the digitizer. Press the second button and observe the circles on the screen.
7. Use the QUIT command to redisplay the Main Menu.

MODIFY THE SCREEN MENU Now change the AutoCAD Root Menu to include an item named BALLOON, which draws 1-inch diameter circles. One possible definition is [BALLOON] ^ CCIRCLE; \ 1;. This sequence uses the characters ^ C to cancel any unfinished command, issues the CIRCLE command and a **Return**, waits for user input (which can come either from the screen cursor, or by typing the coordinates at the keyboard), providing the number 1 as the diameter, and pressing **Return**.

1. Use your word processor or editor to modify MENU.MNU as shown.

```
***SCREEN
**S
[ROOT]
[MENU]

[BLOCKS]$S=BL
[DIM:]$S=DIM ^CDIM
[DISPLAY]$S=DS
[DRAW]$S=DR
[EDIT]$S=ED
[HATCH:]^CHATCH $S=HATCH
[INQUIRY]$S=INQ
[LAYERS]$S=LY
[MODES]$S=MD
[PLOT}$S=PLOT
[UTILITY]$S=UT

[BALLOON]^CCIRCLE;\1;


**0
```

2. Save the file and exit your word processor or text editor.
3. Start AutoCAD and edit the drawing named MENU.
4. Pick BALLOON from the screen menu.
5. Pick a spot on the screen for the circle.
6. Pick BALLOON from the screen menu.
7. Type the coordinates **5,5** and press **Return**.
8. Use **QUIT** to redisplay the Main Menu.
9. Use the AutoCAD file utilities to erase the file MENU.MNU.
10. Quit the AutoCAD file utilities, redisplaying the AutoCAD Main Menu.
11. Turn to Module 18 to continue the learning sequence.

Module 51

MINSERT

```
Command: MINSERT
Block name (or ?):
```

DESCRIPTION

The MINSERT command was introduced in AutoCAD version 2.5. You use MINSERT to perform multiple insertions of a block in a rectangular array. The MINSERT command combines the features of the INSERT and ARRAY commands. When MINSERT is entered at the Command prompt, a series of prompts are displayed.

```
Command: MINSERT
Block name (or ?):
 Insertion point:
 X scale factor <1> / Corner / XYZ:
 Y scale factor (default=X):
 Z scale factor (default=X):    (This is an optional prompt)
 Rotation angle <0>:
Number of rows (---) <1>:
Number of columns (|||) <1>:
Unit cell or distance between rows (---):
Distance between columns (|||):
```

Each MINSERT prompt is described in the following list.

Block name	The first prompt asks for the name of the block you wish to multiple insert.

Insertion point

You may pick the point or enter the coordinates from the keyboard.

X scale factor

The default value is 1. If you press **Return**, the block is inserted using the original X value. If you provide a new X value, AutoCAD multiplies the X scale dimension of your block by the number. You may "show" AutoCAD the dimension by typing the or picking the coordinates of two corners. You may type **DRAG** to drag the X, Y, Z scale factors. Type **XYZ** to tell AutoCAD that you want to specify a Z scale factor. Entering a negative scale factor produces a mirror image of the block.

Y scale factor

The Y scale factor operates in a fashion similar to the X scale factor, but along the Y axis.

Z scale factor

The Z scale factor operates in a fashion similar to the X scale factor, but along the Z, or three dimensional axis. You are not prompted for a Z scale unless you type **XYZ** in response to the X scale factor prompt.

Rotation Angle

The rotation angle rotates the entire array of insertions. The insertion point is used as the basis of all rotations.

Number of rows (- - -) <1>:

Rows are defined across the drawing page.

Number of columns (¦ ¦ ¦) <1>:

Columns are defined down the drawing page.

Unit cell or distance between rows (- - -):

You may type the distance, or you may show AutoCAD the distance by picking points on the screen.

Distance between columns (¦ ¦ ¦):

This prompt appears when the number of columns is greater than one, and you did not specify the size of a unit cell. You may type the distance, or you may show AutoCAD the distance by picking points on the screen.

APPLICATIONS

Apply the MINSERT command any time you need to make multiple insertions of a block into a rectangular array. The MINSERT command is faster and easier to use than having to use the INSERT and ARRAY commands in combination.

Some typical electrical design applications of the MINSERT command include the placement of components, such as gates, on semiconductor circuits and the placement of solder pads and sockets on printed circuit boards.

The placement of seats in an auditorium or stadium is an ideal application for MINSERT. Designing orchard or forestry plantings requires both the insertion of blocks and the creation of rectangular arrays. This combination is an ideal application for MINSERT. You can also use MINSERT to place glass panes on a facade or French door.

The MINSERT command is not limited to creating two-dimensional arrays. One-dimensional arrays are also easy. For example, a row of columns in front of a building is an ideal application for the MINSERT command.

TYPICAL OPERATION

In this operation you create a bubble pattern to be used in an optical scanner. Many data entry operations are handled through the use of opscan forms, and the creation of custom-designed forms is a straightforward operation for AutoCAD. From the AutoCAD Main Menu, begin a new drawing named MINSERT. Then follow the procedure to create a single "bubble" as shown in the following drawing.

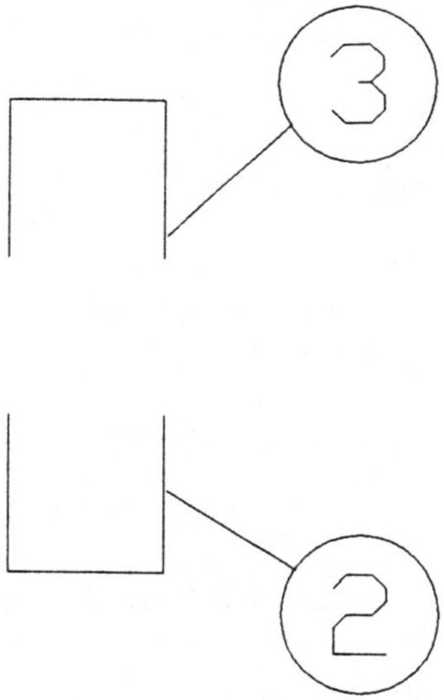

1. ZOOM to a small area of the screen for the construction of a single bubble. Set the SNAP to 0.05 and let the GRID follow the SNAP.

```
Command: ZOOM <CR>
All/Center/Dynamic/Extents/Left/Previous/Window/<Scale(X)>: W <CR>
First corner: .9,.9 <CR>
Other corner: 1.5,1.5 <CR>
Command: SNAP <CR>
Snap spacing or ON/OFF/Aspect/Rotate/Style <1.0000>: .05 <CR>
Command: GRID
Grid spacing(X) or ON/OFF/Snap/Aspect <0.0000>: S <CR>
```

2. Draw half of a bubble.

```
Command: LINE <CR>
From point: 1,1.1 <CR>
To point:  1,1 <CR>
To point: 1.1,1 <CR>
To point: 1.1,1.1 <CR>
To point: <CR>
```

3. Use the MIRROR command to create the other half of the bubble.

```
Command: MIRROR <CR>
Select objects: W <CR>
First corner: 0,0 <CR>
Other corner: 2,2 <CR>
3 found.
Select objects: <CR>
First point of mirror line: 1,1.15 <CR>
 Second point: 1.1,1.15 <CR>
Delete old objects? <N> <CR>
```

4. Define the bubble as a block.

```
Command: BLOCK  <CR>
Block name (or ?): BUBBLE <CR>
Insertion base point: 1.05,1.15 <CR>
Select objects: W <CR>
First corner: 1,1 <CR>
Other corner: 2,2 <CR>
6 found.
Select objects: <CR>
```

5. Turn off the GRID and ZOOM to a full-page view.

```
Command: GRID <CR>
Grid spacing(X) or ON/OFF/Snap/Aspect <0.0000>: OFF <CR>
Command: ZOOM <CR>
All/Center/Dynamic/Extents/Left/Previous/Window/<Scale(X)>: A <CR>
Regenerating drawing.
```

6. Use the MINSERT command to create a rectangular array of bubbles on the page.

```
Command: MINSERT <CR>
Block name (or ?): BUBBLE <CR>
 Insertion point: 1,1 <CR>
 X scale factor <1> / Corner / XYZ: <CR>
 Y scale factor (default=X): <CR>
 Rotation angle <0>: <CR>
Number of rows (---) <1>: 10 <CR>
Number of columns (|||) <1>: 50 <CR>
Unit cell or distance between rows (---): 0.5 <CR>
Distance between columns (|||): 0.18 <CR>
```

Your completed drawing should resemble the following illustration.

7. Type **QUIT** and press **Return**; then type **Y** and press **Return** to display the AutoCAD Main Menu.
8. Turn to Module 30 to continue the learning sequence.

Module 52

MIRROR

```
Command: MIRROR
Select objects or Window or Last: W
```

DESCRIPTION

After you have drawn an object, you can reproduce a mirror image. The MIRROR command flips the object over a vertical or horizontal axis. When mirroring an object, you can either retain the original object or erase it at the time of mirroring. To use the MIRROR command, type **MIRROR** and press **Return** from the command prompt. AutoCAD responds with the following series of prompts.

```
Command: MIRROR
Select objects: W <CR>
First point: (Pick)
Second point: (Pick)
3 found.
Select objects: <CR>
First point of mirror line: (Pick)
Second point: (Pick)
Delete old objects? <N> <CR>
```

When you pick the mirror line, it becomes the mirror axis. In AutoCAD versions prior to 2.5, the mirror line must be either horizontal or vertical. In versions 2.5 and later, the mirror line may be placed at any angle. With version 2.5 and later, you can drag the second point of the mirror line. Dragging allows you to visualize tentative positions of the mirrored object before final placement. When you mirror text, use the SETVAR command to assign the system variable MIRRTEXT a value of 0. This produces readable mirrored text. The default value for MIRRTEXT is 1, which reverses the text when the MIRROR command is used.

APPLICATIONS

The MIRROR command has many applications for increasing your productivity. Any time a drawing needs to have objects repeated around a horizontal or vertical line, the MIRROR command is available to reproduce the object. The figure that is mirrored can be any group of drawing entities.

TYPICAL OPERATION

In this session you use the LINE, ARC, and MIRROR commands to produce the object shown in the following drawing.

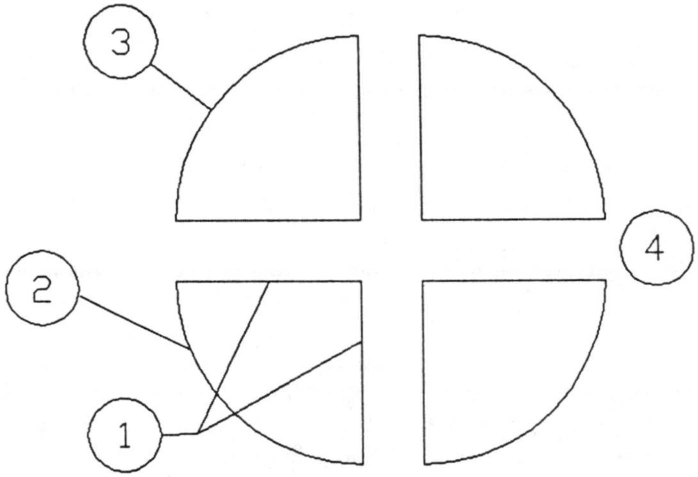

1. Begin a new drawing named MIRROR. Set SNAP to .25 and turn GRID on. Draw two perpendicular lines.

NOTE

You may either pick the points with the screen cursor or type them at the keyboard. If your screen coordinates display in terms of angle and displacement instead of showing the absolute coordinate position, press the <coords> function key to change the display format.

```
Command: LINE <CR>
From point: 4.00,4.25 <CR>
To point: 5.50,4.25 <CR>
To point: 5.50,2.75 <CR>
To point: <CR>
```

2. Draw an arc with its center located at the vertex of the two straight lines:

```
Command: ARC <CR>
Center/<Start point>: C <CR>
Center: 5.50,4.25 <CR>
Start point: 4.00,4.25 <CR>
Angle/Length of chord/<End point>: 5.50,2.75 <CR>
```

3. Reproduce the object with the MIRROR command:

```
Command: MIRROR <CR>
Select objects: W <CR>
First point: 3.75,2.50  <CR>
Second point: 5.75,4.50 <CR>
3 found.
Select objects: <CR>
First point of mirror line: 2.75,4.50  <CR>
Second point: @ 3.50<0 <CR>
Delete old objects? <N> <CR>
```

4. Reproduce the two objects with the MIRROR command:

```
Command: MIRROR <CR>
Select objects: W <CR>
(Create a window around the two pie slices)
First point: (Pick lower left corner of window)
Second point: (Pick upper right corner of window)
6 found.
Select objects: <CR>
First point of mirror line: 5.75,2.50 (Pick)
Second point: @4.75<90 <CR>
Delete old objects? <N> <CR>
```

Your drawing now resembles the one in the illustration.

5. Use **QUIT** to redisplay the Main Menu.
6. Turn to Module 55 to continue the learning sequence.

Module 53

MOVE

```
Command: MOVE
Select objects:
Base point or displacement:
Second point of displacement:
```

DESCRIPTION

The MOVE command is used to reposition one or more objects on a drawing. Begin by verifying that you are at the command prompt. Then type **MOVE** and press **Return** or pick MOVE from the Edit submenu. The MOVE command has three options: Pick, Window, and Last. These are described in the following list.

Pick — Select an object with the screen cursor.

Window — Type **W** and press **Return** (or pick "window" on the screen menu) to specify copying all objects in a window. You are then prompted:

First point:
Second point:

You may either type the coordinates on the keyboard or pick them with the screen cursor.

Last — Selects the most recently used object for the move operation.

You can select more than one object in a single copy operation. You can also mix the Last, Pick, and Window options. To terminate the object selection process, press **Return**.

AutoCAD version 2.6 introduced the SELECT command for identifying a selection set. You may use SELECT to identify the selection set for use with the MOVE command, or you may use any of the object selection techniques more fully described in the SELECT module.

After selecting the object(s), AutoCAD confirms the selection with a message.

```
nn found.
Base point or displacement:
```

You must either select a reference point for your object or specify a displacement in terms of a distance and an angle. You can either type the information on the keyboard or you can pick a point on the screen. The point you pick does not have to be part of the object, but it can be.

AutoCAD 2.6 provides the MOVE command with the ability to accept a Z-coordiante for either the base point or the displacement of an object. For example, specifying a base point of 0,0,0 and a displacement of 0,0,6 moves an object vertically (along the Z-axis) 6 drawing units.

If you choose to type the point, the following prompt appears:

```
Second point of displacement:
```

You may either type the position where the base point of the copy appears or drag the object there with the screen cursor.

APPLICATIONS

MOVE is used to relocate a single entity or group of entities on a drawing. The COPY and the MOVE commands are similar. The major difference between the two commands is that the MOVE command repositions one or more selected objects from one place to another, while the COPY command duplicates one or more selected objects.

TYPICAL OPERATION

This operation moves the elements of the tank drawing made in the COPY Module. Starting at the Main Menu, edit the TANK drawing by typing **2**, pressing **Return**, and then typing **TANK** and pressing **Return** again. If you didn't save the TANK drawing, refer to Module 14 for drawing instructions. The numbered balloons in the following illustration correspond to the steps in the session.

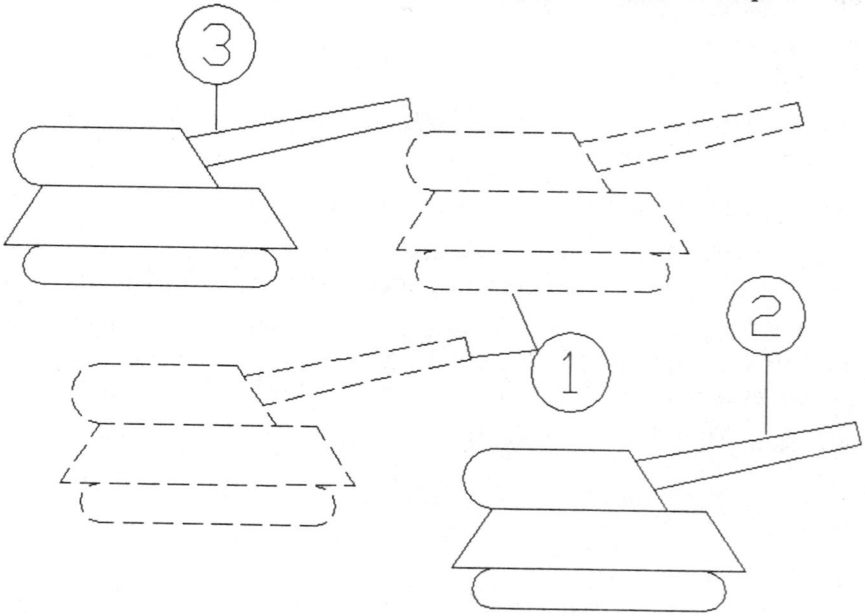

1. Start a new drawing called MOVE. Get to AutoCAD's Main Menu and follow the instructions shown below. This will rename the drawing named TANK that you drew when you did the typical operation for the COPY module.

```
Enter selection: 1  <CR>

Enter NAME of drawing (default XXXXXX): MOVE=TANK <CR>
```

2. Begin the process of moving the lower tank.

```
Command: MOVE <CR>
Select objects: W <CR>
First point: 1.5,1.5 <CR>
Second point: 7.25,4.5 <CR>
13 found.
Select objects: <CR>
```

3. Pick a point on the tank and then drag it to the right.

```
Base point or displacement: 5.5,2.25 <CR>
Second point of displacement: DRAG (to position location
10.25,1.5 and press the pick button)
```

4. Begin the process of moving the upper tank to the left.

```
Command: MOVE <CR>

Select objects: W <CR>
First point: 5.75,4.5 <CR>
Second point: 11.5,7.5 <CR>
13 found.

Select objects or Window or Last: <CR>
```

5. Move the upper tank to the left.

```
Base point or displacement: 6.0,5.25 <CR>
Second point of displacement:  @5.0559<171 <CR>
```

The next picture illustrates how the drawing looks now.

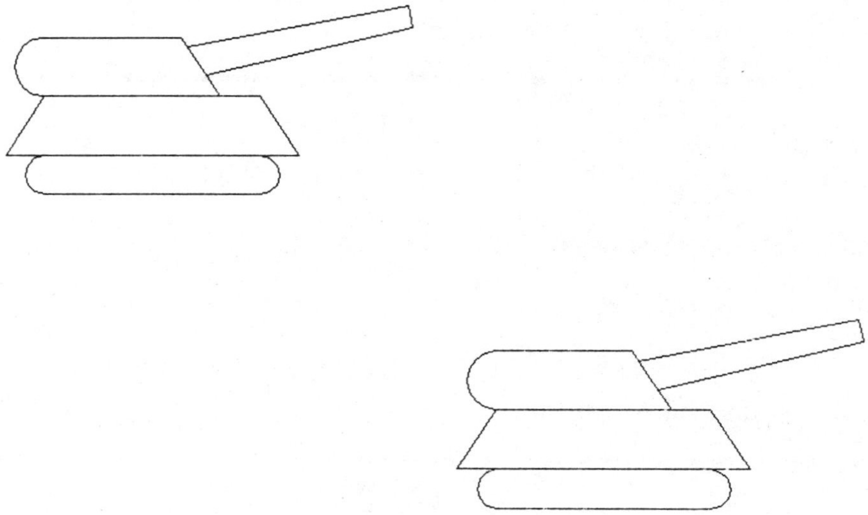

6. Type **QUIT** and press **Return**; then type **Y** and press **Return** to redisplay the Main Menu.
7. Turn to Module 77 to continue the learning sequence.

Module 54

MSLIDE, VSLIDE, SCRIPT, RSCRIPT, AND DELAY

```
Command: MSLIDE
Slide file <filename>:

Command: VSLIDE
Slide file <filename>:

Command: SCRIPT
Script file <filename>:
```

DESCRIPTION

The MSLIDE and VSLIDE commands are used to make and view slide files. Slide files, which have the extension .SLD, are created with the drawing editor and saved with MSLIDE. They are viewed using the VSLIDE command by specifying the slide filename.

The SCRIPT command is used to call a script file, which is an ASCII text file containing a series of AutoCAD commands. Script files should have the extension .SCR. The AutoCAD commands within a script file are executed from top to bottom as they are encountered. The DELAY command is followed by a value that pauses operation. A value of 1000 represents one second. Finally, the RSCRIPT command is used at the bottom of a script file to restart the script from the beginning. This puts a presentation into a continuous loop.

Look at the following example of a script file:

	Remarks (Not part of script file.)
VSLIDE GRAF1	Display slide GRAF1
DELAY 5000	Delay 5 seconds
VSLIDE GRAF2	Display slide GRAF2
DELAY 5000	Delay 5 seconds
VSLIDE GRAF3	Display slide GRAF3
DELAY 5000	Delay 5 seconds
RSCRIPT	Rerun the presentation

A variation of the slide command lets you load the next slide in memory to speed up access time. This is achieved by placing an asterisk in front of the filename. This technique makes the transition from one slide to the next almost instantaneous. Expanding upon the previous example, see how slides are queued into memory using the asterisk.

```
                        Remarks (Not part of script file.)
VSLIDE GRAF1            Display slide GRAF1
VSLIDE *GRAF2           Queues slide GRAF2 in memory
DELAY 5000              Delay 5 seconds
VSLIDE                  Displays slide GRAF2 from memory
VSLIDE *GRAF3           Queues slide GRAF3 in memory
DELAY 10000             Delay 5 seconds
VSLIDE                  Display slide GRAF3 from memory
DELAY 10000             Delay 5 seconds
RSCRIPT                 Rerun the presentation
```

Be sure to terminate each script file line with a hard Return. Press Ctrl-C to interrupt the slide presentation.

APPLICATIONS

The MSLIDE command is important to AutoCAD users who are integrating slide files (with the extension .SLD) with other programs. For example, Ventura Publisher 1.1 readily accepts .SLD files created with AutoCAD versions through 2.62. The ability to combine the power of multiple programs, like AutoCAD and Ventura Publisher, gives microcomputer users capabilities that were unavailable only a short time ago. MSLIDE is additionally useful to users of Release 9 and beyond for the construction of icons for custom screen menus.

The VSLIDE, DELAY, and RSCRIPT commands give AutoCAD a slide presentation capability. You can write script files with any ASCII word processor, like WordStar or the Sidekick editor, and call the script file with the SLIDE command, which starts the presentation. This capability is often used for sales and trade show presentations and in the classroom as an educational tool.

TYPICAL OPERATION

In this session you create a small presentation graphic. Then you save it as a slide file. Next, the UNDO command is used to eradicate the displayed drawing. Finally, VSLIDE is used to display the slide file. Begin a new drawing named MSLIDE.

1. Use the TEXT command to create three lines of text.

```
Command: TEXT <CR>
Start point or Align/Center/Fit/Middle/Right/Style: 1.75,5.3 <CR>
Height <0.2000>: <CR>
Rotation angle <0>: <CR>
Text: REGIONAL SALES <CR>
Command: <CR>
TEXT Start point or Align/Center/Fit/Middle/Right/Style: <CR>
Text: EASTERN $105,345.00 <CR>
Command: <CR>
TEXT Start point or Align/Center/Fit/Middle/Right/Style: <CR>
Text: WESTERN $112,200.00 <CR>
Command:
```

2. Enclose the text using lines to draw a box.

```
Command: LINE <CR>
From point: 1.5,5.9
To point: 5.3,5.9
To point: 5.3,4.4
To point: 1.5,4.4
To point: C
```

3. Make a slide file of the drawing. The drawing is saved as MSLIDE.SLD (the default name uses the drawing filename) and the graphic screen is regenerated.

```
Command: MSLIDE <CR>
Slide file <mslide>: <CR>
Command:
```

4. Discard the slide drawing using the UNDO command.

```
Command: UNDO <CR>
Auto/Back/Control/End/Group/Mark/<number>: 10 <CR>
MSLIDE LINE TEXT TEXT TEXT
Everything has been undone
```

5. Display the slide drawing using the VSLIDE command.

```
Command: VSLIDE <CR>
Slide file <mslide>: <CR>
Command:
```

6. Type **QUIT** and press **Return**; then type **Y** and press **Return** to display the Main Menu.
7. Turn to Module 86 to continue the learning sequence.

Module 55

OFFSET

```
Command: OFFSET
Offset distance or Through <last>:

Last is the last specification given to OFFSET: either a
distance or the word "Through."
```

DESCRIPTION

The OFFSET command was introduced in AutoCAD 2.5. You may type a distance, show AutoCAD a distance by picking two points, or type "Through" (or simply "T") to indicate that the offset goes through a specific point. The distance is always a positive number. Remember to measure the distance from a wide polyline from the center of the polyline. The second prompt, "Select object to offset:," is displayed. Pick the reference object on the screen or type coordinates lying on the object. You may not use alternate methods of object selection. You can offset from a line, polyline, circle, or arc. OFFSET displays the prompt "Side to offset:" when you specify an offset distance.

You must pick or type the coordinates of a point on the proper side of the reference object. It does not matter exactly where you pick the point, as long as it is on the correct side of the reference object. If you specify that the new object goes "Through" a point, OFFSET displays the prompt "Through point:." You must pick or type the coordinates of a point through which the new object is drawn.

APPLICATIONS

The OFFSET command eases the effort involved in constructing parallel entities. While parallel lines are relatively straightforward to draw using conventional methods, OFFSET is especially useful for constructing parallels to curved polylines. You should be aware, however, that the parallel to a curve is not necessarily a well-defined entity. There is more than one way to define the parallel to a complex curve. AutoCAD's methods are reasonable and probably provide the desired curve. However, you should be prepared to fine tune the results with PEDIT.

TYPICAL OPERATION

In this session you construct a polyline parallel to another polyline. From the AutoCAD Main Menu, begin a new drawing named OFFSET.

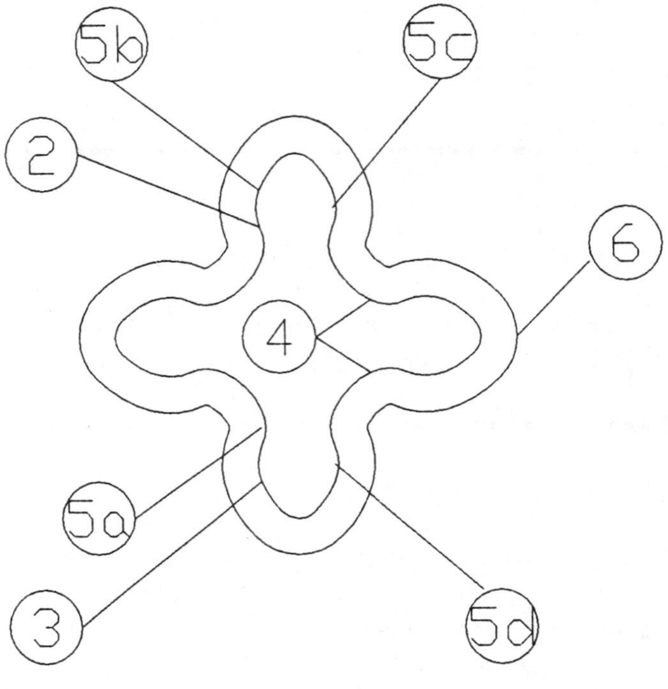

1. Set the SNAP to 0.5, and let the GRID follow the SNAP.

```
Command: SNAP <CR>
Snap spacing or ON/OFF/Aspect/Rotate/Style <1.0000>: .5 <CR>
Command: GRID <CR>
Grid spacing(X) or ON/OFF/Snap/Aspect <0.0000>: S <CR>
Command:
```

2. Draw a segmented polyline with a width of 0.

```
Command: PLINE <CR>
From point: 1.5,4.5 <CR>
Current line-width is 0.0000
Arc/Close/Halfwidth/Length/Undo/Width/<Endpoint of line>: 2,5 <CR>
Arc/Close/Halfwidth/Length/Undo/Width/<Endpoint of line>: 3,5 <CR>
Arc/Close/Halfwidth/Length/Undo/Width/<Endpoint of line>: 3.5,5.5 <CR>
Arc/Close/Halfwidth/Length/Undo/Width/<Endpoint of line>: 3.5,6.5 <CR>
Arc/Close/Halfwidth/Length/Undo/Width/<Endpoint of line>: 4,7 <CR>
Arc/Close/Halfwidth/Length/Undo/Width/<Endpoint of line>: <CR>
Command:
```

3. Mirror the line vertically.

```
Command: MIRROR <CR>
Select objects: (Pick the polyline.) 1 selected, 1 found.
Select objects: <CR>
First point of mirror line: 1,4.5 <CR>
 Second point: 4,4.5 <CR>
Delete old objects? <N> <CR>
Command:
```

4. Mirror both lines horizontally.

```
Command: MIRROR <CR>
Select objects: (Pick one polyline.) 1 selected, 1 found.
Select objects: (Pick the other polyline) 1 selected, 1 found.
Select objects: <CR>
First point of mirror line: 4,0 <CR>
 Second point: 4,1
Delete old objects? <N> <CR>
Command:
```

5. Join the segments and fit a curve.

```
Command: PEDIT <CR>
Select polyline: (Pick 5a.)
Close/Join/Width/Edit vertex/Fit curve/Decurve/Undo/eXit <X>: J <CR>
```

```
Select objects: (Pick 5b.) 1 selected, 1 found.
Select objects: (Pick 5c.) 1 selected, 1 found.
Select objects: (Pick 5d.) 1 selected, 1 found.
Select objects: <CR>
14 segments added to polyline
Open/Join/Width/Edit vertex/Fit curve/Decurve/Undo/eXit <X>: F <CR>
Open/Join/Width/Edit vertex/Fit curve/Decurve/Undo/eXit <X>: X <CR>
Command:
```

6. Offset a second polyline through the point 7,4.5.

NOTE

It takes the offset several moments to generate. Do not give up.

```
Command: OFFSET <CR>
Offset distance or Through <Through>: T <CR>
Select object to offset: (Pick on the polyline.)
Through point: 7,4.5 <CR>
Select object to offset: <CR>
Command:
```

Your drawing should resemble the following illustration.

7. Type **QUIT** and press **Return**; then type **Y** and press **Return** to display the AutoCAD Main Menu.
8. Turn to Module 49 to continue the learning sequence.

Module 56

OOPS

```
Command: OOPS
```

DESCRIPTION

The OOPS command restores drawing elements that have been erased by accident. The OOPS command can undo only the last erasure. However, the erasure can be a single object or several objects that were erased within a window.

APPLICATIONS

The OOPS command is used to bring back something that has been erased. The erasure can be either planned or accidental. Sometimes it is convenient to remove an object from the screen and then restore it with the OOPS command. AutoCAD only remembers one step in reverse. A common use of OOPS is when a block is created. The objects defined within the block disappear when identified. Use the OOPS command to quickly restore the objects to the drawing.

TYPICAL OPERATION

In this session the OOPS command is used to restore drawing elements. Starting at the Main Menu, begin a new drawing named TEMP.

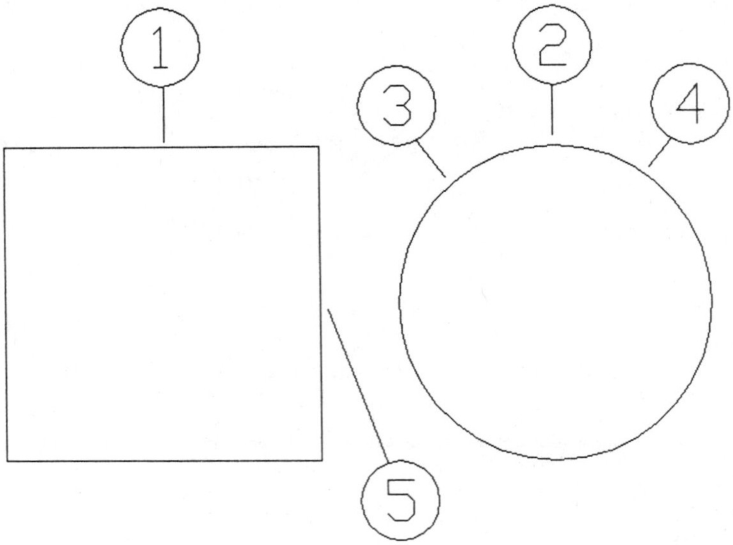

1. Draw a line using the LINE command.

```
Command: LINE <CR>
From point: 3,3 <CR>
To point: 5,5 <CR>
To point: <CR>
```

2. Draw a circle using the CIRCLE command.

```
Command: CIRCLE <CR>
3P/2P/<Center point>: 4,4 <CR>
Diameter/<Radius>: 1 <CR>
```

3. Erase the circle with the ERASE last command.

```
Command: ERASE <CR>
Select objects: L <CR>
1 found
Select objects: <CR>
```

4. Notice that the circle disappears.
5. Use the OOPS command to restore the circle.

```
Command: OOPS <CR>
Command:
```

6. Notice that the circle is redrawn.
7. Type **QUIT** and press **Return**; then type **Y** and press **Return** to redisplay the Main Menu.
8. Turn to Module 19 to continue the learning sequence.

Module 57

ORTHO

```
Command: ORTHO
ON/OFF <Off>: ON
```

DESCRIPTION

If the SNAP grid has a style of "standard" and is not rotated, then the ORTHO command forces all lines and traces specified with the screen cursor to be either horizontal or vertical. It is not possible to draw diagonal when ORTHO is turned on. ORTHO mode also works when the SNAP grid has been rotated or when the style of the SNAP grid has been changed to isometric. The lines are still held orthogonally with respect to the type of projection being produced. To see how ORTHO works with each type of SNAP grid, it is best to toggle the ORTHO mode on and try drawing some experimental lines. It becomes quickly apparent if the ORTHO mode is going to aid your drawing activities. If ORTHO impedes your productivity, it is easy to toggle it off.

APPLICATIONS

The ORTHO command speeds the entry of points in a drawing which are aligned with the rotation of the SNAP grid. This normally refers to horizontal and vertical lines, but is also applicable to a rotated grid or an isometric style.

If your drawing has only a few diagonals, it is easiest to draw with ORTHO on, pick the points on the horizontal and vertical lines, then toggle ORTHO off and specify the diagonals.

The ORTHO command is seldom typed from the keyboard. In most cases, it is easiest to press the Function key or Control key combination assigned to ORTHO to toggle ORTHO on or off. Using the Function key or Control key combinations, ORTHO can be toggled on and off at either the command prompt, or in the middle of another command. For example, ORTHO can be toggled on and off in the middle of drawing a series of lines with the LINE command. The Function key assignments are as follows:

Apricot	Ctrl-O	DEC Mate V	Fnc-Funct 18
Data General	F8 or Ctrl-O	NEC APC	PF3 or Ctrl-O
Dec Rainbow	F8 or Ctrl-O	Tandy 2000	Ctrl-O
Fujitsu Micro 16	Ctrl-O	Texas Instruments	F4 or Ctrl-O
Hewlett Packard	F4	Wang P. C.	PF2 or Ctrl-O
IBM	F8 or Ctrl-O	Zenith Z-100	F7 or Ctrl-O
NCR	Fnc-Funct 18		

TYPICAL OPERATION

Create the following drawing by picking the points on the screen.

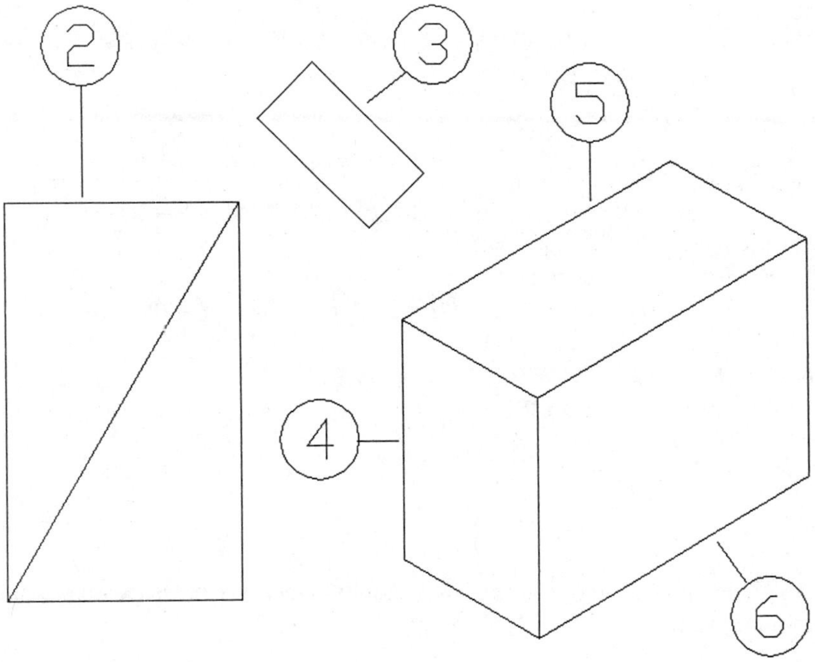

1. Begin a new drawing named ORTHO. Set SNAP, GRID, and COORDS ON. Turn ORTHO on by typing the command.

```
Command:  <SNAP ON>  <GRID ON>  <COORDS ON> ORTHO <CR>
On/Off <Off>: ON <CR>
Command:
```

2. Draw a rectangle and its diagonal by picking the points on the screen. Notice that you must turn ORTHO off to draw the diagonal.

```
Command: (Pick DRAW then pick LINE) LINE From point: (Pick 1,1)
To point:  <COORDS ON> (Pick 1,6)
To point:  (Pick 4,6)
To point:   <Ortho Off>(Pick 6,1)
To point:  (Pick 1,1)
To point:  (Pick 4,6)
To point: (Pick CANCEL) *Cancel*
Command:
```

3. Use the ORTHO Function key to turn ORTHO on. Rotate the SNAP grid to a 45 degree angle and draw a small rectangle.

```
Command: SNAP <CR>
Snap spacing or ON/OFF/Aspect/Rotate/Style <1.0000>: R <CR>
Base point <0.0000,0.0000>: <CR>
Rotation angle <0>: 45 <CR>
Command: (Pick LINE) LINE From Point: (Pick 4.9497,7.7782)
To point: (Pick 4.2426,7.0711)
To point: (Pick 5.6569,5.6569)
To point: (Pick 6.3640,6.3640)
To point: (Pick CLOSE)
Command:
```

4. Restore the SNAP rotation to 0. Set the SNAP style to isometric. Draw an isometric projection of a solid. Begin with the left side.

```
Command:SNAP <CR>
Snap spacing or ON/OFF/Aspect/Rotate/Style <1.0000>: R <CR>
Base point <0.0000,0.0000>: <CR>
Rotation angle <45>: 0 <CR> <CR>
Snap spacing or ON/OFF/Aspect/Rotate/Style <1.0000>: STYLE <CR>
Standard/Isometric: I <CR>
```

```
Vertical spacing <1.0000>: <CR>
Command: LINE <CR>
From point: (Pick 6.0622,4.5)
To point: (Pick 6.0622,1.5)
To point: (Pick 7.7942,0.5)
To point: (Pick 7.7942,3.5)
To point: (Pick 6.0622,4.5)
To point: (Pick CANCEL) *Cancel*
Command:
```

5. Draw the top view of the solid.

```
Command: ISOPLANE <CR>
Left/Top/Right/(Toggle): <CR>
Current Isometric plane is: Top
Command: LINE <CR>
From point: (Pick 6.0622,4.5)
To point: (Pick 9.5263,6.5)
To point: (Pick 11.2583,5.5)
To point: (Pick 7.7942,3.5)
To point: (Pick CANCEL) *Cancel*
```

6. Draw the right view of the solid.

```
Command: ISOPLANE <CR>
Left/Top/Right/(Toggle): <CR>
Current Isometric plane is: Right
Command: (Pick LINE) LINE  From point: (Pick 7.7942,0.5)
To point: (Pick 11.2583,2.5)
To point: (Pick 11.2583,5.5)
To point: (Pick CANCEL) *Cancel*
Command:
```

The drawing is complete.

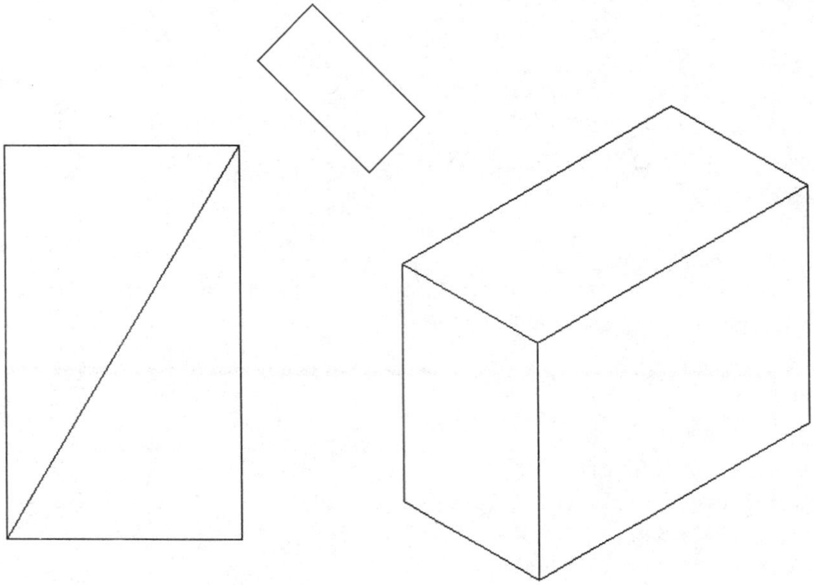

7. Type **QUIT** and press **Return**, then type **Y** and press **Return** to redisplay the Main Menu.
8. Turn to Module 17 to continue the learning sequence.

Module 58

OSNAP

```
Command: OSNAP
```

DESCRIPTION

The OSNAP command makes it possible to snap to an exact position within an object or drawing. Specify the desired Object Snap modes by typing either the entire selection name or only the first three letters of the name.

Center	Locate the exact center of a circle or arc.
Endpoint	Snap to the endpoint of a line, polyline segment, 3DLINE, or arc.
Midpoint	Snap to the midpoint of a line, polyline segment, 3DLINE, or arc.
Perpendicular	Snaps to the place on a line, polyline segment, circle, or arc that is perpendicular or normal to the figure.
Intersection	Snap to the intersection of two objects, including the intersection of two edges of a 3DFACE.
Insert	Snap to the origin of a block.
Nearest	Snap to the nearest point on an object.
Node	Snap to a point.
Tangent	Snap tangent to a circle or arc from the last point entered.
Quadrant	Snap to the nearest 0, 90, 180, or 270 degree position of an arc or circle.
Quick	Used in combination with other OSNAP command options, the Quick option finds the first point meeting the OSNAP criteria. Without the Quick option, OSNAP examines all possible entities before selecting one.

You may specify any number of Object Snap modes simultaneously. When OSNAP is selected, a square target appears at the intersection of the screen cross hairs. The portion of the object you wish to snap to must be inside the square target when it is picked.

APPLICATIONS

The OSNAP command is used any time it is necessary to automatically locate the end of a line, the midpoint of a line, the perpendicular of a line, the center of a circle, or the tangent to a circle. The OSNAP target eliminates the need to specify an exact point, which could take a long period of time. You can alter the dimensions of the target with the APERTURE command.

The OSNAP command is selected in two basic ways. First, you can type **OSNAP** and press **Return**. The following information is displayed.

```
Command: OSNAP <CR>
Object Snap modes:
```

Respond to the "Object Snap modes" prompt by typing the first three letters of any of the options listed at the beginning of this module. If you plan to snap to the ends, midpoints, and tangents of objects many times during your drawing session, respond as follows:

```
Command: OSNAP <CR>
Object Snap modes: END,MID,QUA <CR>
```

To disable a selected option, type **OSNAP** and press **Return**. Then press **Return** in response to the "Object Snap modes:" prompt. This is a "null response."

The second method of activating OSNAP, which is probably the most useful and popular, is to use "Single Point Override." This activation of OSNAP is a one time only activation. In other words it is turned on for only one operation and then it is automatically turned off. This "Single Point Override" method is activated by typing the option's three letter activator at any time AutoCAD prompts for a location. This is illustrated in the following operation.

TYPICAL OPERATION

This session illustrates the operation of the OSNAP command by letting you locate the center of a circle, the end of a line, the midpoint of a line, perpendicular to a line, and tangent to a circle.

1. Begin a new drawing named OSNAP. Set the value of the SNAP grid. Turn the GRID on. Then ZOOM the screen.

```
Command:  SNAP <CR>
Snap spacing or ON/OFF/Aspect/Rotate/Style <1.0000>: .25 <CR>

Command: GRID <CR>
Grid spacing(X) or ON/OFF/Snap/Aspect <0.0000>:  ON <CR>

Command: ZOOM <CR>
All/Center/Dynamic/Extents/Left/Previous/Window/<Scale(X)>:  A <CR>
```

2. Draw a circle.

```
Command: CIRCLE <CR>
3P/2P/<Center point>: 3,5 <CR>
Diameter/<Radius>: 2 <CR>
```

3. Draw two lines and redraw the screen.

```
Command: LINE <CR>
From point: 3,.75 <CR>
To point: 8,.75 <CR>
To point: 8,8 <CR>
To point: <CR>

Command: REDRAW <CR>
```

The graphics screen should now look like the following illustration, except for the letters. They are added in the following procedure.

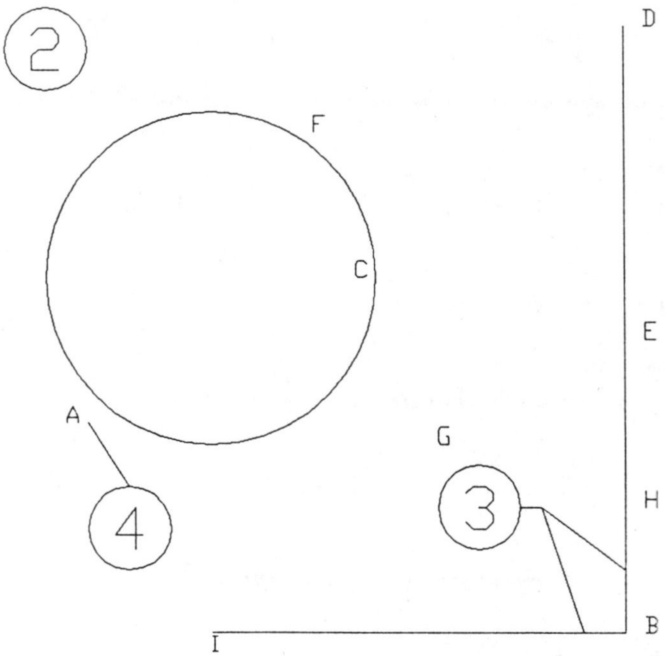

4. Add letters A through I to the drawing.

Command: **TEXT <CR>**
Start point or Align/Center/Fit/Middle/Right/Style: **1.25,3.25 <CR>**
Height <0.2000>: **<CR>**
Rotation angle <0>: **<CR>**
Text: **A <CR>**

Command: **TEXT <CR>**
Start point or Align/Center/Fit/Middle/Right/Style: **8.25,.75 <CR>**
Heignt <0.2000>: **<CR>**
Rotation angle <0>: **<CR>**
Text: **B <CR>**

Command: **TEXT <CR>**
Start point or Align/Center/Fit/Middle/Right/Style: **4.75,5 <CR>**
Height <0.2000>: **<CR>**
Rotation angle <0>: **<CR>**
Text: **C <CR>**

Command: **TEXT <CR>**
Start point or Align/Center/Fit/Middle/Right/Style: **8.25,8 <CR>**
Height <0.2000>: **<CR>**
Rotation angle <0>: **<CR>**
Text: **D <CR>**

Command: **TEXT <CR>**
Start point or Align/Center/Fit/Middle/Right/Style: **8.25,5 <CR>**
Height <0.2000>: **<CR>**
Rotation angle <0>: **<CR>**
Text: **E <CR>**

Command: **TEXT <CR>**
Start point or Align/Center/Fit/Middle/Right/Style: **4.25,6.75 <CR>**
Height <0.2000>: **<CR>**
Rotation angle <0>: **<CR>**
Text: **F <CR>**

Command: **TEXT <CR>**
Start point or Align/Center/Fit/Middle/Right/Style: **5.75,3 <CR>**
Height <0.2000>: **<CR>**
Rotation angle <0>: **<CR>**
Text: **G <CR>**

Command: **TEXT <CR>**
Start point or Align/Center/Fit/Middle/Right/Style: **8.25,2.25 <CR>**
Height <0.2000>: **<CR>**
Rotation angle <0>: **<CR>**
Text: **H <CR>**

Command: **TEXT <CR>**
Start point or Align/Center/Fit/Middle/Right/Style: **3,.5 <CR>**
Height <0.2000>: **<CR>**
Rotation angle <0>: **<CR>**
Text: **I <CR>**

Your AutoCAD screen should look like the following:

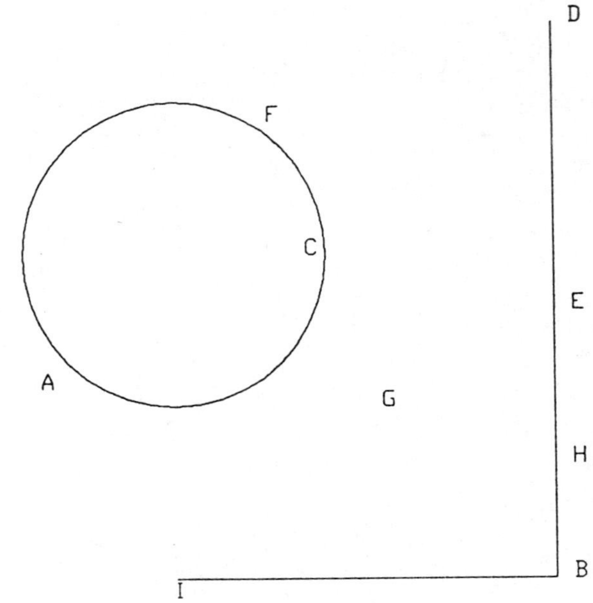

NOTE

The term "Target" refers to a square that is displayed at the intersection of the screen cross hairs. Ensure that you have the portion of the drawing within the target as instructed. Steps 5 through 9 correspond to the numbered balloons on the following drawing.

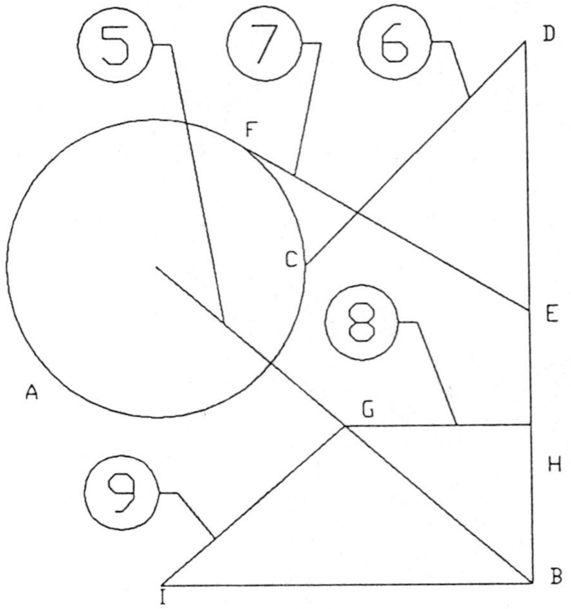

5. Add a line from the center of the circle to the intersection of the two perpendicular lines.

```
Command: LINE <CR>
From point: CEN <CR>
of (Pick with circumference of circle inside target, near "A")
To point: INT <CR>
of (Pick with intersection of two lines inside target, near "B")
To point: <CR>
```

6. Add a line connecting the "zero quadrant" of the circle near the letter "C" to the end of the line near letter "D".

```
Command: LINE <CR>
From point: QUA <CR>
of (Pick with circumference of circle inside target, near "C")
To point: END <CR>
of (Pick with end of line inside of target, near "D")
To point: <CR>
```

7. Add a line from the midpoint of the vertical line near letter "E" to the tangent point of the circle near letter "F".

```
Command: LINE  <CR>
From point: MID <CR>
of (Pick with line inside of target, near "E")
To point: TAN <CR>
to (Pick with circumference of circle inside target, near "F")
To point: <CR>
```

8. Draw a line from the midpoint of the line near letter "G" to a point perpendicular to the line near letter "H".

```
Command: LINE <CR>
From point: MID <CR>
of (Pick with line inside of target, near "G")
To point: PER <CR>
to (Pick with line inside of target, near "H")
To point: <CR>
```

9. Draw a line from the end of the line near letter "I" to the mid point of the line near letter "G".

```
Command: LINE <CR>
From point: END <CR>
of (Pick with line inside of target, near "I")
To point: MID <CR>
of (Pick with line inside of target, near "G")
To point: <CR>
```

The graphics screen should now look like the following drawing.

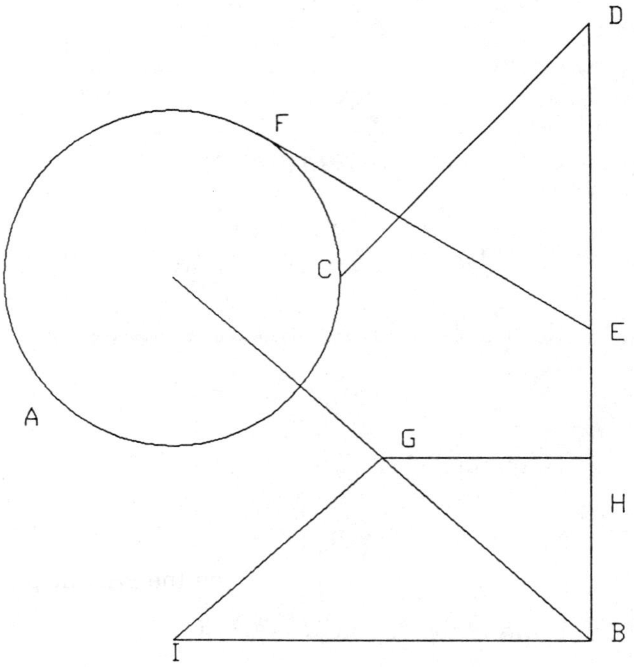

10. Type **QUIT** and press **Return**; then type **Y** and press **Return** to redisplay the Main Menu.
11. Turn to Module 6 to continue the learning sequence.

Module 59

PAN

```
Command: PAN
Displacement: x,y
Second Point: x,y or <R>
```

DESCRIPTION

The PAN command lets you reposition the drawing to a new position within the drawing window. You can move the drawing to the left, right, up, down, or diagonally.

DISPLACEMENT METHOD PAN gives you two ways to specify the drawing displacement. The first method is to type a displacement value. A positive number for *x* moves the drawing to the right. A negative *x* value moves the drawing left. A positive number for *y* moves the drawing up; a negative *y* value moves the drawing down. All displacements are expressed in drawing units. Press **Return** in response to the prompt "Second Point:."

TWO POINT METHOD The second method of specifying the PAN displacement is to specify two points on the drawing. You may either pick the points with the screen cursor or type the coordinates on your keyboard. If you type the coordinates, it is not necessary for either point to be visible on the screen. Using this method, AutoCAD computes the displacement between the two points and pans the drawing. When the PAN command operation is complete, the first specified point is moved to the second point.

APPLICATIONS

When the portion of a drawing you want to view or edit is off the screen, the PAN command is used to slide the desired portion of the drawing into view on your screen. Use the ZOOM command when the magnification of the drawing must change. Use the PAN command when the size relationship of the drawing should not change.

TYPICAL OPERATION

In this session you create a figure that is partially off the screen. Then you use the PAN command to view the hidden portion of the drawing. Begin a new drawing named PAN.

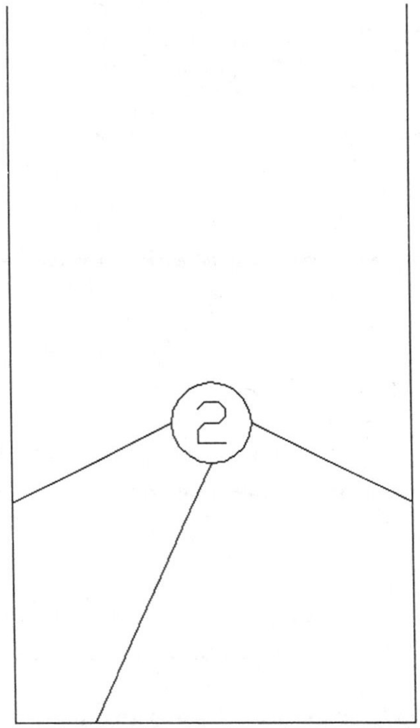

1. Set SNAP to .5, set the drawing LIMITS to 12,20, and turn GRID on.

```
Command: SNAP <CR>
Snap spacing or ON/OFF/Aspect/Rotate/Style <1.0000>: .5 <CR>

Command: LIMITS <CR>
ON/OFF/<Lower left corner> <0.0000,0.0000>: <CR>
Upper right corner <12.0000,9.0000>: 12,20 <CR>

Command: GRID <CR>
Grid spacing(X) or ON/OFF/Snap/Aspect <0.0000>: ON <CR>
```

2. Draw an open box. Notice that the top of the figure extends off the screen.

```
Command: LINE <CR>
From point: 3,15 <CR>
To point: 3,1 <CR>
To point: 8,1 <CR>
To point: 8,15 <CR>
To point: <CR>
```

3. Bring the top of the figure into view with the PAN command using the two-point method of specifying displacement.

```
Command: PAN <CR>
Displacement: 3,15 <CR>
 Second point: 3,3 <CR>
```

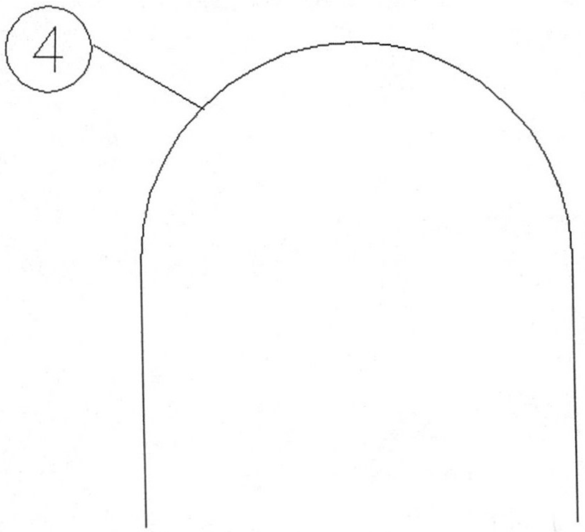

4. Draw an arc joining the top of the figure.

```
Command: ARC <CR>
Center/<Start point>: 8,15 <CR>
Center/End/<Second point>: E <CR>
End point: 3,15 <CR>
Angle/Direction/Radius/<Center point>: 5.5,15 <CR>
```

5. Type **QUIT** and press **Return**; then type **Y** and press **Return** to redisplay the Main Menu.
6. Turn to Module 42 to continue the learning sequence.

Module 60

PEDIT

```
Command: PEDIT
Select a polyline:
```

DESCRIPTION

The PEDIT command is used to edit polylines. You can use PEDIT to perform any of the following operations:

- Alter a polyline to achieve a uniform width.
- Change individual segments of polylines to alter the width and taper.
- Open and close polylines.
- Smooth a polyline.
- Break a polyline into more than one polyline.
- Join entities into a single polyline.
- Add or move vertices.
- Perform curve fitting on polyline vertices.

The PEDIT command is selected by typing **PEDIT** at the command prompt and pressing **Return**. The first step in using PEDIT is to respond to the "Select polyline" prompt by placing the screen cursor on the polyline you intend to edit and pressing **Return**. You can also pick with your mouse or other device. You may find it difficult to pick a polyline with SNAP on. If necessary, turn SNAP off. Then move the cursor slightly and try picking again. If the object you select is not a polyline, AutoCAD responds with the following prompt.

```
Entity selected is not a polyline.
Do you want it to turn into one?
```

If you want to convert a line or arc into a polyline, type **Y** and press **Return**. You can now manipulate the newly converted polyline with PEDIT.

After a polyline is selected, AutoCAD responds with the following prompt.

```
Close/Join/Width/Edit vertex/Fit curve/Spline curve/Decurve/Undo/eXit <X>:
```

NOTE

If the selected polyline is already "Closed," the preceding prompt begins with "Open." You can select any option by typing the capital letter shown on the prompt line and pressing **Return**, i.e., type **J** for Join and press **Return**.

Each PEDIT command option is briefly explained in the following list. The most complex option is Edit vertex. It is given special attention in the explanations.

Close — If the beginning and end of a polyline do not visibly join, the Close option will join the two ends by adding an additional section of polyline between the two ends. If the ends of the polyline are already touching, the Close option does not produce any visible change.

Open — If you have performed a Close on a polyline, the Open option removes the effects caused by the Close. If the ends of the polyline originally touched, the Open option does not produce any visible change.

Join — The Join option prompts for a selection of objects, Window, or Last. You may also elect to join polylines, arcs, and lines. You can also include the original polyline in this selection. The Join option does not necessarily join all the entities you have selected. The Join option only works on polylines that are "Open." Only those entities that touch each other end-to-end are joined. After joining is accomplished, you may wonder which objects have actually been joined. You can use the LIST command to highlight the polyline to reveal what has been joined. Use **Ctrl-C** to cancel the further consequences of the LIST command.

Width — This option changes polylines of varying widths to ones of uniform width. When the Width option is selected, AutoCAD prompts you for a new width. The new value is either entered from the keyboard or entered by selecting two points on the screen.

Edit vertex — This option is one of the most powerful parts of PEDIT. The Edit vertex option lets you select a vertex in the polyline for editing.

Fit curve — Performs "curve fitting" on each segment of the polyline. This is accomplished by replacing each segment with an arc. The Fit curve option automatically adds vertices to the polyline to create the curve. A curve produced by the Fit curve option always passes through all the points on the original polyline.

Spline curve — Introduced in Release 9, this option performs curve fitting using the cubic B-spline method on the polyline. The resultant curve passes through the endpoints of the polyline, and is "pulled" toward other vertices as if they were magnets. The closer the spacing between vertices, the stronger their "pull." The number of line segments representing each spline curve is determined by the SPLINESEGS system variable, accessible through the SETVAR command.

Decurve — Reverses the action of either a Fit curve or a Spline curve, discarding any vertices automatically added in the curve fitting process.

Uncurve — Performs the actions of Decurve in AutoCAD versions prior to 2.5.

Undo — Introduced in version 2.5, the Undo option reverses the action of the most recently performed PEDIT operation.

eXit — Exits the PEDIT command and displays the command prompt.

The Edit vertex option produces its own line of options.

```
Next/Previous/Break/Insert/Move/Regen/Straighten/Tangent/Width/
eXit <N>
```

When the Edit vertex option is selected, an "X" appears on the last polyline selected. You can move the "X" from vertex to vertex using the Next and Previous options.

Next and Previous — You should experiment with the "N" and "P" suboptions to see how the "X" moves to each vertex of a polyline. The "X" only moves to the ends of the polyline, even if you have closed and/or joined the polyline. After moving to the end of the polyline, you can toggle the "N" to "P", or vice versa, and then start pressing **Return** to step the "X" in the opposite direction.

Break — If you want to break a polyline between two vertices, position the "X" to one end of the break with the Next or Previous suboption. After positioning the "X," type **B** and type **N** or **P** to move the "X" to the other end of the break. Then type **G** (for Go) to complete the break. The polyline segment between the two vertices disappears. Typing **X** at any time exits Break and returns you to Edit vertex.

Insert — The Insert suboption lets you choose a position for a new vertex to be added to the existing vertices in the polyline. The new vertex is always added to the polyline after the vertex marked with the "X."

Move — The vertex that contains the "X" can be moved to another location with this suboption. After typing **M**, you are prompted for a new location. Once this location is established, the marked vertex is moved.

Regen — This suboption regenerates the polyline so you can see the true results of suboptions such as "Width."

Straighten — If polyline segments between vertices are arcs, the Straighten suboption produces a straight polyline segment between the vertices to replace the arc. The Straighten suboption works like the Break option. If **G** is typed without adding another vertex to the original position, the following segment is straightened if it is an arc.

Tangent — This suboption works with the curve fitting option. The direction of tangent is either entered as a value from the keyboard or by picking the desired angle with the cursor. After the tangent angle is entered, an arrow is appended to the "X" marked vertex.

Width — This suboption lets you modify the beginning and ending widths of polyline segments. The specified width changes the next segment following the vertex marked with the "X." You can find out which direction is "next" using "N" or "P" to move the "X" on the polyline. This suboption is different from the Width option in PEDIT, which causes a uniform width for the whole polyline. When this suboption is active, it prompts you for a beginning and ending width. After the widths are entered, the polyline will not have any apparent change. In order to see the change, you must use the Regen option.

eXit — This suboption returns you to PEDIT.

APPLICATIONS

The PEDIT command is used to edit polylines. The editing commands used with lines and arcs do not work with polylines. For example, the BREAK command does not work with polylines (prior to version 2.5); you must use the Break option of the PEDIT command to break a polyline. However, the reverse is true; an ordinary line or arc can be changed to a polyline with the PEDIT command. Once a line or arc is changed to a polyline, there is no way to change the polyline back to a line or arc.

Polylines are especially useful to describe shapes which are not composed of lines and arcs, but are defined by a function. A large example of this is the St. Louis Arch, a smaller example is a cam. You define a complex curved shape by plotting a series of points on the curve. The points can come from your calculations of a function, or from a sourcebook such as *Machinery's Handbook*.

In a mapping application, polylines are excellent for depicting contour lines on a topographic map, where the points come from analysis of aerial photographs and field study. If the shape is described by multiple polylines, the second step is to join the multiple polylines into a single polyline with the PEDIT Join option. The final step in the process is to select the PEDIT Fit option, which creates a "best fit" curve passing through all the points on the polyline.

TYPICAL OPERATION

In this session you create an archway based on the quadratic y = x ^ 2. Begin a new drawing named PLINE.

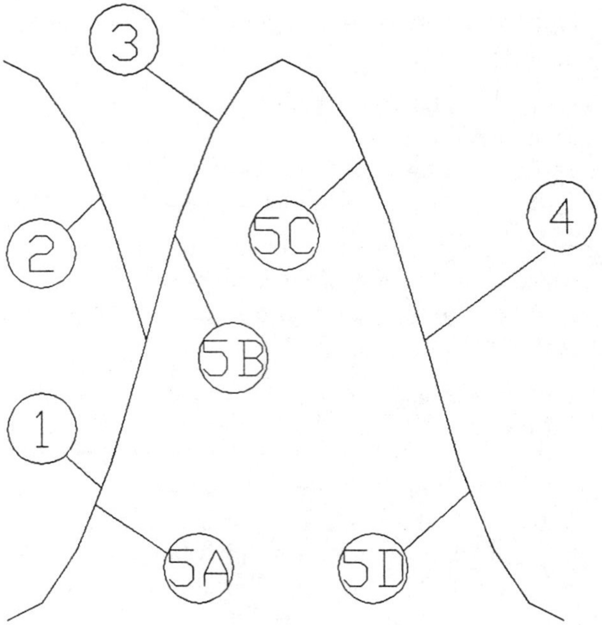

1. Create the lower left portion of the arch.

```
Command: PLINE <CR>
From point: 0,0 <CR>
Current line-width is 0.0000
Arc/Close/Halfwidth/Length/Undo/Width/<Endpoint of line>: .5,.25 <CR>
Arc/Close/Halfwidth/Length/Undo/Width/<Endpoint of line>: 1,1 <CR>
Arc/Close/Halfwidth/Length/Undo/Width/<Endpoint of line>: 1.5,2.25 <CR>
Arc/Close/Halfwidth/Length/Undo/Width/<Endpoint of line>: 2,4 <CR>
Arc/Close/Halfwidth/Length/Undo/Width/<Endpoint of line>: <CR>
Command:
```

2. Use the MIRROR command to replicate the polyline.

```
Command: MIRROR <CR>
Select objects: L <CR>
1 found
```

```
Select objects: <CR>
First point of mirror line: 0,4 <CR>
 Second point: 3,4 <CR>
Delete old objects? <N> <CR>
```

3. MIRROR the polyline around a vertical line, deleting the polyline just created.

```
Command: MIRROR <CR>
Select objects: L <CR>
1 found
Select objects: <CR>
First point of mirror line: 2,4 <CR>
 Second point: 2,8 <CR>
Delete old objects? <N> Y <CR>
```

4. Use the MIRROR command to replicate both polylines around a vertical line, forming the right side of the arch.

```
Command: MIRROR <CR>
Select objects: L <CR>
1 found
Select objects: (Pick the lower-left polyline)
1 selected, 1 found.
Select objects: <CR>
First point of mirror line: 4,0 <CR>
 Second point: 4,1 <cr>
Delete old objects? <N> <CR>
```

5. Join the four polylines.

```
Command:PEDIT <CR>
Select polyline: (Pick A)
Close/Join/Width/Edit vertex/Fit curve/Spline curve/Decurve/Undo/eXit <X>: J <CR>
Select objects: (Pick B) 1 selected, 1 found.
Select objects: (Pick C) 1 selected, 1 found.
Select objects: (Pick D) 1 selected, 1 found.
Select objects: <CR>
12 segments added to polyline
```

6. Replace the segmented polyline with a smooth curve.

```
Close/Join/Width/Edit vertex/Fit curve/Spline curve/Decurve/Undo/eXit <X>: F <CR>
Close/Join/Width/Edit vertex/Fit curve/Spline curve/Decurve/Undo/eXit <X>: <CR>
Command:
```

The segments are redrawn as a smooth curve,

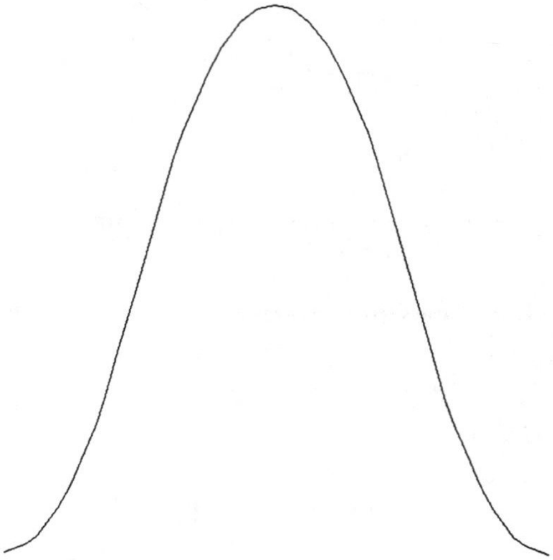

7. Type **QUIT** and press **Return**; then type **Y** and press **Return** to redisplay the Main Menu.
8. Turn to Module 34 to continue the learning sequence.

Module 61

PLINE

```
Command: PLINE
From point:
```

DESCRIPTION

The term PLINE is short for the word polyline. A polyline is a line made up of multiple traces. Therefore, the PLINE command incorporates some of the features of the LINE command and the TRACE command. If the width of the PLINE is set to zero, it draws a normal line. A line drawn with the LINE command is a single entity. A line drawn with the PLINE command is also stored as one entity when drawn in one PLINE sequence.

Polylines are displayed as traces with a designated width. They are displayed solid if FILL is turned on. The main advantage of PLINE over TRACE, besides the fact that PLINE is saved as one entity, is that PLINE can vary in width. There are a number of other advantages. Among these is the ability to be joined together as one entity. This takes advantage of curve fitting. You can also use a polyline to create a dot-dash linetype.

The polyline is available with the AutoCAD ADE-3 package. The polyline is edited with the PEDIT command. The FILLET and CHAMFER commands have special parameters available for use with polylines.

With AutoCAD version 2.5 and later you may additionally modify polylines with the BREAK, TRIM, and EXTEND commands.

APPLICATIONS

Polylines are versatile drawing entities. They are used for drawing lines which have a defined width, lines which taper, and for drawing curves and arcs based on a "best fit" function through a series of points.

WIDE LINES The PLINE command is used for drawing lines that need to be wider than is possible with the LINE command. The PLINE command is more efficient for disk storage, because a PLINE is saved as a single entity, in spite of being made up of several different PLINE segments. PLINE is also used to draw a tapered line.

To use the PLINE command, make sure you are at the command prompt. Type **PLINE**, press **Return** and notice the "From point" prompt.

After you have picked a beginning point on the drawing, you see the prompt:

```
Current line-width is 00.00
```

The line width is set to the last PLINE width used. If this is the first use of PLINE, it uses zero as the default. A zero line width draws a line that looks like a line produced with the LINE command. You may press **Return** to retain the default line width or supply a new width value from the keyboard and press **Return**. Next, you see the prompt:

```
Arc/Close/Halfwidth/Length/Undo/Width/<Endpoint of line>:
```

CURVES To create a curve which passes through a series of known points, draw the curve as a multi-segment polyline. Then use the FIT option on the PEDIT (Polyline Edit) command to transform the series of segments into a smooth curve. This technique is useful for drawing cams and parabolic shapes. It would be ideal for drawing a structure such as the St. Louis Arch.

TYPICAL OPERATION

This session lets you draw an outline of a printed wiring board, including the contacts, called *edge connectors*.

The following drawing contains numbered balloons that correspond to the following steps. Begin a new drawing named PLINE.

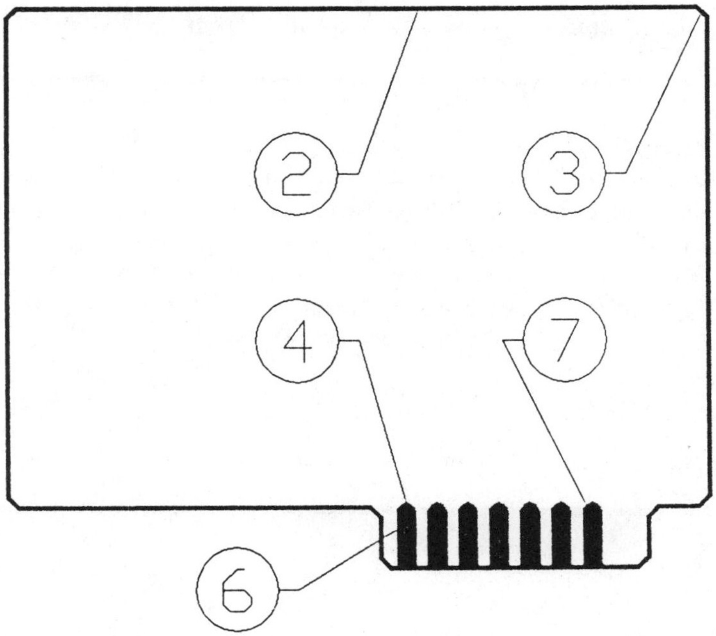

1. Set the SNAP value, turn GRID on, and ZOOM the screen to see it at its maximum size.

```
Command: SNAP Snap spacing or ON/OFF/Aspect/Rotate/Style <1.0000>: .25 <CR>
Command: GRID Grid spacing(X) or ON/OFF/Snap/Aspect <0.0000>: ON <CR>
Command: ZOOM All/Center/Dynamic/Extents/Left/Previous/Window/<Scale(X)>: A <CR>
```

2. Draw the outline of the printed wiring board with the PLINE command.

```
Command: PLINE <CR>
From point: .5,2 <CR>
Current line-width is 0.0000
Arc/Close/Halfwidth/Length/Undo/Width/<Endpoint of line>: W <CR>
Starting width <0.0000>: .0625 <CR>
Ending width <0.0625>: <CR>
Arc/Close/Halfwidth/Length/Undo/Width/<Endpoint of line>:.5,8 <CR>
Arc/Close/Halfwidth/Length/Undo/Width/<Endpoint of line>:9,8 <CR>
Arc/Close/Halfwidth/Length/Undo/Width/<Endpoint of line>:9,2 <CR>
Arc/Close/Halfwidth/Length/Undo/Width/<Endpoint of line>:8.25,2 <CR>
Arc/Close/Halfwidth/Length/Undo/Width/<Endpoint of line>:8.25,1.25 <CR>
Arc/Close/Halfwidth/Length/Undo/Width/<Endpoint of line>:5,1.25 <CR>
Arc/Close/Halfwidth/Length/Undo/Width/<Endpoint of line>:5,2 <CR>
Arc/Close/Halfwidth/Length/Undo/Width/<Endpoint of line>:C <CR>
```

3. Chamfer all of the printed wiring board's corners.

```
Command: CHAMFER <CR>
Polyline/Distances/<Select first line>: D <CR>
Enter first chamfer distance <0.0000>: .125 <CR>
Enter second chamfer distance <0.1250>:<CR>
Command: <CR>
Chamfer Polyline/Distances/<Select first line>: P <CR>
Select polyline: (Pick somewhere on the polyline.)
```

Eight lines were chamfered.

4. Produce the radius for the end of the edge connector.

```
Command: PLINE <CR>
From point: 5.375,1.9375 <CR>
Current line-width is 0.0625 <CR>
Arc/Close/Halfwidth/Length/Undo/Width/<Endpoint of line>: W <CR>
Starting width <0.0625>: .1250 <CR>
Ending width <0.1250>: <CR>
Arc/Close/Halfwidth/Length/Undo/Width/<Endpoint of line>: A <CR>
Angle/CEnter/CLose/Direction/Halfwidth/Line/Radius/Second pt/
Undo/Width/<Endpoint of arc>: CE <CR>
Center point: 5.3125,1.9375 <CR>
Angle/Length/<End point>: A <CR>
Included angle: 180 <CR>
```

5. Press **Ctrl-C** to cancel the pline series.
6. Draw the remainder of the first edge connector.

```
Command: PLINE <CR>
From point: 5.3125,1.9375 <CR>
Current line-width is 0.1250 <CR>
Arc/Close/Halfwidth/Length/Undo/Width/<Endpoint of line>: W <CR>
Starting width <0.1250>: .250 <CR>
Ending width <0.2500>: <CR>
Arc/Close/Halfwidth/Length/Undo/Width/<Endpoint of line>: 5.3125,1.25 <CR>
Arc/Close/Halfwidth/Length/Undo/Width/<Endpoint of line>: Ctrl-C
*Cancel*
```

7. Use a rectangular array to repeat the one edge connector enough times to finish it.

```
Command: ARRAY <CR>
Select objects: W <CR>
First point: 5.125,1.25 <CR>
Second point: 5.5,2.125 <CR>
2 found.
Select objects: <CR>
Rectangular or Polar array (R/P): R <CR>
Number of rows (---) <1>: 1 <CR>
Number of columns (|||) <1>: 7 <CR>
Distance between columnd (|||): 5.25,2.125 <CR>
Second point: 5.625,2.125 <CR>
```

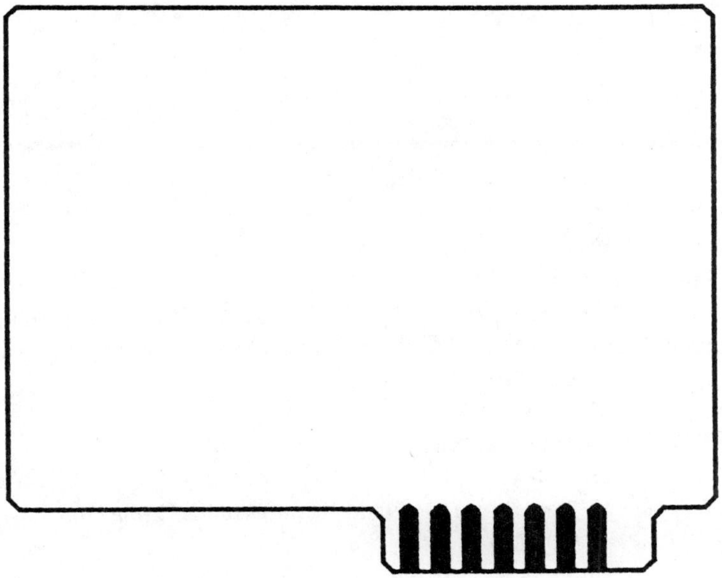

Now, circles called "pads" are drawn. Then three polylines are used to connect one of the circles to the edge connector. Finally, the three polylines are filleted. The remaining steps correspond to the numbered balloons in the following illustration.

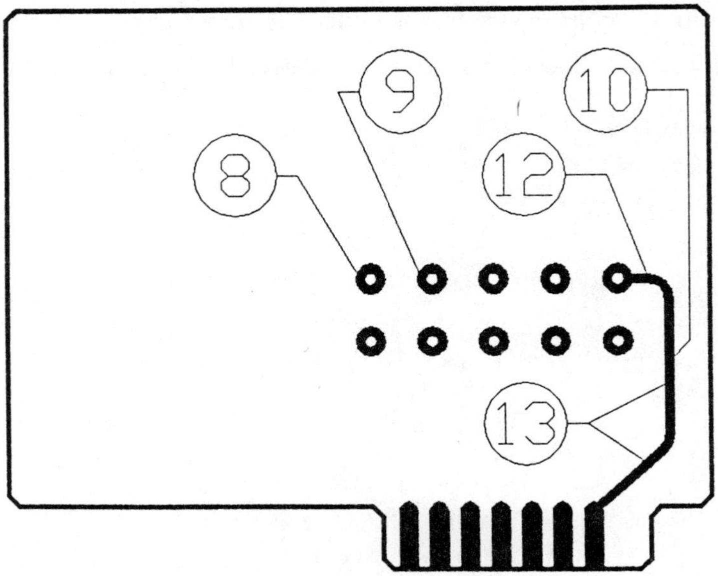

8. Add a soldering pad to the board and redraw the screen.

```
Command: PLINE <CR>
From point: 5,4 <CR>
Current line-width is 0.1250
Arc/Close/Halfwidth/Length/Undo/Width/<Endpoint of line>: A <CR>
Angle/CEnter/CLose/Direction/Halfwidth/Line/Radius/Second pt/Undo/Width/
<Endpoint of arc>: CE <CR>
Center point: 4.875,4.0 <CR>
Angle/Length/<Endpoint>: A <CR>
Included angle: 180 <CR>
Angle/CEnter/CLose/Direction/Halfwidth/Line/Radius/Second pt/Undo/Width/
<Endpoint of arc>: CL <CR>

Command: REDRAW <CR>
```

9. Add nine more pads with the ARRAY command.

```
Command: ARRAY <CR>
Select objects: L <CR>
1 found.
Select objects: <CR>
Rectangular or Polar array (R/P): R <CR>
Number of rows  (---)  <1>: 2 <CR>
Number of columns  (¦¦¦)  <1>: 5 <CR>
Unit cell or distance between rows: .75 <CR>
Distance between columns: .75 <CR>
```

10. Add a polyline to connect one of the pads with one of the edge connectors.

```
Command: PLINE <CR>
From point: 8,4.75 <CR>
Current line-width is 0.250
Arc/Close/Halfwidth/Length/Undo/Width/<Endpoint of line>:8.5,4.75 <CR>
Arc/Close/Halfwidth/Length/Undo/Width/<Endpoint of line>:8.5,2.75 <CR>
Arc/Close/Halfwidth/Length/Undo/Width/<Endpoint of line>:7.625,2 <CR>
Arc/Close/Halfwidth/Length/Undo/Width/<Endpoint of line>: ^Ctrl-C
```

11. Set the fillet radius to .25 inches.

```
Command: FILLET <CR>
Polyline/Radius/<Select two objects>: R <CR>
Enter fillet radius <0.7500>: .25 <CR>
```

12. Place a fillet on one corner of the pline produced in step 10.

```
Command: <CR>
FILLET Polyline/Radius/<Select two objects>: P <CR>
```

13. Select polyline: (Pick the horizontal line which connects to the circle by locating the cross hairs on the line and pressing **Return**.)

```
Command: <CR>
FILLET Polyline/Radius/<Select two objects>: P <CR>
Select polyline: (Pick the vertical line)
Select polyline: (Pick the angled line connected to the edge connector)
2 lines were filleted
```

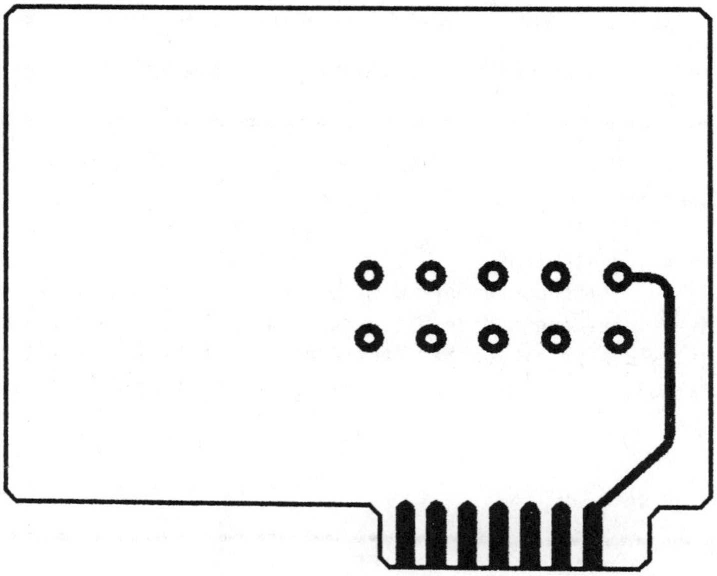

14. Type **QUIT** and press **Return**; then type **Y** and press **Return** to redisplay the Main Menu.
15. Turn to Module 60 to continue the learning sequence.

Module 62

PLOT

```
Command: PLOT
What to plot — Display, Extents, Limits, View, or Window <D>:
```

DESCRIPTION

The PLOT command is used to plot a drawing on an X-Y plotter. AutoCAD drives your plotter directly, or, starting with AutoCAD version 2.5, you may write the plotter output to a disk file for plotting at a later time, possibly on a different computer system. You can select a PLOT command option from the AutoCAD Main Menu, or you can plot from within the Drawing Editor by typing **PLOT** on the command line or picking it from the Screen Menu. The PLOT command options are described in the following list.

D (Display) — Plots what is on the screen. If you select PLOT from the Main Menu, there is nothing on the screen. In this case, AutoCAD plots whatever was on the screen when the drawing was saved.

E (Extents) — The plot consists of the parts of the drawing which contain entities. The effect is similar to the Extents option on the ZOOM command.

L (Limits) — Defines the drawing in terms of the drawing limits. If the drawing extends past the drawing limits, that part of the drawing is not plotted.

V (View) — (ADE-2 option) If you have saved a view with the VIEW command, you can plot that view with this option. If no views have been saved, the option is meaningless.

W (Window) — Plots any rectangular portion of your drawing that you specify with a window. If you are in the Drawing Editor, you can pick the lower-left and upper-right corners on the screen. If you select PLOT from the Main Menu, you have to type the coordinates from the keyboard. Specify the points in drawing units.

```
Plot will NOT be written to a selected file
Sizes are in Inches
Plot origin is at (0.00,0.00)
Plotting area is 44.72 wide by 35.31 high (MAX size)
Plot is NOT rotated 90 degrees
Pen width is 0.010
Area fill will NOT be adjusted for pen width
Hidden lines will NOT be removed
Plot will be scaled to fit available area

Do you want to change anything? <N>
```

AutoCAD uses the defaults set when you configured your plotter. If the defaults are not acceptable for this plot, type **Y** and press **Return**.

```
Layer         Pen  Line  Pen      Layer     Pen  Line  Pen
Color         No.  Type  Speed    Color     No.  Type  Speed
1 (red)        1    0     36      9          1    0     36
2 (yellow)     1    0     36      10         1    0     36
3 (green)      1    0     36      11         1    0     36
4 (cyan)       1    0     36      12         1    0     36
5 (blue)       1    0     36      13         1    0     36
6 (magenta)    1    0     36      14         1    0     36
7 (white)      1    0     36      15         1    0     36
8              1    0     36

Line types     0 = continuous line
               1 = ................................
               2 = ----    ----    ----    ----
               3 = -----   -----   -----   -----
               4 = ------. ------. ------. ------.
               5 = ---- -  ---- -  ---- -  ---- -
               6 = --- - - --- - - --- - - --- - -
Do you want to change any of the above parameters? <N> y
```

Remember that AutoCAD does not know what color pen has been placed in each position in the plotter. It is up to you to ensure that the correct color pen is in each location. If your plotter does not have adjustable speeds, no pen speed information is shown.

The line types are the plotter-defined line types. Only an AutoCAD continuous line is plotted in a line type other than continuous. Mixing a plotter-generated line type and an AutoCAD-generated line type produces undesirable results.

Answering Yes produces the following display:

```
Enter values, blank=Next value, Cn=Color n, S=Show current values, X=Exit

Layer        Pen  Line  Pen
Color        No.  Type  Speed
3 (green)     1    0     36      Pen speed <36>:
```

This display cycles through each layer for each specification. The only way to stop is to type **X** for Exit.

The following screen is displayed by AutoCAD versions 2.5 and later.

```
Write the plot to a file? <N>
```

This option allows you to write the plotter output to a disk file instead of sending it directly to the plotter.

```
Size units (Inches or Millimeters) <I>:
```

Specify whether you want to work in inches or millimeters. The current default is shown in brackets.

```
Plot origin in Inches <0.00,0.00>:
```

The plot origin is specified in inches or millimeters, depending upon your answer to the previous question. The origin of a pen plotter is normally the lower-left corner of the paper. The origin of a printer is the upper-left corner of the paper. You can position your plot anywhere on the paper by specifying the plot origin using current units.

```
Standard values for plotting size

Size     Width    Height
A        10.50     8.00
B        16.00    10.00
C        21.00    16.00
D        33.00    21.00
E        43.00    33.00
MAX      44.72    35.31

Enter the Size or Width,Height (in Inches) <MAX>:
```

If the origin is set at (0,0), your plotter's maximum size (specified when AutoCAD was installed) is listed as MAX. If you move the origin, you reduce the maximum plotting size. Standard sizes which are smaller than your plotter's maximum size are also listed. You may either accept the default, type the letter of the standard size you want, or specify the width and height by typing two numbers separated by commas.

```
Rotate 2D plots 90 degrees clockwise? <N>
```

If you rotate the plot, the rotation is performed in a clockwise direction.

```
Pen width <0.010>:
```

The size is specified in either inches or millimeters, whichever you selected.

```
Adjust area fill boundaries for pen width? <N>
```

When producing printed circuit boards, it is necessary to move the boundaries of filled regions inward by half the width of the pen. For most applications, this is unnecessary.

If you have the ADE-3 options, the following screen appears:

```
Remove hidden lines? <N>
```

If you want hidden line removal, type **Y**.

```
Specify scale by entering:
Plotted Inches=Drawing Units or Fit or ? <F>:
```

The following screen is displayed if you elect to send the plotter output to a file.

```
Enter file name for plot <drawname>:
```

You may either accept the default file name (AutoCAD uses the drawing name.) or type a valid file name, including a drive and path, as appropriate for your computer system.

If you want a specific scale for the drawing, type the scale in drawing units. For example, to specify a full-scale plot, where the drawing was produced in inches, specify 1 = 1. If you want to specify a scale of 1 foot = 1 mile for a mapping application, you could type 12 = 5280. If you have created your drawing in feet and inches and want to plot for ¼ inch = 1 foot, you can type either 1/4" = 1' or 0.25 = 12. In summary:

Notation	Description
1 = 1	Full scale plot
12 = 5280	1 foot = 1 mile
1/4" = 1' or .25 = 12	1/4 inch = 1 foot

Select Fit if you want to make your drawing as large as possible on the paper with no particular scale. If you forget these options, type ? for a short description.

```
Effective plotting area:  44.72 wide by 27.28 high
Position paper in plotter.
Press RETURN to continue or S to Stop for hardware setup
```

When ready, press **Return**.

```
Processing vector: 1854
Plot complete.
```

AutoCAD organizes the plotting to produce the fastest plot possible.

APPLICATIONS

The PLOT command is used with a pen plotter, while the PRPLOT command is used with a dot matrix or laser printer. Printer plots are more limited than pen plots in resolution, size, and color. However, printer plots are generally faster to produce than pen plots.

On plotters with adjustable pen speed, adjust the speed to produce a uniform flow of ink. Ball point pens and fiber tip pens are normally operated at the plotter's maximum speed. Liquid ink pens normally require a slower pen speed. To establish the optimum pen speed, make a multilayer drawing where the same figure appears in each layer. Plot the drawing specifying a different pen speed for each layer. The optimum plot speed is the fastest speed that achieves uniform lines.

TYPICAL OPERATION

In this session you plot a drawing to fit on C-size paper. Begin at the Main Menu.

1. Type **2** and press **Return** to edit an existing drawing.

```
Main Menu

  0.  Exit AutoCAD
  1.  Begin a NEW drawing
  2.  Edit an EXISTING drawing
  3.  Plot a drawing
  4.  Printer Plot a drawing

  5.  Configure AutoCAD
  6.  File Utilities
  7.  Compile shape/font description file
  8.  Convert old drawing file

Enter selection: 2 <CR>

Enter NAME of drawing: COLUMBIA <CR>
```

2. Type **COLUMBIA** and press **Return** to specify the name of the drawing.

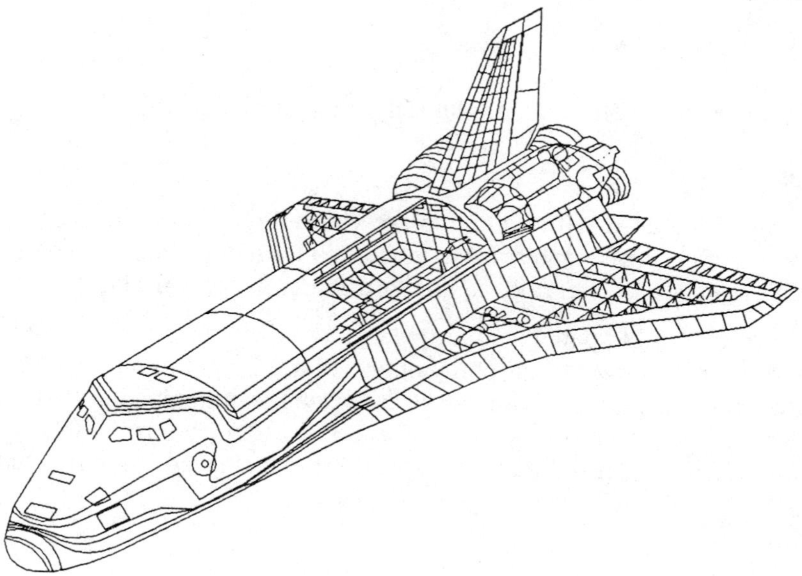

3. Type **PLOT** and press **Return**.

```
COMMAND: PLOT <CR>
What to plot -- Display, Extents, Limits, View, or Window <D>: <CR>
```

4. Type **D** and press **Return** to plot the displayed view.

```
Plot will NOT be written to a selected file
Sizes are in Inches
Plot origin is at (0.00,0.00)
Plotting area is 44.72 wide by 35.31 high (MAX size)
Plot is NOT rotated 90 degrees
Pen width is 0.010
Area fill will NOT be adjusted for pen width
Hidden lines will NOT be removed
Plot will be scaled to fit available area

Do you want to change anything? <N>
```

5. Accept the defaults by pressing **Return**.

AutoCAD displays the status of its vector processing during the plot. On complex drawings plotted with hidden line removal, you may wish to perform some other task while waiting for AutoCAD to remove the hidden lines.

6. When the plot is completed, press **Return** to return to the Drawing Editor.
7. Use **QUIT** to redisplay the Main Menu.
8. Turn to Module 50 to continue the learning sequence.

Module 63

POINT

```
Command: POINT
Point:
```

DESCRIPTION

Points are small marks that are placed on a drawing. The position of a point is selected by typing a location from the keyboard, or by picking a location with the screen cursor.

AutoCAD versions prior to 2.5 display points only as small points on the screen. Starting with AutoCAD version 2.5, use the system variables PDMODE and PDSIZE, to controll the size and shape of point representation on the screen.

It is important to note that a line is not made up of a series of points. A point is a distinct entity which has no length, width, nor depth. When you plot a point, the width is controlled by the thickness of the plotter pen.

APPLICATIONS

The POINT command places a point on the screen, which is often useful for establishing reference coordinates within a drawing. When working with the screen cursor, you can OSNAP to a point. This gives you quick and precise access to a specific reference point on your drawing.

With AutoCAD version 2.5 + , use SETVAR to change the values of PDMODE and PDSIZE to make points more readily visible on the screen.

TYPICAL OPERATION

In this session you use the POINT command to establish two reference points on your drawing screen. Next, you use OSNAP to jump from one point to the other. Begin a new drawing named POINT.

1. Use the POINT command to establish two reference points.

```
Command: POINT <CR>
Point: 1,1 <CR>
Command: <CR>
POINT Point: 5,5 <CR>
Command:
```

2. Use OSNAP to jump from one point to the other.

```
Command: OSNAP <CR>
Object snap modes: NODE <CR>
Command:
```

3. Draw a line between the points.

```
Command:LINE <CR>
From point: (Pick with aperature enclosing 1,1.)
To point: (Pick with aperature enclosing 5,5.)
To point: <CR>
Command:
```

4. Type **QUIT** and press **Return**; then type **Y** and press **Return** to redisplay the Main Menu.
5. Turn to Module 7 to continue the learning sequence.

Module 64

POLYGON

```
Command: POLYGON   Number of sides:
Edge/<Center of polygon>:   (enter a point)
Inscribed in circle/Circluscribed about circle (I/c):
Radius of circle:
```

DESCRIPTION

The POLYGON command, introduced in AutoCAD 2.5, lets you construct a regular polygon with from three to 1,024 sides. The size of the polygon is specified in one of three ways. First, you can specify the size of the inscribed circle (a circle that fits inside the polygon). Second, you can specify the size of the circumscribed circle (a circle that fits outside the polygon). The location of the polygon is selected by specifying its center point. Third, you can describe the polygon in terms of an edge.

Using the inscribed or circumscribed circle methods, you must describe the polygon relative to its center point, size of the inscribed or circumscribed circle, and number of sides in the polygon. Using this method, AutoCAD computes the required length for each side of the polygon. The second method requires that you describe the polygon relative to the length and position of one side; you must also provide the number of sides in the polygon. Use the method that takes maximum advantage of the information you know, and minimizes your required computation.

APPLICATIONS

Although polygons are often constructed using lines and angles, the POLYGON command provides a drawing shortcut that is more convenient. The POLYGON command eliminates the need to compute the magnitude of angles and either the length of sides or the radius of the inscribed/circumscribed circle. Of course, this depends on the construction technique you use. You can use the POLYGON command to draw regular polygons, such as equilateral triangles, squares, pentagons, hexagons, and octagons.

TYPICAL OPERATION

In this session you construct a polygon representing the floor-level outline of a geodesic dome. If the dome is to have a nominal diameter of 45 feet, then the construction resembles the following illustration. From the AutoCAD Main Menu begin a new drawing named POLYGON.

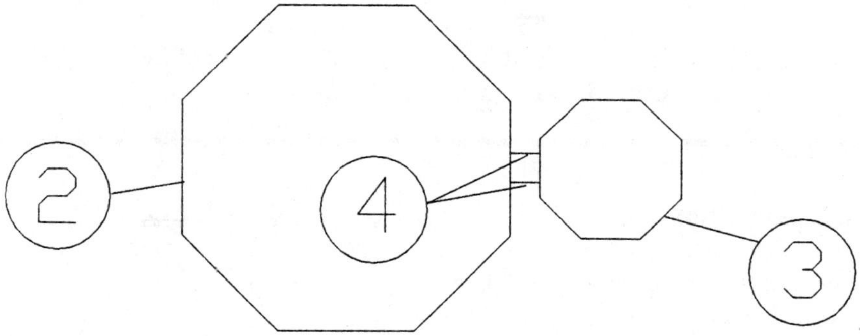

1. Set the limits to 300 x 200 drawing units (feet) to represent a large lot; then ZOOM to the drawing limits.

```
Command: LIMITS <CR>
ON/OFF/<Lower left corner> <0.0000,0.0000>: <CR>
Upper right corner <12.0000,9.0000>: 300,200  <CR>
Command: ZOOM <CR>
All/Center/Dynamic/Extents/Left/Previous/Window/<Scale(X)>: A <CR>
Regenerating drawing.
Command:
```

2. Construct the main living dome based on an octagon in a 45' inscribed circle.

```
Command: POLYGON <CR>
Number of sides: 8 <CR>
Edge/<Center of polygon>: 100,100 <CR>
Inscribed in circle/Circumscribed about circle (I/C): C <CR>
Radius of circle: 45 <CR>
Command:
```

3. Construct a smaller entry foyer, basing the dimension on an 16' linear dimension for each side rather than an overall dimension for the octagon.

```
Command: POLYGON <CR>
Number of sides: 8 <CR>
Edge/<Center of polygon>: E  <CR>
First endpoint of edge: 153,108  <CR>
Second endpoint of edge: 153,92  <CR>
Command:
```

4. Connect the two polygons with a passageway.

```
Command: LINE  <CR>
From point: 145,96 <CR>
To point: 153,96  <CR>
To point: <CR>
Command: <CR>
LINE From point: 145,104 <CR>
To point: 153,104 <CR>
To point: <CR>
Command:
```

Your completed drawing resembles the following illustration.

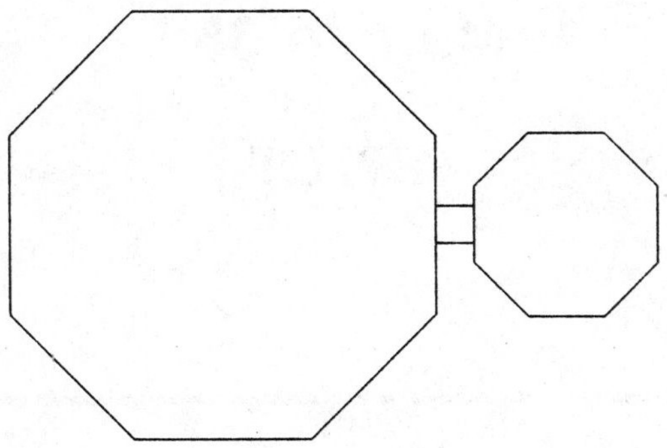

5. Type **QUIT** and press **Return**; then type **Y** and press **Return** to display to the AutoCAD Main Menu.
6. Turn to Module 76 to continue the learning sequence.

Module 65

PRPLOT

```
Command: PRPLOT
What to plot — Display, Extents, Limits, View, or Window <D>:
```

DESCRIPTION

The PRPLOT command lets you plot drawings with a dot matrix or laser printer. AutoCAD drives your printer directly, or, starting with AutoCAD version 2.5, you may write the plotter output to a disk file for printing at a later time, possibly on a different computer system. There are two major requirements for performing a PRPLOT. First, you must have an AutoCAD-supported printer. Second, the necessary software driver must have been selected at AutoCAD installation. The software drivers available for PRPLOTs at this writing drive the following printers.

```
Available printer plotters:

    1.  None
    2.  ADI printer plotter
    3.  AMT Office Printer
    4.  Datacopy Model 90
    5.  Epson
    6.  HP Laser Jet
    7.  IBM Color Jetprinter
    8.  IBM Proprinter
    9.  JDL 750
   10.  Mitsubishi G500
   11.  Okidata
   12.  Printronix
   13.  TI 800
   14.  Toshiba 3-in-One
```

Autodesk continues to add device drivers with product updates.

The printer plot is initiated in two ways. First, you can start a plot by typing **4** from the Main Menu. Starting a PRPLOT from the Main Menu allows you to plot any drawing by typing in its name. Second, you can use the PRPLOT command while in the Drawing Editor. It is either entered from the keyboard or picked from the screen menu. If you want to printer-plot the current drawing, choose the PRPLOT command option from the screen menu or type in PRPLOT from the keyboard.

You can stop PRPLOT at any time by pressing **Ctrl-C**. Sometimes it takes PRPLOT some time to stop because of memory buffers built into the printer.

There are a number of PRPLOT command options that you should know about. These are described in the following list.

D (Display) Plots what is on the screen. If you select PRPLOT from the Main Menu, there is nothing on the screen. In this case, AutoCAD plots whatever was on the screen when the drawing was saved.

E (Extents) The plot consists of the parts of the drawing which contain entities. The effect is similar to the Extents option on the ZOOM command.

L (Limits) Defines the drawing in terms of the drawing limits. If the drawing extends past the drawing limits, that part of the drawing is not plotted.

V (View) (ADE-2 option) If you have saved a view with the VIEW command, you can plot that view with this option. If no views have been saved, the option is meaningless.

W (Window) Plots any rectangular portion of your drawing that you specify with a window. If you are in the Drawing Editor, you can pick the lower-left and upper-right corners on the screen. If you select PRPLOT from the Main Menu, you have to type the coordinates from the keyboard. Specify the points in drawing units.

After selecting what to plot, the next prompt is displayed.

```
Plot will NOT be written to a selected file
Sizes are in Inches
Plot origin is at (0.00,0.00)
Plotting area is 8.00 wide by 11.00 high (MAX size)
Plot is NOT rotated 90 degrees
Hidden lines will NOT be removed
Plot will be scaled to fit available area

Do you want to change anything? <N>
```

All of the above options were set at the time AutoCAD was configured. You can change them at this time. The changes are retained by AutoCAD until changed again. The best way to find out what happens when changing each of the options is to run a series of PRPLOT tests. You can save each plotted sheet with a notation of what options were used when plotted.

When entering the size of the PRPLOT, you cannot exceed a size larger than that specified by MAX. Plot origin is considered as the upper-left-hand corner of the paper on a printer plotter. This origin is altered by changing the values at the Plot origin query.

APPLICATIONS

PRLPLOT is used any time you wish to produce a drawing plot on a dot matrix or laser printer. The size and resolution of the printer plot is determined by the resolution of the printer in use. The resolution of dot matrix printers is fixed. Laser printers have different levels of resolution which are related to the amount of memory in the printer. For example, the supported Hewlett Packard Laserjet Plus printer can print either a full page of graphics at 150 dots per inch, or a half page of graphics at its maximum resolution of 300 dots per inch. You must choose the most appropriate compromise between drawing size and resolution.

Many printers are advertised as being "compatible" with other popular printers. The AutoCAD PRPLOT routines make use of the features of supported printers to their full extent. If you have difficulty with a compatible printer, it is probably not as compatible as you thought.

TYPICAL OPERATION

In this session you perform a printer plot from the Main Menu. A supplied drawing file is selected. The session requires that you have a supported dot-matrix or laser printer attached to your computer.

1. Type **4** and press **Return**; then type **COLUMBIA** and press **Return**.

```
Main Menu

    0.  Exit AutoCAD
    1.  Begin a NEW drawing
    2.  Edit an EXISTING drawing
    3.  Plot a drawing
    4.  Printer Plot a drawing

    5.  Configure AutoCAD
    6.  File Utilities
    7.  Compile shape/font description file
    8.  Convert old drawing file

Enter selection: 4 <CR>

Enter NAME of drawing: COLUMBIA <CR>
```

2. Notice the following display.

```
            A U T O C A D
Copyright (C) 1982,83,84,85,86,87 Autodesk, Inc.
Release X.XXz (MM/DD/YY) IBM PC
Advanced Drafting Extensions 3
Serial Number: 99-999999
Current drawing:  COLUMBIA

Specify the part of the drawing to be plotted by entering:
Display, Extents, Limits, View, or Window <D>:
```

3. Accept the default values by pressing **Return**. The next prompt is displayed.

```
Plot will NOT be written to a selected file
Sizes are in Inches
Plot origin is at (0.00,0.00)
Plotting area is 8.00 wide by 11.00 high (MAX size)
Plot is NOT rotated 90 degrees
Hidden lines will NOT be removed
Plot will be scaled to fit available area

Do you want to change anything? <N>
```

4. Respond to this prompt by pressing **Return** to accept the AutoCAD defaults. The following prompt appears.

```
Effective plotting area:  8.00 wide by 6.18 high
Position paper in printer.
Press RETURN to continue:
```

5. Check your printer, then press **Return** to start the plot. The PRPLOT begins and the following message appears on the screen:

```
Processing vector: nnnn
```

6. When the plot is completed, press **Return** to return to the Main Menu.

NOTE

If you start the PRPLOT from the Drawing Editor, AutoCAD returns to the Drawing Editor when the plot is complete.

7. Turn to Module 62 to continue the learning sequence.

Module 66

PURGE

```
Command: PURGE
Purge unused Blocks/LAyers/LTypes/SHapes/STyles/All: (select one)
```

DESCRIPTION

AutoCAD maintains names for blocks, layers, line types, text styles, and named views. Some names, such as text styles and line types, are provided by AutoCAD. You must supply the name for items like blocks and layers.

Object names are up to 31 characters in length. They consist of uppercase letters, the dollar sign ($), the hyphen (-), and the underscore (_). You can type the name in lowercase if you prefer. AutoCAD converts all lowercase letters to uppercase.

The PURGE command must be the first command issued upon entering the Drawing Editor. Only unused objects may be purged. Layer 0, the Continuous line type, and the Standard text style cannot be purged. Named views cannot be purged. However, a named view can be eliminated with the Delete option of the VIEW command.

APPLICATIONS

After creating an object, you may decide that it is no longer needed. All named objects require storage space in your drawing file. If you find that you no longer need some of the objects you created, the PURGE command eliminates them and restores the storage space.

TYPICAL OPERATION

Because the use of the PURGE command requires that you only type **PURGE** and press **Return**, no practice session is necessary.

Turn to Module 32 to continue the learning sequence.

Module 67

QTEXT

```
Command: QTEXT
On/Off <current>:
```

DESCRIPTION

The QTEXT (Quick-Text) command increases regeneration and plotting speed. It is turned on and off by typing **QTEXT** and pressing **Return**. Then type **on** or **off** and press **Return** to toggle QTEXT on or off.

APPLICATIONS

In drawings having a moderate amount of text, the speed of the REDRAW, REGEN, PLOT, and PRPLOT operations is reduced while calculations are made to regenerate text material. The QTEXT command substitutes a rectangular area in place of text. This feature increases the redraw and plotting time significantly.

When QTEXT is turned back off, text is not redisplayed until you use a REGEN command.

TYPICAL OPERATION

In this session you use the QTEXT command to speed up the regeneration of the following drawing. Begin a new drawing named QTEXT.

Function Keys

F1 Flip Screen
F3 Grid
F6 Coords
F8 Ortho
F9 Snap

1. Create the text with the TEXT command. Use the Roman text style created in the STYLE module.

```
Command: STYLE
Text style name (or ?): ROMAN <CR>
Font file <TXT>: COMPLEX <CR>
Height <0.20>: 0 <CR>
Width factor <1>: 1 <CR>
Obliquing angle <0>: 15 <CR>
Backwards? <N>: N <CR>
Upside-down? <N>: N <CR>

Command: TEXT <CR>
Starting point or (ACRS): S <CR>
Style name <STANDARD>: ROMAN <CR>
Start point or Align/Center/Fit/Middle/Right/Style:
```

2. Pick the starting point for the text with the screen cursor.

```
Height <0.5000>: .75 <CR>
Rotation angle <0>:<CR>
Text: Function Keys <CR>
Command: TEXT <CR>
Start point or Align/Center/Fit/Middle/Right/Style:
```

3. Pick the starting point for the second line of text.

```
Height <0.7500>: .5 <CR>
Rotation angle <0>: <CR>
Text: F1 Flip Screen <CR>
Command: <CR>
TEXT
Text: F3 Grid <CR>
Command: <CR>
TEXT
Text: F6 Coords <CR>
Command: <CR>
TEXT
Text: F8 Ortho <CR>
Command: <CR>
TEXT
Text: F9 Snap <CR>
Command:
```

4. Use QTEXT to display the text as rectangles.

```
Command: QTEXT <CR>
On/Off <On>: ON <CR>
Command:REGEN <CR>
Command:
```

The text is displayed as rectangles.

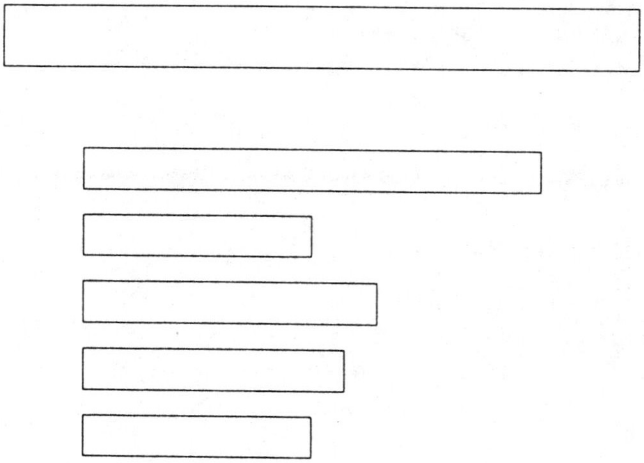

5. Use QTEXT and REGEN to recreate the text.

```
Command: QTEXT <CR>
On/Off <On>: OFF <CR>
Command:REGEN <CR>
Command:
```

The text is regenerated as before.

6. Type **QUIT** and press **Return**; then type **Y** and press **Return** to redisplay the Main Menu.
7. Turn to Module 25 to continue the learning sequence.

Module 68

QUIT

```
Command: QUIT
```

DESCRIPTION

The QUIT command leaves the drawing screen and redisplays the Main Menu.

APPLICATIONS

The QUIT command exits the Drawing Editor and redisplays the Main Menu. It does not update the drawing file. It is useful when examining drawings which are not changed. It is invaluable if you inadventently destroy part of your drawing and need to restart the session. Because the QUIT command has the potential to loose changes you want to keep, it requires verification:

TYPICAL OPERATION

In this operation the QUIT command is used to exit the drawing screen.

1. Type **QUIT** and check the following screen.

```
Command: QUIT
Do you really want to discard all changes to drawing?
```

An answer of No returns you to the Drawing Editor.

2. Type **Y** and press **Return** to redisplay the Main Menu.
3. Turn to Module 75 to continue the learning sequence.

Module 69

REDO

```
Command: REDO
```

DESCRIPTION

The REDO command, introduced in AutoCAD 2.5, is used in combination with the UNDO and U commands to replace entities that have been undone with U or UNDO. The REDO command is always used immediately following an UNDO operation. Otherwise, it has no effect.

APPLICATIONS

The only application for REDO is to reverse an UNDO operation. The REDO command relates to UNDO like the OOPS command relates to ERASE. The UNDO-REDO command pair gives you the freedom to experiment without worrying about permanent contamination of your work, especially when trying new construction techniques.

TYPICAL OPERATION

In this operation you create several entities, remove them with UNDO, and then restore them with REDO. Begin a new drawing named REDO.

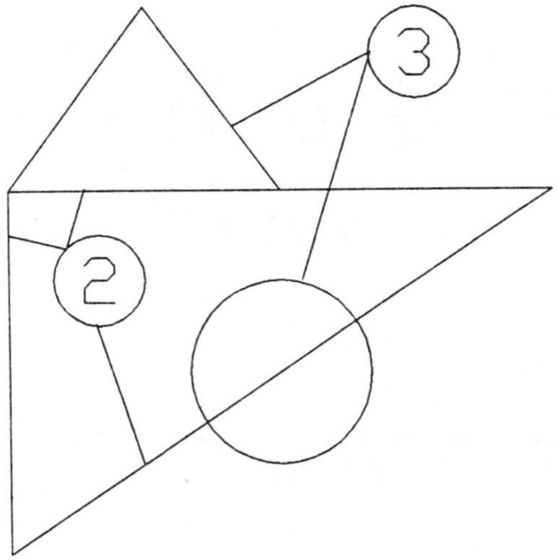

1. Set SNAP to .5. Turn on GRID and ZOOM the screen.

```
Command: SNAP <CR>
Snap spacing or ON/OFF/Aspect/Rotate/Style <1.0000>: .5 <CR>
Command: GRID <CR>
Grid spacing(X) or ON/OFF/Snap/Aspect <0.0000>: ON <CR>
Command: ZOOM <CR>
All/Center/Dynamic/Extents/Left/Previous/Window/<Scale(X)>: A <CR>
Regenerating drawing.
```

2. Draw some entities and remove one with the U command. Then restore the entity with the REDO command.

```
Command: LINE <CR>
From point: 1,1 <CR>
To point: 1,5 <CR>
To point: 7,5 <CR>
To point: C <CR>

Command: U <CR>
LINE
Command: REDO <CR>
```

3. Add an UNDO Mark. Draw more entities. Use the UNDO and replace with REDO.

```
Command: UNDO <CR>
Auto/Back/Control/End/Group/Mark/<number>: M <CR>

Command: CIRCLE <CR>
3P/2P/TTR/<Center point>: MID <CR>
of 2.5,2 <CR>
Diameter/<Radius>: 1 <CR>

Command: LINE <CR>
From point: MID <CR>
of 2.5,5 <CR>
To point: 2.5,7 <CR>
To point: 1,5 <CR>
To point: <CR>

Command: UNDO <CR>
Auto/Back/Control/End/Group/Mark/<number>: 5 <CR>
LINE CIRCLE
Mark encountered

Command: REDO <CR>
```

Your drawing should resemble the following illustration.

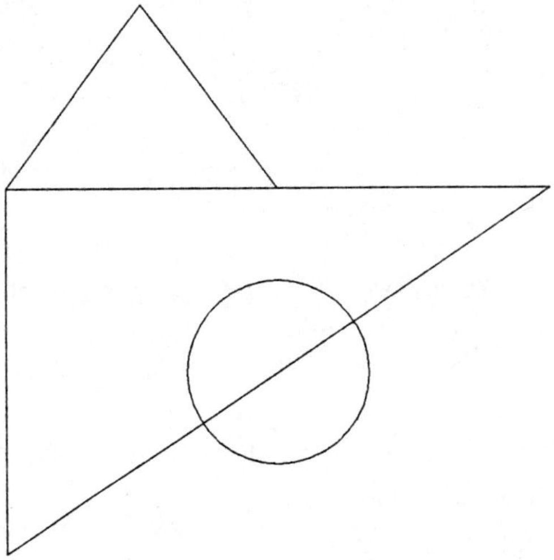

4. Type **Quit** and press **Return**; then type **Y** and press **Return** to display the Main Menu.
5. Turn to Module 27 to continue the learning sequence.

Module 70

REDRAW

```
Command: REDRAW
```

DESCRIPTION

When picking points on the screen, AutoCAD displays "blips" to designate the position of the points. These small crosses are not actually part of the drawing; they are used only for visual reference. They also let you know that AutoCAD has accepted your input.

The REDRAW command refreshes your screen, which eliminates the blips. The REDRAW command does not recompute the drawing vectors for the drawing. If you want to force a complete regeneration of the drawing, use the REGEN command.

If you have a digitizing device with three buttons, the REDRAW command is typically assigned to the third button.

APPLICATIONS

When you perform an ERASE, MOVE, or COPY operation with the drawing grid on, AutoCAD does not regenerate portions of the grid which are removed. To clean up the drawing, use the REDRAW command.

TYPICAL OPERATION

This session lets you use REDRAW to eliminate blips from a simple drawing. Starting at the Main Menu, begin a new drawing named TEMP.

1. Type **LINE** and press **Return**.

2. Type the following points:

```
from point: 5,5 <CR>
to point: 6,6 <CR>
to point: 5,7 <CR>
to point: 4,6 <CR>
to point: <CR>
```

3. Type **REDRAW** and press **Return**.

```
Command:  REDRAW <CR>
```

4. Notice the blips are gone.
5. Type **QUIT** and press **Return**; then type **Y** and press **Return** to redisplay the Main Menu.
6. Turn to Module 71 to continue the learning sequence.

Module 71

REGEN

```
Command: REGEN
```

DESCRIPTION

The REDRAW command refreshes your screen. The REGEN command does more; for instance, it forces AutoCAD to recalculate all points of the drawing from the latest database of information.

APPLICATIONS

The only way you can be certain that a true picture of what you have drawn is displayed is to use the REGEN command. To use this command, type **REGEN** at the command prompt and press **Return**.

TYPICAL OPERATION

Because REGEN is a single entry command, there is no need for a practice session. However, you may use REGEN at any time to see how it regenerates a drawing.

Turn to Module 72 to continue the learning sequence.

Module 72

REGENAUTO

```
Command: REGENAUTO
ON/OFF <current>:
```

DESCRIPTION

The total regeneration of the AutoCAD drawing screen is sometimes a time-consuming process. This is particularly true where complex drawings are involved. There are several AutoCAD commands that produce automatic screen regeneration. These commands are:

ATTEDIT	When doing global editing
BLOCK	When redefining a block
INSERT	When inserting a block
LAYER	When using freeze/thaw or line type
LTSCALE	When changing scale of line type
STYLE	If the font file is changed

To activate the REGENAUTO function, type **REGENAUTO** and press **Return**. AutoCAD responds with the "On/Off <current>:" prompt.

```
Command: REGENAUTO <CR>
On/Off <current>: OFF
```

To suppress automatic screen regeneration, respond with **OFF**. If you want to turn automatic screen regeneration back on, type **REGENAUTO** and press **Return** again. Then type **ON** and press **Return**.

```
Command: REGENAUTO <CR>
On/Off <current>: ON
```

The automatic regeneration process is now turned back on.

There are several commands that produce an automatic regeneration, whether the REGENAUTO command is on or off. These are:

ZOOM
PAN
VIEW
RESTORE
REGEN

APPLICATIONS

Anytime you want to speed up the drawing process, you can suspend automatic screen regeneration using REGENAUTO. Automatic screen regeneration that is caused by the preceding commands is suspended.

The addition of the VIEWRES command in AutoCAD version 2.5 provides additional control over automatic regeneration of drawings. See Module 92 for additional information.

TYPICAL OPERATION

Because REGENAUTO is a simple ON/OFF command, no purpose is served by a practice session. However, when you are producing a drawing that uses any of those commands that cause automatic screen regeneration, try REGENAUTO to see how it speeds up the drawing process. You may want to try it with the BLOCK or INSERT sessions (Module 13 or 41).

Turn to Module 92 to continue the learning sequence.

Module 73

RENAME

```
Command: RENAME
Block/LAyer/LType/Style/View: (select one)
Old (object) name: (name)
New (object) name: (name)
```

DESCRIPTION

AutoCAD maintains names for blocks, layers, line types, text styles, and named views. Some names, such as text styles and line types are provided by AutoCAD. You must supply names for objects like blocks and layers. The RENAME command lets you change the name of an object. You cannot rename layer 0 or the Continuous line type.

Object names are up to 31 characters in length. They consist of uppercase letters, the dollar sign ($), the hyphen (-), and the underscore (_). You can type the name in lowercase if you prefer. AutoCAD converts all lowercase letters to uppercase.

APPLICATIONS

After naming an object, you may decide that the name is inconsistent with the purpose of the object, it may be hard to remember, or it may conflict with an existing name.

TYPICAL OPERATION

In this session you change the name of the default line type from "Standard" to "Ordinary." Begin a new drawing named NAME.

1. Type the command **RENAME** (or pick it from the Utility submenu).

```
Command: RENAME <CR>
Block/LAyer/LType/Style/View:
```

2. Select Style.

```
Command: RENAME <CR>
Block/LAyer/LType/Style/View: STYLE <CR>
Old text style name:
```

3. Type **STANDARD** and press **Return**.

```
Command: RENAME <CR>
Block/LAyer/LType/Style/View: STYLE <CR>
Old text style name: STANDARD <CR>
New text style name:
```

4. Type **ORDINARY** and press **Return**.

```
Command: RENAME <CR>
Block/LAyer/LType/Style/View: STYLE <CR>
Old text style name: STANDARD <CR>
New text style name: ORDINARY <CR>
Command:
```

The operation is complete.

5. Use **QUIT** to redisplay the Main Menu.
6. Turn to Module 66 to continue the learning sequence.

Module 74

ROTATE

```
Command: ROTATE
Select objects:
Base point:
<Rotation angle>/Reference:
```

DESCRIPTION

The ROTATE command, introduced in AutoCAD 2.5, rotates an object or group of objects around a point. First, you select the objects to rotate using any object selection method. Next, you pick a base point. The base point may be anywhere on the drawing. It does not have to be on or inside the object to rotate. You may rotate an object around itself, or you may rotate it around some external point. The amount of the rotation is specified in several ways.

Number — You can type the measure of an angle using the current units.

Drag — If you wish, you can drag the angle. The dragging is relative to the base point you previously specified.

R — Type **R** and press **Return**. You are then prompted for a reference angle and a new length. You may specify these angles either by typing the angle measure at the keyboard, or by picking points on the screen corresponding to the angles. You do not have to specify each angle in the same manner. The objects are rotated so that lines drawn at the reference angle are rotated to the new angle.

APPLICATIONS

With the introduction of AutoCAD 2.5, rotation capabilities that were previously available with BLOCKS and WBLOCKS extended to entities and groups of entities with the introduction of the ROTATE command. Object rotation lets you rotate selected portions of a drawing without having to define the objects as a block and insert the block with rotation. This saves steps and allows the original objects to remain single entities, rather than become part of a block.

TYPICAL OPERATION

In this session you use the LOGO drawing that was created in the TRIM module and modified in the SCALE module. If the drawing is not on your disk, review the TRIM and SCALE operations to create the drawing.

1. From the AutoCAD Main Menu, edit the existing drawing LOGO.

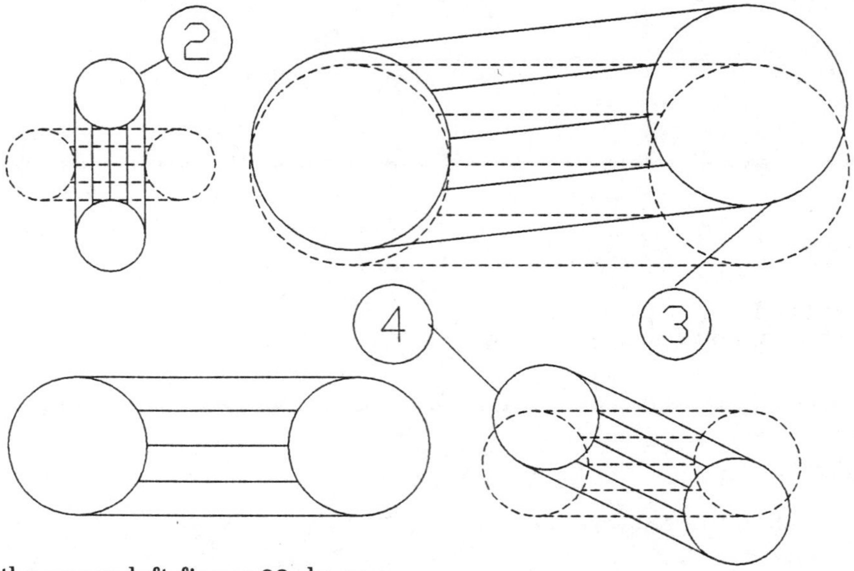

2. Rotate the upper left figure 90 degrees.

```
Command: ROTATE <CR>
Select objects: W <CR>
First corner: 0,11 <CR>
Other corner: 6,15 <CR>
7 found.
Select objects: <CR>
Base point: 3,13 <CR>
<Rotation angle>/Reference: 90 <CR>
Command:
```

3. Rotate the upper right figure around an external point by dragging the rotation on the screen.

```
Command: ROTATE <CR>
Select objects: W <CR>
First corner: 6,9 <CR>
Other corner: 24,17 <CR>
```

```
7 found.
Select objects: <CR>
Base point: 6,13 <CR>
<Rotation angle>/Reference: 24,15 <CR>
Command:
```

4. Rotate the lower right figure around itself by showing AutoCAD the angles on the screen.

```
Command: ROTATE <CR>
Select objects: W <CR>
First corner: 13,1 <CR>
Other corner: 24,7 <CR>
7 found.
Select objects: <CR>
Base point: 18,4.5 <CR>
<Rotation angle>/Reference: R <CR>
Reference angle <0>: 15,3 <CR>  (Bottom of the left circle.)
 Second point: 21,6 <CR>         (Top of the right circle.)
New angle: 21,4.5 <CR>
Command:
```

Your completed drawing looks like the following.

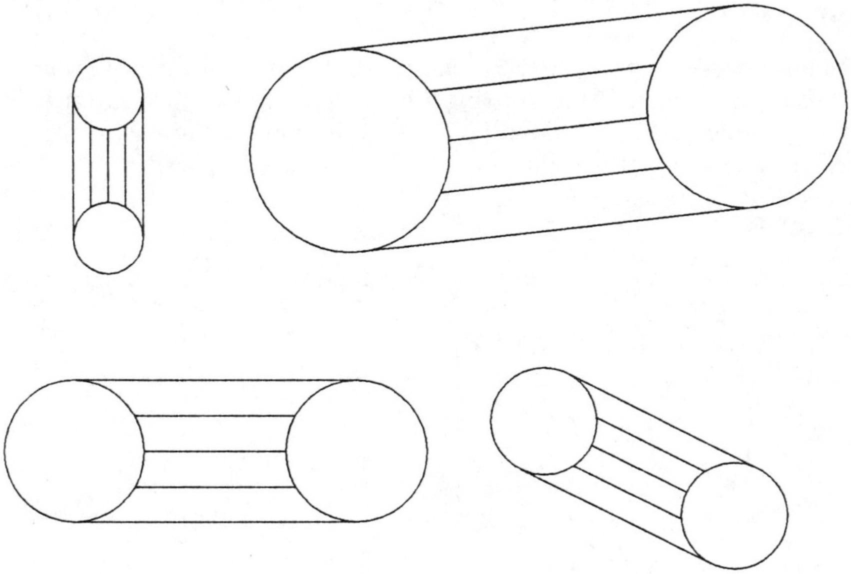

5. Type **END** and press **Return** to display the AutoCAD Main Menu.
6. Turn to Module 52 to continue the learning sequence.

Module 75

SAVE

```
Command: SAVE
```

DESCRIPTION

When you type **SAVE** and press **Return**, your drawing file is saved to your disk. Once it is saved, you can resume your drawing work.

APPLICATIONS

The SAVE command provides protection against power failures, hardware failures, and human error. The SAVE command updates the drawing file without forcing you to exit the Drawing Editor. The old "current" version is renamed with a .BAK extension, and any existing .BAK version is discarded. Saving your work often is an excellent insurance policy.

TYPICAL OPERATION

Because operation of the SAVE command is self-evident, no step-by-step exercise is necessary.

Next 28

Module 76

SCALE

```
Command: SCALE
Select objects:
Base point:
<Scale factor>/Reference:
```

DESCRIPTION

The SCALE command, intoduced in AutoCAD 2.5, lets you re-size anything from an entity to an entire drawing. To use SCALE, you can select any group of entities in the drawing for scaling. If you wish, you can enclose the entire drawing in a window and re-scale it. Next, you select a base point. The location of the base point remains constant after the scaling operation is complete. The location of all other points are re-computed with reference to the base point. The last prompt requests the scale factor or reference.

There are several ways to specify the amount of scaling to take place:

Number — First, you can type a scale factor. A scale factor of one does nothing. A scale factor less than one reduces the size of the drawing. A scale factor greater than one increases the size of the drawing. Use numbers greater than zero.

Drag — If you want to, you can drag the scale factor. The dragging is relative to the base point you previously specified. Dragging less than one drawing unit away from the base point reduces the drawing, dragging more than one drawing unit away from the base point enlarges the drawing. It does not matter which direction you move from the base point. The SCALE command relates to the distance you move, not the direction.

R Type **R** and press **Return**. You are prompted for a reference length and a new length. You specify these lengths either by typing a length at the keyboard, or by picking points on the screen corresponding to the lengths. You do not have to specify each length in the same way. The objects are scaled so that the reference length becomes the new length.

APPLICATIONS

The SCALE command provides a simple way to change the size of objects within a drawing, or to change the size of an entire drawing. If you determine that your original choice of drawing units is inappropriate, the SCALE command provides an easy method to change your choice.

TYPICAL OPERATION

In this session you use the SCALE command to change the size of existing entities in a drawing. This activity makes use of the LOGO drawing produced in the TRIM module. If the drawing is not on your disk, refer to the TRIM module to create the drawing.

1. From the AutoCAD Main Menu, edit the existing drawing LOGO.

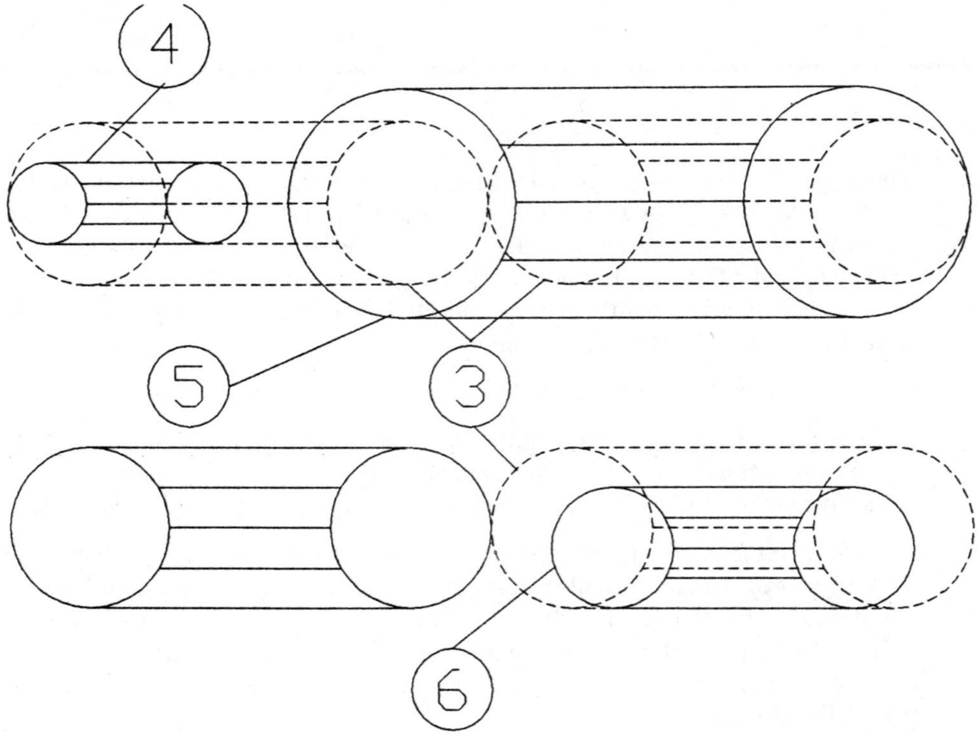

2. Reset the drawing limits to make room for additional copies of the figure. ZOOM to the new limits.

```
Command: LIMITS <CR>
ON/OFF/<Lower left corner> <0.0000,0.0000>: <CR>
Upper right corner <12.0000,9.0000>: 24,18 <CR>
Command: ZOOM <CR>
All/Center/Dynamic/Extents/Left/Previous/Window/<Scale(X)>: A <CR>
Regenerating drawing.
Command:
```

3. Make 3 copies of the figure.

```
Command: COPY <CR>
Select objects: W <CR>
First corner: 0,2 <CR>
Other corner: 13,9 <CR>
7 found.
Select objects:
<Base point or displacement>/Multiple: M <CR>
Base point: Second point of displacement:  0,13 <CR>
Second point of displacement: 12,13 <CR>
Second point of displacement: 12,5 <CR>
Second point of displacement: <CR>
Command:
```

4. Scale the first copy. Define the objects with a window. Set the base point at the leftmost point in the figure. Specify the scale as an absolute scale factor.

```
Command: SCALE
Select objects: W
First corner: 0,10
Other corner: 12,16
7 found.
Select objects: <CR>
Base point: 0,13 <CR>
<Scale factor>/Reference: .5 <CR>
Command:
```

5. Scale the second copy of the figure. In this operation you use a scale factor of the square root of two. However, you specify this value as the diagonal of a unit square rather than computing the value and typing it.

```
Command: SCALE <CR>
Select objects: W <CR>
First corner: 12,10 <CR>
Other corner: 24,16 <CR>
7 found.
Select objects: <CR>
Base point: 24,13 <CR>
<Scale factor>/Reference: 23,14 <CR>
Command:
```

6. Scale the third copy. This time, select the base point as the midpoint of the bottom line in the figure. Specify the scale as rescaling a length of two to a length of 1.5.

```
Command: SCALE <CR>
Select objects: W <CR>
First corner: 12,2 <CR>
Other corner: 24,8 <CR>
7 found.
Select objects: <CR>
Base point: 18,3 <CR>
<Scale factor>/Reference: R <CR>
Reference length <1>: 2 <CR>
New length: 1.5 <CR>
Command:
```

Your completed drawing looks like the following one.

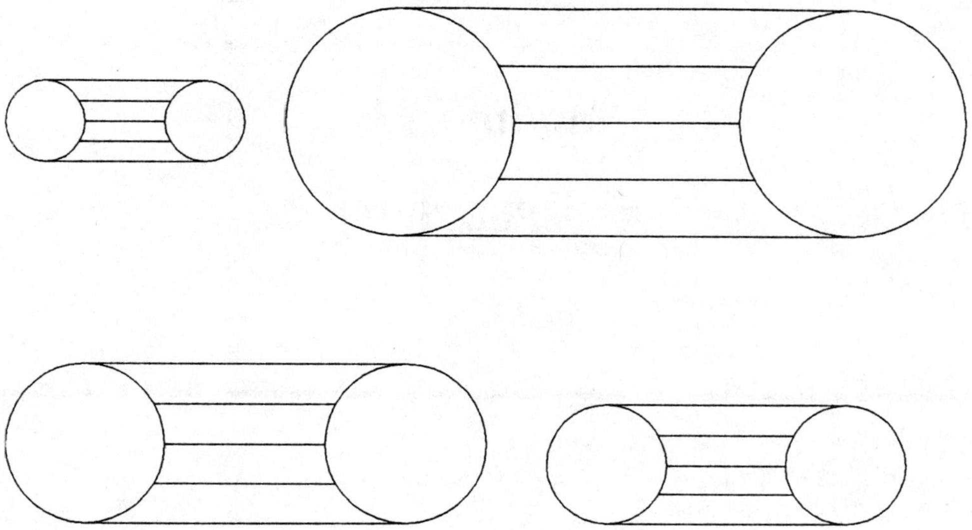

7. Type **END** and press **Return** to display the AutoCAD Main Menu. This drawing is used again in the ROTATE module.
8. Turn to Module 74 to continue the learning sequence.

Module 77

SELECT

```
Command: SELECT
Select objects:
```

DESCRIPTION

The SELECT command, introduced in AutoCAD 2.5, lets you define a set of objects for use with other AutoCAD commands. Many commands, such as COPY, MOVE, SCALE, ROTATE, MIRROR, require you to select one or more objects in the performance of an operation. You have your choice of selecting each entity individually, or grouping objects together in a selection set with the SELECT command. If this is done, the current selection set can serve as the object of other commands.

The following commands and techniques apply to building a selection set within the SELECT command, and to selecting objects with an individual editing or inquiry command.

Point	You may respond by picking a point on the screen or typing its coordinates from the keyboard. You may adjust the size of the screen cursor's target box with the APERTURE command. When you select a solid, trace, or polyline, point to an edge instead of a solid-filled region.
M	Multiple object selection. When you pick a point on the screen, AutoCAD scans the drawing to locate the object. If the drawing is large and complex, the search delay may be excessive. To select multiple objects, type **M** and press **Return**; then pick the multiple objects on the screen. Press **Return** again to begin AutoCAD's search for the selected objects.
W	Window selection. This lets you to select all the objects enclosed within a window. If only part of an object displayed on the screen is in a window, the object is ignored. If part of an object is displayed, and the remainder is off the screen, window adds the object to the selection set if all the visible portions are enclosed within the window. Window selection only applies to objects that are visible on the screen.

C — Crossing selection. Similar to Window selection, Crossing selection includes all objects touched by the window. The objects do not have to be completely enclosed within the window for selection.

L — Last selection. Selects the most recently created object visible on the screen. There is only one "last" object.

P — Previous selection. Uses the set of objects used for the previous command. Use SELECT to create a selection set; then use P (Previous) to use that set of objects in another command.

U — Undo. Removes the most recently selected object or group of objects from a selection set. Undo may be used repeatedly to step backward to undo a selection set.

R — Remove. Normally when you select an object, it is added to the selection set. Selecting Remove allows you to remove selected objects from the selection set. Selection set construction continues in Remove mode until you use the Add command to place it back in Add mode.

A — Add. The default setting for building a selection set, add mode allows you to use any of the object selection techniques to add entities to the selection set.

Null — Pressing **Return** or **Spacebar** terminates the selection of objects, indicating that you have completed construction of the desired selection set.

Ctrl-C — Cancels the construction of the current selection set and terminates the command.

? — Displays a listing of the valid object selection responses.

Box — This option, introduced in Release 9, must be spelled out, there is no abbreviation. The action is dependent on the way points are picked. If the second point of the box is to the left of the first point, Box is equivalent to the Window option. If the second point of the box is to the right of the first point, Box is equivalent to the Crossing option. The Box option is useful in constructing menu systems.

AUto — Automatic selection, introduced in Release 9 and abbreviated AU, allows the method of picking to determine the object selection criteria. If the first point picked identifies an object, AUto is equivalent to single item selection. If the first point does not identify an object, AUto operates like Box. The AUto option is more useful in constructing menu systems than in typing selecting criteria interactively from the keyboard.

SIngle — Single object selection, introduced in Release 9 and abbreviated SI, suppresses the normal dialog for object selection, and ends the selection process when a single selection is made.

Use these responses singly or in combination to construct the required selection set for each operation.

APPLICATIONS

When you perform a series of operations on the same group of objects, first use the SELECT command to define a selection set. Then, for each required operation, specify the selection set at the "Select objects" prompt. You are thereby freed from the tedium of repeatedly picking or otherwise defining the same group of drawing entities several times.

TYPICAL OPERATION

In this session you draw a group of objects, construct a selection set from these objects, and then perform two operations that use the selection set. Begin a new drawing named SELECT.

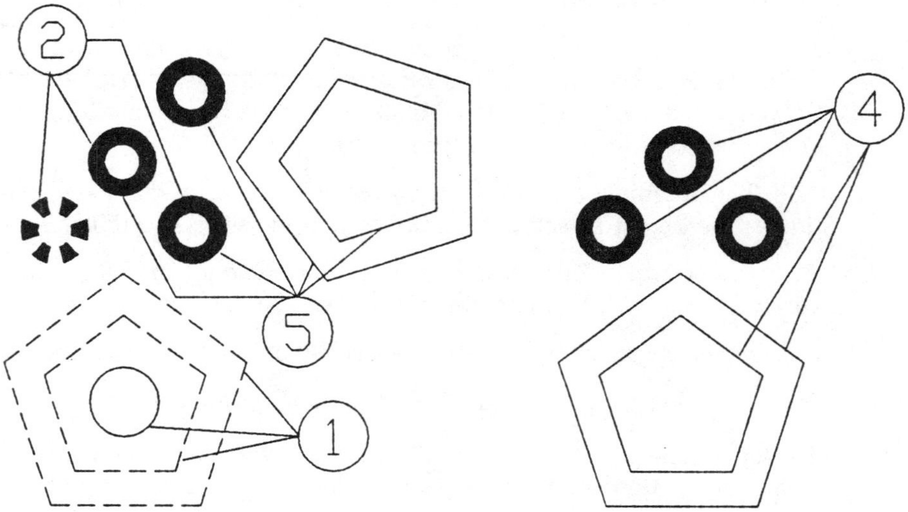

1. Draw two pentagons with a circle in the middle.

```
Command: POLYGON <CR>
Number of sides: 5 <CR>
Edge/<Center of polygon>:  2,2 <CR>
Inscribed in circle/Circumscribed about circle (I/C): C <CR>
Radius of circle: 1.5 <CR>
Command: POLYGON <CR>
Number of sides: 5 <CR>
Edge/<Center of polygon>: 2,2 <CR>
Inscribed in circle/Circumscribed about circle (I/C): C <CR>
Radius of circle: 1 <CR>
Command: CIRCLE <CR>
3P/2P/TTR/<Center point>: 2,2 <CR>
Diameter/<Radius>: 0.5 <CR>
Command:
```

2. Draw three donuts above the pentagons.

```
Command: DONUT <CR>
Inside diameter <0.5000>:  <CR>
Outside diameter <1.0000>:  <CR>
Center of doughnut: 1,4.5 <CR>
Center of doughnut: 3,4.5 <CR>
Center of doughnut: 2,5.5 <CR>
Center of doughnut: <CR>
```

3. Construct a selection set consisting of all the objects except the circle.

```
Command: SELECT <CR>
Select objects: W <CR>
First corner: 0,0 <CR>
Other corner: 4,6 <CR>
6 found.
Select objects: R <CR>
Remove objects: (Pick the circle.)
1 selected, 1 found, 1 removed.
Remove objects: <CR>
```

4. Copy the objects in the current selection set.

```
Command: COPY <CR>
Select objects: P <CR>
5 found.
Select objects: <CR>
<Base point or displacement>/Multiple: 2,2 <CR>
Second point of displacement: @8<0 <CR>
```

5. Rotate the objects in the current selection set. Notice that the selection set includes the original objects, not the group in the new location.

```
Command: ROTATE <CR>
Select objects: P <CR>
5 found.
Select objects: <CR>
Base point: CEN <CR>
of (Pick the top donut.) <CR>
<Rotation angle>/Reference: 90 <CR>
```

Your completed drawing resembles the following illustration.

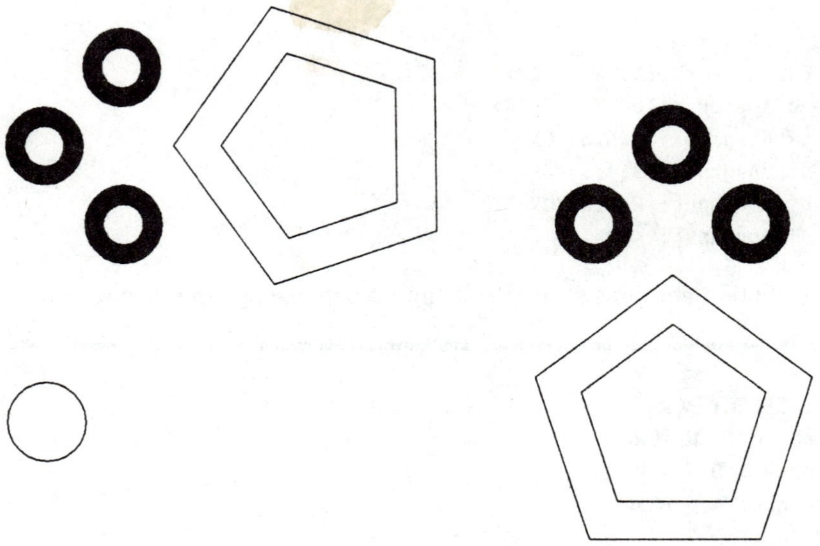

6. Type **QUIT** and press **Return**; then type **Y** and press **Return** to display the Main Menu.
7. Turn to Module 24 to continue the learning sequence.

Module 78

SETVAR

```
Command: SETVAR
Variable name or ?:
New value for variable-name <current>
```

DESCRIPTION

The SETVAR command was introduced in AutoCAD version 2.5. Many choices you make in an AutoCAD drawing establish default values. This includes text size, snap resolution, elevation, fill mode, and others. These values are saved as predefined AutoCAD system variables. Saving these values establishes them as defaults the next time a command is used. In addition, AutoCAD maintains a number of system variables that are not set by specific commands. These values control various editing features and the way a drawing is displayed. Many of these values are stored with the drawing and are retained from one editing session to the next. Some of the values are stored as part of the AutoCAD configuration file.

The SETVAR command serves two purposes. First, it is used to inspect the current settings of the AutoCAD system variables. Second, it is used to modify selected system variables. The AutoCAD system variables are shown in the following list.

ACADPREFIX	The name of the directory specified by the ACAD environment variable. Normally empty.
ACADVER	This read-only variable provides the current AutoCAD version number. It contains string values such as "2.62" or "9.0."
AFLAGS	Attribute flags bit-code for ATTDEF command (sum of the following): 1 = Invisible, 2 = Constant, 4 = Verify.
ANGBASE	Angle 0 direction.

ANGDIR	1 = clockwise angles, 0 = counterclockwise angles.
APERTURE	Object snap target height expressed in pixels.
AREA	Area computed by AREA, LIST, or DBLIST (read-only).
ATTDIA	If zero, AutoCAD issues text prompts for the INSERT command. If 1, AutoCAD uses a dialogue box. (Release 9 +)
ATTMODE	Attribute display mode (0 = off, 1 = normal, 2 = on).
ATTREQ	If zero, all default values for attributes are assumed for the INSERT command. If one, Attribute values are requested from the user according to the setting of ATTDIA. (Release 9 +)
AUNITS	Angular units mode (0 = decimal degrees, 1 = degrees/minutes/seconds, 2 = grads, 3 = radians, 4 = surveyor's units).
AUPREC	Angular units decimal places.
AXISMODE	Axis on if 1, off if 0.
AXISUNIT	Axis spacing, X and Y.
BLIPMODE	Marker blips on if 1, off if 0.
CDATE	Calendar date/time (read-only).
CECOLOR	Current entity color (read-only).
CELTYPE	Current entity linetype (read-only).
CHAMFERA	First chamfer distance.
CHAMFERB	Second chamfer distance.
CLAYER	Current layer (read-only).
CMDECHO	When AutoLISP's (command) function is used, prompts and input are echoed if this variable is 1, but not if it is 0.
COORDS	If zero, coordinated display is updated on point picks only. If 1, display of absolute coordinates is continuously updated. If 2, distance and angle from last point are displayed when a distance or angle is requested.
DATE	Julian date/time (read-only).
DIMxxxxx	Dimensioning variables. The values of these variables are displayed and changed using the SETVAR command from the drawing editor; the values are inspected using the STATUS command in the Dimensioning subsystem; values are changed while in the Dimensioning subsystem by typing the name of the variable at the DIM prompt. The full explanation of these variables and their use is explained in Module 18, DIM and DIM1.

DISTANCE	Distance computed by DIST, LIST, or DBLIST (read only).
DRAGMODE	0 = no dragging, 1 = on if requested, 2 = auto.
DRAGP1	Regen-drag input sampling rate.
DRAGP2	Fast-drag input sampling rate.
DWGNAME	Drawing name (read-only).
DWGPREFIX	Drive/directory prefix for drawing (read-only).
ELEVATION	Current 3D elevation.
EXPERT	0 issues all prompts normally. 1 suppresses the REGEN prompt "About to regen, proceed?," and the LAYER prompt, "Do you really want to turn the current layer off?" 2 suppresses the BLOCK prompt "Block already defined. Redefine it?," and the WBLOCK prompt "A drawing with this name already exists. Overwrite it?," in addition to the prompts suppressed by EXPERT = 1. 3 suppresses prompts displayed by LINETYPE warning that you are trying to load a linetype already loaded, or that you are creating a duplicate definition of a linetype.
EXTMAX	Upper-right "drawing uses" extents (read-only).
EXTMIN	Lower-left "drawing uses" extents (read-only).
FILLETRAD	Fillet radius.
FILLMODE	Fill mode on if 1, off if 0.
GRIDMODE	0 = off, 1 = on.
GRIDUNIT	Grid spacing, X and Y.
HIGHLIGHT	Object selection highlighting (0 = off, 1 = on).
INSBASE	Insertion base point (set by BASE command).
LASTANGLE	The end angle of the last arc entered (read-only).
LASTPOINT	Referenced by "@" during keyboard entry of points in two (X and Y) dimensions.
LASTPT3D	Referenced by "@" during keyboard entry of points in three (X, Y and Z) dimensions.
LIMCHECK	Limits checking. 0 = off, 1 = on.
LIMMAX	Upper-right drawing limits.
LIMMIN	Lower-left drawing limits.

LTSCALE	Global linetype scale factor.
LUNITS	Linear units mode (1 = scientific, 2 = decimal, 3 = engineering, 4 = architectural).
LUPREC	Linear units decimal places or denominator.
MENUECHO	The value represents the sum of the following bit codes: 0 = menu input is echoed and prompts are displayed normally. 1 = menu input is not echoed (but ^P in a menu item toggles echoing on). 2 = prompts are suppressed if input is coming from a menu item. 4 = the use of ^P for menu toggling is disabled. For example, a value of 3 means that echoing and prompts are both suppressed.
MENUNAME	The name of the current menu file. (Read only)
MIRRTEXT	MIRROR reflects text if nonzero, retains text direction if zero.
ORTHOMODE	0 = Ortho off, 1 = Ortho on.
OSMODE	Object snap modes bit-code (sum of the following): 1 = Endpoint, 2 = Midpoint, 4 = Center 8 = Node, 16 = Quadrant, 32 = Intersection 64 = Insert, 128 = Perpendicular, 256 = Nearest 512 = Quick
POPUPS	If 1, the advanced user interface is available. If 0, only the standard interface is available. (Read only)
PDMODE	Point display mode.
PDSIZE	Point display size.
PERIMETER	Perimeter computed by AREA, LIST, or DBLIST.
PICKBOX	Object selection target height, in pixels.
QTEXTMODE	0 = Quick text mode off, 1 = Quick text mode on.
REGENMODE	0 = Regenauto is off, 1 = Regenauto is on.
SCREENSIZE	Graphics screen size in pixels, X and Y (read-only).
SKETCHINC	Sketch record increment.
SKPOLY	0 = SKETCH generates lines, 1 = SKETCH generates polylines.
SNAPANG	Snap/grid rotation angle.

SNAPBASE	Snap/grid origin point.
SNAPISOPAIR	Current isometric plane (0 = left, 1 = top, 2 = right).
SNAPMODE	0 = Snap off, 1 = Snap on.
SNAPSTYL	Snap style (0 = standard, 1 = isometric).
SNAPUNIT	Snap spacing, X and Y.
SPLFRAME	If one, the control polygon for spline-fit polylines is displayed. If zero, the control polygon is not displayed.
SPLINESEGS	The number of segments generated for each spline when the PEDIT Spline fit option is used.
TDCREATE	Time and date of drawing creation (read-only).
TDINDWS	Total editing time (read-only).
TDUPDATE	Time and date of last update/save (read-only).
TDUSRTIMER	User elapsed timer (read-only).
TEMPPREFIX	Contains the directory name used for temporary files. May include a path. The default is empty.
TEXTEVAL	Controls the evaluation of text for the TEXT command. (The value of this variable is ignored by the DTEXT command.) 0 All text values are taken literally. This is the default. 1 Text starting with "(" or "!" is interpreted as an AutoLISP statement.
TEXTSIZE	Default text height.
TEXTSTYLE	The current text style.
THICKNESS	Current 3D thickness.
TRACEWID	Default trace width.
VIEWCTR	Center of current view (read-only).
VIEWSIZE	Current view height, in drawing units (read-only).
VPOINTX	X component of current 3D viewpoint (read-only).
VPOINTY	Y component of current 3D viewpoint (read-only).
VPOINTZ	Z component of current 3D viewpoint (read-only).
VSMAX	The upper-right corner of the current virtual screen (read-only).
VSMIN	The lower-left corner of the current virtual screen (read-only).

APPLICATIONS

Many of AutoCAD's system variables are most easily modified through their related command. These system variables include settings for snap specifications, text height, axis display, and similar variables for which AutoCAD provides a special command. However, some of AutoCAD's variables can only be set through the SETVAR command. Two examples of this are PDMODE and PDSIZE. A good use for the SETVAR command is to review the parameters of a drawing created by someone else. This is particularly valuable if you must edit the drawing. Knowing the variable settings lets you predict the consequences of using a number of AutoCAD commands.

TYPICAL OPERATION

In this session you use the SETVAR command to view the settings of the AutoCAD system variables. A further example of SETVAR is included in the MEASURE module. Begin a new drawing named SETVAR.

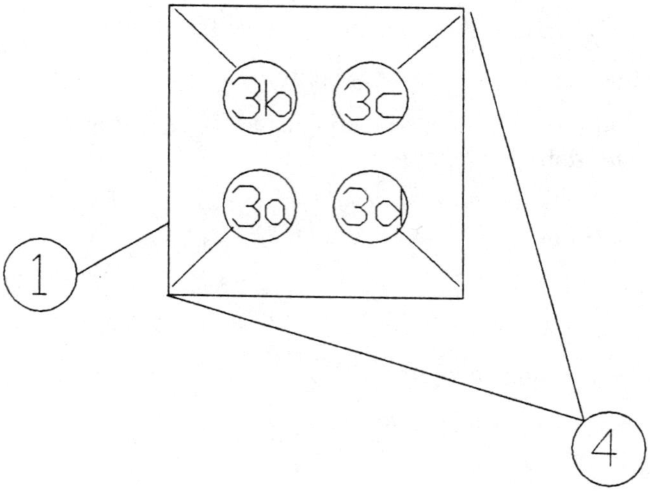

1. Draw a rectangle.

```
Command: LINE <CR>
From point: 3,3 <CR>
To point: 3,7 <CR>
To point: 7,7 <CR>
To point: 7,3 <CR>
To point: C <CR>
Command:
```

2. Set Object snap to "intersection." This automatically snaps to the intersection of two lines.

```
Command: OSNAP <CR>
Object snap modes: INT <CR>
Command:
```

3. Use the AREA command to find the area of the rectangle.

```
Command: AREA <CR>
<First point>/Entity/Add/Subtract: (Pick 3a, the lower left corner.)
Next point: (Pick 3b, the upper left corner.)
Next point: (Pick 3c, the upper right corner.)
Next point: (Pick 3d, the lower right corner.)
Next point: (Pick 3a, the lower left corner.)
Next point: <CR>
Area = 16.0000, Perimeter = 16.0000
```

4. Use the DIST command to find the length of the diagonal.

```
Command: DIST <CR>
First point: (Pick the lower left corner.)
Second point: (Pick the upper right corner.)
Distance = 5.6569   Angle = 45
Delta X = 4.0000   Delta Y = 4.0000   Delta Z = 0.0000
```

5. Inspect the AutoCAD system variables.

```
Command: SETVAR <CR>
Variable name or ?: ? <CR>
```

Your screen flips to the text screen and displays the first screen of system variables.

```
ACADPREFIX     ""                                    (read only)
AFLAGS         0
ANGBASE        0
ANGDIR         0
APERTURE       10
AREA           16.0000                               (read only)
  :            :                                       :
  :            :                                       :
CMDECHO        1
COORDS         0
DATE           2447058.60239021                      (read only)
-- Press RETURN for more --
```

Notice the system variable AREA has the value you computed with the AREA command.

6. Press **Return** to view the second screen of system variables.

```
DIMALT         0
DIMALTD        2
DIMALTF        25.4000
  :            :
  :            :
DIMSHO         0
DIMTAD         0
DIMTIH         1
-- Press RETURN for more --
```

7. Press **Return** to see the third screen of system variables.

```
DIMTM          0.0000
DIMTOH         1
  :            :                                       :
  :            :                                       :
DISTANCE       5.6569                                (read only)
  :            :                                       :
```

```
  :              :                                      :
DWGPREFIX      "C:\ACAD26\"                          (read only)
ELEVATION      0.0000
EXPERT         0
EXTMAX         7.0000,7.0000                         (read only)
EXTMIN         3.0000,3.0000                         (read only)
  :              :                                      :
  :              :                                      :
GRIDUNIT       0.0000,0.0000
HIGHLIGHT      1
-- Press RETURN for more --
```

Notice the system variable DISTANCE has the value you computed with the DIST command. The drawing name is "SETVAR." The value of DWGPREFIX shows the disk drive letter and subdirectory name you used to store your drawing. EXTMAX shows the point 7,7, the upper rightmost point used in your drawing. EXTMIN has the value 3,3, the lower leftmost point used in the drawing. The value of EXTMAX and EXTMIN are used when you PLOT, PRPLOT, or ZOOM with the "Extents" option.

8. Press **Return** to see the fourth screen of system variables.

```
INSBASE        0.0000,0.0000
LASTANGLE      0                                     (read only)
LASTPOINT      3.0000,3.0000
  :              :                                      :
  :              :                                      :
OSMODE         32
PDMODE         0
PDSIZE         0.0000
PERIMETER      16.0000                               (read only)
  :              :                                      :
  :              :                                      :
SKETCHINC      0.1000
```

Notice that the LASTPOINT is 3,3 and could be referenced by @ in the next drawing command. PERIMETER has the value 16, the perimeter computed with the AREA command. Notice that OSMODE has the value 32, corresponding to intersection snap.

9. Press **Return** to see the fifth screen of system variables.

```
SKPOLY        0
SNAPANG       0
SNAPBASE      0.0000,0.0000
  :           :                                  :
  :           :                                  :
VPOINTX       0.0000                             (read only)
VPOINTY       0.0000                             (read only)
VPOINTZ       1.0000                             (read only)
```

10. Press **Return** to view the final screen of system variables and return to the Command prompt.

```
VSMAX         14.7563,9.0000                     (read only)
VSMIN         0.0000,0.0000                      (read only)
Command:
```

11. Type **Quit** and press **Return**; then type **Y** and press **Return** to display to the AutoCAD Main Menu.
12. Turn to Module 82 to continue the learning sequence.

Module 79

SHELL AND SH

```
Command: SHELL                  Command: SH
DOS command:                    DOS command:
```

DESCRIPTION

The SHELL command allows you to run another program without exiting AutoCAD. It is called-up by typing **SHELL** and pressing **Return**. You can run any DOS command or other program that fits into the available memory.

The SH command, introduced in AutoCAD version 2.5, reserves only enough memory to run "internal" DOS commands. Consult your DOS reference manual for information on internal v.s. external DOS commands.

AutoCAD is a big program and makes use of all available memory. However, it is capable of stepping aside, when requested, to make room for another application. If you are unsure about the amount of memory required, try it and see. The worst thing that can happen is to get an insufficient memory message.

APPLICATIONS

If you want to use only one DOS command before returning to AutoCAD (maybe you want to back up your hard disk during lunch), type the name of the command. If you want to use several DOS commands or run more than one program prior to returning to AutoCAD, press **Return** to display a modified DOS prompt.

```
DOS Command:

Type EXIT to return to AutoCAD


The IBM Personal Computer DOS
Version 3.10 (C)Copyright International Business Machines Corp 1981, 1985
             (C)Copyright Microsoft Corp 1981, 1985

C>>
```

Notice that the DOS command prompt is C> > instead of the more familiar C>. This alerts you that you are using DOS inside AutoCAD. To get back to the AutoCAD command prompt, type **EXIT** and press **Return.**

EXTERNAL COMMANDS With the ADE-3 package, the SHELL command is just one part of an entire external command facility. The ADE-3 version of AutoCAD is distributed with an ASCII file named ACAD.PGP. You can use the DOS TYPE command to display this file on your screen or printer, or you can edit it with the DOS EDLIN line editor. If your favorite word processor or text editor has an ASCII or non-document mode, you can use your word processor instead of EDLIN. For example, to use WordStar™ you type **N** for non-document instead of D for document at the Opening Menu. The file, as distributed, looks similar to the following:

```
C>TYPE ACAD.PGP

SHELL,,80000,*DOS Command: ,0
DIR,DIR,64000,File specification: ,0
catalog,DIR /W,120000,*Files: ,0
```

Each command in this file is described on a single line. Each command requires four specifications, separated by commas. The first entry on each line is the command that AutoCAD recognizes at the AutoCAD command prompt. When you type a command that is not an AutoCAD command, AutoCAD looks at the file ACAD.PGP to see if the command is defined as an external command. The first entry of each line in the file is where AutoCAD looks for this information. The commands defined in ACAD.PGP above are SHELL, DIR, and CATALOG. (AutoCAD is not case sensitive in this field.)

The second item on each line is the command that AutoCAD passes to the DOS command interpreter. This is what you would type to start the program or perform the operation. The item may include parameters or switches. In the example above, notice that the SHELL command sends nothing to the command interpreter, DIR sends the string "DIR," and CATALOG sends "DIR/W."

The third item on each line is the amount of memory required to execute the command or program. Because your program is run under a second copy of the DOS command interpreter (typically COMMAND.COM), the memory requirement is equal to the memory required for the program plus the memory required for the command interpreter. The command interpreter typically requires 17-23K, depending on your DOS version. Add to this number the number of bytes required for program operation.

When software publishers publish minimum hardware configurations for programs, they often specify the minimum memory requirements. Memory requirements published in this way often include up to 64K for operating system overhead. For example, if your word processor requires a minimum of 96K of memory, subtract 64K for system overhead, and then add 23K for COMMAND.COM. Try running with 55K as a start (55 × 1024 is 56,320). If it doesn't work, experiment! At least you have a starting point.

The third item on the specification line is a prompt that is displayed when you type the name of the AutoCAD external command. It is used to get additional information from the user. In the example above, notice that the DIR command prompts the user for a "File specification:." The user's response is passed to DOS along with the actual command string. If the first character is an asterisk "*," the response may contain spaces, and the user must press **Return** to terminate the input. Otherwise, the input is terminated by either a space or a blank.

The fourth specification is an integer return code. A code of 0 does nothing. Codes of 1 and 2 are used for loading and constructing blocks—a topic beyond the scope of this book. A code of 4 restores the graphics/text configuration on a single monitor system. AutoCAD switches to text mode on a single monitor system any time an external command is used. A return code of 0 leaves the screen in text mode at the conclusion of the command. A return code of 4 restores the screen to the mode that was active when the command was entered.

SIDE EFFECTS There are potential difficulties and side effects in using the SHELL command, or external commands from inside AutoCAD.

Corruption of Files When you execute a command from inside AutoCAD, AutoCAD remains resident in memory and maintains several files in an open condition. If you use the CHKDSK program to check the available space on your disk, it reports those open files as errors in disk space allocation.

CAUTION

Never use CHKDSK/F from inside AutoCAD. You will loose important files if you do so. There is no problem in using CHKDSK without the /F switch.

Too Many File Handles If the program you run opens several files, you may exceed the operating system's limit for the number of files that can be open at the same time. This number of files is set by DOS when the system is started. The default value is 8. If you receive an error message indicating that you have too many files open, you may increase the number of available file handles available to DOS by modifying the FILES = specification in the file CONFIG.SYS on your root directory. If you do not have a file named CONFIG.SYS, you can either create one with your word processor in non-document mode, use the EDLIN line editor supplied with DOS, or copy it directly from the keyboard to the disk.

If you do not have a CONFIG.SYS file, you may create it directly from the keyboard by performing the following steps:

1. Make sure the DOS prompt is displayed.
2. Type **CD** and press **Return** to access the root directory of your disk.
3. Type **COPY CON: CONFIG.SYS** and press **Return.**

Pick a number greater than the default value of 8 for the maximum number of available file handles.

4. Type **FILES=12** and press **Return.**

While you are at it, use the BUFFER command to allow DOS to make more efficient use of your disk.

5. Type **BUFFERS=20** and press **Return.**
6. Press **Ctrl-Z** and press **Return.**

The message "1 file copied" is displayed.

You must restart your system for the new CONFIG.SYS specification to take effect.

Graphics Memory Conflict AutoCAD stores the screen image for some graphics output devices in memory. It is possible for the external command or program to overwrite this memory area. If this happens, AutoCAD can easily restore the graphics screen with the REDRAW command.

TYPICAL OPERATION

In this session you check the amount of disk space available on the fixed disk.

1. Begin a drawing named TEMP. Type **SHELL** and press **Return.**

```
DOS Command:
```

Assuming that CHKDSK.COM is located in another subdirectory on the fixed disk with the name of DOS, you would access it from the DOS command line by typing **\DOS\CHKDSK**. Therefore, access it now the same way.

2. Type **\DOS\CHKDSK** and press **Return**.

```
DOS Command: \DOS\CHKDSK
Volume HARDDISK    created Jul 2, 1985 11:48p

 21225472 bytes total disk space
   180224 bytes in 11 hidden files
   311296 bytes in 38 directories
 19398656 bytes in 1246 user files
  1335296 bytes available on disk

   655360 bytes total memory
    78336 bytes free

Command:
```

You are back at the AutoCAD command prompt.

3. Type **QUIT** and press **Return**; then type **Y** and press **Return** to redisplay the Main Menu.
4. Turn to Module 65 to continue the learning sequence.

Module 80

SNAP

```
Command: SNAP
Snap spacing or ON/OFF/Aspect/Rotate/Style <1.0000>:
```

DESCRIPTION

For the options other than Value, you may respond to the prompt by picking the subcommand from the menu or by typing the subcommand (or its first letter) and then pressing **Return**. For the Value option, type the desired number and press **Return**.

On	Turns the snap feature on using the values previously specified for the snap resolution and rotation. If you have not previously specified a snap resolution, you are prompted for one at this time.
Off	Turns the snap feature off but retains the values describing the snap resolution and rotation.
Snap spacing	Typing a number specifies the snap resolution for both the horizontal and vertical dimensions.
Aspect	Typing A or Aspect causes AutoCAD to display two additional prompts, allowing you to specify different resolutions for the horizontal and vertical dimensions of the snap resolution.
Rotate	Typing R or Rotate causes AutoCAD to display prompts for the rotation base point and the angle of rotation. The default base point is (0,0), and the default rotation angle is 0 degrees. It is possible to rotate the snap grid any angle from -90 degrees to +90 degrees. Positive angles produce counterclockwise rotation; negative angles produce clockwise rotation. Starting with AutoCAD version 2.5, rectangular arrays can be rotated via the Snap rotation angle.

Style — Typing S or Style allows you to choose between a standard snap and isometric snap. The default is *Standard*, producing a rectangular coordinate system. Choosing *Isometric* causes AutoCAD to provide an additional prompt for the vertical spacing of the grid.

APPLICATIONS

When using a pointing device, exact alignment of points can be tedious. To streamline this process, the SNAP command is used to force all points picked on the screen into alignment with a rectangular grid. To specify a new snap value, type **SNAP**, then type the number of drawing units for the snap value. If the grid is activated, SNAP produces a visible change on the screen. Without GRID, there is no change in the appearance of the screen.

Once the snap paramaters are set, it is convenient to activate and deactivate SNAP with a function key. The function keys used for this purpose on various computers are as follows:

Apricot	Ctrl-B	DEC Mate V	F7 or Ctrl-B
Data General	F9 or Ctrl-B	NEC APC	FNC-FUNCT 19
DEC Rainbow	F9 or Ctrl-B	NEC APC III	PF4 or Ctrl-B
Fujitsu Micro 16	Ctrl-B	Tandy 2000	Ctrl-B
Hewlett Packard	F5	Texas Instruments	F5 or Ctrl-B
IBM	F9 or Ctrl-B	Wang PC	PF3 or Ctrl-B
NCR	F7 or Ctrl-B	Zenith Z-100	F8 or Ctrl-B

IBM compatible computers use the same function key assignments as their IBM counterparts.

The function keys can only toggle SNAP on or off. They are not used to set the snap parameters. You can, however, use the snap function keys to activate or deactivate SNAP while performing another command. For example, in drawing a series of lines, you could turn SNAP on to specify some of the points, and SNAP off for other points, without having to terminate the LINE command.

The SNAP specification applies only to points specified with the screen cursor. Any coordinates typed at the keyboard are accepted at those values, whether or not they correspond to the current SNAP setting.

TYPICAL OPERATION

If a drawing is dimensioned in inches, and the smallest fractional unit is 0.25, the speed of entry of points is greatly increased by setting the snap to 0.25.

1. Begin a new drawing named SNAP. Set the snap value to .25.

```
Command: SNAP <CR>
Snap spacing or ON/OFF/Aspect/Rotate/Style <1.0000>: .25 <CR>
```

There is no visible change on the screen, unless the GRID command is also in use. However, it is now possible to only pick points which lie at the intersection of a rectangular grid .25 by .25 inches.

2. Move the screen cursor to check its response with the SNAP feature on.
3. Type **QUIT** and press **Return**; then type **Y** and press **Return** to redisplay the Main Menu.
4. Turn to Module 95 to continue the learning sequence.

Module 81

SOLID

```
Command: SOLID
First point:
Second point:
Third point:
Fourth point:
```

DESCRIPTION

Solid and filled quadrilaterals and triangles are produced using the SOLID command.

The solid areas produced by the SOLID command are either filled or open, depending upon whether the FILL command is on or off.

APPLICATIONS

When you have a need to draw a solid object on the graphics screen, the SOLID command does the job. The SOLID command is particularly helpful when drawing in AutoCAD's 3-D mode. An object that is drawn in the 3-D mode is displayed as a solid when viewed with the VPOINT command.

TYPICAL OPERATION

In this session you draw a parallelogram, a rectangle, and a "bowtie."

NOTE

The SOLID command is sensitive to the sequence of point entry used to produce a parallelogram or a bowtie shape. This Typical Operation has each step carefully marked to enable you to follow the exact steps to get the results you want with the SOLID command. The numbers in the balloon correspond to the points within the steps.

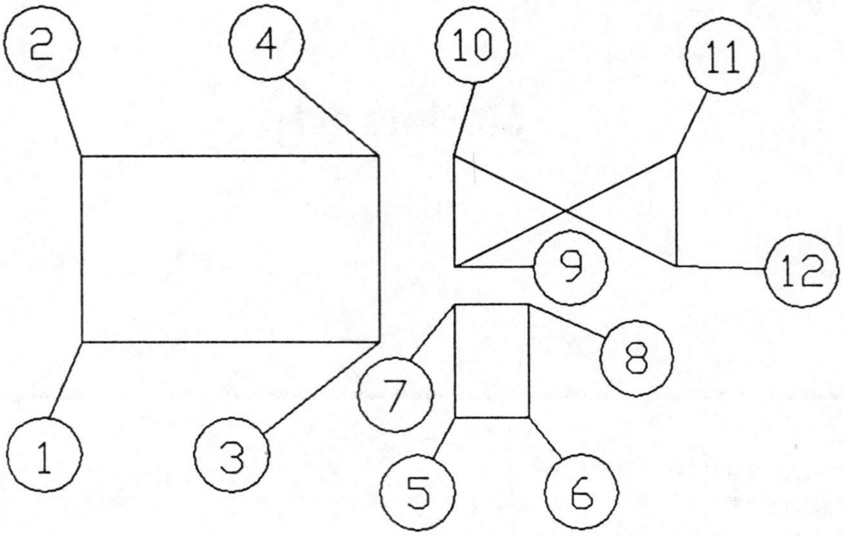

1. Begin a new drawing named SOLID.
2. Draw a solid parallelogram.

```
Command: SOLID <CR>
First point: 1,3 <CR>
Second point: 1,6 <CR>
Third point: 5,3 <CR>
Fourth point: 5,6 <CR>
Third point: <CR>
```

3. Use the SOLID command to create a rectangle.

```
Command: SOLID <CR>
First point: 5.75,1.5 <CR>
Second point: 5.75,3.5 <CR>
Third point: 7.75,1.5 <CR>
Fourth point: 7.75,3,5 <CR>
Third point: <CR>
```

4. Use the SOLID command to draw a "bowtie."

```
Command: <CR>
First point: 5.75,4.0 <CR>
Second point: 5.75,6 <CR>
Third point: 10.75,6 <CR>
Fourth point: 10.75,4 <CR>
Third point: <CR>
```

If you have followed the steps, your drawing resembles the following one.

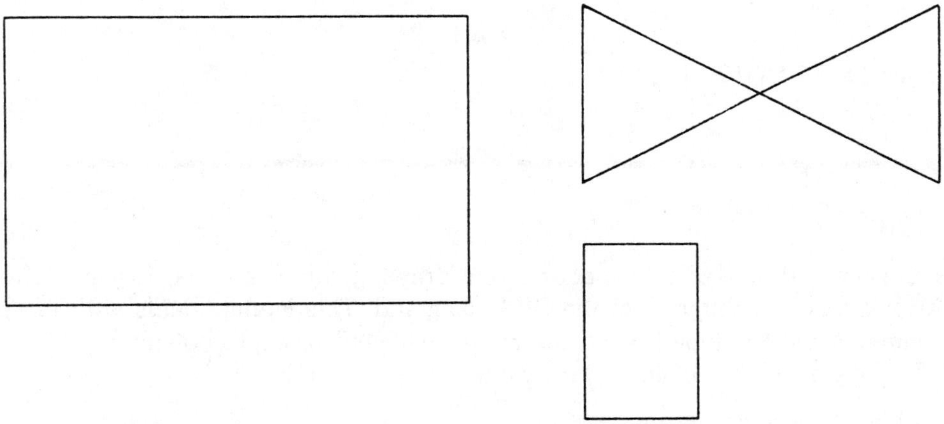

5. Type **QUIT** and press **Return**; then type **Y** and press **Return** to display the Main Menu.
6. Turn to Module 70 to continue the learning sequence.

Module 82

STATUS

```
Command: STATUS
```

DESCRIPTION

The STATUS command is used to inspect current drawing values and hardware configuration parameters. It is also a suboption of the DIM command. This module deals with the primary STATUS command, as it is typed when the main Command prompt is displayed. The STATUS command displays a number of important values. These include:

- Number of drawing entities
- Limits, including the notation "(OFF)" if limit checking is turned off
- Drawing extents, including the notation "** Over" if the drawing exceeds the drawing limits
- Display extents
- Insertion base point
- Snap and grid resolution
- Current layer setting
- Current color setting
- Current linetype
- Current elevation and thickness
- Toggle settings for AXIS, FILL, GRID, ORTHO, QTEXT, SNAP, and TABLET
- Object snap modes

All coordinates and distances are displayed in the current units format.

Additionally, on MS-DOS/PC-DOS systems, use the STATUS command to examine your hardware and operating system values including

- Free RAM
- Free Disk space
- I/O page space
- Extended I/O page space on systems equipped with memory conforming to the Lotus/Intel/Microsoft extended memory specification.

The values of "Free RAM," "I/O page space," and "Extended I/O page space" show how much RAM is available for AutoCAD to use as temporary storage. When AutoCAD runs out of space in RAM for temporary storage it uses disk storage, resulting in slower system performance.

The value of "Free Disk" refers to the amount of space remaining on the disk drive containing the current drawing. If you run out of disk space, AutoCAD automatically saves the current version of your drawing and exits the drawing editor.

APPLICATIONS

Unlike the SETVAR command which displays and modifies *system* values, the STATUS command lets you inspect *drawing* values that are changed by other commands, or reflect the *status* of your MS-DOS/PC-DOS hardware system.

Using the STATUS command is easier than typing each of the individual commands that modify and display individual values reported by STATUS. STATUS is especially useful for determining the drawing values at the start of a work session when an existing drawing requires editing. Using STATUS first helps prevent missteps, such as using the wrong color or linetype on the wrong layer or finding the snap set to an inconvenient value while in the middle of a construction.

Inspecting the I/O page space values helps you determine whether or not adding memory to your system would help increase system performance. If you have little RAM available for I/O page space, the addition of memory to your system (either conventional or extended as appropriate for your hardware configuration) improves system performance by reducing disk access time.

TYPICAL OPERATION

In this operation you use the STATUS command to inspect the values of drawing variables before and after creating a drawing. Begin a new drawing named STATUS.

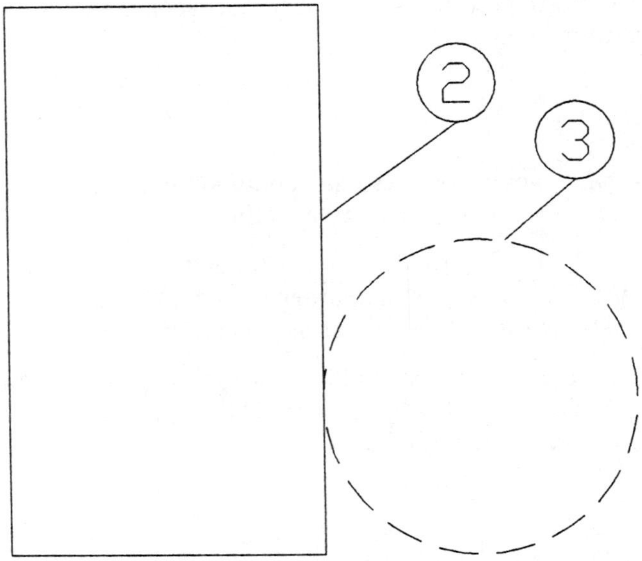

1. Type **STATUS** and press **Return** to inspect the status of the drawing variables before beginning the drawing.

```
    0 entities in status
Limits are           X:     0.0000     12.0000  (Off)
                     Y:     0.0000      9.0000
Drawing uses         *Nothing*
Display shows        X:     0.0000     14.7563
                     Y:     0.0000      9.0000
Insertion base is    X:     0.0000    Y:     0.0000    Z:     0.0000
Snap resolution is   X:     1.0000    Y:     1.0000
Grid spacing is      X:     0.0000    Y:     0.0000

Current layer:     0
Current color:     BYLAYER -- 7 (white)
Current linetype: BYLAYER -- CONTINUOUS
Current elevation:     0.0000  thickness:    0.0000
Axis off  Fill on  Grid off  Ortho off  Qtext off  Snap off
Tablet off
Object snap modes: None
Free RAM:  4346 bytes        Free disk: 17217536 bytes
I/O page space:  40K bytes   Extended I/O page space: 1664K bytes

Command:
```

Notice that before beginning there are no entities in the drawing. The snap resolution is set to 1.0, the current layer is 0, the current color is white, and the linetype is continuous. The values displayed for RAM, Free disk, I/O page space, and Extended I/O page space are probably different for your system. Extended memory is only displayed if your system contains a Lotus/Intel/Microsoft extended memory board and its software driver.

2. Set the SNAP on; then construct the rectangle at the left of the drawing.

```
Command:  <Snap on>   LINE <CR>
From point: 1,1 <CR>
To point:  1,8 <CR>
To point: 5,8 <CR>
To point: 5,1 <CR>
To point: C <CR>
Command:
```

3. Construct a new layer named DIFFERENT. Set its color to green and its linetype to dashed.

```
Command:  LAYER <CR>
?/Make/Set/New/ON/OFF/Color/Ltype/Freeze/Thaw: M <CR>
New current layer <0>: DIFFERENT <CR>
?/Make/Set/New/ON/OFF/Color/Ltype/Freeze/Thaw: C <CR>
Color: GREEN <CR>
Layer name(s) for color 3 (green) <DIFFERENT>:  <CR>
?/Make/Set/New/ON/OFF/Color/Ltype/Freeze/Thaw: S <CR>
New current layer <DIFFERENT>: <CR>
?/Make/Set/New/ON/OFF/Color/Ltype/Freeze/Thaw: L <CR>
Linetype (or ?) <CONTINUOUS>: DASHED <CR>
Layer name(s) for linetype DASHED <DIFFERENT>: <CR>
?/Make/Set/New/ON/OFF/Color/Ltype/Freeze/Thaw: <CR>
Regenerating drawing.
```

4. Draw a circle in the new layer.

```
Command: CIRCLE <CR>
3P/2P/TTR/<Center point>: 7,3 <CR>
Diameter/<Radius>: 2 <CR>
Command:
```

5. Type **STATUS** and press **Return** to display the system status.

```
    5 entities in STATUS
Limits are           X:    0.0000     12.0000  (Off)
                     Y:    0.0000      9.0000
Drawing uses         X:    1.0000      9.0000
                     Y:    1.0000      8.0000
Display shows        X:    0.0000     14.7563
                     Y:    0.0000      9.0000
Insertion base is    X:    0.0000   Y:    0.0000   Z:     0.0000
Snap resolution is   X:    1.0000   Y:    1.0000
Grid spacing is      X:    0.0000   Y:    0.0000

Current layer:     DIFFERENT
Current color:     BYLAYER -- 3 (green)
Current linetype:  BYLAYER -- DASHED
Current elevation:    0.0000  thickness:    0.0000
Axis off  Fill on  Grid off  Ortho off  Qtext off  Snap on
Tablet off
Object snap modes: None
Free RAM:  3318 bytes      Free disk: 17217536 bytes
I/O page space:  40K bytes   Extended I/O page space: 1664K bytes

Command:
```

Notice that the drawing contains five entities (four lines and a circle). "Drawing Uses" changes from "*Nothing*" to the drawing extents. DIFFERENT is reflected as the current layer, and green is shown as the color. The current linetype changed to DASHED from CONTINUOUS.

6. Type **QUIT** and press **Enter**; then type **Y** and press **Enter** to abandon this drawing and display the AutoCAD Main Menu.

7. Turn to Module 20 to continue the learning sequence.

Module 83

STRETCH

```
Command: STRETCH
Select objects to stretch by window . . .
Select objects:
```

DESCRIPTION

The STRETCH command, introduced in AutoCAD 2.5, allows you to move part of an object while retaining connections to other parts of the object. Connections made with lines, arcs, traces, solids, and polylines may be stretched. You must select the portion of the object to move by enclosing it in a window. You select additional objects for stretching by picking them on the screen. When one endpoint of an object lies inside the window and the other lies outside the window, the endpoint in the window is moved, the other endpoint remains fixed, and the entity connecting the endpoints is elongated.

APPLICATIONS

The STRETCH command lets you elongate any object constructed with lines, arcs, traces, solids, and polylines. If you wish to lengthen an object in the middle, but the endpoints must remain constant, use the STRETCH command. For example, an automotive chassis can be stretched by moving the rear assembly back several inches. A floorplan can be stretched by moving part of the structure, stretching the connecting walls.

TYPICAL OPERATION

In this session you draw a chair. You then use STRETCH to convert the chair into a couch. Begin a new drawing named STRETCH.

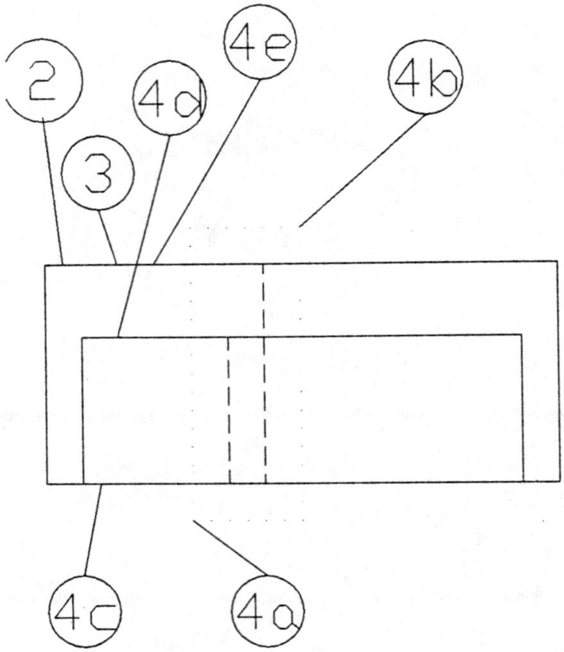

1. Set the SNAP to .5 and turn it on. Turn on the GRID.

```
Command: SNAP <CR>
Snap spacing or ON/OFF/Aspect/Rotate/Style <1.0000>: .5 <CR>
Command: GRID <CR>
Grid spacing(X) or ON/OFF/Snap/Aspect <0.0000>: ON <CR>
Command:
```

2. Draw the outline of the chair.

```
Command: LINE <CR>
From point: .5,2.5 <CR>
To point: .5,5.5 <CR>
To point: 3.5,5.5 <CR>
To point: 3.5,2.5 <CR>
To point: C <CR>
Command:
```

3. Draw the cushions on the chair.

```
Command: LINE <CR>
From point: 1,2.5 <CR>
To point: 1,4.5 <CR>
To point: 3,4.5 <CR>
To point: 3,2.5 <CR>
To point: <CR>
Command:
```

4. Stretch the chair into a couch. (If necessary, refer to Module 3 for the COORDS function key.)

```
Command: STRETCH <CR>
Select objects to stretch by window...
Select objects: W <CR>
First corner: (Pick 4a.) Other corner: (Pick 4b.) 2 found.
Select objects: (Pick 4c.) 1 selected, 1 found.
Select objects: (Pick 4d.) 1 selected, 1 found.
Select objects: (Pick 4e.) 1 selected, 1 found.
Select objects: <CR>
Base point: 3.5,5.5 <CR>
New point: 7.5,5.5 <CR>
Command:
```

Your drawing should resemble the following illustration.

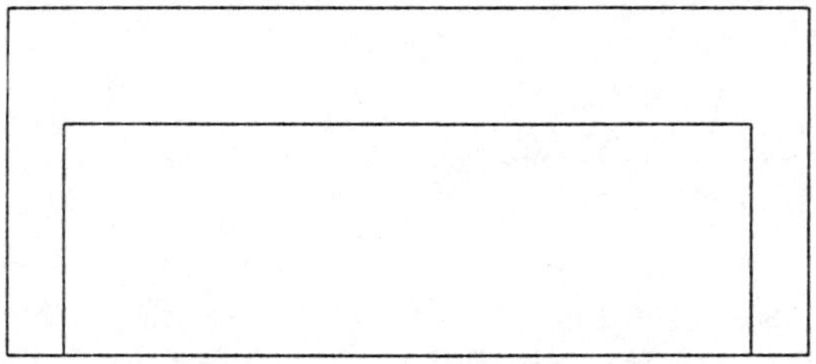

5. Type **QUIT** and press **Return**; then type **Y** and press **Return** to display the Main Menu.
6. Turn to Module 23 to continue the learning sequence.

Module 84

STYLE

```
Command: STYLE
Text style name (or ?): (name)
```

DESCRIPTION

AutoCAD provides one built-in text style named Standard. You can create additional text styles.

Specify a name for the new text style or the old text style you wish to modify. Names are 1-31 characters in length, and may contain letters, digits, and special characters including the dollar sign ($), hyphen (-), and underscore (_). Names may not contain spaces.

If you want to see a list of the available styles, type **?** and press **Return**. When you pick STYLE from Release 9's drop-down menu, the available fonts are displayed as screen icons. You may choose the text style by picking it on the screen instead of typing its name at the keyboard.

```
Command: STYLE
Text style name (or ?): MYOWNSTYLE
Font file <default>: (font name)
```

You must specify a font to use as a base for your text style. AutoCAD versions prior to version 2.5 provide five text fonts: TXT, VERTICAL, SIMPLEX, COMPLEX, and ITALIC. Version 2.5 adds the provision to create your own vertical fonts from the included horizontal fonts. Release 9 adds 20 new fonts. Three of the new fonts are replacements for the SIMPLEX, COMPLEX, and ITALIC fonts. The Release 9 software includes these old fonts for compatiblity with earlier drawings. Use the new fonts for creating new drawings. The following diagram shows the available fonts.

AutoCAD Text Fonts

Fonts provided in all versions of AutoCAD.

txt	The standard text font. It can be redrawn rapidly.
simplex	Use romans instead if working with Release 9.
complex	Use romanc instead if working with Release 9.
italic	*Use italicc instead if working with Release 9.*
vertical	A vertical version of txt. Dropped in version 2.5.

Fonts introduced with Release 9 of AutoCAD.

romans	A Roman font composed of many short line segments.
scripts	*A script font that is faster to draw than scriptc.*
greeks	A simplex Greek character set. ΑΒΧΔΕΦΓ αβχδεφγ
romand	**A duplex (double stroke) sans serif font.**
romanc	A complex (double stroke) serif font.
italicc	*An italic version of the romanc font.*
scriptc	*A complex script font, smoother than scripts.*
greekc	A complex Greek character set. ΑΒΧΔΕΦΓ αβχδεφγ
cyrillic	An alphabetical Cyrillic character set. АБВГДЕЖ абвгдеж
cyriltic	A transliteration Cyrillic character set. АБЧДЕФГ абчдефг
romant	**A triplex serif font.**
italict	***An italic version of romant.***
gothice	**A Gothic English font.**
gothicg	**A Gothic German font.**
gothici	**A Gothic Italian font.**
syastro	Astronomical symbols, such as ☉☿♀⊕♂♃♄♅♆♇☾☄✱☊☋♈
symap	Mapping symbols, such as ○□△◊☆+×*●■▲◀▼▶★
symeteo	Mathematical symbols, such as ℵ′|‖±∓×·÷=≠≡<>≦≧
symusic	Music symbols, such as ·╮╯oo●♯♮♭▬-×┐𝄞𝄢𝄂

Several of the fonts do not correspond to the Roman alphabet. The alphabetic assignments for these fonts is shown in the following table.

Character Mapping for Non-Roman and Symbol Fonts

	A	B	C	D	E	F	G	H	I	J	K	L	M	N	O	P	Q	R	S	T	U	V	W	X	Y	Z	[	\	]	^	_	‘
cyrillic	А	Б	В	Г	Д	Е	Ж	З	И	Й	К	Л	М	Н	О	П	Р	С	Т	У	Ф	Х	Ц	Ч	Ш	Щ	Ъ	Ы	Ь	Э	Ю	Я
cyriltlc	А	Б	Ч	Д	Е	Ф	Г	Х	И	Щ	К	Л	М	Н	О	П	Ц	Р	С	Т	У	В	Ш	Ж	Й	З	Ь	Ы	Ъ	Ю	Э	Я
greekc	Α	Β	Χ	Δ	Ε	Φ	Γ	Η	Ι	ϑ	Κ	Λ	Μ	Ν	Ο	Π	Θ	Ρ	Σ	Τ	Υ	∇	Ω	Ξ	Ψ	Ζ	[	\	]	^	_	‘
greeks	Α	Β	Χ	Δ	Ε	Φ	Γ	Η	Ι	ϑ	Κ	Λ	Μ	Ν	Ο	Π	Θ	Ρ	Σ	Τ	Υ	∇	Ω	Ξ	Ψ	Ζ	[	\	]	^	_	‘
syastro	☉	☿	♀	⊕	♂	♃	♄	♅	♆	♇	☾	☄	✱	☊	☋	♈	♉	♊	♋	♌	♍	♎	♏	♐	♑	♒	[	\	]	^	_	‘
symap	○	□	△	◊	☆	+	×	*	●	■	▲	◀	▼	▶	★	⚑	⚓	†	✕	⩓	⛪	⛳	✧	©	✡	🔔	[	\	]	^	_	‘
symath	ℵ	′	|	‖	±	∓	×	·	÷	=	≠	≡	<	>	≦	≧	∝	∼	√	⊂	∪	⊃	∩	∈	→	↑	[	\	]	^	_	‘
symeteo	,	•	•	▲	▬	◣	^	⌒	∩	◡	‿	›	’	‘	S	∿	∞	☈	ϭ	—	/	|	\	‾	⟋	/	[	\	]	^	_	‘
symusic	·	╮	╯	o	o	●	♯	♮	♭	▬	-	×	┐	𝄞	𝄢	𝄂	•	›	---	┌┐	^	≑	▽				[	\	]	^	_	‘

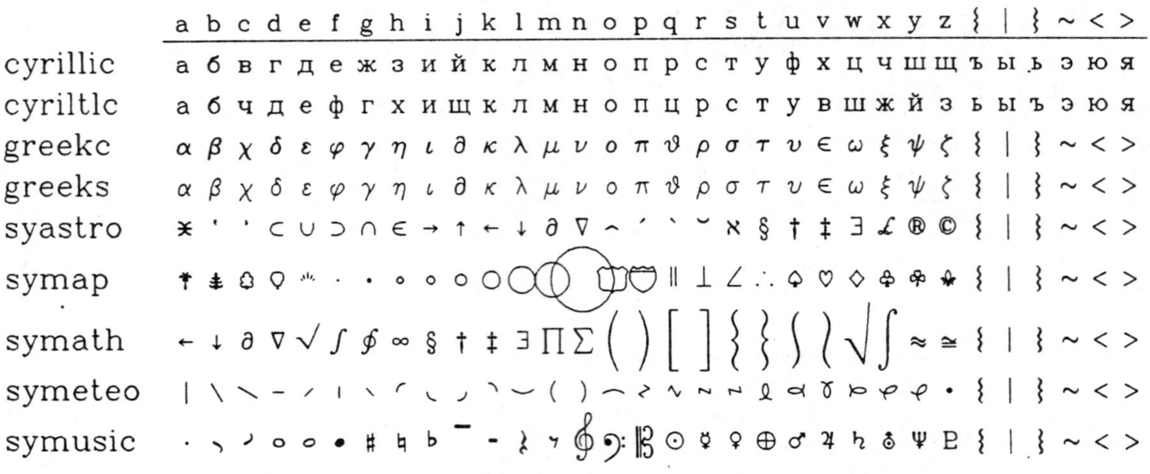

The following screen displays the text height prompt.

```
Command: STYLE Text style name (or?): MYOWNSTYLE
Font file <default>: (font name)
Height <0.20>: (value)
```

If you want all the text of this style drawn the same height, specify the height here and AutoCAD skips the Height specification on the TEXT command when this font is selected. Specify a height of 0 if you want AutoCAD to prompt you for the height in the TEXT command.

```
Command: STYLE Text style name (or ?): MYOWNSTYLE
Font file <default>: (font name)
Height <0.20>: (value)
Width factor <default>: (scale factor)
```

A width factor of 1 produces a normally proportioned character. A width factor less than 1 produces a tall thin character, and a width factor greater than 1 produces a short wide character.

```
Command: STYLE Text style name (or ?): MYOWNSTYLE
Font file <default>: (font name)
Height <0.20>: (value)
Width factor <default>: (scale factor)
Obliquing angle <default>: (scale factor)
```

The obliquing angle, specified in degrees, is an offset from vertical. A positive offset slants letters to the right; a negative offset slants letters to the left.

```
Command: STYLE Text style name (or ?): MYOWNSTYLE
Font file <default>: (font name)
Height <0.20>: (value)
Width factor <default>: (scale factor)
Obliquing angle <default>: (scale factor)
Backwards? <Y/N> (Y or N)
```

In special circumstances you want characters reversed. Normally, the answer to this question is no.

```
Command: STYLE Text style name (or ?): MYOWNSTYLE
Font file <default>: (font name)
Height <0.20>: (value)
Width factor <default>: (scale factor)
Obliquing angle <default>: (scale factor)
Backwards? <Y/N> (Y or N)
Upside-Down? <Y/N> (Y or N)
```

In special circumstances you want characters upside-down. Normally, the answer to this question is no.

The ability to create a vertical font from any base font was added to AutoCAD in version 2.5. These versions display the following additional prompt.

```
Command: STYLE  Text style name (or ?):  (name)
Font file <default>:  (file name)
Height <default>:  (value)
Width factor <default>:  (scale factor)
Obliquing angle <default>: (angle)
Backwards? <Y/N>
Upside-down? <Y/N>
Vertical? <Y/N>
(name) is now the current text style.
```

In version 2.5 and later the newly defined or modified style is set as the current style for new text entries. With versions prior to 2.5 it is necessary to use the Style option of the TEXT command to set the current style to the newly defined or modified font.

APPLICATIONS

AutoCAD is supplied with one text style and multiple fonts. You use the STYLE command to create additional text styles from the supplied fonts. You cannot use the font names in the TEXT command.

The most rapid plotting and screen regeneration is accomplished through the use of text styles based on the TXT font. The characters contain the fewest drawing elements. The more complex fonts, however, provide an asthetically pleasing touch to your drawings, and can provide additional readability for some applications.

TYPICAL OPERATION

Create a variable height Roman style with a forward slant of 15 degrees.

1. Type **STYLE** and press **Return**.

```
Command: STYLE <CR>
Text style name (or ?):
```

2. Name the new style ROMAN.

```
Command: STYLE <CR>
Text style name (or ?): ROMAN <CR>
Font file <TXT>:
```

3. Select the COMPLEX font.

NOTE

The fonts are stored on disk with a filename extension of .SHX. Do not type the file extension; type only the name of the font.

```
Command: STYLE <CR>
Text style name (or ?): ROMAN <CR>
Font file <TXT>: COMPLEX <CR>
Height <0.20>:
```

4. You specify a font with variable height by specifying a height of 0 in the STYLE definition.

```
Command: STYLE <CR>
Text style name (or?): ROMAN <CR>
Font file <TXT>: COMPLEX <CR>
Height <0.20>: 0 <CR>
```

5. For ordinary lettering, a width factor of 1 generally produces pleasing results.

```
Command: STYLE <CR>
Text style name (or?):  ROMAN <CR>
Font file <TXT>: COMPLEX <CR>
Height <0.20>: 0 <CR>
Width factor <1>: <CR>
Obliquing angle <0>:
```

6. To slant the character set towards the right at a 15 degree angle, type **15** and press **Return**.

```
Command: STYLE <CR>
Text style name (or?):  ROMAN <CR>
Font file <TXT>: COMPLEX <CR>
Height <0.20>: 0 <CR>
Width factor <1>: <CR>
Obliquing angle <0>: 15 <CR>
Backwards? <N>:
```

7. Press **Return** to accept the default of forward lettering.

```
Command: STYLE <CR>
Text style name (or?): ROMAN <CR>
Font file <TXT>: COMPLEX <CR>
Height <0.20>: 0 <CR>
Width factor <1>:  <CR>
Obliquing angle <0>:  15 <CR>
Backwards? <N>:  <CR>
Upside-down? <N>:
```

8. Press **Return** to accept right-side-up lettering.

```
Command: STYLE Text style name (or ?): ROMAN <CR>
Font file <TXT>: COMPLEX <CR>
Height <0.20>: 0 <CR>
Width factor <1>: 1 <CR>
Obliquing angle <0>: 15 <CR>
Backwards? <N>: <CR>
Upside-down? <N>: <CR>
```

9. With version 2.5 and later, press **Return** again to decline the use of vertical lettering.

Your definition of a new type style is now complete. To use this style, you must specify ROMAN in the Style option of the TEXT command.

Starting with AutoCAD version 2.5, the STYLE command sets the style as the current default style for the TEXT and DTEXT commands. It is no longer necessary to use the Style option of the TEXT command to use the style.

10. Turn to Module 67 to continue the learning sequence.

Module 85

TEXT

```
Command: TEXT
Start point or Align/Center/Fit/Middle/Right/Style:
```

DESCRIPTION

The TEXT command lets you enter letters and numbers on your drawing. TEXT options let you position the text, size it, and choose a text style. These are:

Starting point	Specify a point by picking it on the screen or by typing its coordinates. The text is left-justified starting at the point. The point specifies the bottom or baseline for the text.
A (Aligned)	You specify the starting point and the ending point for the text. The height and width of each character is computed by AutoCAD automatically so that the text exactly fits the specified area.
C (Centered)	You specify the midpoint of the text baseline.
M (Middle)	(Version 2.5 +) Similar to centered text, the Middle specification additionally provides vertical centering.
R (Right)	(Version 2.5 +) You specify a point on the baseline of the right margin. AutoCAD then right-justifies the text based on the selected point.
S (Style)	You specify a new text style.

The Aligned option automatically computes the height and rotation angle for the text. The left-justified, centered, and right-justified options require additional information:

The default text height is the most recent height used.

```
Command: TEXT
Start point or Align/Center/Fit/Middle/Right/Style: 3,5
Height <0.25>:
```

The default rotation is the most recent rotation used. A rotation angle of 0 is horizontal text.

```
Command: TEXT
Start point or Align/Center/Fit/Middle/Right/Style: 3,5
Height <0.25>: 0.5
Rotation angle <0>: 0
Text:
```

Last, you enter the text.

```
Command: TEXT
Start point or Align/Center/Fit/Middle/Right/Style: 3,5
Height <0.25>: 0.5
Rotation angle <0>: 0
Text: THIS IS THE TEXT THAT IS PLACED ON THE DRAWING
Command:
```

If you repeat the command by pressing **Return**, AutoCAD assumes that you want to continue entering text immediately below the previous line of text, using the same justification, height, and rotation as the previous line. For the purpose of repetition, Aligned text is considered to be left-justified.

APPLICATIONS

All text is added to AutoCAD drawings with the TEXT command. You control the style of the text. AutoCAD is supplied with one text style, Standard. You create additional styles with the STYLE command.

AutoCAD uses control codes starting with double percent signs to add special symbols to your text.

%%o	Toggle overscore on/off
%%u	Toggle underscore on/off
%%d	Draw "degrees" symbol
%%p	Draw "plus/minus" symbol
%%c	Draw "circle diameter" dimensioning symbol

%%%	Force a single percent sign to be drawn
%%nnn	Draw special character number "nnn"

The single percent sign is handled as an ordinary character. There are, however, circumstances where this could be ambiguous (for example, turning off underscore immediately after a percent sign). In this case, you need the %%% symbol to force the printing of a single percent sign. For example, Maximum Variation %%u5%%%%%u draws "Maximum Variation 5%."

You can produce two percent signs in a row with the sequence %%%%%%.

TYPICAL OPERATION

In this session you center the text PUMP HANDLE on the screen. Starting at the Main Menu, begin a new drawing named TEMP.

PUMP HANDLE

1. Select the TEXT command.

```
Command: TEXT <CR>
Start point or Align/Center/Fit/Middle/Right/Style:
```

2. Type **C** (or pick Center from the screen menu) and press **Return**.

```
Command: TEXT <CR>
Start point or Align/Center/Fit/Middle/Right/Style: C <CR>
Center point:
```

3. Center the text at 5,5 on the screen.

```
Start point or Align/Center/Fit/Middle/Right/Style: C <CR>
Center point: 5,5 <CR>
Height <0.20>:
```

4. Specify the height as 0.5 drawing units.

```
Center point: 5,5 <CR>
Height <0.20>: 0.5 <CR>
Rotation angle <0>:
```

5. No rotation is appropriate for this title. Accept the default of 0.

```
Height <0.20>: 0.5 <CR>
Rotation angle <0>: <CR>
Text:
```

6. Type **PUMP HANDLE** and press **Return**.

```
Height <0.20>: 0.5 <CR>
Rotation angle <0>: <CR>
Text: PUMP HANDLE <CR>
```

The text is centered at the specified point.

7. Type **QUIT** and press **Return**; then type **Y** and press **Return** to redisplay the Main Menu.
8. Turn to Module 84 to continue the learning sequence.

Module 86

TIME

```
Command: TIME
Display/ON/OFF/Reset:
```

DESCRIPTION

The AutoCAD TIME command, introduced in AutoCAD 2.6, displays the following information:

```
Command: TIME

Current time:              23 Feb 1987 at 07:38:03.830
Drawing created:           18 Feb 1987 at 17:42:55.850
Drawing last updated:      18 Feb 1987 at 22:29:16.380
Time in drawing editor:  0 days 03:51:40.990
Elapsed timer:             0 days 03:51:40.990
Timer on.
Display/ON/OFF/Reset:
```

Current time: This line displays the current date and the time of day that corresponds to the computer's clock. AutoCAD uses the time maintained by DOS. AutoCAD does not have a separate time and date function.

Drawing created: This line displays the date and time that a drawing was created. Normally this is the time you select "Begin a NEW drawing" from the AutoCAD Main Menu. If the drawing is created as a WBLOCK, the creation time is the time that a WBLOCK is saved. If the drawing was created with a version of AutoCAD prior to version 2.5, the creation time is the time that the drawing was first saved from the version 2.5 drawing editor.

Drawing last updated: This line displays the last time the drawing was saved through the use of either the SAVE or END command. (The creation time and update time are the same prior to the first save operation.)

Time in drawing editor: This line displays the total time spent on this drawing while in the drawing editor. Although the time is continually updated, it is only saved when you SAVE the drawing or END the editing session. If you QUIT an editing session, the time between the last SAVE and the QUIT operation is not added to the total time. The timer does not run during plotting operations, even if the drawing is plotted with the PLOT or PRPLOT commands from within the drawing editor.

Elapsed timer: This timer runs at the same time as the time in drawing editor timer; however, the elapsed timer is turned on, turned off, and reset with the TIME command. (When you create a drawing, the elapsed timer is turned on and left on until you turn it off. If you do not turn off the elapsed timer, or reset it, the elapsed time is the same as the drawing editor time.)

Timer on This line shows the current status of the elapsed timer.

Display/ON/OFF/Reset: Press **Return** to end the TIME command and return to the drawing editor. Display repeats the time screen with updated time. ON turns on the elapsed timer. OFF turns off the elapsed timer but does not clear the timer value. Reset clears the elapsed timer to zero.

APPLICATIONS

To make best use of the TIME command, set your computer's clock before starting AutoCAD. The clock may be set automatically when you start your computer, or you may be prompted to type the correct values on the keyboard. Setting the clock establishes the creation and save times and dates recorded by AutoCAD. The computer's clock does not have to be correct to maintain the correct total drawing time or elapsed timer values.

The TIME functions add greatly to your ability to manage and account for AutoCAD projects. The elapsed timer is excellent for accounting for the time spent by several people working on the same drawing, for accurately accounting for the time required to make drawing changes, or for establishing productivity indices. Remember that PLOTS and PRPLOTS are accounted for separately. The time to perform plotting operations is not reflected in the drawing timer.

TYPICAL OPERATION

There is no sample session for the TIME command. As you work through the remaining modules, try the TIME command occasionally and examine the information provided.

Turn to Module 5 to continue the learning sequence.

Module 87

TRACE

```
Command: TRACE
Width:
From point:
To point:
```

DESCRIPTION

The TRACE command is used to draw thick, solid lines. Traces are entered in the same way as lines. The only difference between the TRACE and the LINE command is that TRACE prompts you for a line width. There are two methods for specifying the width of a trace.

- Type the trace width in terms of drawing units.
- Type or pick coordinates that correspond to the desired trace width. When you type or pick a point in response to the Width prompt, AutoCAD provides the additional prompt "To point." This prompt lets you enter the second point, which completes your definition of the trace width.

The ends of a TRACE line are located at the center of the TRACE. A TRACE is not drawn on the screen until the next TRACE is entered or until TRACE is terminated by pressing **Return**.

The trace is displayed as a solid line if the FILL command is on. If FILL is off, the TRACE is displayed as a quadrilateral (open line).

To use TRACE, type **TRACE** and press **Return**. Supply the width and proceed as you would with the LINE command.

APPLICATIONS

An ideal use for the TRACE command is for drawing the walls in a floor plan of an architectural drawing. Leave FILL off while drawing. This speeds up the generation of screen redraws. If you want the walls drawn solid, turn FILL on before producing the final plot. You can also use TRACE to designate the electrical conductors on printed circuit boards.

TYPICAL OPERATION

In this session you draw a set of three consecutive traces having a single width. Next, you draw two additional traces that use different parameters. The following drawing contains numbered balloons that correspond to the steps in the session. Begin a new drawing named TRACE.

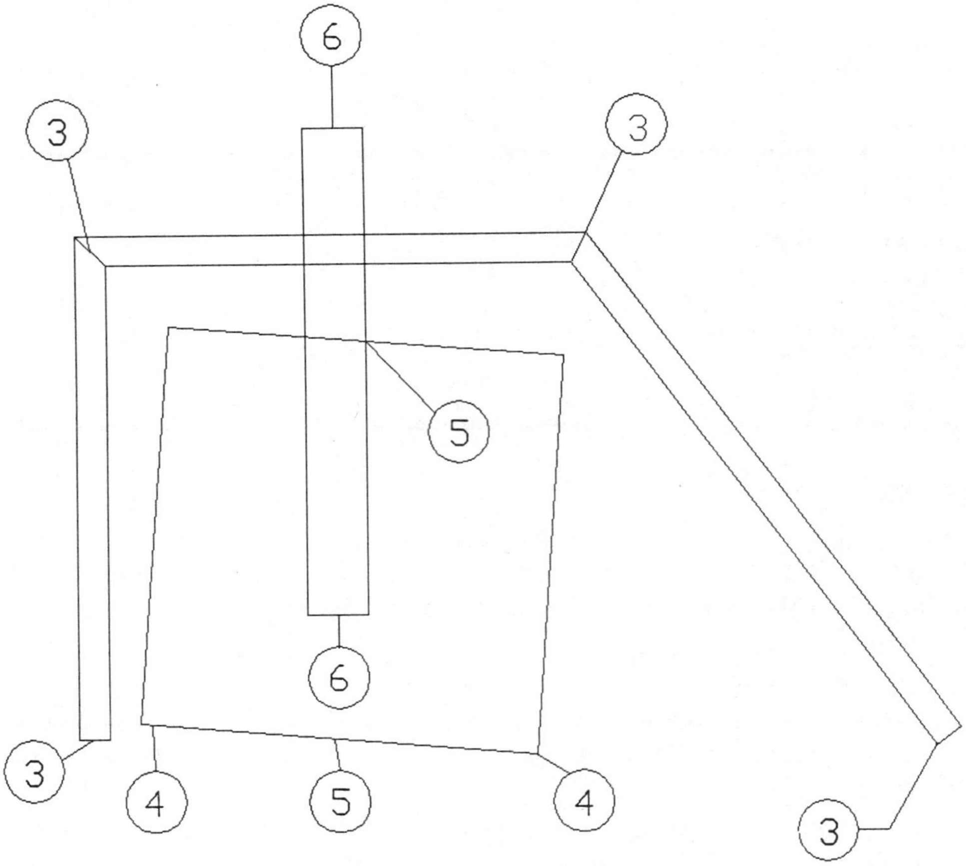

1. Set the SNAP to .25 and turn GRID on.

```
Command: SNAP <CR>
Snap spacing or ON/OFF/Aspect/Rotate/Style <1.0000>: .25 <CR>

Command: GRID <CR>
Grid spacing(X) or ON/OFF/Snap/Aspect <0.0000>: ON <CR>
```

2. Turn FILL off to speed generation of the drawing.

```
Command: FILL <CR>
On/Off <On>: OFF <CR>
```

3. Draw three ¼-inch-wide lines using the TRACE command.

```
Command: TRACE <CR>
Width: .25 <CR>
From point: 1,1 <CR>
To point:  1,5 <CR>
To point: 5,5 <CR>
To point: 8,1 <CR>
To point: <CR>
```

4. Set the trace width by specifying two points on the drawing.

```
Command: TRACE <CR>
Width: 1.5,1 <CR>
 Second point: 4.75,1 <CR>
From point:
```

5. Draw a wide trace. Notice that the trace always starts and ends square or at 90 degrees.

```
Command: TRACE
Width: 1.5,1
 Second point: 4.75,1
From point: 3,1 <CR>
To point: 3.25,4.25 <CR>
To point: <CR>
```

6. Draw another trace with a ½-inch width. Notice that when FILL is off, the trace does not hide what is underneath.

```
Command: TRACE <CR>
Width: .5 <CR>
From point: 3,2 <CR>
To point: 3,6 <CR>
To point: <CR>
```

7. Turn FILL on and use the REGEN command to repaint the screen. Notice that when FILL is on, the trace hides what is underneath.

```
Command: FILL <CR>
On/Off <Off>: ON <CR>
Command: REGEN <CR>
```

Your drawing should resemble the following illustration.

8. Type **QUIT** and press **Return**; then type **Y** and press **Return** to redisplay the Main Menu.
9. Turn to Module 57 to continue the learning sequence.

Module 88

TRIM

```
Command: TRIM
Select cutting edge(s)...
Select objects:
Select object to TRIM:
```

DESCRIPTION

The TRIM command, intoduced in AutoCAD 2.5, is used to snip the end of a drawing entity so that it ends exactly at an edge. After issuing the TRIM command, you are prompted to specify one or more cutting edges. Pressing **Return** produces the prompt "Select object to TRIM:," allowing you to pick any number of objects to trim. The side of the object you pick is always the side that is discarded.

APPLICATIONS

The TRIM command performs similar actions to the BREAK command. However, when using TRIM it is not necessary to use object snap to force the break to occur at the intersection of two entities. You can also TRIM polylines. When two lines meet in a corner, the FILLET command assures a clean corner. When two lines meet in a "T" intersection, the TRIM command assures a precise intersection.

TYPICAL OPERATION

In this exercise you use the TRIM command to draw lines between two circles. In this example, the circles are the cutting edge and the lines are the objects that are cut. Start a new drawing named TRIM. The numbers in the balloons correspond to the numbers of the steps.

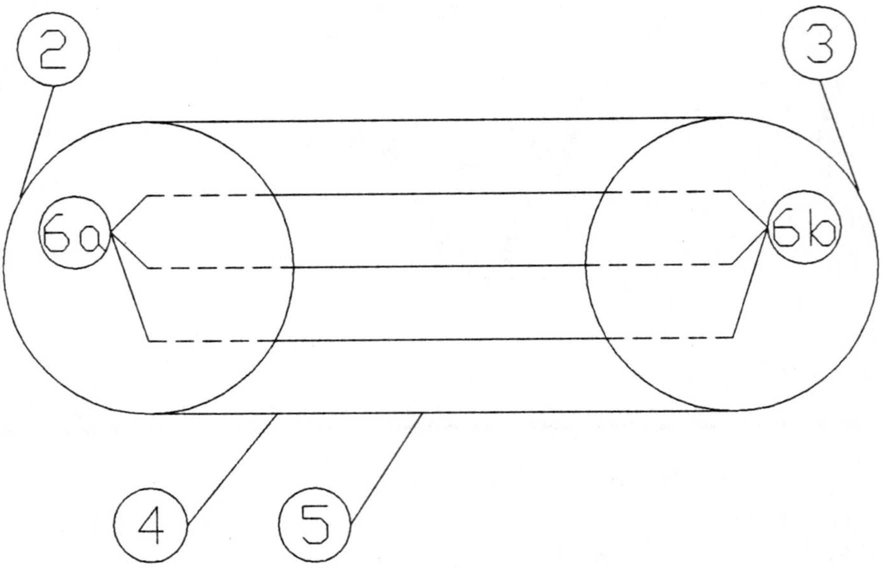

1. Turn the SNAP on and set its value to 1. Let the GRID follow the SNAP.

```
Command: SNAP <CR>
Snap spacing or ON/OFF/Aspect/Rotate/Style <1.0000>: ON <CR>
Command: GRID <CR>
Grid spacing(X) or ON/OFF/Snap/Aspect <0.0000>: ON <CR>
Command:
```

2. Draw the left circle.

```
Command: CIRCLE <CR>
3P/2P/TTR/<Center point>:  2,5 <CR>
Diameter/<Radius>: 2 <CR>
Command:
```

3. Draw the right circle.

```
Command: CIRCLE <CR>
3P/2P/TTR/<Center point>: 10,5 <CR>
Diameter/<Radius>: 2 <CR>
Command:
```

4. Draw a line connecting the bottom points of the circles.

```
Command: LINE <CR>
From point: 2,3 <CR>
To point:  10,3 <CR>
To point: <CR>
Command:
```

5. Use the ARRAY command to replicate the line.

```
Command: ARRAY <CR>
Select objects: (Pick the line.) 1 selected, 1 found.
Select objects: <CR>
Rectangular or Polar array (R/P): R <CR>
Number of rows (---) <1>: 5 <CR>
Number of columns (|||) <1>: <CR>
Unit cell or distance between rows (---): 1 <CR>
Command:
```

6. TRIM the ends of the lines inside the circles. (Turning the SNAP off makes this step easier—see Module 3 for function keys.)

```
Command: TRIM <CR>
Select cutting edge(s)...
Select objects:  <Snap off>  (Pick a circle) 1 selected, 1 found.
Select objects: (Pick the other circle) 1 selected, 1 found.
Select objects: <CR>
Select object to trim: (Pick a line inside a circle.)
Select object to trim: (Pick a line inside a circle.)
Select object to trim: (Pick a line inside a circle.)
Select object to trim: (Pick a line inside a circle.)
Select object to trim: (Pick a line inside a circle.)
Select object to trim: (Pick a line inside a circle.)
Select object to trim: <CR>
Command:
```

Your drawing looks like the following.

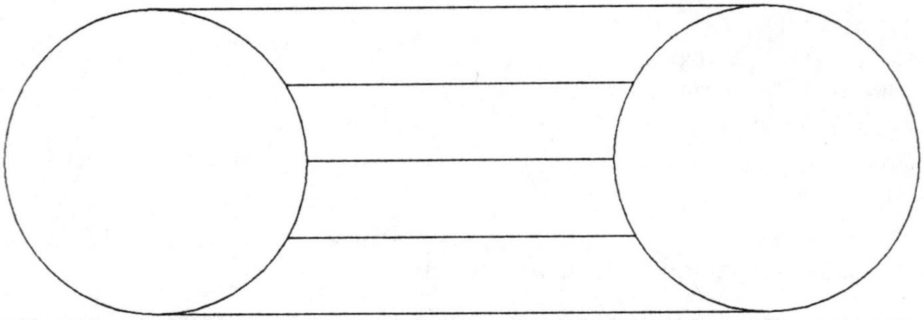

7. Type **QUIT** and press **Return**; then type **Y** and press **Return** to display the Main Menu.
8. Turn to Module 31 to continue the learning sequence.

Module 89

U AND UNDO

```
Command: U
Command: UNDO
Auto/Back/Control/End/Group/Mark/<Number>:
```

DESCRIPTION

The UNDO command, introduced in AutoCAD 2.5, performs multiple undo operations in the reverse order of construction. A list of previous commands is listed for your examination beneath the command line. You can respond by typing a number that corresponds to the number of UNDO operations you wish to perform. In contrast, the U command only undoes the last operation performed.

For safety sake, the UNDO command lets you "mark" a series of commands. This keeps you from accidentally discarding a command by performing more UNDO operations than intended. Marks, which are UNDO barriers, are entered by typing **UNDO** and then typing **M**. The multiple UNDO stops at an UNDO Mark even though more UNDO operations have been specified. For safety sake, you should periodically insert UNDO marks.

If you accidentally UNDO the wrong construction, you can use the REDO command to restore undone entities. Refer to Module 69 for a complete description of the REDO command.

UNDO is disabled by typing **C** for Control and **N** for None in response to the UNDO prompts. This sometimes releases enough disk space to avoid a disk full problem. Keep this in mind when you think you are approaching a disk full condition.

APPLICATIONS

The U and UNDO commands are used to remove the last operation or operations performed. This is easier than using the ERASE Last command to remove the last entity created. When experimenting with an operation, the UNDO command is convenient for backing out undesired results. Remember to add an UNDO Mark before proceeding with uncharted drawing territory. This UNDO boundary can prevent you from destroying valuable work.

TYPICAL OPERATION

In this activity you create some lines and circles. Then you use the U and UNDO commands to help you understand their effect. Begin a new drawing named UNDO.

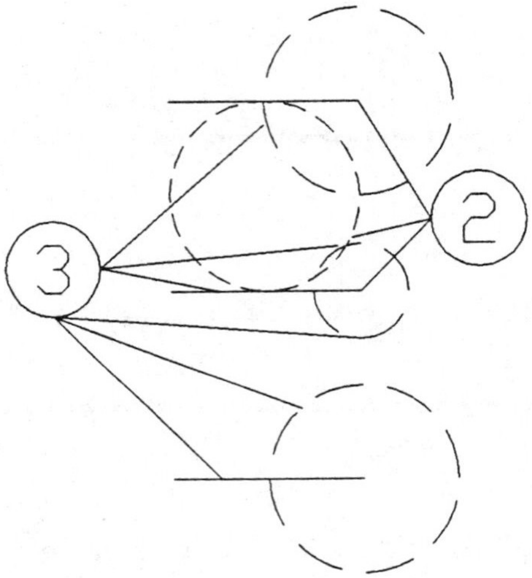

1. Set the Snap to .25, turn on the GRID and ZOOM the screen.

```
Command: SNAP <CR>
Snap spacing or ON/OFF/Aspect/Rotate/Style <0.2500>: .25 <CR>
Command: GRID <CR>
Grid spacing(X) or ON/OFF/Snap/Aspect <0.0000>: ON <CR>
Command: ZOOM <CR>
All/Center/Dynamic/Extents/Left/Previous/Window/<Scale(X)>: A <CR>
Regenerating drawing.
```

2. Draw two lines and a circle. Use the UNDO command to remove the last two commands, leaving only the first line. Redraw the screen. Notice that the UNDO operation listed the names of the commands that were undone.

```
Command: LINE <CR>
From point: 2,8 <CR>
To point:  4,8 <CR>
To point: <CR>

Command: LINE <CR>
From point: 2,6 <CR>
To point: 4,6 <CR>
To point: <CR>

Command: CIRCLE <CR>
3P/2P/TTR/<Center point>: 3,7 <CR>
Diameter/<Radius>:  1 <CR>

Command: UNDO <CR>
Auto/Back/Control/End/Group/Mark/<number>: 2 <CR>
CIRCLE LINE
Command: REDRAW <CR>
```

3. Draw more entities using an UNDO Mark to stop the undoing process at a specific point in the drawing process. This Mark can be thought of as a safety barrier that limits UNDO operations. Notice that even though five UNDO operations are requested, UNDO stops at the mark.

```
Command: LINE <CR>
From point: 2,6 <CR>
To point: 4,6 <CR>
To point: <CR>
Command: LINE <CR>
From point: 2,4 <CR>
To point: 4,4 <CR>
To point: <CR>

Command: UNDO <CR>
Auto/Back/Control/End/Group/Mark/<number>: M <CR>
```

```
Command: CIRCLE <CR>
3P/2P/TTR/<Center point>: 4,8 <CR>
Diameter/<Radius>: 1 <CR>

Command: CIRCLE <CR>
3P/2P/TTR/<Center point>: 4,6 <CR>
Diameter/<Radius>: .5 <CR>

Command: CIRCLE <CR>
3P/2P/TTR/<Center point>: 4,4 <CR>
Diameter/<Radius>: 1 <CR>

Command: UNDO <CR>
Auto/Back/Control/End/Group/Mark/<number>: 5 <CR>
CIRCLE CIRCLE CIRCLE
Mark encountered
```

Your drawing should resemble the following illustration.

4. Type **Quit** and press **Return**; then type **Y** and press **Return** to display the AutoCAD Main Menu.
5. Turn to Module 69 to continue the learning sequence.

Module 90

UNITS

```
Command: UNITS
```

DESCRIPTION

There are five available systems of units. These are:

1. Scientific
2. Decimal
3. Engineering
4. Architectural
5. Fractional (Added in version 2.5)

Decimal is the default unit. The default system of units is always set to the current system of units.

You can either pick the UNITS command from the Utility submenu or type UNITS on the command line. When you select your system of units, AutoCAD responds with a prompt for the precision of numeric display.

If you select 1, 2, or 3:

```
Enter choice, 1 to 5 <2>: 2
Number of digits to right of decimal point, 1 to 8 <4>:
```

If you select 4 or 5:

```
Enter choice, 1 to 5 <2>: 4
Denominator of smallest fraction to display
(1, 2, 4, 8, 16, 32, or 64) <16>:
```

You can accept the default value, which is shown in brackets, by pressing **Return**, or supply a number from the keyboard.

The next required specification is the angle measurement system. Here again, there are five choices. These are:

1. Decimal degrees
2. Degrees/minutes/seconds
3. Grads
4. Radians
5. Surveyor's units (Added in version 2.5)

The first choice provides for the measure of angles in decimal degrees. The second choice also uses degrees, but expresses fractional degrees in minutes and seconds. The third option uses the gradient system of angle measure. The fourth uses radians. You may keep the current system of angle measure by pressing **Return** to accept the default value.

The final step is to select the precision of angle measurement for display purposes.

```
Enter choice, 1 to 5 <1>: 1
Number of fractional places for display of angles (0 to 8) <0>:
```

You may either accept the default value by pressing **Return** or supply a number. If you are using decimal degrees, gradients, or radian angle measure, the selection of the number of fractional places is readily apparent. If you are using the degrees/minutes/seconds display format, the selection is less obvious. In this format, the following chart demonstrates the action of various selections:

Selection	*Display*	*Example*
0	Degrees only	89d
1-2	Degrees and minutes	89d12'
3-4	Degrees, minutes, and seconds	89d12'8"
5	Degrees, minutes, & seconds (one fractional decimal)	89d12'8.4"
6	Degrees, minutes, and seconds (two fractional decimal places)	89d12'8.43"
7	Degrees, minutes, and seconds (three fractional decimal places)	89d12'8.432"
8	Degrees, minutes, and seconds (four fractional decimal places)	89d12'8.4321"

Effective with AutoCAD version 2.5, you may also select the direction for the zero angle and whether you want angles measured in a clockwise or counterclockwise direction.

```
Direction for angle 0:
   East     3 o'clock  =  0
   North   12 o'clock  =  90
   West     9 o'clock  =  180
   South    6 o'clock  =  270
Enter direction for angle 0 <0>: <CR>

Do you want angles measured clockwise? <N> <CR>
```

APPLICATIONS

Your selection of precision of both linear measure and angular measure does not limit the precision of AutoCAD's internal calculations. AutoCAD always makes use of the maximum available precision which the computer can supply. The precision selection affects only the precision which is displayed on the screen coordinates display and the precision used in dimensioning. (See DIM for a further discussion of precision in dimensioning.) Furthermore, it does not limit the precision of values which you type from the keyboard. For example, if the number of decimal places is specified as 1, typing 2.9678 as an input value provides AutoCAD with all the precision specified. Only the first decimal digit is displayed, but all digits are used for internal operations.

TYPICAL OPERATION

In this session you change the units from decimal to architectural. At the Main Menu, start a new drawing named UNITS.

1. Check the default values for UNITS.

```
Command: UNITS
Systems of units:        (Examples)

    1.  Scientific        1.55E+01
    2.  Decimal           15.50
    3.  Engineering       1'-3.50"
    4.  Architectural     1'-3 1/2"
    5.  Fractional        15 1/2

Enter choice, 1 to 5 <2>: <CR>
Number of digits to right of decimal point (0 to 8) <4>: <CR>
```

```
Systems of angle measure:        (Examples)

    1.  Decimal degrees               45.0000
    2.  Degrees/minutes/seconds       45d0'0"
    3.  Grads                         50.0000g
    4.  Radians                       0.7854r
    5.  Surveyor's units              N 45d0'0" E


Enter choice, 1 to 5 <1>: <CR>
Number of fractional places for display of angles (0 to 8) <0>: <CR>


Direction for angle 0:
   East     3 o'clock  =  0
   North   12 o'clock  =  90
   West     9 o'clock  =  180
   South    6 o'clock  =  270
Enter direction for angle 0 <0>: <CR>

Do you want angles measured clockwise? <N> <CR>

Command: (Press the flip screen key to return to the graphics
screen [F1 on the IBM PC].)
```

Notice that the defaults reflect the current setting of UNITS. Check the coordinates in the upper-right corner of the screen just to the left of the Root Menu. The coordinates are in decimal inches, and there are four digits to the right of the decimal point.

3. Change the UNITS to architectural.

```
Command: UNITS <CR>
Systems of units:        (Examples)

    1.  Scientific       1.55E+01
    2.  Decimal          15.50
    3.  Engineering      1'-3.50"
    4.  Architectural    1'-3 1/2"
    5.  Fractional       15 1/2

Enter choice, 1 to 5 <1>: 4 <CR>
Denominator of smallest fraction to display (1, 2, 4, 8, 16, 32, or 64) <16>: <CR>
```

```
Systems of angle measure:        (Examples)

    1.  Decimal degrees            45.0000
    2.  Degrees/minutes/seconds    45d0'0"
    3.  Grads                      50.0000g
    4.  Radians                    0.7854r
    5.  Surveyor's units           N 45d0'0" E


Enter choice, 1 to 5 <1>: <CR>
Number of fractional places for display of angles (0 to 8) <0>: <CR>


Direction for angle 0:
   East     3 o'clock  =  0
   North   12 o'clock  =  90
   West     9 o'clock  =  180
   South    6 o'clock  =  270
Enter direction for angle 0 <0>: <CR>

Do you want angles measured clockwise? <N> <CR>

Command: (Press the flip screen key to return to the graphics
screen [F1 on the IBM PC].)
```

Notice that the defaults reflect the current setting of UNITS. Check the coordinates in the upper-right corner of the screen just to the left of the Root Menu. The coordinates are in feet and inches. The changing of UNITS in AutoCAD works the same way for all of the other values. Decide what units you want to use and then select them with the UNITS command.

4. End the session by typing **QUIT** and pressing **Return**. Then type **Y** and press **Return** to redisplay the Main Menu.
5. Turn to Module 36 to continue the learning sequence.

Module 91

VIEW

```
Command: VIEW
?/Delete/Restore/Save/Window:
View Name:
```

DESCRIPTION

The VIEW command provides a convenient way to quickly view different parts of a large drawing. Without the VIEW command, the ZOOM and PAN commands would be required. A view is plotted by specifying a view name. Views are called immediately from AutoCAD's Main Menu by giving the drawing name and the view name separated by a comma (e.g., KITCHEN,CABINET). Views are recalled while in the drawing editor by using the VIEW Restore command.

APPLICATIONS

The VIEW command is typically used in conjunction with large drawings. A city map is a good example of a large drawing. Different portions of the city are assigned view names such as: DOWNTOWN, TOWNLAKE, CITYPARK, and other meaningful names.

When drawing a house plan, it is convenient to make a VIEW Window of each room. In this way, each room is quickly displayed with the VIEW command.

If you anticipate the need to plot different sections of a drawing, it is a good idea to give VIEW names to the specific drawing areas. This practice makes plotting much more efficient and saves the time necessary to isolate specific views. When you are in the drawing editor and are about to save the drawing, you may wish to name the view so you can resume work using the displayed view. When you return to AutoCAD and the Main Menu asks for the drawing name of an existing drawing, use the View name to recall the last display.

TYPICAL OPERATION

In this session you create a drawing, ZOOM to different portions of the drawing, and create views. Begin a new drawing named VIEW.

1. Change the drawing Limits to 120,90, set the SNAP to 12, and turn on the GRID and ZOOM the screen.

```
Command: LIMITS <CR>
ON/OFF/<Lower left corner> <0.0000,0.0000>: <CR>
Upper right corner <12.0000,9.0000>: 120,90 <CR>

Command: SNAP <CR>
Snap spacing or ON/OFF/Aspect/Rotate/Style <1.0000>: 12 <CR>

Command: GRID <CR>
Grid spacing(X) or ON/OFF/Snap/Aspect <0.0000>: ON <CR>

Command: ZOOM <CR>
All/Center/Dynamic/Extents/Left/Previous/Window/<Scale(X)>: A <CR>
Regenerating drawing.
```

2. Draw the outline of a large object.

```
Command: LINE <CR>
From point: 12,12 <CR>
To point: 12,72 <CR>
To point: 108,72 <CR>
To point: 108,60 <CR>
To point: 96,60 <CR>
To point: 96,24 <CR>
To point: 24,24 <CR>
To point: 24,12<CR>
To point: C <CR>
```

3. Add detail to two extreme ends of the drawing using a block. Name the view before moving to another portion of the drawing.

```
Command: ZOOM <CR>
All/Center/Dynamic/Extents/Left/Previous/Window/<Scale(X)>: W <CR>
First corner: 11,11 <CR>
Other corner: 36,36 <CR>

Command: CIRCLE <CR>
3P/2P/TTR/<Center point>: 18,18 <CR>
Diameter/<Radius>: 3 <CR>

Command: TEXT <CR>
Start point or Align/Center/Fit/Middle/Right/Style: C <CR>
Center point: 18,17 <CR>
Height <0.2000>: 2.5 <CR>
Rotation angle <0>: <CR>
Text: L <CR>

Command: BLOCK <CR>
Block name (or ?): LOCATE <CR>
Insertion base point: 18,18 <CR>
Select objects: W <CR>
First corner: 13,14 <CR>
Other corner: 22,22 <CR>
2 found.
Select objects: <CR>
```

```
Command: OOPS <CR>

Command: VIEW <CR>
?/Delete/Restore/Save/Window: S <CR>
 View name to save: LOWLEF <CR>

Command: ZOOM <CR>
All/Center/Dynamic/Extents/Left/Previous/Window/<Scale(X)>: A <CR>
Regenerating drawing.
```

4. ZOOM in the upper-right portion of the drawing and insert the block. Create a View for that part of the drawing. Experiment with the VIEW command.

```
Command: ZOOM <CR>
All/Center/Dynamic/Extents/Left/Previous/Window/<Scale(X)>: W <CR>
First corner: 84,48 <CR>
Other corner: 120,84 <CR>
Regenerating drawing.

Command: VIEW <CR>
?/Delete/Restore/Save/Window: S <CR>
 View name to save: UPPRIG <CR>

Command: INSERT <CR>
Block name (or ?): LOCATE <CR>
 Insertion point: 102,66 <CR>
 X scale factor <1> / Corner / XYZ: 1.5 <CR>
 Y scale factor (default=X): 1 <CR>
 Rotation angle <0>: 45 <CR>

Command: ZOOM <CR>
All/Center/Dynamic/Extents/Left/Previous/Window/<Scale(X)>: A <CR>
Regenerating drawing.

Command: VIEW <CR>
?/Delete/Restore/Save/Window: R <CR>
 View name to restore: LOWLEF <CR>

Command: VIEW <CR>
```

```
?/Delete/Restore/Save/Window: R <CR>
 View name to restore: UPPRIG <CR>
Regenerating drawing.

Command: VIEW <CR>
?/Delete/Restore/Save/Window: ? <CR>

Saved views:

View name          Scale        Center point

LOWLEF             3.60     X=  28.8977  Y=  23.5000
UPPRIG             2.50     X= 109.7727  Y=  66.0000
```

Press the Graphscreen key (usually F1). Your drawing should resemble the illustration shown at the beginning of this activity.

5. Type **Quit** and press **Return**; then type **Y** and press **Return** to display the AutoCAD Main Menu.
6. Turn to Module 54 to continue the learning sequence.

Module 92

VIEWRES

```
Command: VIEWRES
Do you want fast zooms? <Y>
Enter circle zoom percent (1-20000) <100>:
```

DESCRIPTION

The VIEWRES command was introduced in AutoCAD 2.5. On your graphics screen, circles and arcs are actually composed of short line segments. AutoCAD computes an optimum number of segments for the current display magnification. You can modify AutoCAD's choice with the VIEWRES command. The VIEWRES command only controls the number of line segments used to display a circle on your graphics screen. It does not affect the results shown on a printer or plotter. These results are always displayed at the optimum resolution. The first prompt, "Do you want fast zooms? <Y>," sets the REGEN threshold when ZOOM, PAN, or VIEW are used. Answering "No" to this prompt forces AutoCAD to perform a REGEN with every ZOOM, PAN, and VIEW Restore operation. Answering "Yes" to this prompt allows AutoCAD to perform these operations at REDRAW speed, until you exceed your allowable limits. Each time you exceed the limits you specify, a REGEN is performed automatically.

The second prompt, "Enter circle zoom percent (1-20000) <100>:," is displayed only if you respond with "Yes" to the first prompt. The default value of 100 causes AutoCAD to use its internal formulas without modification. Setting the circle zoom percent to 1000 causes AutoCAD to generate enough vectors to display the circle at ten times the current magnification. Therefore, if you zoom in by any factor up to ten, the new display is drawn at REDRAW speed instead of REGEN speed. This setting speeds up the action of ZOOM, PAN, and VIEW Restore, but it slows down the generation of screens at the current magnification, because many more vectors are computed than are necessary for the current magnification. No matter how large you set the zoom percentage, AutoCAD never generates more vectors than are necessary to zoom to the largest magnification available without a REGEN.

Setting the circle zoom to a value less than 100 lets AutoCAD generate fewer vectors for each circle. Circles generate faster, but the line segments are more obvious. No matter how small you make the zoom percentage, however, AutoCAD never draws a circle with fewer than eight sides.

APPLICATIONS

As an AutoCAD drawing becomes more complex, the time to perform a REGEN becomes more significant. AutoCAD provides several tools for increasing its screen-handling speed:

- QTEXT speeds up text generation
- Turning off FILL eliminates the time required to fill solids
- Freezing selected layers removes entire layers from the regeneration and drawing process
- Setting REGENAUTO to OFF suspends drawing regeneration for selected commands
- VIEWRES controls the resolution maintained in handling circles.

Which of these techniques, or combination of techniques, is most effective in improving your productivity? This depends upon:

- Your computer's processor and graphics display
- The complexity of the image
- The mix of different types of drawing entities
- The amount of zooming and panning required.

In general, however, the VIEWRES command can appreciably speed up zooms and pans when a drawing contains large numbers of circles and arcs.

Use a zoom percentage greater than 100 when you must always see circles at maximum resolution on your screen but want to perform zooms and pans with a minimum number of REGENs. Select a zoom percentage, if possible, that is larger than the difference between your largest and smallest zoom magnification for each phase of your drawings. Use a zoom percentage less than 100 when you can accept less resolution in drawing circles.

Remember that the display mode you select has no effect on AutoCAD's internal representation of your circles and arcs. The definition of your drawing is always maintained at the maximum possible accuracy.

TYPICAL OPERATION

In this activity you use the VIEWRES command to alter the appearance of entities on your AutoCAD screen. The VIEWRES command does not alter the appearance of printed or plotted drawings. Begin a new drawing named VIEWRES.

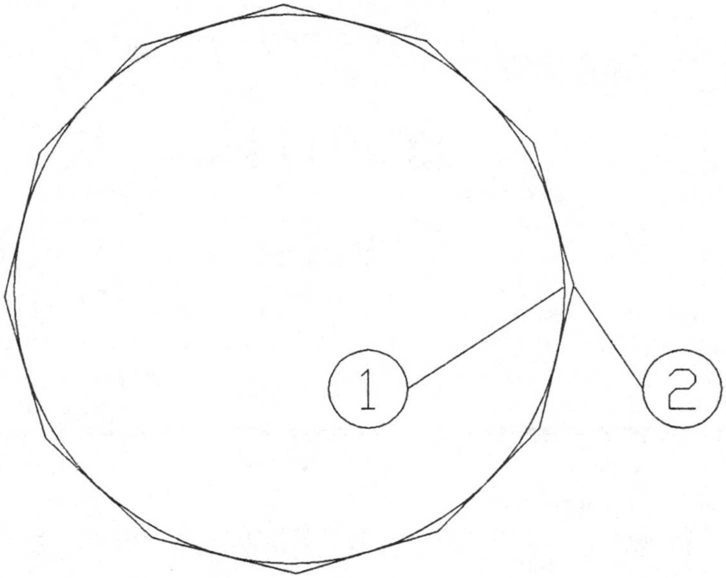

1. Draw a circle.

```
Command: CIRCLE <CR>
3P/2P/TTR/<Center point>: 5,4 <CR>
Diameter/<Radius>: 3.5 <CR>
```

2. Alter the VIEWRES setting.

```
Command: VIEWRES <CR>
Do you want fast zooms? <Y> <CR>
Enter circle zoom percent (1-20000) <100>: 10 <CR>
Regenerating drawing.
```

3. Compare the circle to the previous display.
4. Type **QUIT** and press **Return**; then type **Y** and press **Return** to display the Main Menu.
5. Turn to Module 12 to continue the learning sequence.

Module 93

VPOINT

```
Command: VPOINT
Rotate/<View point> <0.0000,0.0000,1.0000>:
```

DESCRIPTION

The VPOINT command produces a parallel projection with the X, Y, and Z coordinates of the object rotated at any angle you wish to specify. You can specify the view point in two ways. If you are at the Command prompt line, type **VPOINT**, press **Return**, and the following prompt is displayed.

```
Command: VPOINT
Rotate/<View point> <0.0000,0.0000,1.0000>:
```

The default method requires you to enter the X, Y, and Z values from the keyboard. A typical keyboard entry that designates top, right, and front view is 1, −1, 1 for X, Y, and Z.

A second method is to type **VPOINT** and press **Return** twice. A compass and axes tripod screen is displayed. The compass contains a small cross hair. The cross hair is manipulated with the pointing device until located in the appropriate position. Next, the view point is chosen by pressing the pick button on the mouse or by pressing **Return.**

The VPOINT command is used any time you want to view a drawing in three dimensions. Usually the drawing is produced by using the ELEV command to add the third (or Z) dimension to the traditional X and Y dimensions of the AutoCAD drawing.

For effective use of the compass and axes tripod screen, refer to the following illustration. It provides examples of where to position the cross hairs on the compass to produce various views.

VPOINT Compass schematic

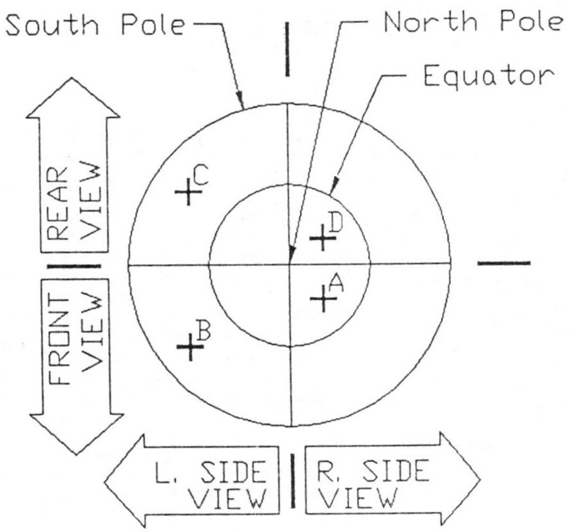

PICK POINT AND RESULT

A = TOP, RIGHT, FRONT VIEW
(above the equator, right Hemisphere, and bottom half of Compass)

B = BOTTOM, LEFT, FRONT VIEW
(below the equator, left Hemisphere, and bottom half of Compass)

C = BOTTOM, LEFT, REAR VIEW
(below the equator, left Hemisphere, and top half of Compass)

D = TOP, RIGHT, REAR VIEW
(above the equator, right Hemisphere, and top half of Compass)

The illustration gives you some clues about how to experiment with the VPOINT command. You can use these clues to view the drawing produced with elevation and thickness at any desired angle.

You can also enter the rotation coordinates directly. Coordinates of 0, 0, 1 display the drawing as drawn. Because AutoCAD three-dimensional drawings are always created in plan (or top) view, 0, 0, 1 corresponds to a plan view presentation. You can also view objects from the front, rear, bottom, or even display a pictorial view that reveals three sides. The following table lets you experiment with the rotation of three-dimensional objects.

VPOINT Setting	*Displayed View(s)*
0, 0, 1	Top
0, 0, −1	Bottom
0, −1, 0	Front
0, 1, 0	Rear
1, 0, 0	Right Side
−1, 0, 0	Left Side
1, −1, 1	Top, Front, Right Side
−1, −1, 1	Top, Front, Left Side
1, 1, 1	Top, Rear, Right Side
−1, 1, 1	Top, Rear, Left Side
1, −1, −1	Bottom, Front, Right Side
−1, −1, −1	Bottom, Front, Left Side
1, 1, −1	Bottom, Rear, Right Side
−1, 1, −1	Bottom, Rear, Left Side

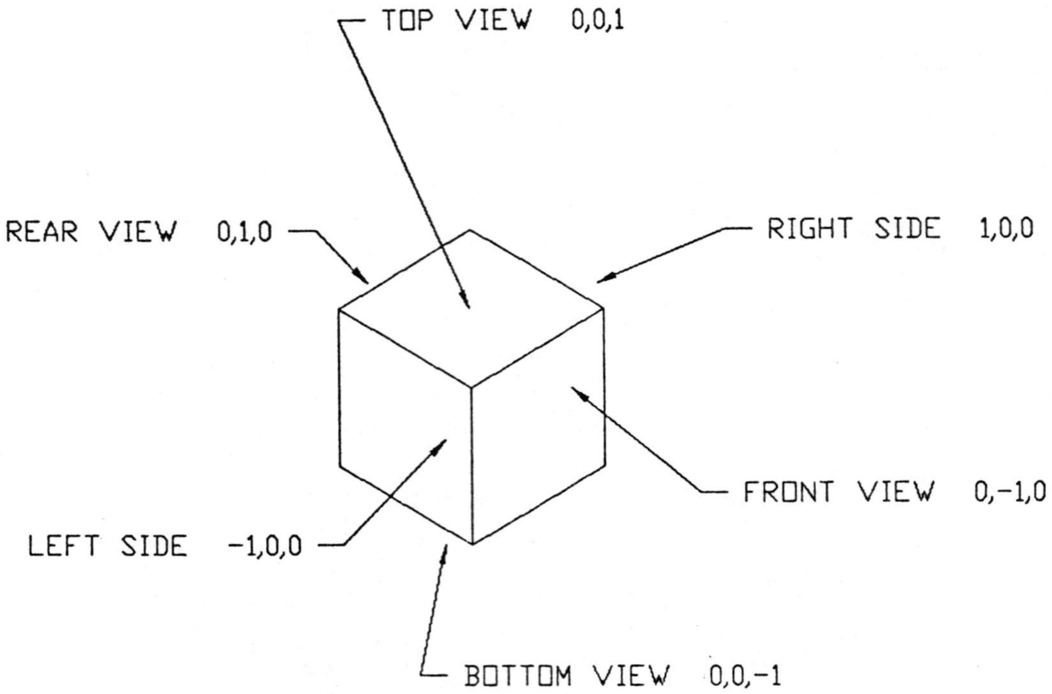

AutoCAD Release 9 introduced a Rotate option for the VPOINT command. When you select the Rotate option, the system supplies two additional prompts.

```
Enter angle in X-Y plane from X axis <270>:
Enter angle from X-Y plane <90>:
```

The Rotate command is intuitively similar to the spherical coordinate system, with the exception that no distances are specified. The angles required are illustrated in the following diagram.

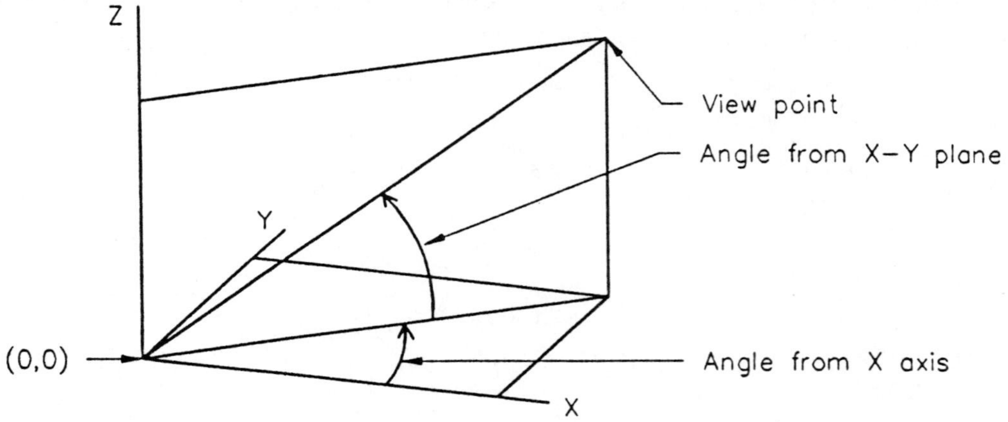

APPLICATIONS

Three-dimensional visualization is a powerful tool for viewing an object from any point. It allows front, back, top, bottom, rear, and angular views. The views do not have to be selected to conform to a specific type of projection. AutoCAD creates the three-dimensional visualization through the production of a wire-frame drawing. In addition to providing the designer with an alternative perspective of the work, wire-frame visualizations are especially appropriate for communicating three-dimensional views to lay persons who are not skilled at visualizing a third dimension from a three-view drawing.

TYPICAL OPERATION

In this session you draw an object with several elevations and thicknesses. Next you view the drawing from four different view points. After the objects are in view, the HIDE command is used to remove the hidden lines to further reveal the finished view. When the VPOINT command is requested for positions A, B, C, and D, refer to the preceding VPOINT compass schematic. The numbered balloons in the following drawing correspond to the numbered steps.

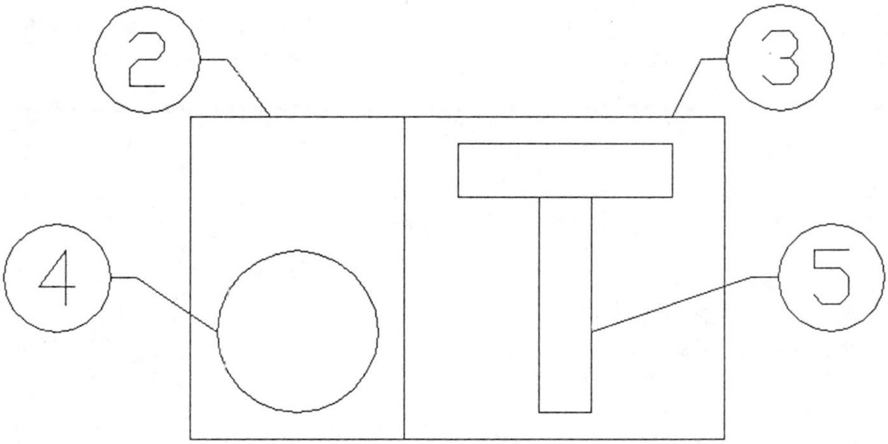

1. Begin a new drawing named VPTAC. Set the values for SNAP, GRID, and ELEV.

```
Command: SNAP <CR>
Snap spacing or ON/OFF/Aspect/Rotate/Style <1.0000>: .25 <CR>

Command: GRID <CR>
Grid spacing(X) or ON/OFF/Snap/Aspect <0.0000>: ON <CR>

Command: ELEV <CR>
New current elevation <0.0000>: <CR>
New current thickness <0.0000>: .25 <CR>
Command:
```

2. Use the SOLID command to draw a polygon. Turn FILL off and regenerate the screen with the REGEN command.

```
Command: SOLID <CR>
First point: 2,2 <CR>
Second point: 4,2 <CR>
Third point: 2,5 <CR>
Fourth point: 4,5 <CR>
Third point: <CR>

Command: FILL <CR>
On/Off <On>: OFF <CR>

Command: REGEN <CR>
```

3. Draw another polygon with the SOLID command and another elevation value. This time you also change the elevation from zero.

```
Command: ELEV <CR>
New current elevation <0.0000>: <CR>
New current thickness <0.2500>: 2.0 <CR>

Command: SOLID <CR>
First point: 4,2 <CR>
Second point: 7,2 <CR>
Third point: 4,5 <CR>
Fourth point: 7,5 <CR>
Third point: <CR>
```

4. Change the elevation again and draw a circle.

```
Command: ELEV <CR>
New current elevation <0.0000>: .25 <CR>
New current thickness <2.0000>: .50 <CR>

Command: CIRCLE <CR>
3P/2P/<Center point>: 3,3 <CR>
Diameter/<Radius>: .75 <CR>
```

5. Change the elevation and thickness and use the TRACE command to continue drawing the "T" shape.

```
Command: ELEV <CR>
New current elevation <0.2500>: 2 <CR>
New current thickness <0.5000>: .25 <CR>

Command: TRACE <CR>
Width: .5 <CR>
From point: 5.5,2.25 <CR>
To point:   5.5,4.25 <CR>
To point: <CR>

Command: TRACE <CR>
Width: .5 <CR>
From point: 4.5,4.5 <CR>
To point: 6.5,4.5 <CR>
To point: <CR>
Command:
```

6. Use the VPOINT command. Locate the cross hairs at position "A" shown on the VPOINT compass schematic. After locating the cross hair, press the pick button or **Return** Use the HIDE command and produce the equivalent of a view that can be described as a front, top, right.

```
Command: VPOINT <CR>
Rotate/<View point> <0.0000,0.0000,1.0000>: <CR>
(Locate cross hair at position "A" and press the pick button.)

Command: HIDE <CR>
Command:
```

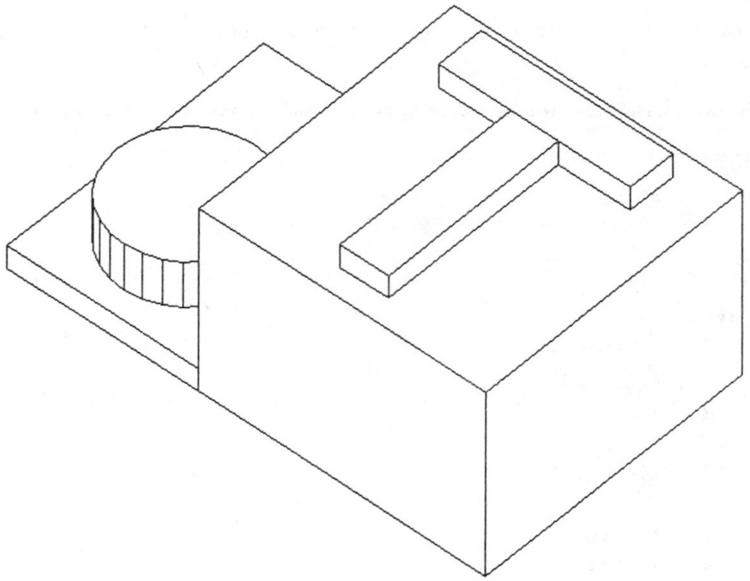

7. Use the VPOINT command. Locate the cross hairs at position "B" shown on the VPOINT compass schematic. After locating the cross hairs, press your pick button or **Return**. Use the HIDE command and produce the equivalent of a view that can be described as a front, bottom, left.

```
Command: VPOINT <CR>
Rotate/<View point> <0.0000,0.0000,1.0000>: <CR>
(Locate cross hair at position "B" and press the pick button.)

Command: HIDE <CR>
Command:
```

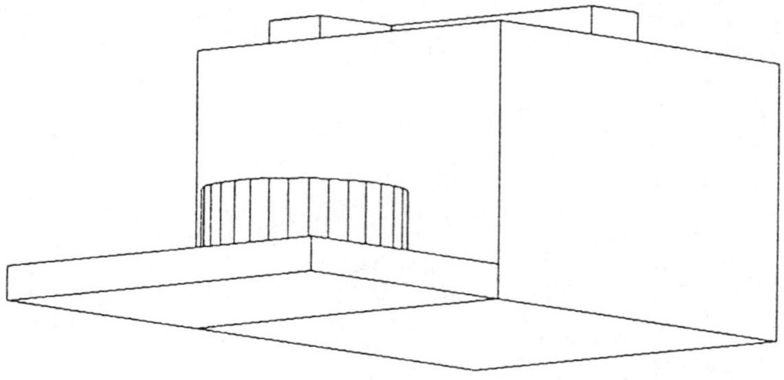

8. Use the VPOINT command. Locate the cross hairs at position "C" on the VPOINT compass schematic. After locating the cross hair, press your pick button or **Return**. Use the HIDE command and produce the equivalent of a view that can be described as a back, bottom, left.

```
Command: VPOINT <CR>
Rotate/<View point> <0.0000,0.0000,1.0000>: <CR>
(Locate cross hair at position "C" and press the pick button.)

Command: HIDE <CR>
Command:
```

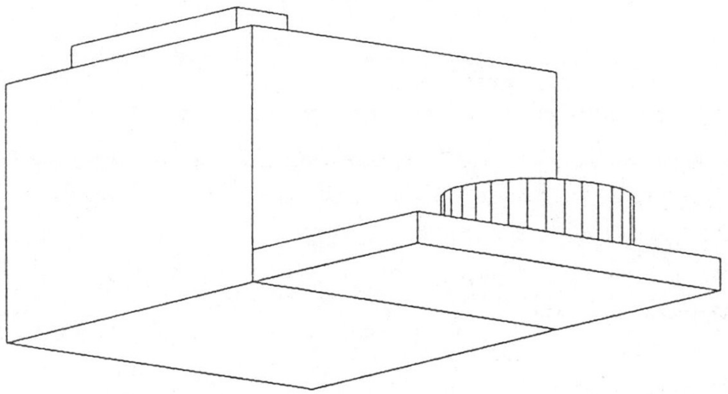

9. Use the VPOINT command. Locate the cross hairs at position "D" shown on the VPOINT compass schematic. After locating the cross hair, press your pick button or **Return**. Use the HIDE command and produce the equivalent of a view that can be described as a back, top, right.

```
Command: VPOINT <CR>
Rotate/<View point> <0.0000,0.0000,1.0000>: <CR>
(Locate cross hair at position "D" and press the pick button.)

Command: HIDE <CR>
```

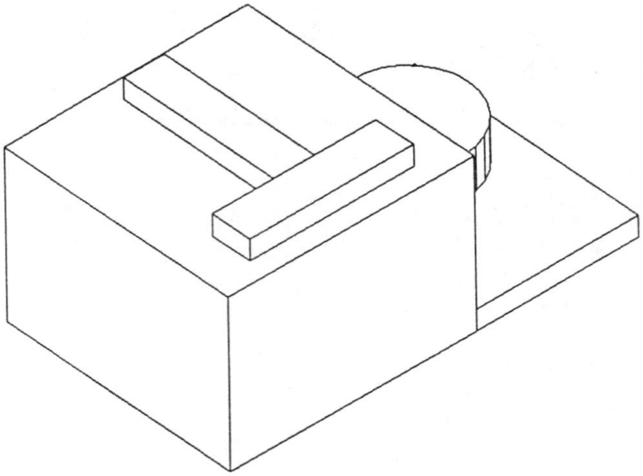

10. Use the VPOINT command to return to the original drawing shown in the plan view. Type the VPOINT coordinates of **0,0,1** from the keyboard to restore the original view.

```
Command: VPOINT <CR>
Rotate/<View point> <0.0000,0.0000,0.0000>: 0,0,1 <CR>
Command:
```

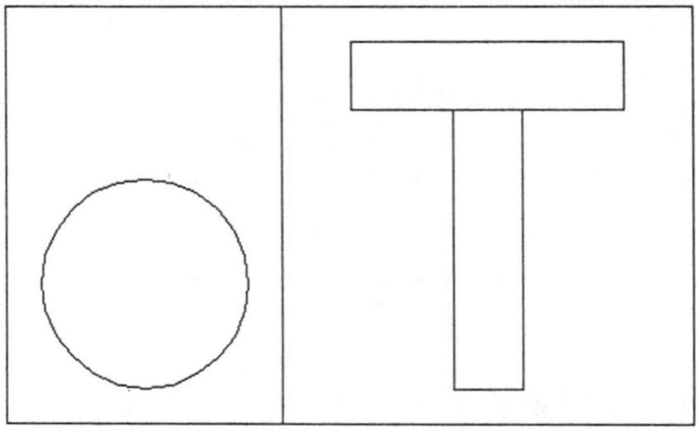

11. Type **QUIT** and press **Return**; then type **Y** and press **Return** to redisplay the Main Menu.
12. Turn to Module 39 to continue the learning sequence.

Module 94

WBLOCK

```
Command: WBLOCK
File name:
```

DESCRIPTION

The WBLOCK command is used to give your drawing a name and save it to disk. In this respect, it is similar to the SAVE command. A WBLOCK is also similar to a BLOCK. However, a BLOCK can only be inserted back into the drawing where it was created, while a WBLOCK can be inserted into any drawing. The ".DWG" file extension is given to a WBLOCK file name. If you type **WBLOCK** and press **Return**, the following prompt is displayed.

```
Command: WBLOCK <CR>
File name: (Type a file name) <CR>
Block name: (An asterisk entered here saves the whole drawing
with the insertion point as 0,0; a blank entry causes a series
of prompts similar to the entry of a regular block)
```

Answering the WBLOCK "Block name" prompt with an asterisk and a **Return** operates satisfactorily only after the entire drawing has been saved. Pressing **Return** at the "Block name" prompt produces a WBLOCK that reacts much the same way as a BLOCK. See Typical Operation to clarify the use of the "Block name" prompt.

APPLICATIONS

The WBLOCK command is similar to the BLOCK command. Both are used to define groups of objects and refer to them by name (for example, a plumbing fixture, a light fixture, a truss, a wheel assembly, a bolt, a screw, or a gear). You should remember that the only difference between a WBLOCK and a BLOCK is that a WBLOCK can be inserted into any drawing and a BLOCK can only be inserted into its original drawing. AutoCAD saves BLOCKS as entities within your drawing file. AutoCAD saves WBLOCKS as separate drawing files on the disk.

TYPICAL OPERATION

In this session you draw an electrical resistor symbol and use WBLOCK to name and save the drawing. Begin a new drawing named WBLOCK.

1. Set COORDS on. Set the SNAP resolution to .25.

```
Command: <COORDS ON> SNAP <CR>
Snap spacing or ON/OFF/Aspect/Rotate/Style <1.0000>: .25 <CR>
```

2. Now turn the GRID on.

```
Command: GRID <CR>
Grid spacing(X) or ON/OFF/Snap/Aspect <0.0000>: ON <CR>
```

3. Now enter the LINE command and draw the resistor symbol.

```
Command: LINE <CR>
From point: 1.5,4.0 <CR>
To point: @.5<0 <CR>
To point: @.5590<63 <CR>
To point: @1.0280<284 <CR>
To point: @1.0296<76 <CR>
To point: @1.0300<284 <CR>
To point: @1.0304<76 <CR>
To point: @1.0308<284 <CR>
To point: @1.0311<76 <CR>
To point: @1.0314<284 <CR>
To point: @.5602<63 <CR>
To point: @.4973<0 <CR>
To point: <CR>
```

4. Save the resistor as a WBLOCK and name it RESISTOR. The WBLOCK is saved as the entire drawing sheet with the insertion point at 0,0. This is accomplished at the Block name prompt by entering an asterisk (*).

```
Command: WBLOCK <CR>
File name: RESISTOR <CR>
Block name: * <CR>
```

5. Now save the resistor as a WBLOCK and name the file ELECRESI. The WBLOCK is saved much the same way as a BLOCK. This is accomplished by pressing **Return** at the Block name prompt.

```
Command: WBLOCK <CR>
File name: ELECRESI <CR>
Block name: <CR>
Insertion base point: 1.5,4.0 <CR>
Select objects: W <CR>
First point: 1.25,3.25 <CR>
Second point: 5.0,4.75 <CR>
11 found.
Select objects: <CR>
```

6. Bring the resistor drawing back to the screen:

```
Command: OOPS <CR>
```

7. The resistor saved as a WBLOCK named RESISTOR is now inserted into the drawing.

```
Command: INSERT <CR>
Block name (or ?) <DEFAULT>: RESISTOR <CR>
 Insertion point: 0,2.0 <CR>
 X scale factor <1> / Corner / XYZ: <CR>
 Y scale factor (default=X):<CR>
 Rotation angle <0>: <CR>
```

8. Now the WBLOCK named ELECRESI is inserted.

```
Command: INSERT <CR>
Block name (or ?) <RESISTOR>: ELECRESI <CR>
 Insertion point: 1.5,2.0 <CR>
 X scale factor <1> / Corner / XYZ: <CR>
 Y scale factor (default=X): <CR>
 Rotation angle <0>: <CR>
```

There are now three resistors on your screen. The resistor in the middle was produced originally with the LINE command and is labeled ORIGINAL. The resistor at the top was produced using the asterisk at the Block name prompt and is called RESISTOR. The resistor on the bottom was produced by pressing **Return** at the Block name prompt and is called ELECRESI. The use of these different techniques should now be clear. If you want to produce the displayed text, refer to the TEXT command (Module 85).

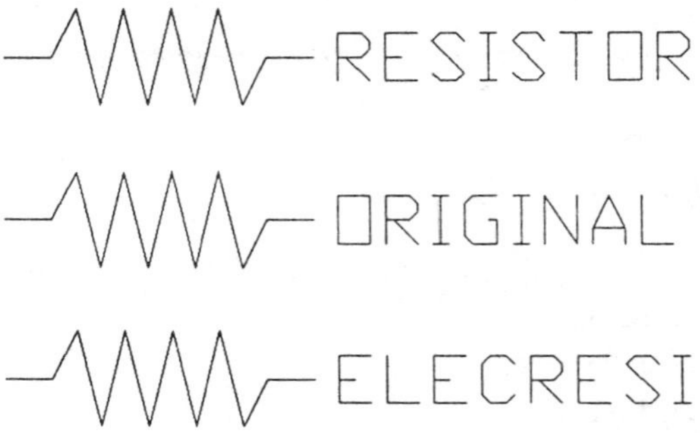

9. Type **QUIT** and press **Return**; then type **Y** and press **Return** to redisplay the Main Menu.
10. Turn to Module 47 to continue the learning sequence.

Module 95

ZOOM

```
Command: ZOOM
All/Center/Dynamic/Extents/Left/Previous/Window/<Scale(X)>:
```

DESCRIPTION

The ZOOM command lets you enlarge and reduce drawing views. When making a large drawing you can "zoom in" on small objects in order to see hidden details. Each ZOOM command option is described in the following list.

Magnification	Type a number and press **Return** to specify a magnification factor relative to the full view. A number greater than 1 increases the magnification relative to the full view; a decimal between 0 and 1 decreases the magnification. If you type a number followed by an X, such as 2X, the magnification is computed relative to the current view.
A (All)	The entire drawing is shown on the screen. The actual size depends on either the drawing limits (set with the LIMITS command) or the current extent of the drawing (if you have extended your drawing beyond the limits).
C (Center)	Allows you to pick a point as the center of the zoomed display and specify a height or magnification factor for the display.
D (Dynamic)	Introduced in version 2.5, allows you to ZOOM and PAN graphically by moving the screen cursor.
E (Extents)	Fills the screen with the drawing elements. This is the maximum magnification capable of displaying all drawing elements.
L (Left)	Allows you to pick a point as the lower-left corner of the zoomed display, and to specify either a height or a magnification factor for the display.

P (Previous) — Restores the previous view. If you have not used the ZOOM command, this option has no effect. You may restore up to three previous views. (Five previous views may be restored starting with version 2.5.)

W (Window) — Allows you to pick the lower-left and upper-right corner of the area (or window) to be zoomed.

APPLICATIONS

The limited size and resolution of the screen make it impractical to create the individual elements of a large drawing when the entire drawing is displayed. Use the ZOOM command to selectively expand portions of the drawing. When the selected portion of the drawing fills the screen, you can begin detail work.

Use of the ZOOM command has no effect on the dimensions of the drawing. It affects only the screen display.

The most basic form of the option, the specification of Magnification, is the least useful form of the command. This form of the command does not change the center point of the display. In typical drawings, it is more common to want to enlarge a portion of the drawing. More often than not, this area is not in the center of the display.

The most useful application of the Magnification option is when you inadvertently zoom in on a portion of an object, but zoom too far. In this instance, a relative zoom, for example 0.9X, would provide approximately 10 percent more of the drawing, while retaining the center point of the zoomed view.

The Window option allows you to select quickly (and intuitively) the area requiring enlargement.

The Previous option is useful when you need to repeatedly zoom in to examine or edit detail in a drawing, and return to a larger view to examine the effect of the change. Since AutoCAD automatically saves the last three views of a drawing, the ZOOM Previous command option produces a faster zoom operation because there is no need to totally regenerate the drawing.

The Dynamic option is possibly the most powerful form of the ZOOM command. It is designed to be used with a pointing device—either a mouse or a tablet. When you type **D** for Dynamic and press **Return** your system displays a special graphic screen containing several boxes that are differentiated by color (or linetype on monochrome systems). A solid white box indicates the drawing extents. A dotted green box highlights the current view. Four red corners identify the portion of the drawing for which AutoCAD has calculated vectors and which are available for display at REDRAW speed.

A view box, initially identical to the current screen, represents the view that AutoCAD generates when you press **Return**. You manipulate both the size and the position of the view box with the screen cursor.

Initially, the view box contains a large X, designating that it is in ZOOM mode. While in ZOOM mode, moving the cursor horizontally changes the size of the view box. The lower-left corner of the view box remains stationary, and the vertical dimension of the box is automatically calculated to correspond to the selected width.

Pressing the pointer's pick button switches the view box into PAN mode, designated by the absence of the large X. In this mode, moving the cursor moves the view box around the drawing, maintaining a constant size.

You may press the pick button any number of times to toggle back and forth between ZOOM mode and PAN mode to adjust the exact size and position of the the view box to match your requirements. When everything is perfect, press **Return**. It does not matter whether the view box in in PAN or ZOOM mode when you press **Return**. AutoCAD updates the screen with the view described by the view box.

TYPICAL OPERATION

This session lets you practice using the ZOOM command by drawing a circle and changing its display size. Starting at the Main Menu, begin a new drawing named CIRCLE.

1. Draw a circle at the point (2,2) with a radius of 1.

```
Command: CIRCLE <CR>
3P/2P/<Center Point>: 2,2 <CR>
Diameter/<Radius>: 1 <CR>
Command:
```

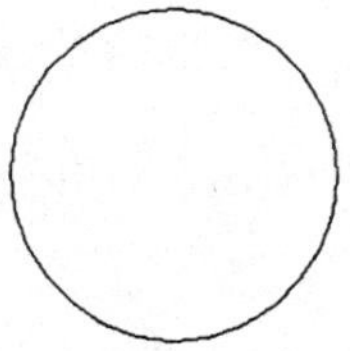

2. Type **ZOOM** and press **Return**; then pick Extents by typing **E** and pressing **Return**.

```
Command: ZOOM <CR>
All/Center/Dynamic/Extents/Left/Previous/Window/<Scale(X)>: E <CR>
```

Notice that the circle expands to fill the screen.

3. Type **ZOOM** and press **Return**; then pick All by typing **A** and pressing **Return**. Notice that the previous display is restored.

```
Command: ZOOM <CR>
All/Center/Dynamic/Extents/Left/Previous/Window/<Scale(X)>: A <CR>
```

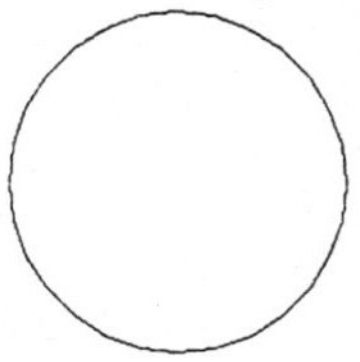

4. Draw a second circle with center point 5,5 and radius 10.

Command: **CIRCLE <CR>**
3P/2P/<Center Point>: **5,5 <CR>**
Diameter/<Radius>: **10 <CR>**

5. Type **ZOOM** and press **Return**; then pick Extents by typing **E** and pressing **Return**.

Command: **ZOOM <CR>**
All/Center/Dynamic/Extents/Left/Previous/Window/<Scale(X)>: **E <CR>**

Notice that the large circle fills the display area.

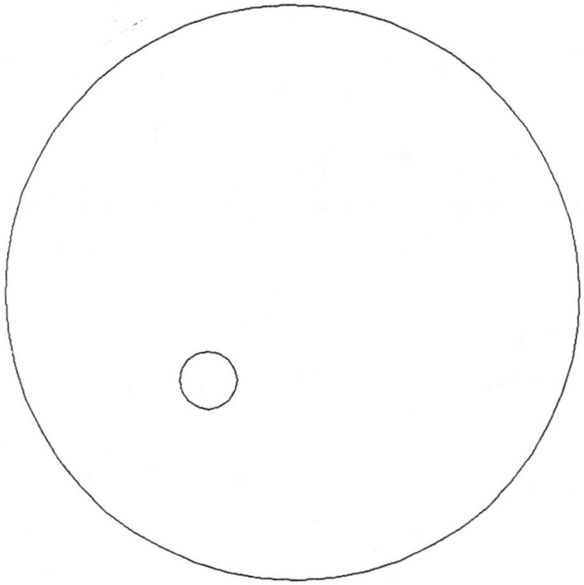

Because the drawing extends beyond the drawing limits, the ZOOM All command option uses the extent of the drawing instead of the drawing limits when performing this zoom.

6. Type **QUIT** and press **Return**; then type **Y** and press **Return** to redisplay the Main Menu.
7. Turn to Module 59 to continue the learning sequence.

Appendix A

RELEASE 9 USER INTERFACE

AutoCAD Release 9 adds capability and functionality to the user interface without removing any features present in previous versions. To take advantage of these features, your hardware system must be capable of supporting the AutoCAD advanced display interface. Not all display systems supported by AutoCAD also support the advanced display capabilities. (A list of supported hardware is included in Module 3.) In addition, your system must be equipped with a a mouse or tablet digitizer. You can't access the advanced user interface through the keyboard. A *menu bar* and *pull-down menus* provide an additional way of executing AutoCAD commands. The menu

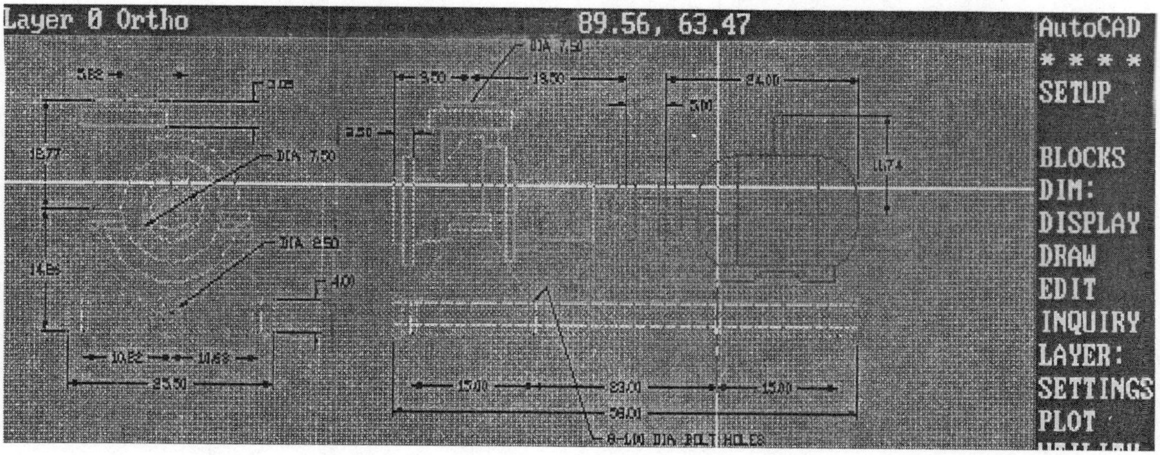

AutoCAD Status line

bar occupies the top line of the screen, which also contains the status line with the layer name, snap indicator, and coordinate display. Move the screen cursor to the top line of the screen to display the menu bar.

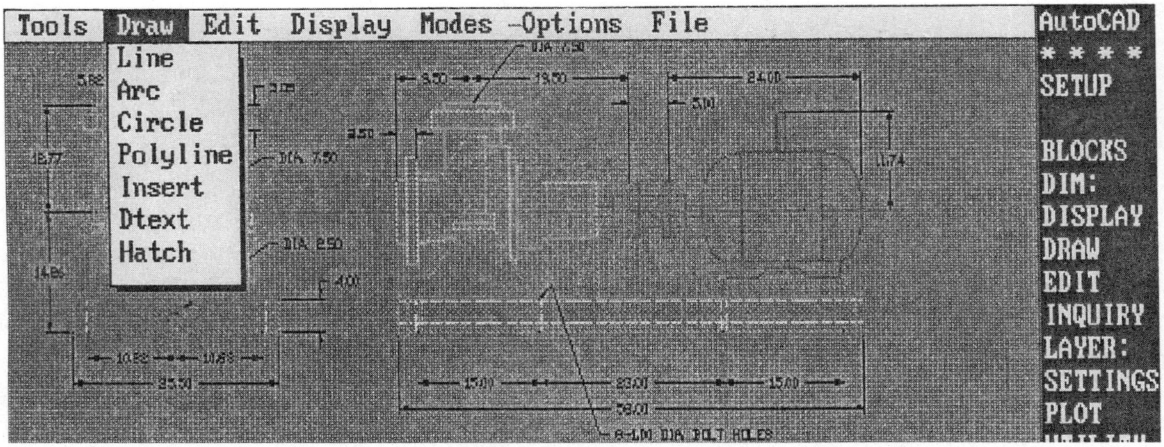

AutoCAD Menu Bar and Drop-Down Menu

Select a drop-down menu by moving the cursor along the menu bar to highlight the desired command menu title and press the pick button on your pointing device. Move the cursor vertically to highlight the desired selection, and press the pick button to activate the command.

You may switch to another drop-down menu without executing a command by picking another menu title from the menu bar.

You may exit the drop-down menu system with one of the following procedures:

- pick an unused area of the menu bar
- pick a point on the graphics screen
- type a character with the keyboard
- pick a command with a tablet or button menu
- move the screen cursor to the regular screen menu.

Some drop-down menus lead to icon-menus. For example, picking HATCH from the drop down menu displays a selection of HATCH patterns. Picking the selection box adjacent the desired option

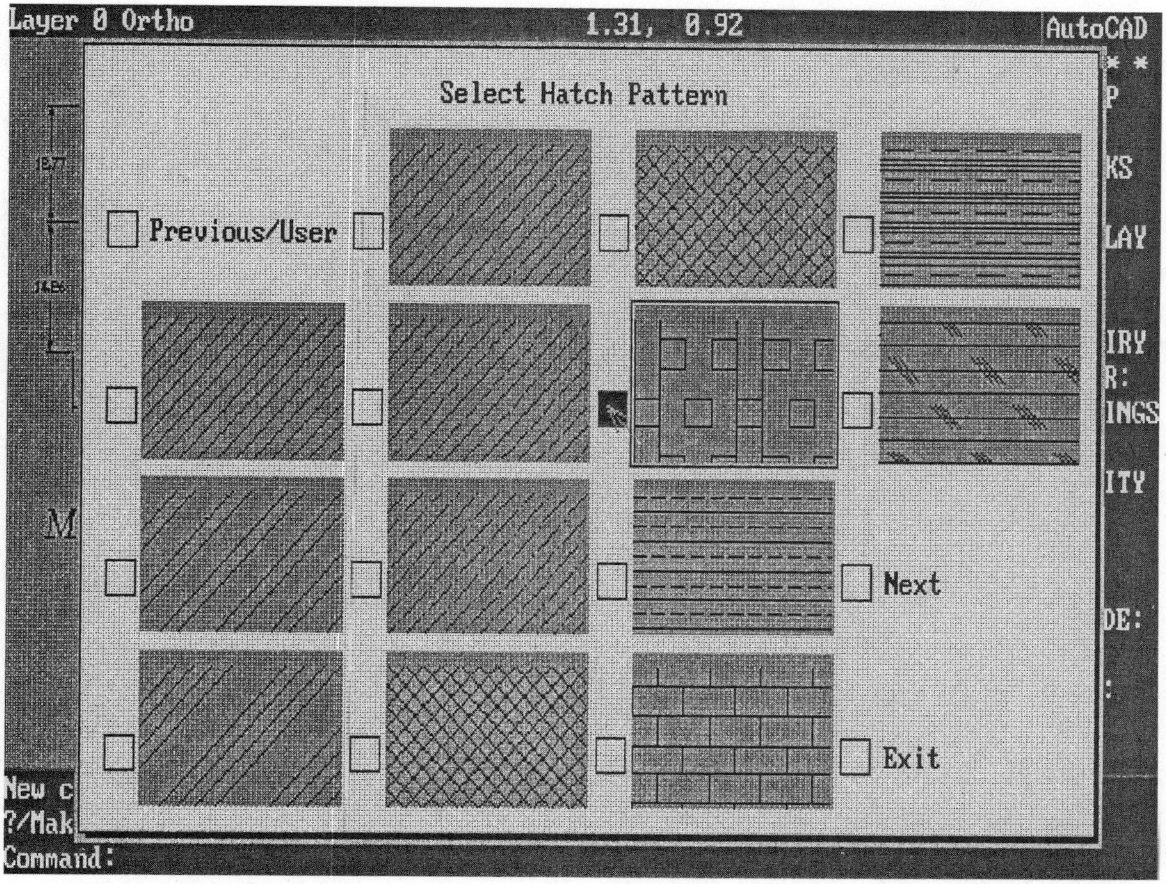

AutoCAD Icon Menu

selects the option. A "Next" option is provided on icon menus that have more than one screen of options. An "Exit" option is provided to exit a screen menu without making a choice. Move the screen cursor into the graphics screen area to restore the status line to the top of the screen.

Other drop-down menu choices lead to dialogue boxes, allowing you to select a number of options at one time. For example, the Drawing Aids Option of the Modes drop-down menu allows you to perform many of the operations of the SNAP, GRID, ORTHO, and ISOPLANE commands.

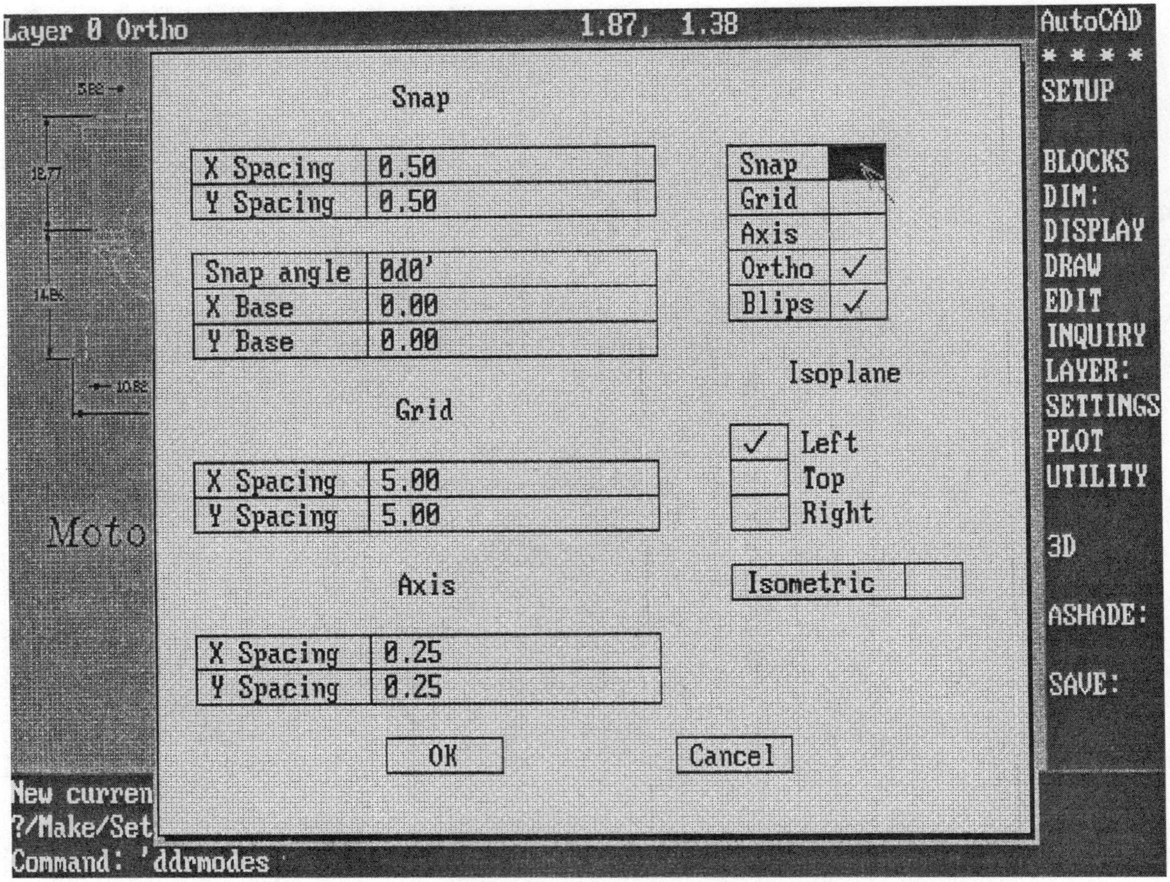

AutoCAD Dialogue Box

To change a numeric value, pick the value with the screen cursor, type the new value, then press Return. To activate or deactivate a toggle, such as SNAP or GRID, pick the check-box adjacent to the toggle name.

AutoCAD Release 9 introduces the word MULTIPLE as a modifier for AutoCAD commands. When typing commands from the keyboard, preceeding a command with the word MULTIPLE, as in MULTIPLE CIRCLE, causes AutoCAD to repeatedly execute the CIRCLE command until you explicitly cancel it. The drop-down menu system included with AutoCAD uses the MULTIPLE modifier automatically for most drawing commands. As a result, when you select CIRCLE from the drop-down menu, the CIRCLE command repeats automatically, allowing you to create multiple circles. To use another command, you must either pick the new command from screen menu, or explicitly cancel the command by pressing Ctrl-C before typing a new command from the keyboard.

The screen menu system is almost always available, even in the middle of other commands. This is especially useful for accessing the Drawing Aids screen of the Modes drop-down menu to modify the SNAP, GRID, AXIS, and similar settings, and to perform pan and zoom operations in the midst of another command sequence. Selecting a command such as CIRCLE from the drop-down menu while the LINE command is active, cancels the LINE command and proceeds with the CIRCLE command. The menu bar and drop-down menu system is not available, however during the following commands:

- DTEXT (after setting the rotation angle)
- SKETCH (after setting the record increment)
- VPOINT (while the axis and compas are displayed)
- ZOOM Dynamic.

The menu system is available at all other times.

As you perform the Typical Operations in each module, there is great flexibility in performing many of the steps. For example, many of the Typical Operation sections begin with setting the SNAP and the GRID. Using Release 9, you may either type the commands from the keyboard (as illustrated in the module) or you may specify the settings using the Drawing Aids option of the Mode drop-down menu. You may find it useful to perform some of the typical operations more than once—use keyboard entry one time, and repeat the operation using the drop-down menu system. The most important thing is to develop a personal style of working with AutoCAD that allows you to work rapidly and accurately, with the least amount of effort.

Appendix B

OTHER AUTOCAD COMMANDS

INTRODUCTION

This Appendix lists each of the AutoCAD commands included in version 2.17B OVL + ADE3 which were not included in the main body of this book. The authors believe that the commands included in the book are all that are necessary to provide a basic working knowledge of AutoCAD. The commands listed in this appendix, accompanied by a short description of their function, should help you decide if you need to consult your AutoCAD manual for further information. The +1, +2, and +3 indicate the ADE level (e.g. +1 = ADE1).

COMMAND LIST

1.	ATTDEF +2	Allows the creation of an Attribute Definition.
2.	ATTDISP +2	Turns the visibility of Attributes on or off.
3.	ATTEDIT +2	Used for editing Attributes.
4.	ATTEXT +2	Allows the extraction of Attribute entities from AutoCAD for use with other programs, such as data bases and spreadsheets.
5.	DXBIN +3	Loads files with the file name extension of .DXB, like those produced by CAD/camera.
6.	DXFIN	Allows the conversion of a drawing interchange file into AutoCAD.
7.	DXFOUT	Generates a drawing interchange file from an AutoCAD drawing.
8.	ENDREP	Used with the REPEAT command to produce rectangular patterns. This command is considered obsolete. The ARRAY command is recommended for producing rectangular patterns. Support was dropped for the ENDREP command effective with AutoCAD version 2.5.
9.	LOAD	Loads Shape files into the drawing.
10.	REPEAT	Used with the ENDREP command to produce rectangular patterns. This command is considered obsolete. The ARRAY command is recommended for producing rectangular patterns. Support was dropped for the REPEAT command effective with AutoCAD version 2.5.

11.	RESUME	Restarts a script that was interrupted with a **Ctrl-C** or **Backspace**.
12.	SHAPE	Used to place shapes into the drawing.
13.	SKETCH +1	Permits freehand drawing.
14.	TABLET	Allows the calibration of the tablet. This command also turns the tablet on and off.
15.	TEXTSCR	Used in command scripts to flip to the text screen.

Appendix C

AUTOCAD EXERCISES

1. *About This Book*
   a. For what kind of CAD user is this book designed?
   b. If you are learning AutoCAD, what sequence should you follow to go through this book?
   c. How are the AutoCAD commands arranged in this book?

2. *Sample Session*
   a. How do you save your drawing on a specific disk drive?
   b. What should you look for on your screen before entering a new command?
   c. What scale do you work in with AutoCAD?
   d. What command changes the size of the drawing view?
   e. What command removes sections of entities?

3. *Hardware/Software Relations*
   a. With how many screens is AutoCAD designed to operate?
   b. Name the two AutoCAD screens.
   c. When you need to switch from one AutoCAD screen to another, which key do you use?
   d. List two reasons why you might not want a screen menu.
   e. How do you speed up or slow down the screen cursor?
   f. List two ways of controling the screen cursor.

4. *3DFACE*
   a. The HIDE command treats the 3DFACE as ______________________.
   b. The 3DFACE command is similar to the two-dimensional command called ________.
   c. What OSNAP command will work with entities produced by the 3DFACE command?

5. *3DLINE*
   a. What entities are produced by the 3DLINE command?
   b. The 3DLINE command is an extension of what older command?
   c. Name three commands that will manipulate the end points of a 3DLINE segment.

6. *APERTURE*
   a. Explain what the APERTURE command alters.
   b. What command is the APERTURE command most closely associated with?

c. The size of the OSNAP target is expressed in what?
d. The physical size of the aperture depends on what?

7. *ARC*
a. In the ARC command, what does the "A" option stand for?
b. In the ARC command, what does the "C" option stand for?
c. In the ARC command, what does the "E" option stand for?
d. In the ARC command, what does the "R" option stand for?
e. What command is typed to dynamically locate an arc?
f. How many ways can you draw arcs in AutoCAD?
g. What is the default method of drawing arcs?

8. *AREA*
a. The AREA command will compute the area of what?
b. What are some common problems that could be solved with the AREA command?
c. The area computation is expressed using?
d. Explain some ways to use the AREA Subtract option.

9. *ARRAY*
a. Columns are sometimes thought of as ____________________.
b. What two types of arrays can you produce?
c. What is the default number of rows and columns?
d. Explain the two basic ways of entering the distance between rows and columns.
e. Why would you enter a negative number at the prompt for quantity or degrees to fill?
f. Why is an item sometimes saved as a block before using it within an array?

10. *AXIS*
a. How is the AXIS ruler line turned on?
b. How is the AXIS ruler line turned off?
c. Explain two ways to set the tick spacing.
d. Explain how to set the "Aspect" ratio.
e. Explain why the tick marks are sometimes different lengths.

11. *BASE*
a. Why is a base point designated for a drawing?
b. If a drawing is inserted without a base point, what happens?
c. Give a rationale for location of a base point.
d. Give two reasons why you should add a base point to a drawing.

12. *BLIPMODE*
a. Explain the purpose of BLIPMODE.
b. Compare the difference between BLIPMODE on and off.
c. What causes the BLIPMODE cross hairs to disappear from the screen when BLIPMODE is on?
d. What is the normal setting for BLIPMODE?

13. *BLOCK*
    a. Define BLOCK.
    b. How does AutoCAD interpret a BLOCK?
    c. Name three AutoCAD commands that can act upon BLOCK.
    d. Name the four commands used for defining and manipulating BLOCKS.
    e. What happens if you try to insert a BLOCK into a frozen layer?

14. *BREAK*
    a. Explain the difference between BREAK and ERASE.
    b. Name an entity on which BREAK does not work.
    c. Explain how the pointing method in BREAK works differently from other commands.

15. *CHAMFER*
    a. What does the CHAMFER command do to a corner?
    b. Does the CHAMFER command work with POLYLINES?
    c. If you did not have the CHAMFER command, explain the sequence you would need to follow in AutoCAD to accomplish the same operation.

16. *CHANGE*
    a. What are the three types of changes you can make using the CHANGE command?
    b. What happens if the ORTHO mode is on when changing lines with CHANGE?
    c. When changing circles with CHANGE, what is altered?
    d. Explain how CHANGE can affect TEXT.
    e. What affect can CHANGE have on BLOCKS?

17. *CIRCLE*
    a. What does a circle have in common with a line in AutoCAD?
    b. Explain the three major methods of defining a circle.
    c. Name two ways of locating points for circles.
    d. Name three types of drawings in which circles are used.

18. *COLOR*
    a. How was color controlled in versions of AutoCAD prior to version 2.5?
    b. What is the default setting of COLOR?
    c. What can the careless use of the COLOR command produce?

19. *COPY*
    a. What does COPY do to entities?
    b. Explain the difference between COPY and MOVE.
    c. Give an example of when you would use COPY.
    d. How is DRAG sometimes used with COPY? Give an example.

20. *DIM and DIM1*
    a. Name the five types of dimensioning capabilities in DIM.
    b. Name the six areas of linear dimensioning in DIM.

c. What does angular dimensioning do on the drawing?
d. What does diameter dimensioning do to circles?
e. What does radius dimensioning do to circles?
f. Name three dimensioning utilities in the DIM command and explain what they do to the drawing.
g. Name six dimensioning variables (DIMVAR), and explain why they may require adjustment before using the DIM command.
h. Why and when is the STATUS command used with DIM?
i. How does DIM differ from DIM1?

21. *DIST*
a. What can you do with the DIST command?
b. List two ways of specifying points for the DIST command.
c. What other AutoCAD command is useful to use with DIST to insure accuracy of point location?

22. *DIVIDE*
a. What does the DIVIDE command do?
b. Give three examples of how you might use the DIVIDE command in a drawing.

23. *DONUT (or DOUGHNUT)*
a. The DONUT command produces an enclosed ______________________________.
b. What command is used to edit a DONUT?
c. What command can be used to cause the DONUT to appear as a solid or as an open entity?
d. List the three things that must be entered to produce a DONUT.
e. What are three examples of ways that the DONUT command may be used in a drawing?

24. *DRAGMODE*
a. If DRAGMODE is On how can it be used in the drawing?
b. If DRAGMODE is set to Auto, how does the command work?
c. If DRAGMODE is turned Off how does the command react to your input?

25. *DTEXT*
a. How does DTEXT differ from the TEXT command?
b. How do you terminate the DTEXT command and cause the produced text to remain on the screen?
c. How do you terminate the DTEXT command cause the produced text to disappear?
d. What happens if you move the screen cursor while the DTEXT command is in progress?

26. *ELEV*
a. What dimension is added when using the ELEV command?
b. What two values are set in the ELEV command?
c. What happens when the thickness value is negative?
d. Why would you want to enter an elevation value as a negative number?

27. *ELLIPSE*
   a. Explain what the ELLIPSE command can do.
   b. If specifying a rotation angle for an ellipse, what inclusive angles are permitted?
   c. How can ELLIPSE be used with isometric snap enabled?

28. *END*
   a. Explain the three things that happen when using END.
   b. Give the difference between using END and ENDSV.
   c. Give the main reason for using END.
   d. Give the main reason for using ENDSV.

29. *ERASE*
   a. What is the ERASE command used for?
   b. Explain specifically what erase does to the drawing.
   c. What command is used for erasing part of a line?
   d. What happens when ERASE is used on a BLOCK?
   e. Explain how the Window option is used with ERASE.
   f. How does the Last option work with ERASE?

30. *EXPLODE*
   a. What does the EXPLODE command do?
   b. Why is it necessary to use the EXPLODE command more than once on some entities?
   c. What blocks will not work with EXPLODE?
   d. What happens to attribute information in blocks that are EXPLODEd?

31. *EXTEND*
   a. What entities can be used to form EXTEND boundaries?
   b. How do you select EXTEND boundaries in AutoCAD?
   c. Give two examples of how EXTEND may be used in practical situations.

32. *FILES*
   a. What are the options listed in the File Utility Menu?
   b. Name two places where you can gain access to the Files Utility Menu.
   c. Explain how to exit the Files Utility Menu and return to the Drawing Editor.

33. *FILL*
   a. Explain why it is good to have FILL off during some drawing sessions.
   b. What causes the FILL on or off to take effect on your screen?

34. *FILLET*
   a. Explain what the FILLET command does.
   b. How do you adjust the length of the two straight lines to get them to match the radius of the fillet?
   c. What happens if you FILLET two lines with a zero radius?

35. *GRAPHSCREEN*
   a. Explain what the GRAPHSCR command does.
   b. What key is used to accomplish the GRAPHSCREEN command on the IBM PC?
   c. When are you unable to use the GRAPHSCR toggle key and are forced to use the command GRAPHSCR by typing it from the keyboard?

36. *GRID*
   a. When is the GRID command most often used?
   b. What does the GRID do to your screen?
   c. Name three GRID options and explain them.
   d. What effect does GRID have on the drawing?
   e. Is the GRID and SNAP spacing always the same?
   f. What happens when GRID is set to 0 (zero)?

37. *HATCH*
   a. What does the HATCH command do?
   b. List 3 HATCH options and explain their function.
   c. List the three style functions in HATCH and explain each.
   d. What two types of hatching can you produce?
   e. How are hatching lines stored?
   f. What line type is used in a layer where hatching is used?
   g. When hatching entities, what two things are required?
   h. How does Normal style hatching react each time it encounters a new boundary?
   i. How does the Ignore style react to boundaries?
   j. How do you prevent HATCH lines from being stored in a block?
   k. In what kinds of mechanical drawings do you usually use HATCH?

38. *HELP*
   a. Explain what the HELP command does.
   b. What are two ways to call up the HELP command?
   c. What are the two types of help that you can get from HELP?
   d. How do you interrupt the HELP command?
   e. How do you get back to the Drawing Editor after getting a listing from HELP?

39. *HIDE*
   a. The HIDE command is used with what other AutoCAD command?
   b. What does the HIDE command do?
   c. How do you trick the HIDE command into thinking that a cylinder is not a solid object?

40. *ID*
   a. What does the ID command do?
   b. What can you find by combining the ID and INT commands?
   c. List three dimensions you can get from the ID command.

41. *INSERT*
   a. What is the INSERT command used for?
   b. When using INSERT, if you don't remember the name of the block to insert, what should you do?
   c. Explain the two ways of designating the insertion point.
   d. What is the default value for the X scale factor?
   e. What does AutoCAD do with the X scale factor you enter?
   f. What is the default value for the Y scale factor?
   g. What does AutoCAD do with the Y scale factor you enter?
   h. What is the default rotation angle for INSERT?
   i. What point is used for the center of rotation?
   j. When is it not advisable to use DRAG with INSERT?

42. *ISOPLANE*
   a. What does the ISOPLANE command do?
   b. What two angles form the left face or plane?
   c. What two angles form the right face or plane?
   d. What two angles form the top face or plane?
   e. What command is called before using the ISOPLANE command?
   f. How is ISOPLANE toggled without typing the command ISOPLANE?

43. *LAYER*
   a. What is the purpose of the LAYER command?
   b. List three layer options and explain them.
   c. What is the maximum number of layers in AutoCAD?
   d. How do you refer to a layer in AutoCAD?
   e. What is the maximum number of characters in a layer name?
   f. How many spaces are allowed in a layer name?
   g. Name the two things that the LAYER command can do to layers and the one thing it cannot do.
   h. How does AutoCAD reference colors for layers?
   i. What are the two places AutoCAD refers to colors associated with layers?
   j. Do you need a color monitor to produce color plots?
   k. Name three line types used with the LAYER command and draw a sketch of each.
   l. What command is used to eliminate unused line types?
   m. Give two examples of why you might use layers.

44. *LIMITS*
   a. What is the LIMITS command used for?
   b. AutoCAD's LIMITS command compares to what in manual drafting?
   c. Explain the effect of LIMITS command being on.
   d. Explain the effect of LIMITS command being off.
   e. What are the two corners set with LIMITS?
   f. Is the LIMITS command only used when first starting a drawing?
   g. What is an important point to remember about scale when setting limits in AutoCAD?

45. *LINE*
   a. What is the LINE command used for?
   b. What is designated whan drawing a line?
   c. Explain two ways to designate the end points of a line.
   d. AutoCAD treats a line as what?

46. *LINETYPE*
   a. How many line types are included with AutoCAD?
   b. How do you get AutoCAD to load a line type?
   c. Give the filename extension for a line type.

47. *LIST and DBLIST*
   a. What does the LIST command do?
   b. What does the DBLIST command do?
   c. Why does the DBLIST command not need options?
   d. Why is the LIST command usually preferred over the DBLIST command?
   e. How do you suspend screen listing so you can examine it?
   f. If you use **Ctrl-C** with LIST or DBLIST commands, what happens?
   g. How can you toggle the printer on or off to print listings?

48. *LTSCALE*
   a. What does the LTSCALE command do?
   b. Give an example of when you would use LTSCALE.

49. *MEASURE*
   a. What does the MEASURE command do?
   b. What markers can be used with MEASURE?
   c. What can you not use to pick an object to measure?
   d. What command is MEASURE similar to?
   e. Give a practical example of how the MEASURE command may be applied to a drawing activity.

50. *MENU*
   a. What kind of file is an AutoCAD menu file?
   b. In a menu file, what does *** indicate?
   c. For menu items of more than eight characters, what symbols are used?
   d. What does the semi-colon (;) mean when used in a menu file?
   e. What is a common first step in creating or customizing an AutoCAD menu?

51. *MINSERT*
   a. What is MINSERT used for?
   b. MINSERT combines the features of what two commands?
   c. MINSERT is faster than using what?
   d. Give an example of how MINSERT can be applied in a drawing.

52. *MIRROR*
    a. What is the purpose of the MIRROR command?
    b. At what angles may mirroring be done?
    c. Does the MIRROR command always mirror the new object and leave the old object in place?
    d. Can you turn off the ORTHO command while mirroring?

53. *MOVE*
    a. When should you use the MOVE command?
    b. In what submenu can you find MOVE?
    c. Name two of the MOVE command options and explain how they work.
    d. Is the MOVE reference point always part of the moved object?
    e. Give an example of how DRAG is used with the MOVE command.

54. *MSLIDE, VSLIDE, SCRIPT, RSCRIPT, AND DELAY*
    a. What are the MSLIDE and VSLIDE commands used for?
    b. When a slide is stored on disk, what is the filename extension given to it?
    c. A script file is what kind of a file?
    d. What is the filename extension given to a script file?
    e. What does the DELAY file do?
    f. A DELAY value of 1000 represents what length of time?

55. *OFFSET*
    a. OFFSET distance is always what kind of number?
    b. When using OFFSET with a polyline the distance should be measured from where on the polyline?
    c. What does the OFFSET command do?
    d. Give an example of how to use the OFFSET comand in a drawing.

56. *OOPS*
    a. How is the OOPS command used with ERASE?
    b. How many erasures does OOPS remember?

57. *ORTHO*
    a. When the ORTHO command is turned on, what kinds of lines are drawn?
    b. Describe why you might use the ORTHO command.
    c. What key combined with the **Ctrl** key toggles ORTHO on and off?

58. *OSNAP*
    a. What is the basic purpose of the OSNAP command?
    b. What three components of a line does OSNAP snap to?
    c. Explain how the Tangent option is used in OSNAP.
    d. Explain what the Quadrant option does in OSNAP.
    e. How many letters of the OSNAP option must be typed to activate the OSNAP command?

f. Explain how the OSNAP command target works.
g. How can you change the size of the OSNAP command target?
h. Explain how to set the OSNAP command for use on a series of command operations when all of the operations require the same basic OSNAP commands.
i. How do you deactivate the Object Snap Modes?
j. Explain "Single Point Overrides" in OSNAP.

59. *PAN*
a. Explain the two ways of specifying drawing displacement with PAN.
b. What other command is used to change the display size of your drawing?

60. *PEDIT*
a. What is the PEDIT command used for?
b. How can the PEDIT command alter line width?
c. Explain what "curve fitting" does in PEDIT.
d. After entering the PEDIT command at the command prompt, what is the first step in its use?
e. How can SNAP affect the use of the PEDIT command?
f. What happens if you select an entity that is not a polyline?
g. Explain the Close option in PEDIT.
h. Explain the Open option in PEDIT.
i. What does the Join option accomplish in PEDIT?
j. Explain how you might use the Width option in PEDIT.
k. There are several suboptions within the Edit Vertex option. Choose two of these suboptions and explain what they do.
l. Why would you use REGEN with the PEDIT command?

61. *PLINE*
a. What does the term PLINE mean?
b. If the width of the PLINE is set to zero, what does the PLINE look like on your screen?
c. What is the major difference between LINEs and a PLINE?
d. What causes a PLINE to be displayed as a solid?
e. Explain two advantages of a PLINE over a TRACE.
f. What command is used to edit a PLINE?

62. *PLOT*
a. Explain two ways to gain access to the PLOT command.
b. What does the Display option do in PLOT?
c. What does the Extents option do in PLOT?
d. What does the Limits option do in PLOT?
e. What does the Window option do in PLOT?
f. What happens to the size of the PLOT area if the origin is moved from the 0,0 point?
g. In what direction does plot rotation take place?
h. If you want your drawing plotted as large as possible, regardless of scale, what command is used for the scale prompt?

63. *POINT*
    a. What does the POINT command do?
    b. How is the POINT located?
    c. Define POINT as it is defined in AutoCAD.

64. *POLYGON*
    a. What does the POLYGON command do?
    b. What is the minimum and maximum number of sides that the POLYGON command will deal with?
    c. Explain the two ways that a polygon size can be designated.
    d. Give an example of how the POLYGON command may be used.

65. *PRPLOT*
    a. What does the PRPLOT command allow you to do?
    b. What kind of output device is used with the PRPLOT command?
    c. What are two ways to gain access to PRPLOT?
    d. How is PRPLOT aborted during printing?

66. *PURGE*
    a. When is the only time you can use PURGE?
    b. What is typically purged from a drawing?
    c. What two things cannot be purged?

67. *QTEXT*
    a. What is the purpose of QTEXT?
    b. Explain how QTEXT is turned on and off.
    c. What does the term QTEXT stand for?
    d. When looking at your drawing, how would you know if you had QTEXT turned on?

68. *QUIT*
    a. What does the QUIT command do?
    b. Does the QUIT command save your drawing?
    c. Give an example of when the QUIT command is helpful.

69. *REDO*
    a. What is the REDO command used for?
    b. When must the REDO command be used?

70. *REDRAW*
    a. What does the REDRAW command do?
    b. Does REDRAW recompute the screen?
    c. What button on the mouse is used for REDRAW?

71. *REGEN*
 a. What does the REGEN command do that the REDRAW command does not do?
 b. What does the REGEN command do to guarantee "what you see is what you save?"
 c. When is the REGEN command typically used?

72. *REGENAUTO*
 a. Name five of the six commands that cause the automatic regeneration of the AutoCAD screen.
 b. What happens in AutoCAD when the REGENAUTO command is turned off?
 c. Name three commands that cause automatic regeneration of the screen whether REGENAUTO is off or on.

73. *RENAME*
 a. What does RENAME let you do in AutoCAD?
 b. What two things are not renamed using the RENAME command?
 c. Why might you want to RENAME an object?

74. *ROTATE*
 a. What does the ROTATE command do?
 b. When using the ROTATE command, what is the first step?
 c. What is the second step when using ROTATE?
 d. Where must the base point be located on the drawing?
 e. Name and explain two ways to specify rotation.

75. *SAVE*
 a. What does the SAVE command do?
 b. Why should you use the SAVE command often?
 c. What happens to the original version of a drawing when you use the SAVE command?

76. *SCALE*
 a. What does the SCALE command allow you to do with a drawing?
 b. What is the base point used for in the SCALE command?
 c. Explain two ways to specify the amount of scaling to be done in SCALE.

77. *SELECT*
 a. Name and explain two ways of building a selection set.
 b. How do you cancel the construction of a selection set?

78. *SETVAR*
 a. What is the SETVAR command used for?
 b. List and describe ten variables that come under the SETVAR command.
 c. Give two reasons for using the SETVAR command.

79. *SHELL*
   a. What does the SHELL command allow you to do?
   b. What does it mean when you see the DOS prompt displayed?
   c. How do you return to AutoCAD from the SHELL mode?
   d. Name a DOS command that you should never use in SHELL.
   e. When returning to a damaged drawing after using SHELL, what AutoCAD command is used to restore your drawing?

80. *SNAP*
   a. What does the SNAP command do?
   b. When using SNAP, if you want to only enter the value, explain how this is done.
   c. What does the Aspect option allow in SNAP?
   d. Explain how the Style option is used.

81. *SOLID*
   a. What does the SOLID command do?
   b. What command is used to cause the object drawn in SOLID to appear solid on the screen?

82. *STATUS*
   a. What is the STATUS command used for?
   b. Where are the two places to use STATUS?
   c. List five items displayed by the STATUS command when it is used at the Command prompt.

83. *STRETCH*
   a. What does the STRETCH command allow you to do?
   b. What selection mode must be used first in the STRETCH command?

84. *STYLE*
   a. What is the name of the Style of text that is built into AutoCAD?
   b. What does the STYLE command do?
   c. What is the maximum length of a Style name?
   d. When you are at the STYLE command prompt, how may you view a list of styles?
   e. If you specify a height of zero for the text Style, what results when you use the text?
   f. What affect does the width factor have on STYLE?
   g. Why would you want to use an obliquing angle?
   h. What text styles are used to gain the most rapid plotting speeds?

85. *TEXT*
   a. What does the TEXT command allow you to do?
   b. Name the three things that TEXT allows you to do.
   c. What is the default text height?

d. What is the default rotation of text?
e. What rotation angle is used for horizontal text?
f. Explain what happens when using the TEXT command if you press **Return** at the end of a text entry.
g. Name three TEXT control codes and describe their affect.

86. *TIME*
a. What information is displayed by the TIME command?
b. What should you do to make the best use of the TIME command?

87. *TRACE*
a. Describe the use of the TRACE command.
b. Explain the difference between TRACE and LINE.
c. What are two ways to enter the TRACE width?
d. When points are entered in the TRACE command, what part of the TRACE do the points designate?
e. Explain what effect FILL has on TRACE.
f. Give an example of when you might use the TRACE command.

88. *TRIM*
a. What is the TRIM command used for?
b. When using the TRIM command, what is the first item asked for?
c. What determines which side of an object is discarded?

89. *U and UNDO*
a. In what order does the UNDO operation work?
b. Explain how you would undo the last 5 commands with the UNDO command.
c. How would you undo the last operation just completed?

90. *UNITS*
a. What does the UNITS command allow you to do in your AutoCAD drawing?
b. What are the four systems of UNITS available in AutoCAD?
c. What is the default for the UNITS command?
d. In what submenu do you find the UNITS command?
e. List the four methods of angle measurement available in the UNITS command.
f. What effect does the choice of UNITS have on AutoCAD's system of internal calculations or precision?

91. *VIEW*
a. What does the VIEW command allow you to do?
b. Without the VIEW command, what commands would be required to perform the same operation?
c. What does the VIEW Restore command do?

92. *VIEWRES*
   a. What effect does the VIEWRES command have on plotting?
   b. What does the VIEWRES command control?
   c. What is the default value of VIEWRES?

93. *VPOINT*
   a. What does the VPOINT command do?
   b. Explain the two ways of specifying VPOINT.
   c. After entering VPOINT at the command prompt, how do you get the Axes Tripod to appear?
   d. What does the Axes Tripod do in the VPOINT command?

94. *WBLOCK*
   a. What other command is similar to WBLOCK?
   b. Explain the difference between BLOCK and WBLOCK.
   c. Give two examples of why you would use WBLOCK.

95. *ZOOM*
   a. What is the purpose of the ZOOM command.
   b. What happens if you type a number greater than 1 for magnification?
   c. What happens if you type a decimal less than 1 for magnification?
   d. What happens if you follow your magnification number with an X?
   e. Explain the results of the following ZOOM suboptions:
      (1) A
      (2) E
      (3) P
      (4) W
   f. How many previous ZOOM views does AutoCAD remember?
   j. What affect does the ZOOM command have on your drawing dimensions?
   k. What is probably the most popular and powerful form of the ZOOM command?

Index

ABOUT THE AUTHOR

Dr. Tom W. Berghauser is Assistant Professor of the Division of Industrial Technology at North Texas State University. He has an extensive industrial background as a designer and CAD technologist. Dr. Paul L. Schleive is Assistant Professor of Education at North Texas State University. He is a computer scientist and *AutoCAD* instructor.